*I HEAR
A VOICE.
IT'S SAYING
THE WORDS
I'VE ALWAYS
LONGED
TO HEAR.*

CONTENTS

{ CHARACTERS }

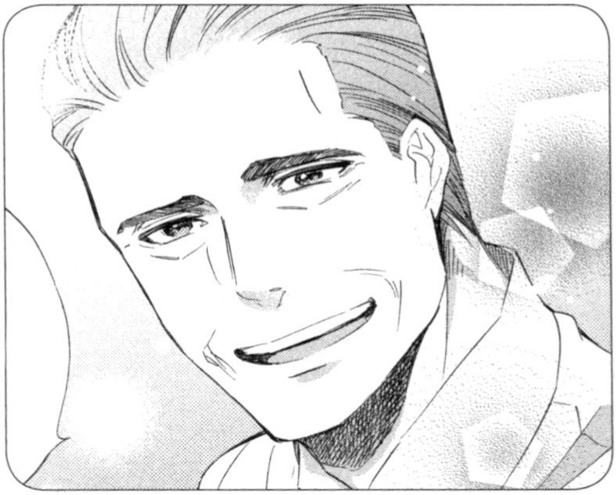

Fuyuki Kanda

The man who lives with Fukumaru. Drawn to Fukumaru from the moment he first laid eyes on the kitty at the pet store, Kanda went on to take Fukumaru home. Kanda was once a celebrated pianist but was unable to return to the stage after his wife's death. He now works as a piano teacher at a music school.

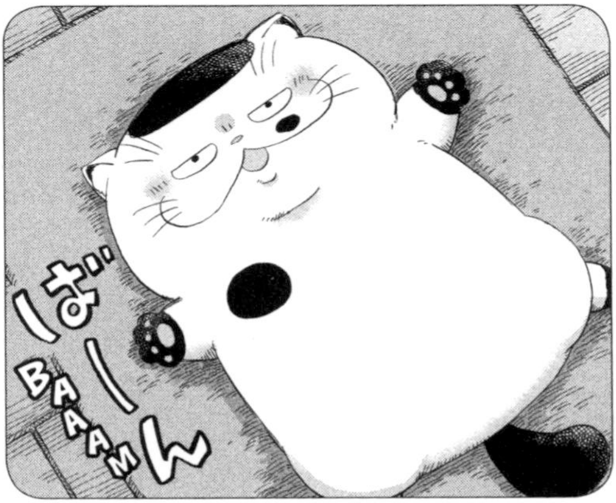
ばーん
BAAAAM

Fukumaru

A cat who lived at the pet store for a long time before Kanda fell in love with him at first sight and adopted him. Fukumaru is an Exotic Shorthair. He adores Kanda, who treasures him, and affectionately calls him "Daddy." He loves food, and he's not so great with baths.

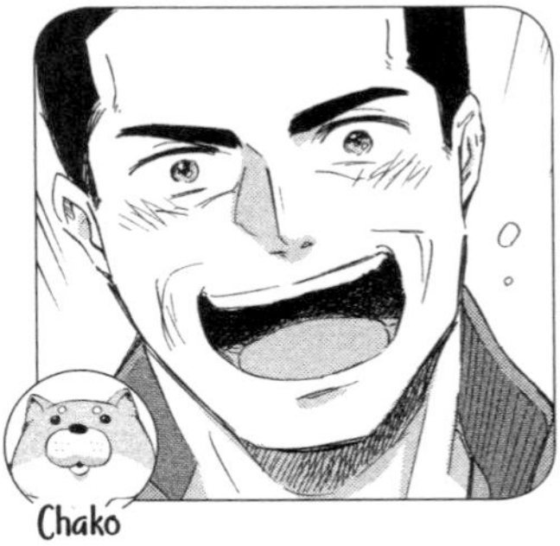
Chako

Natsuhito Kobayashi

Kanda's best friend since early childhood. They're very close, and Kobayashi is always teasing Kanda and cheering him up. He has a Shiba Inu named Chako.

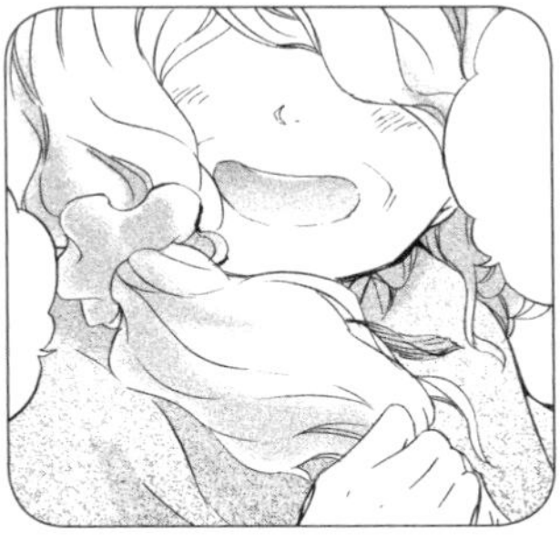

Mrs. Kanda

Kanda's late wife. A great cat lover in life, she inspired her husband to adopt Fukumaru later on.

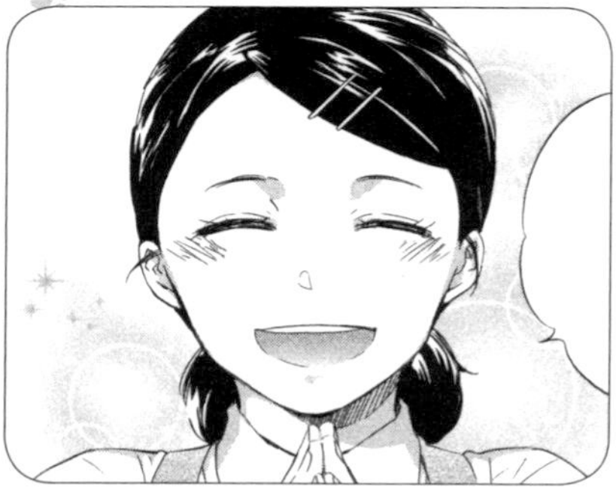

Momiji Sato

An employee at the pet store where Fukumaru used to live. Worried about Fukumaru because no one wanted to buy him, she always made a point of keeping Fukumaru's spirits up.

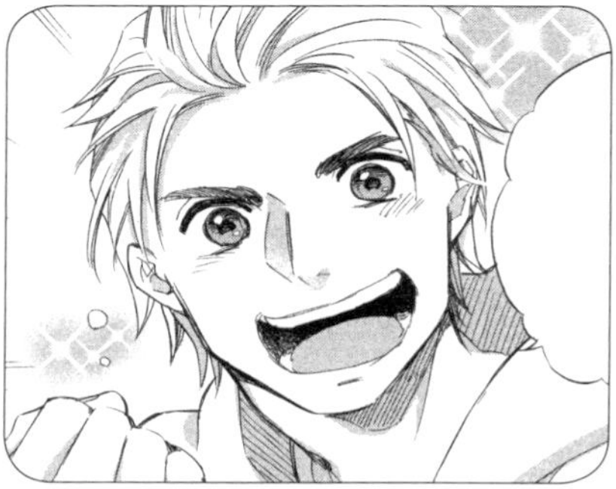

Yoshiharu Moriyama

A teacher at the music school where Kanda works. Moriyama also plays in a band, but he keeps that a secret at work. His dream is to hit it big and play concerts at massive venues.

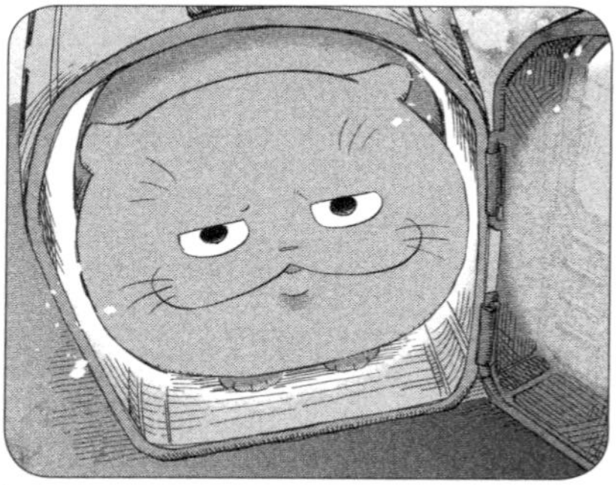

Marin

A female cat who used to belong to Hibino's mother. Forced on Hibino when his mother grew bored of her, Marin is now Hibino's cat.

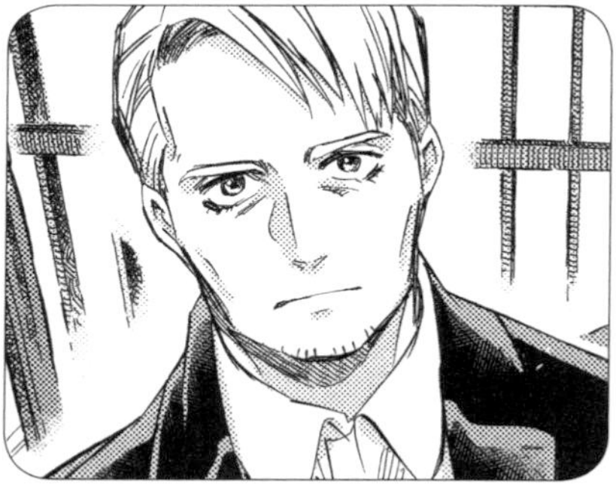

Kanade Hibino

A man shattered by Kanda's talent as a pianist. When Hibino's mother forces him to take in her cat, Marin, he and Kanda meet once again.

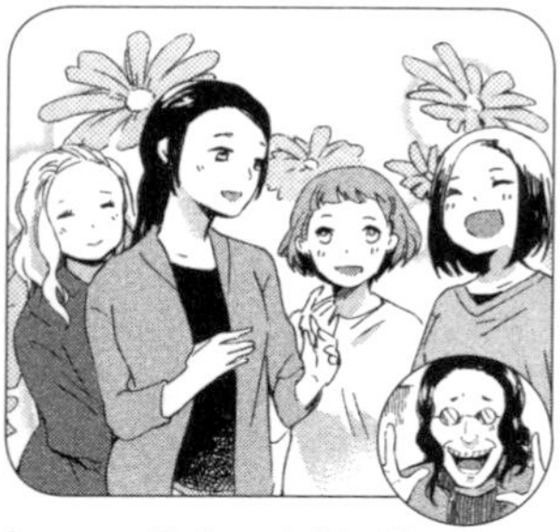

Music School Staff

The employees at the music school where Kanda and Moriyama work. They secretly idolize Kanda. Mostly women, there are very few men among them.

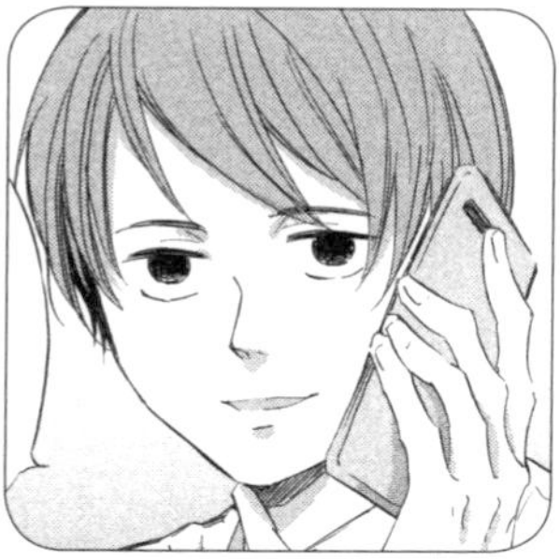

Masato Moriyama

Moriyama's little brother and Hibino's acquaintance. The Moriyama brothers have low opinions of each other.

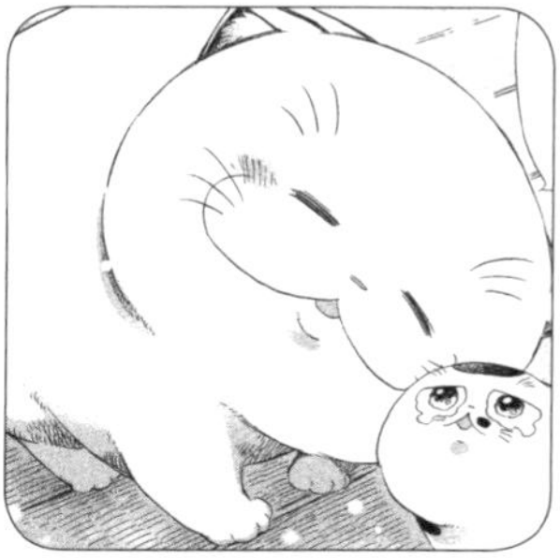

Mom

Fukumaru's mother. Her constant wish is for Fukumaru and her other kittens to be happy.

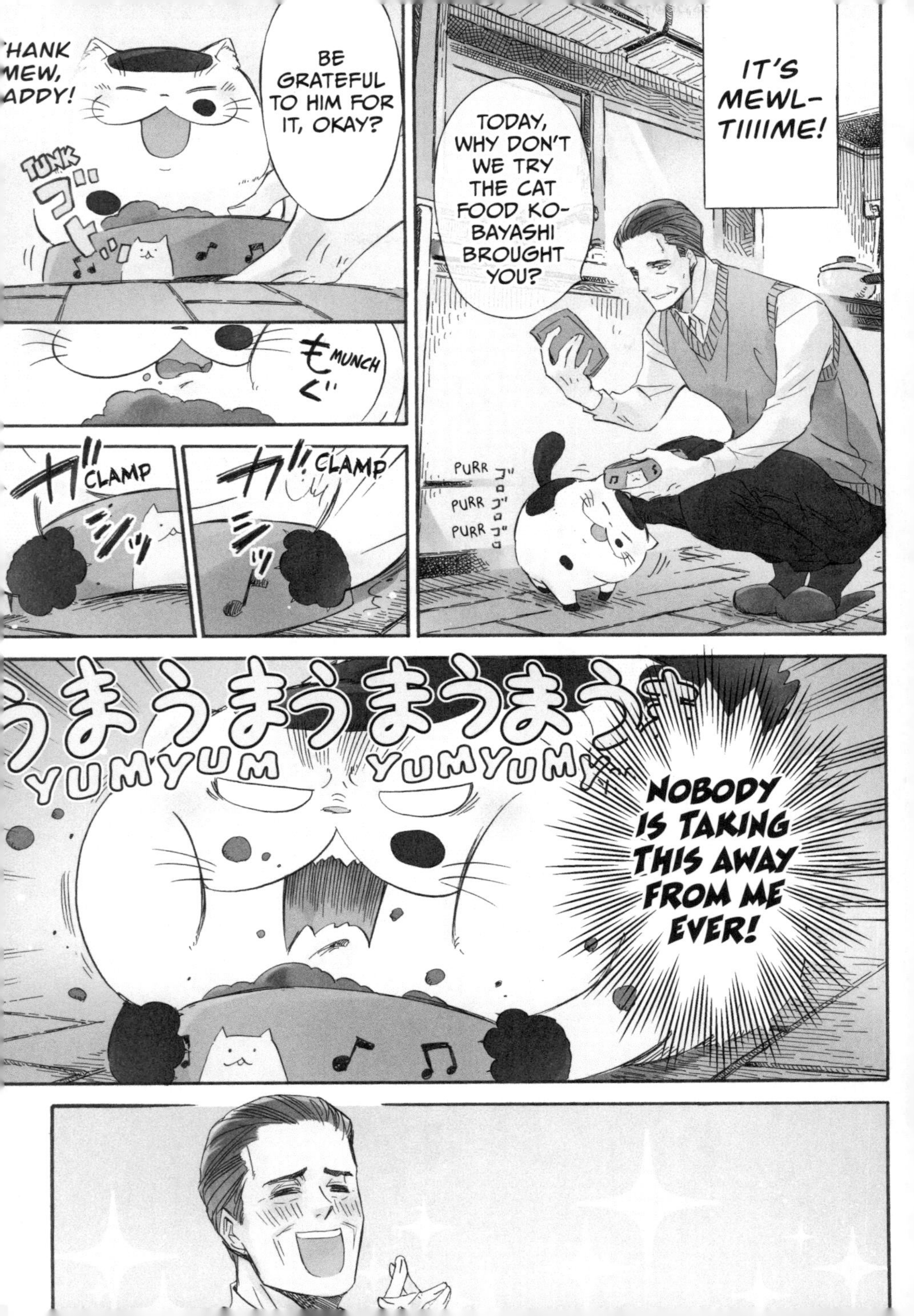
IT'S MEWL-TIIIIME!
TODAY, WHY DON'T WE TRY THE CAT FOOD KO-BAYASHI BROUGHT YOU?
PURR
PURR
PURR
BE GRATEFUL TO HIM FOR IT, OKAY?
THANK MEW, ADDY!
TUNK
MUNCH
CLAMP
CLAMP
YUMYUM YUMYUM
NOBODY IS TAKING THIS AWAY FROM ME EVER!

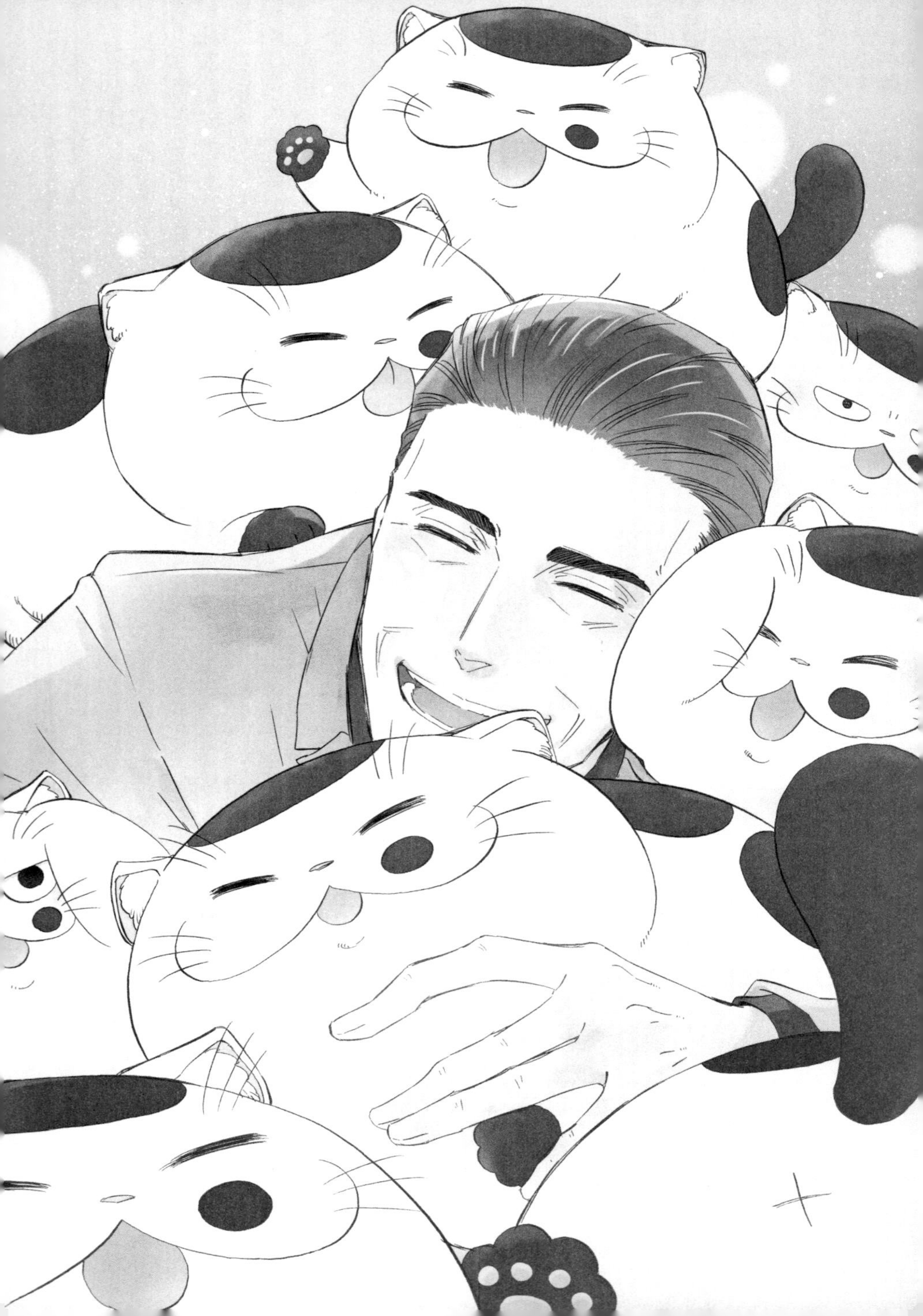

Chapter 39 Cats on the Brain

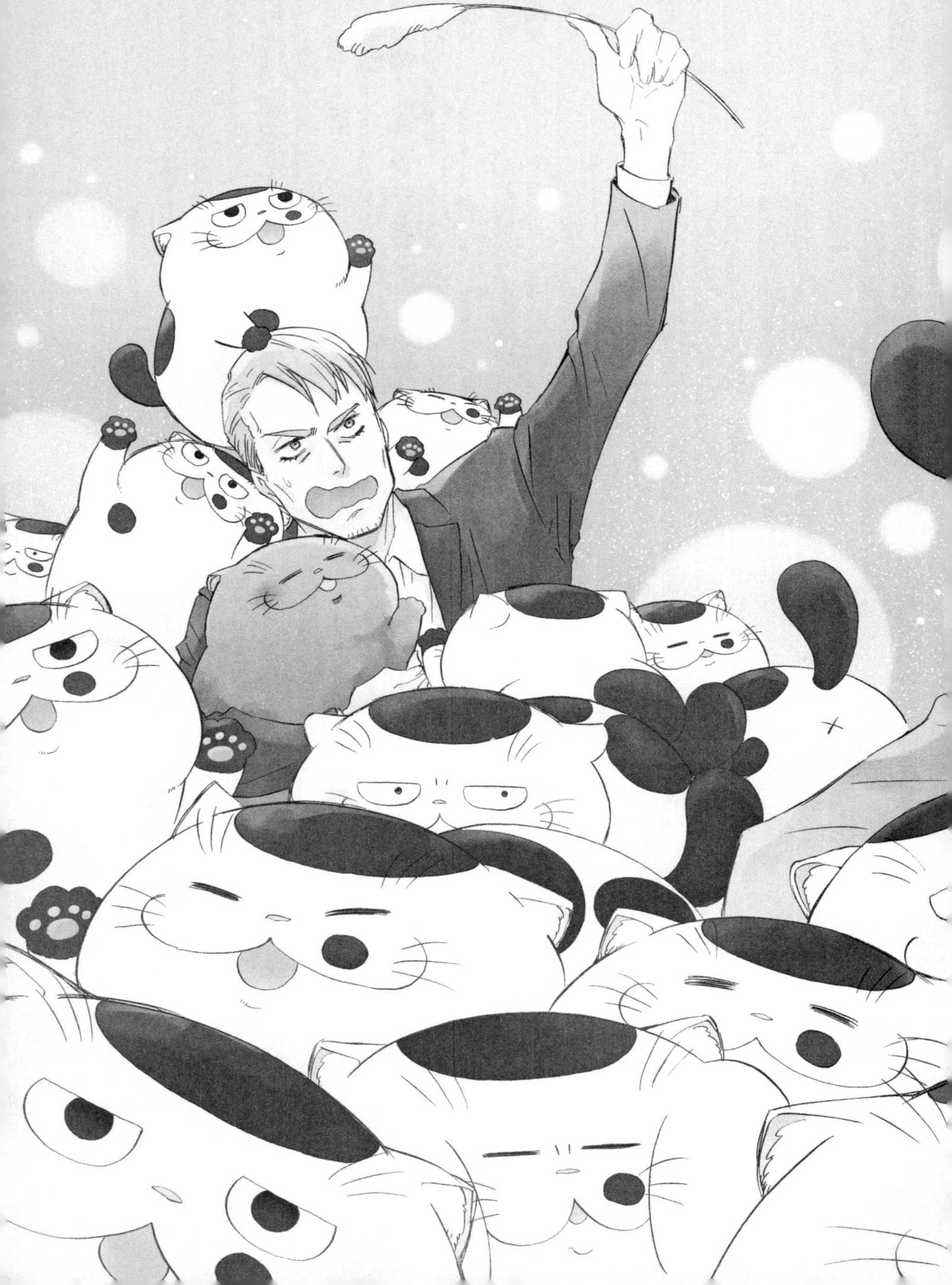

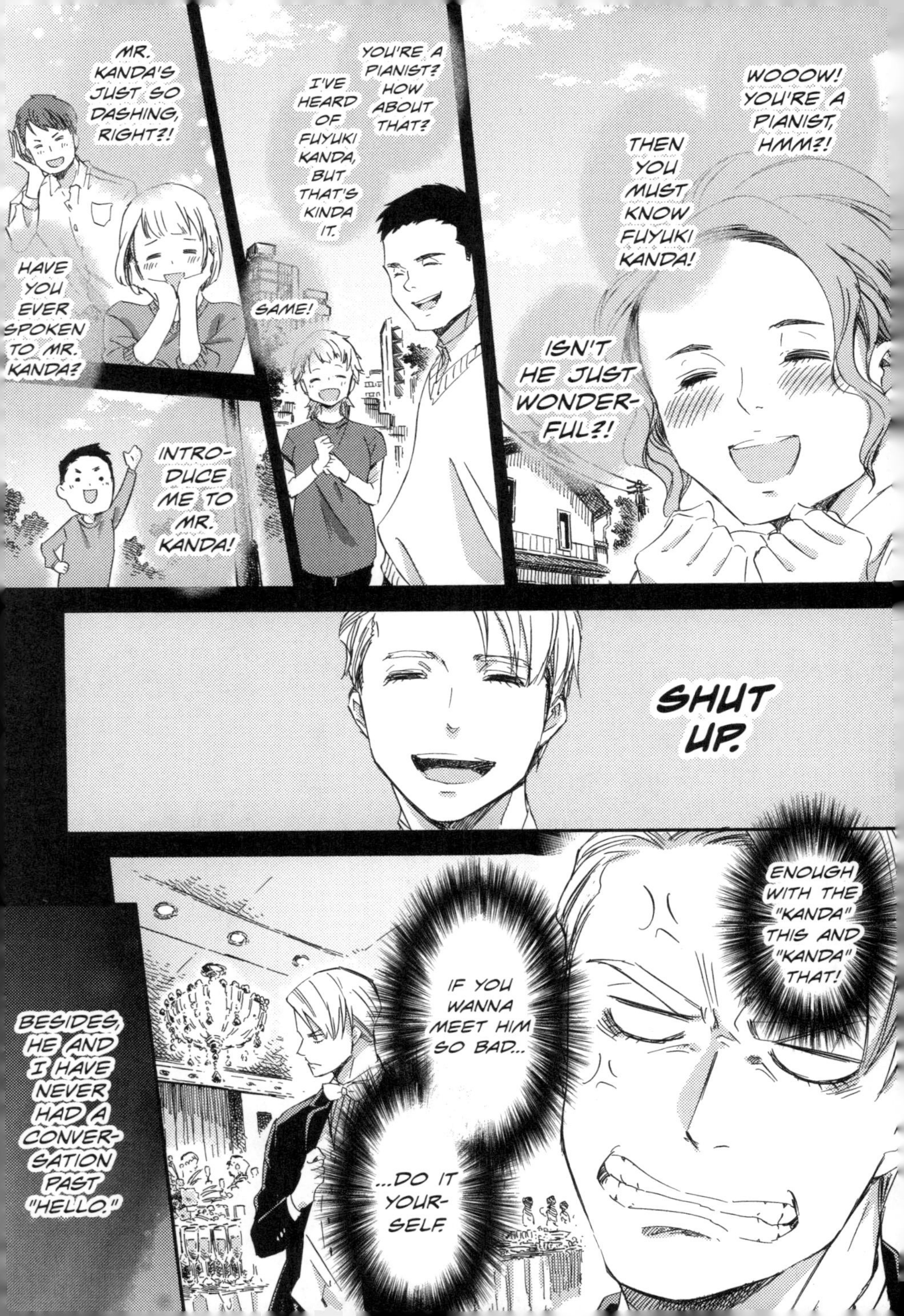
WOOOW! YOU'RE A PIANIST, HMM?!
THEN YOU MUST KNOW FUYUKI KANDA!
ISN'T HE JUST WONDER-FUL?!
YOU'RE A PIANIST? HOW ABOUT THAT?
I'VE HEARD OF FUYUKI KANDA, BUT THAT'S KINDA IT.
SAME!
MR. KANDA'S JUST SO DASHING, RIGHT?!
HAVE YOU EVER SPOKEN TO MR. KANDA?
INTRO-DUCE ME TO MR. KANDA!
SHUT UP.
ENOUGH WITH THE "KANDA" THIS AND "KANDA" THAT!
IF YOU WANNA MEET HIM SO BAD...
...DO IT YOUR-SELF.
BESIDES, HE AND I HAVE NEVER HAD A CONVER-SATION PAST "HELLO."

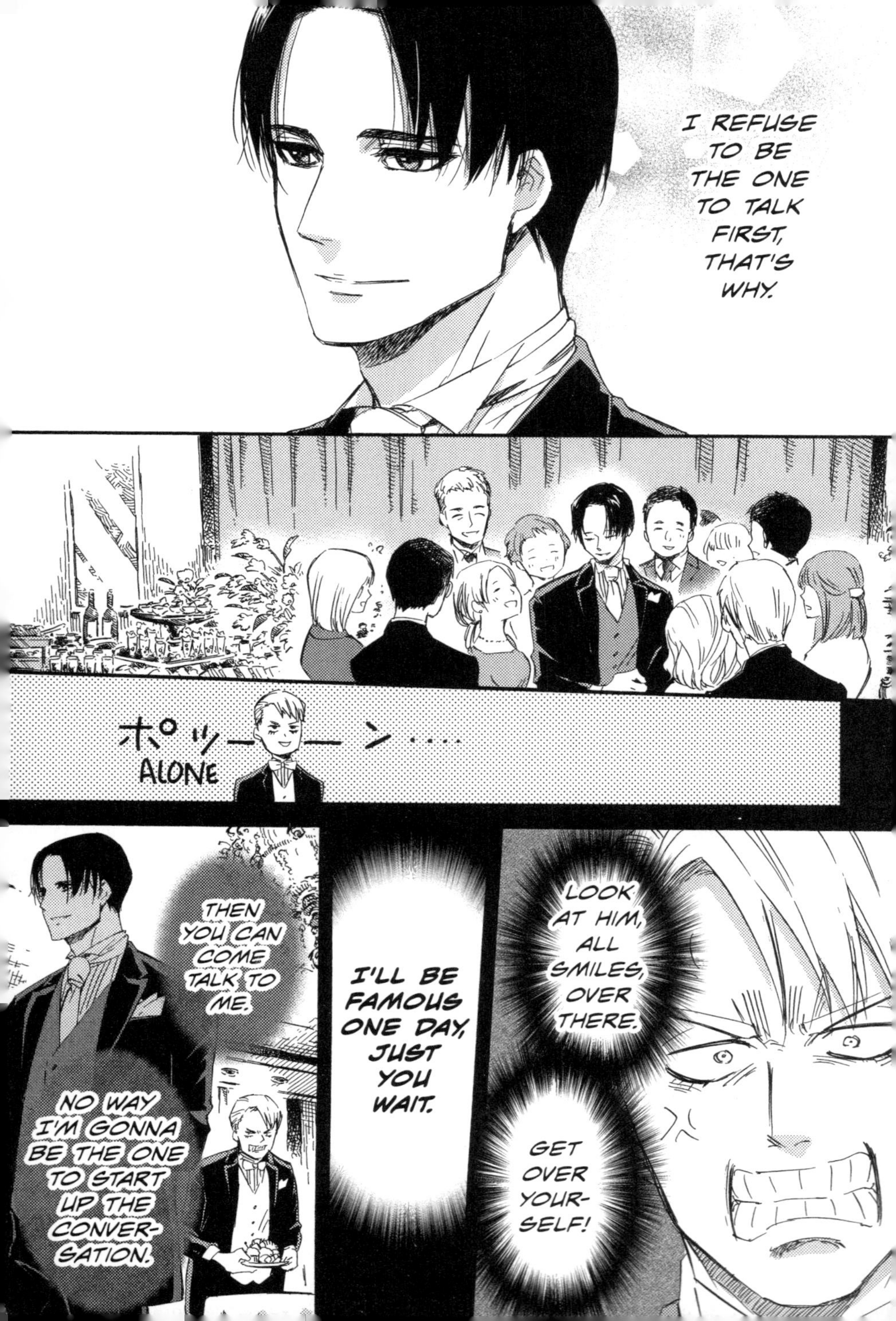
I REFUSE TO BE THE ONE TO TALK FIRST, THAT'S WHY.
ポツーーン…
ALONE
LOOK AT HIM, ALL SMILES, OVER THERE.
GET OVER YOURSELF!
I'LL BE FAMOUS ONE DAY, JUST YOU WAIT.
THEN YOU CAN COME TALK TO ME.
NO WAY I'M GONNA BE THE ONE TO START UP THE CONVER-SATION.

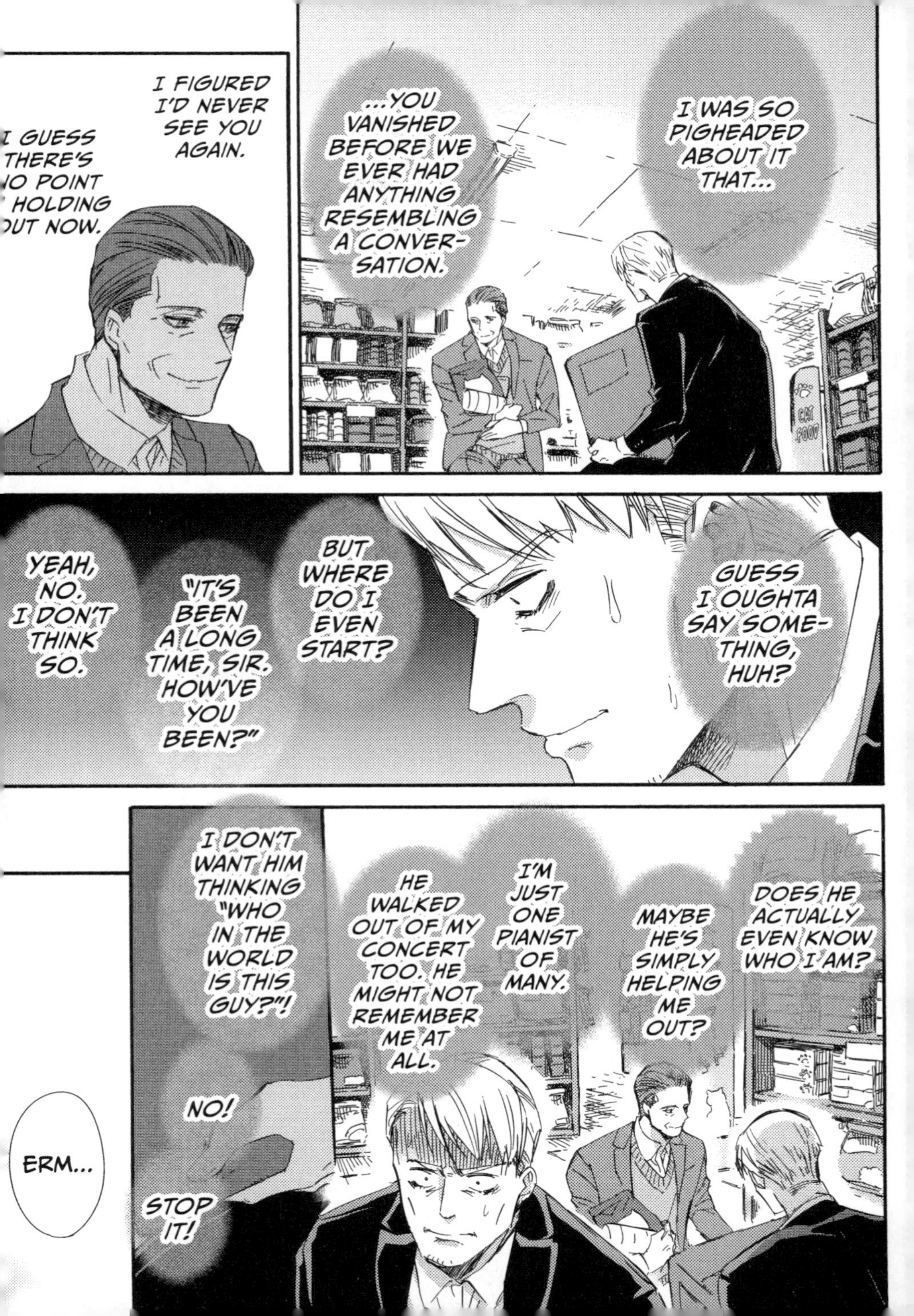
I WAS SO PIGHEADED ABOUT IT THAT...
...YOU VANISHED BEFORE WE EVER HAD ANYTHING RESEMBLING A CONVER-SATION.
I FIGURED I'D NEVER SEE YOU AGAIN.
I GUESS THERE'S O POINT HOLDING OUT NOW.
GUESS I OUGHTA SAY SOME-THING, HUH?
BUT WHERE DO I EVEN START?
"IT'S BEEN A LONG TIME, SIR. HOW'VE YOU BEEN?"
YEAH, NO. I DON'T THINK SO.
DOES HE ACTUALLY EVEN KNOW WHO I AM?
MAYBE HE'S SIMPLY HELPING ME OUT?
I'M JUST ONE PIANIST OF MANY.
HE WALKED OUT OF MY CONCERT TOO. HE MIGHT NOT REMEMBER ME AT ALL.
I DON'T WANT HIM THINKING "WHO IN THE WORLD IS THIS GUY?"!
NO!
STOP IT!
ERM...

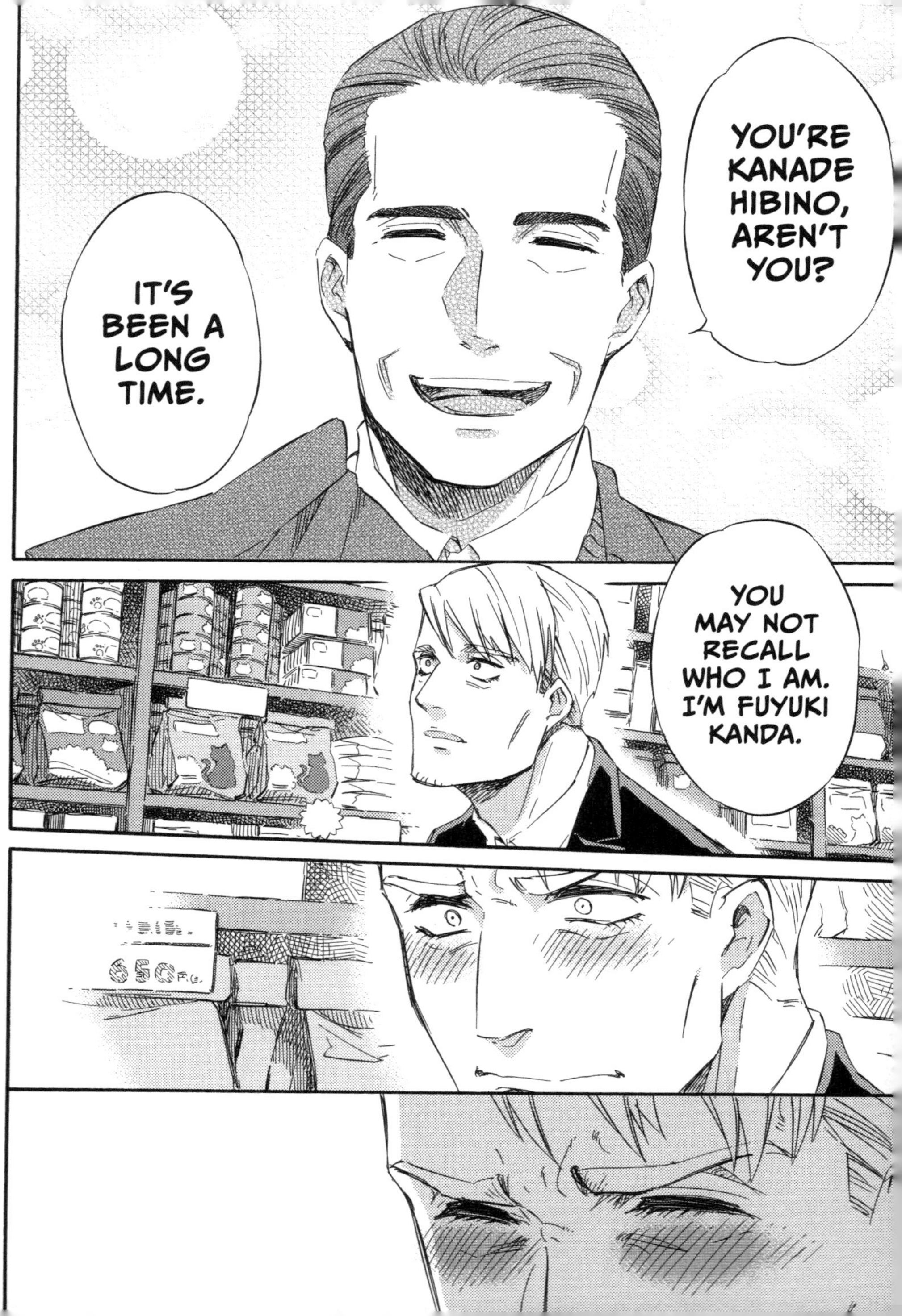
YOU'RE KANADE HIBINO, AREN'T YOU?
IT'S BEEN A LONG TIME.
YOU MAY NOT RECALL WHO I AM. I'M FUYUKI KANDA.

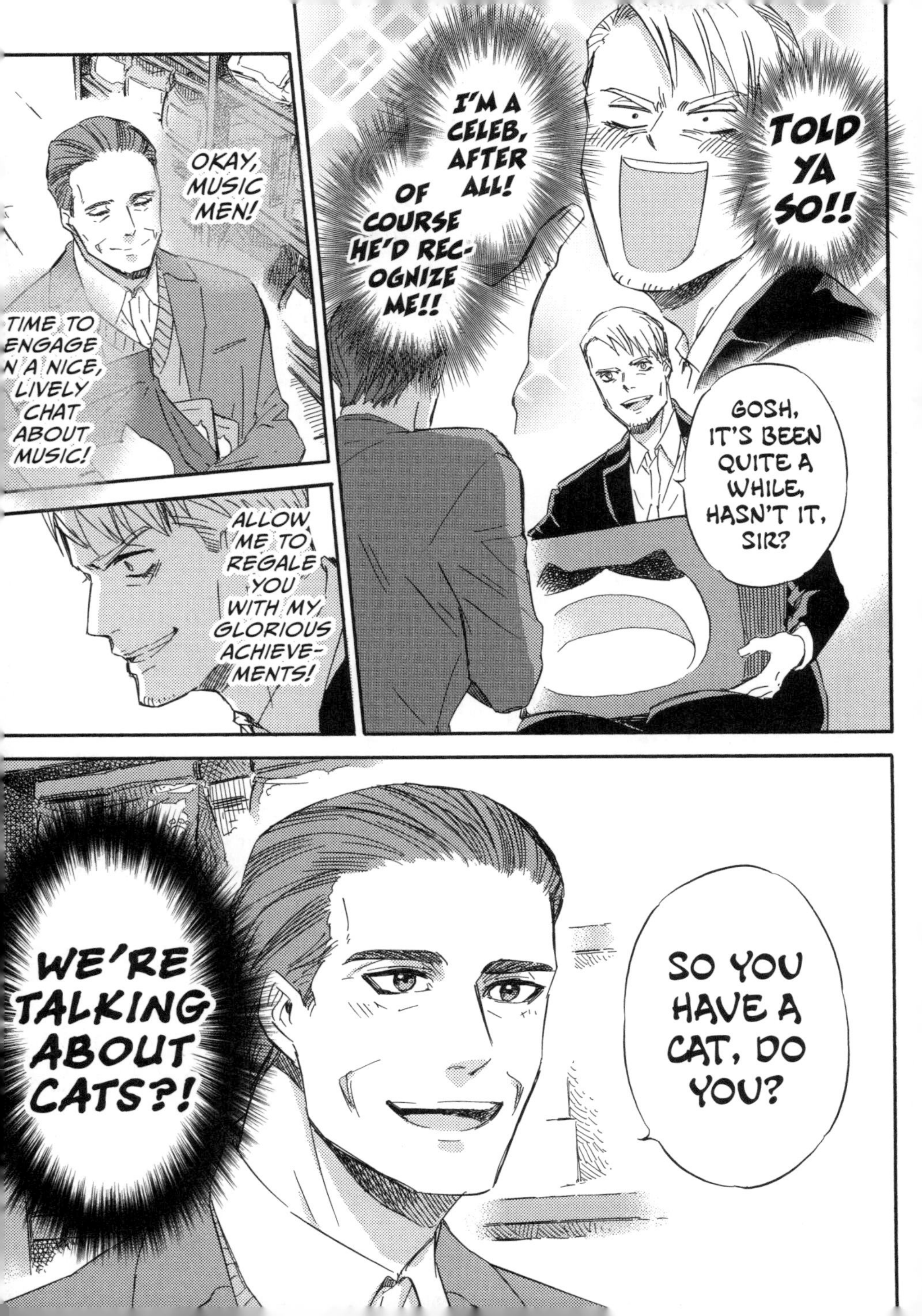
TOLD YA SO!!
I'M A CELEB, AFTER ALL!
OF COURSE HE'D REC-OGNIZE ME!!
GOSH, IT'S BEEN QUITE A WHILE, HASN'T IT, SIR?
OKAY, MUSIC MEN!
TIME TO ENGAGE N A NICE, LIVELY CHAT ABOUT MUSIC!
ALLOW ME TO REGALE YOU WITH MY GLORIOUS ACHIEVE-MENTS!
SO YOU HAVE A CAT, DO YOU?
WE'RE TALKING ABOUT CATS?!

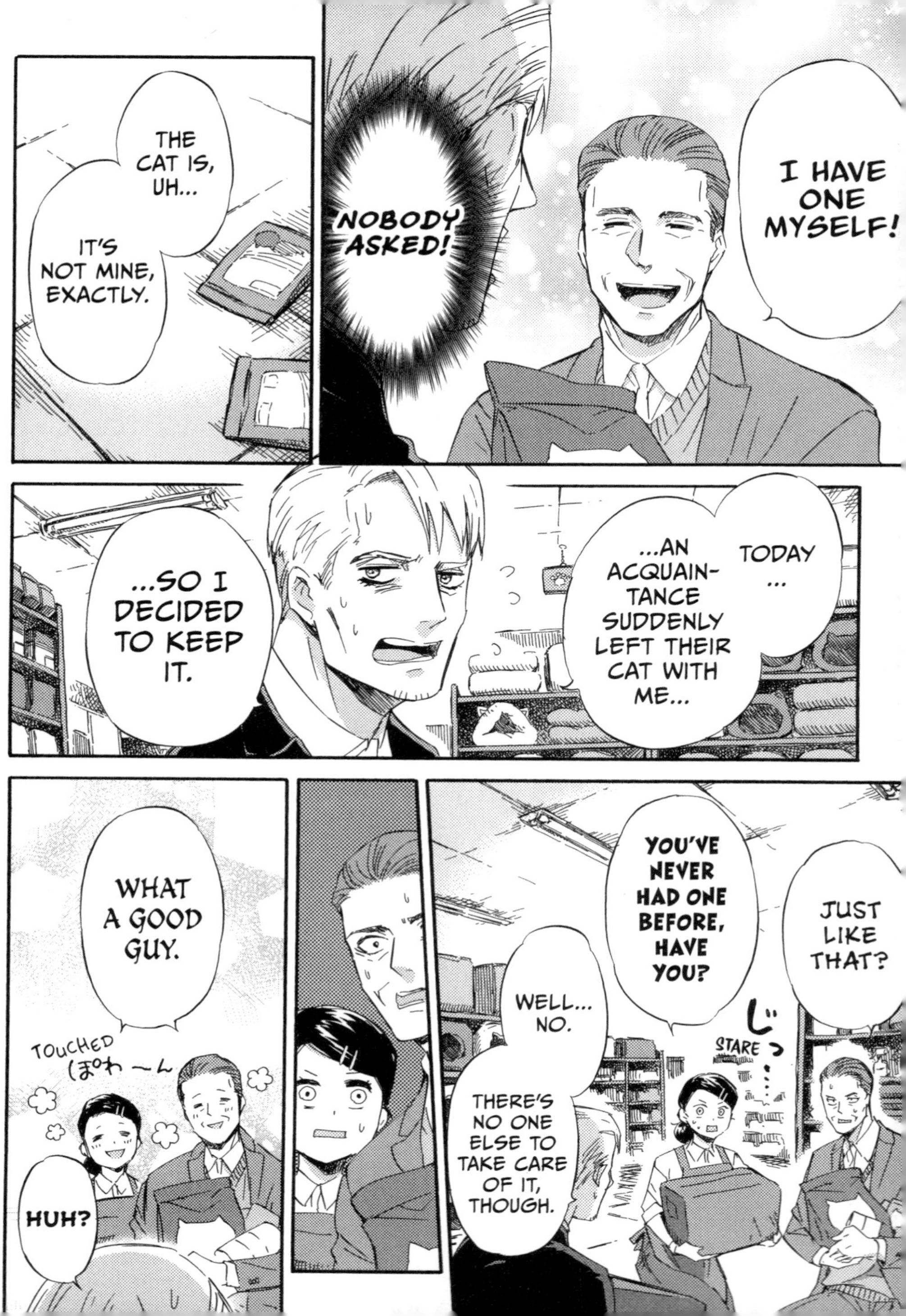
I HAVE ONE MYSELF!
NOBODY ASKED!
THE CAT IS, UH...
IT'S NOT MINE, EXACTLY.
TODAY...
...AN ACQUAIN-TANCE SUDDENLY LEFT THEIR CAT WITH ME...
...SO I DECIDED TO KEEP IT.
JUST LIKE THAT?
STARE
じっ
YOU'VE NEVER HAD ONE BEFORE, HAVE YOU?
WELL... NO.
THERE'S NO ONE ELSE TO TAKE CARE OF IT, THOUGH.
WHAT A GOOD GUY.
TOUCHED
ぽわ~ん
HUH?

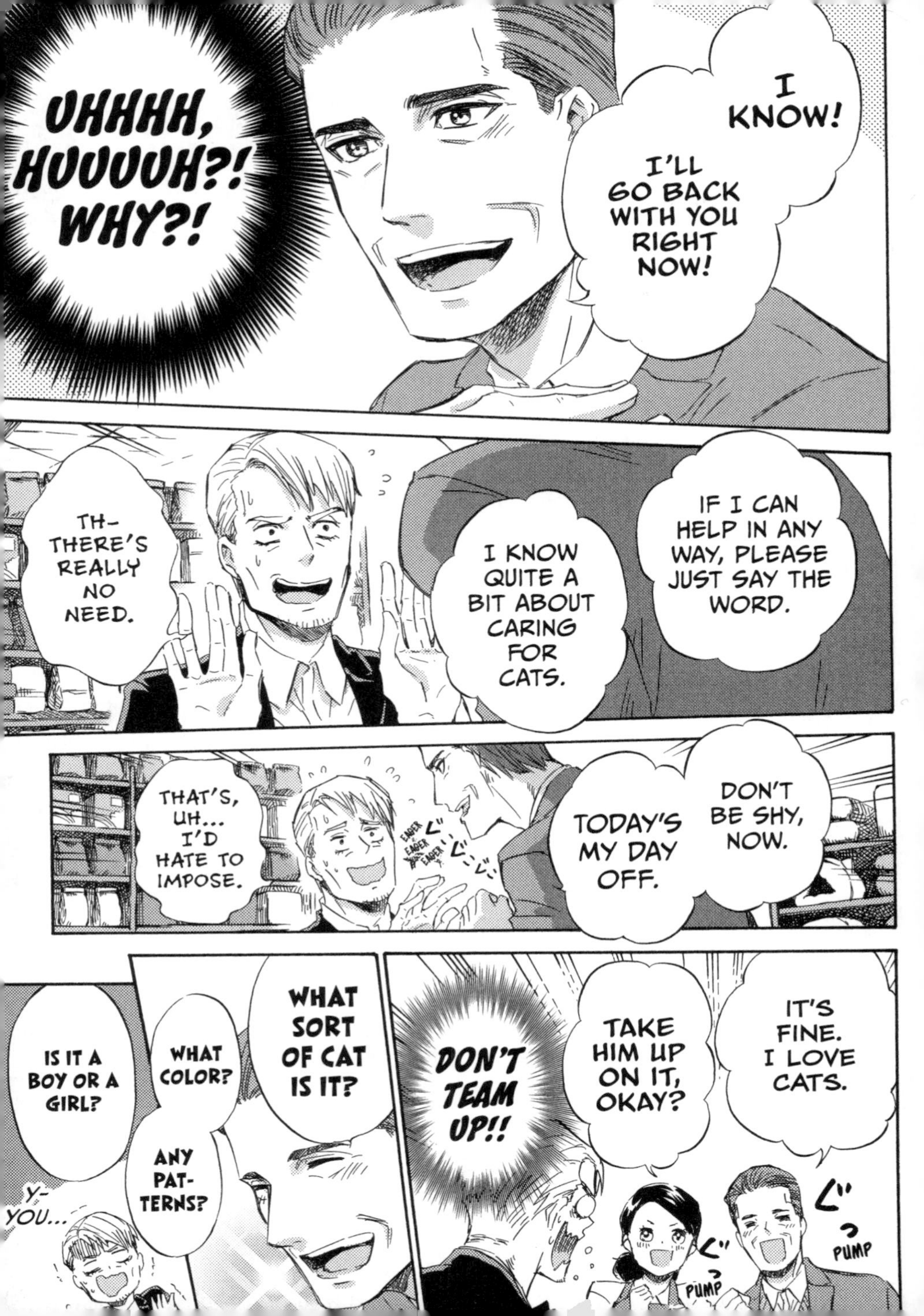
I KNOW!
I'LL GO BACK WITH YOU RIGHT NOW!
UHHHH, HUUUUH?! WHY?!
IF I CAN HELP IN ANY WAY, PLEASE JUST SAY THE WORD.
I KNOW QUITE A BIT ABOUT CARING FOR CATS.
TH- THERE'S REALLY NO NEED.
DON'T BE SHY, NOW.
TODAY'S MY DAY OFF.
EAGER EAGER EAGER
THAT'S, UH... I'D HATE TO IMPOSE.
IT'S FINE. I LOVE CATS.
TAKE HIM UP ON IT, OKAY?
PUMP
PUMP
DON'T TEAM UP!!
WHAT SORT OF CAT IS IT?
WHAT COLOR?
IS IT A BOY OR A GIRL?
ANY PAT-TERNS?
Y- YOU...

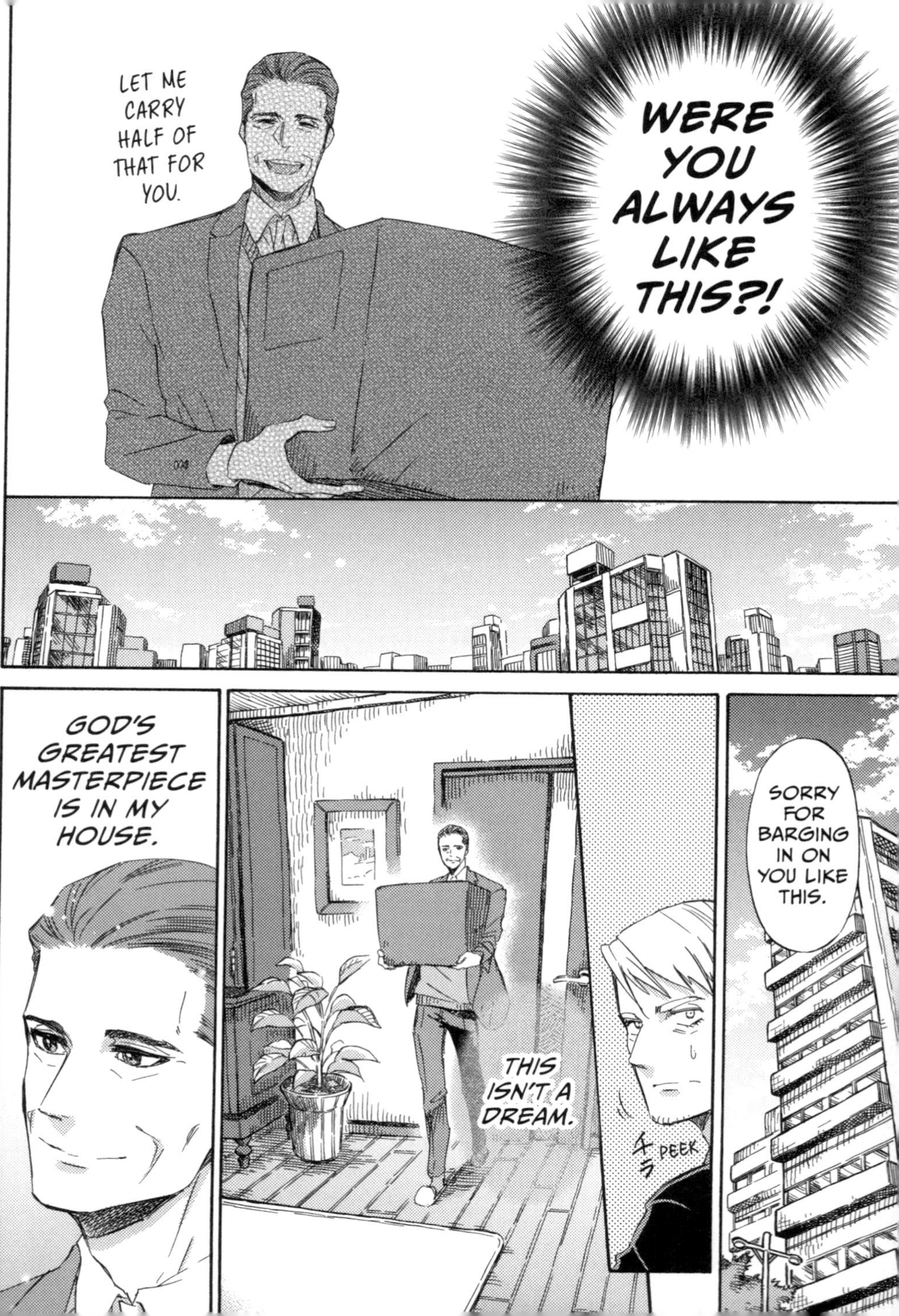
WERE YOU ALWAYS LIKE THIS?!
LET ME CARRY HALF OF THAT FOR YOU.
SORRY FOR BARGING IN ON YOU LIKE THIS.
PEEK
THIS ISN'T A DREAM.
GOD'S GREATEST MASTERPIECE IS IN MY HOUSE.

Chapter 40 | A Kind Voice

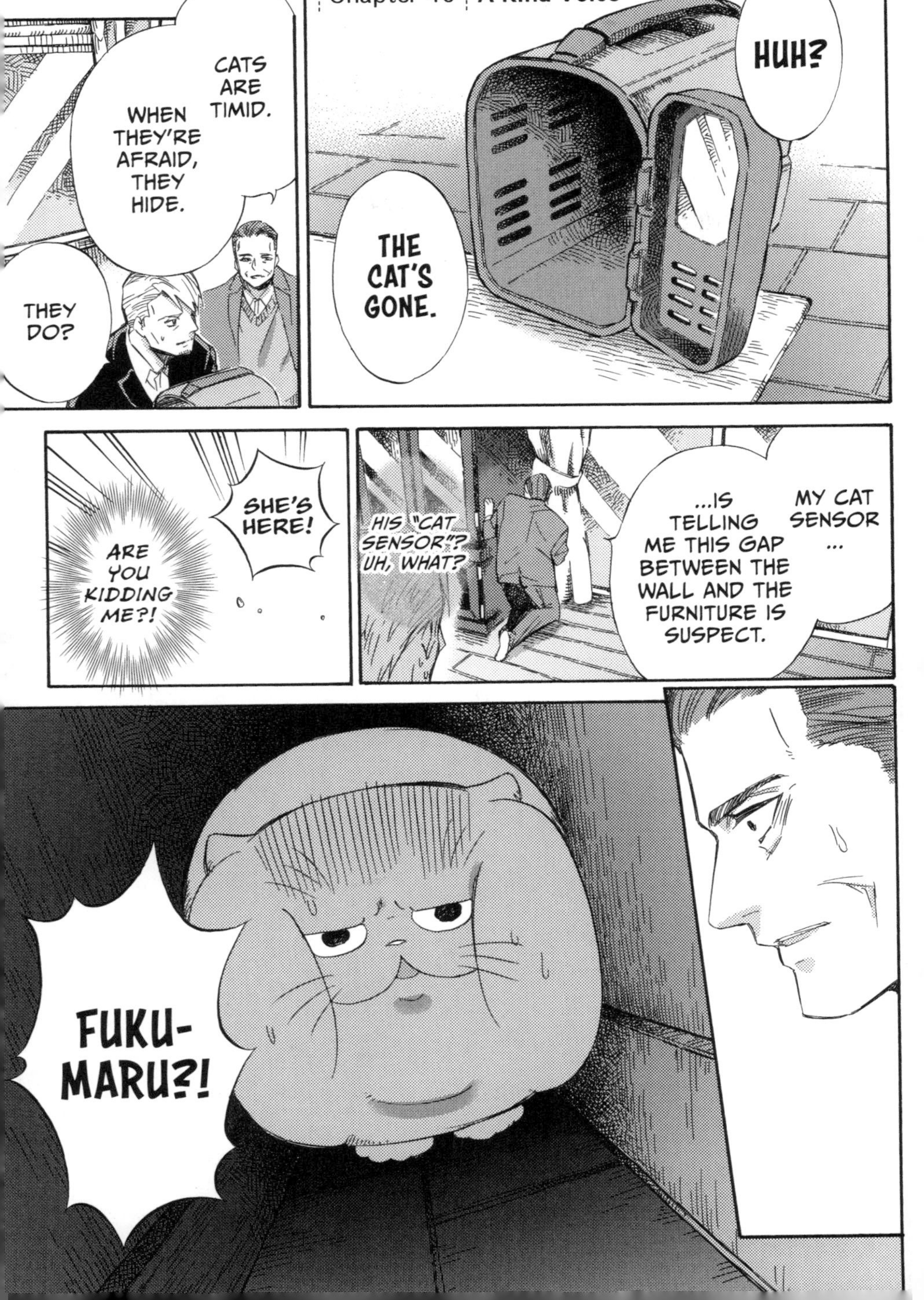
HUH?
THE CAT'S GONE.
CATS ARE TIMID. WHEN THEY'RE AFRAID, THEY HIDE.
THEY DO?
MY CAT SENSOR ...
...IS TELLING ME THIS GAP BETWEEN THE WALL AND THE FURNITURE IS SUSPECT.
HIS "CAT SENSOR"? UH, WHAT?
SHE'S HERE!
ARE YOU KIDDING ME?!
FUKU-MARU?!

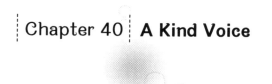

Chapter 40 | A Kind Voice

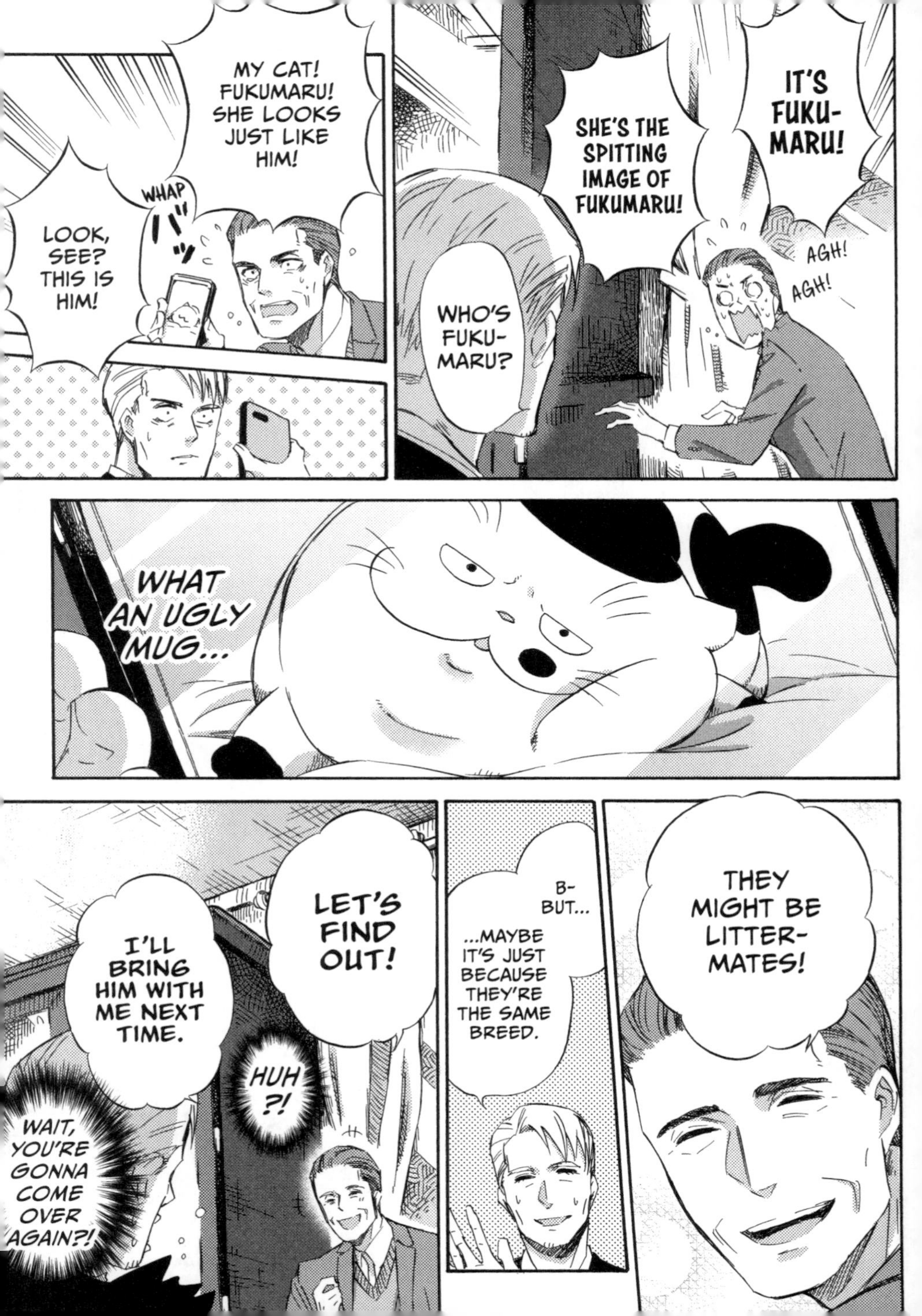
IT'S FUKU-MARU!
SHE'S THE SPITTING IMAGE OF FUKUMARU!
AGH!
AGH!
WHO'S FUKU-MARU?
MY CAT! FUKUMARU! SHE LOOKS JUST LIKE HIM!
WHAP
LOOK, SEE? THIS IS HIM!
WHAT AN UGLY MUG...
THEY MIGHT BE LITTER-MATES!
B-BUT...
...MAYBE IT'S JUST BECAUSE THEY'RE THE SAME BREED.
LET'S FIND OUT!
I'LL BRING HIM WITH ME NEXT TIME.
HUH?!
WAIT, YOU'RE GONNA COME OVER AGAIN?!

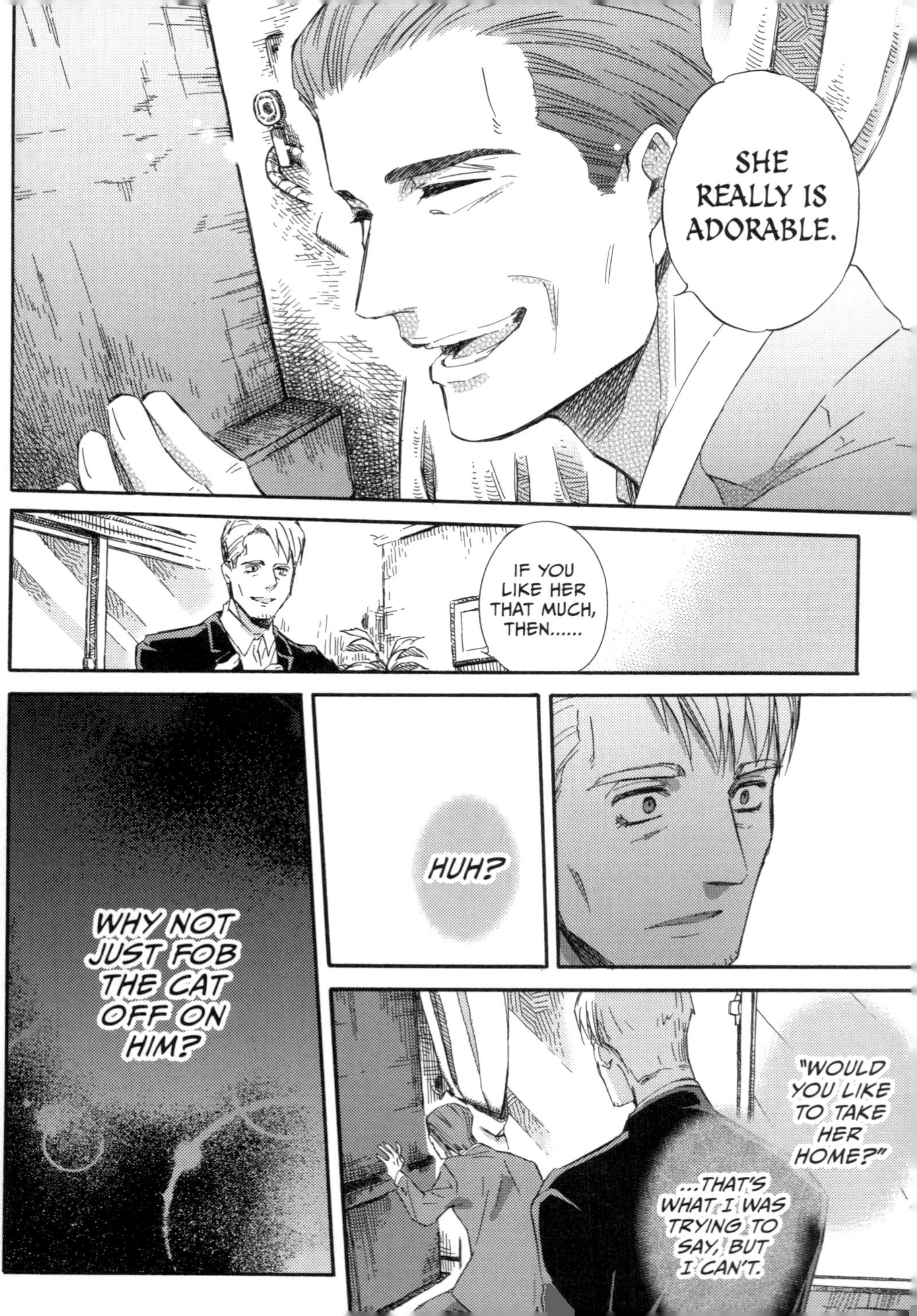
SHE REALLY IS ADORABLE.
IF YOU LIKE HER THAT MUCH, THEN......
HUH?
"WOULD YOU LIKE TO TAKE HER HOME?"
...THAT'S WHAT I WAS TRYING TO SAY, BUT I CAN'T.
WHY NOT JUST FOB THE CAT OFF ON HIM?

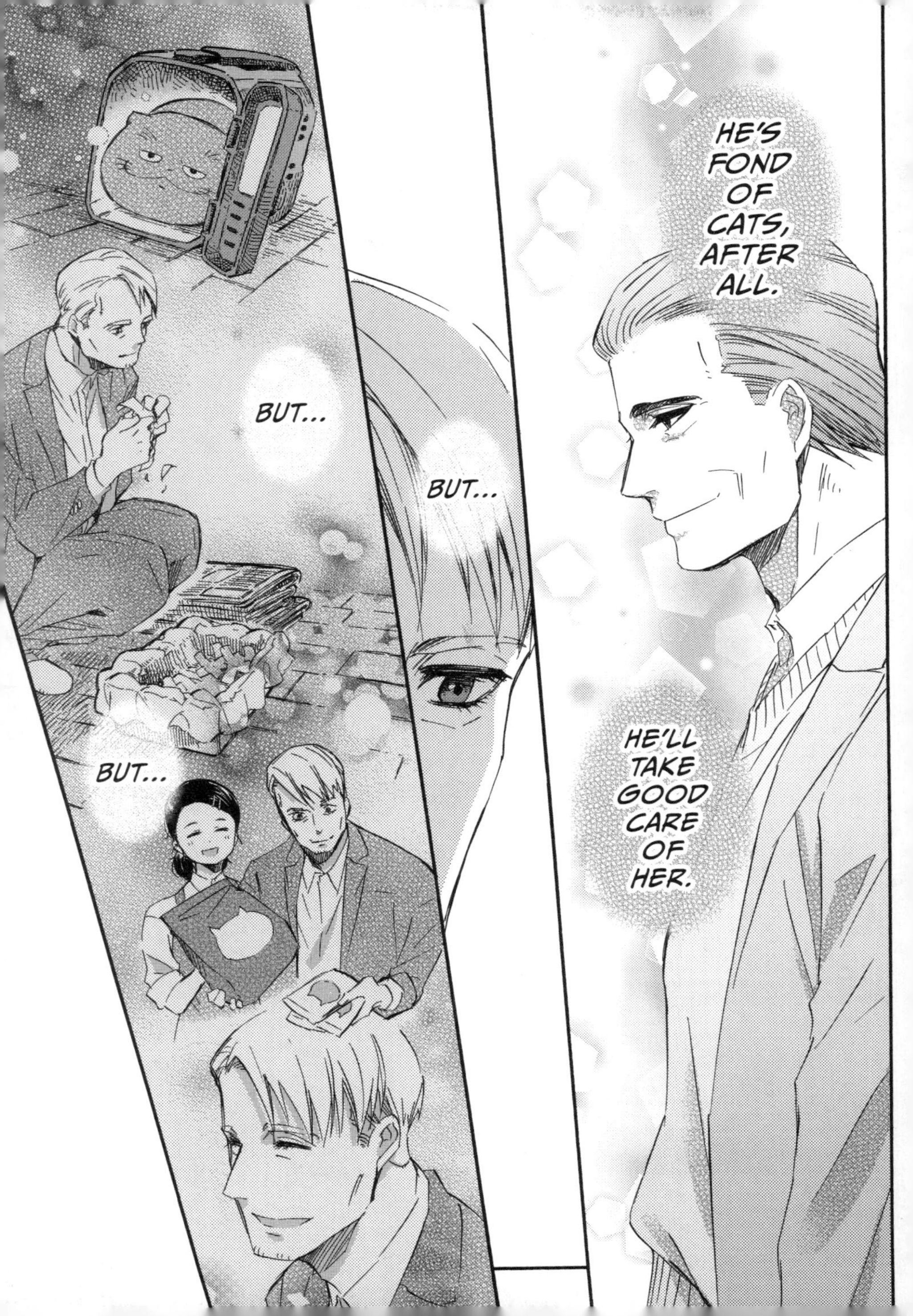
HE'S FOND OF CATS, AFTER ALL.
HE'LL TAKE GOOD CARE OF HER.
BUT...
BUT...
BUT...

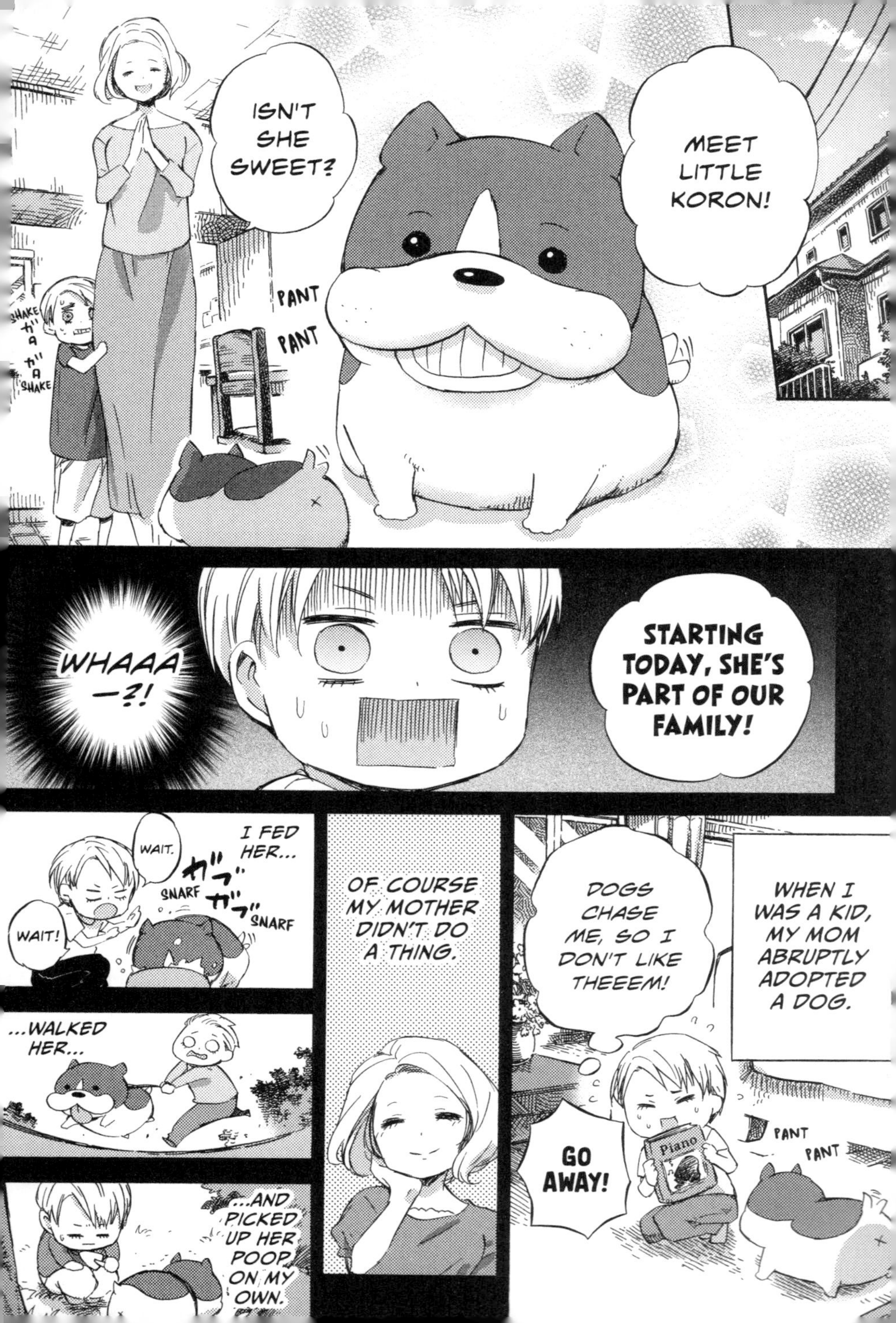
MEET LITTLE KORON!
ISN'T SHE SWEET?
PANT
PANT
SHAKE
SHAKE
STARTING TODAY, SHE'S PART OF OUR FAMILY!
WHAAA—?!
WHEN I WAS A KID, MY MOM ABRUPTLY ADOPTED A DOG.
DOGS CHASE ME, SO I DON'T LIKE THEEEM!
GO AWAY!
PANT
PANT
Piano
OF COURSE MY MOTHER DIDN'T DO A THING.
I FED HER...
WAIT.
WAIT!
SNARF
SNARF
...WALKED HER...
...AND PICKED UP HER POOP ON MY OWN.

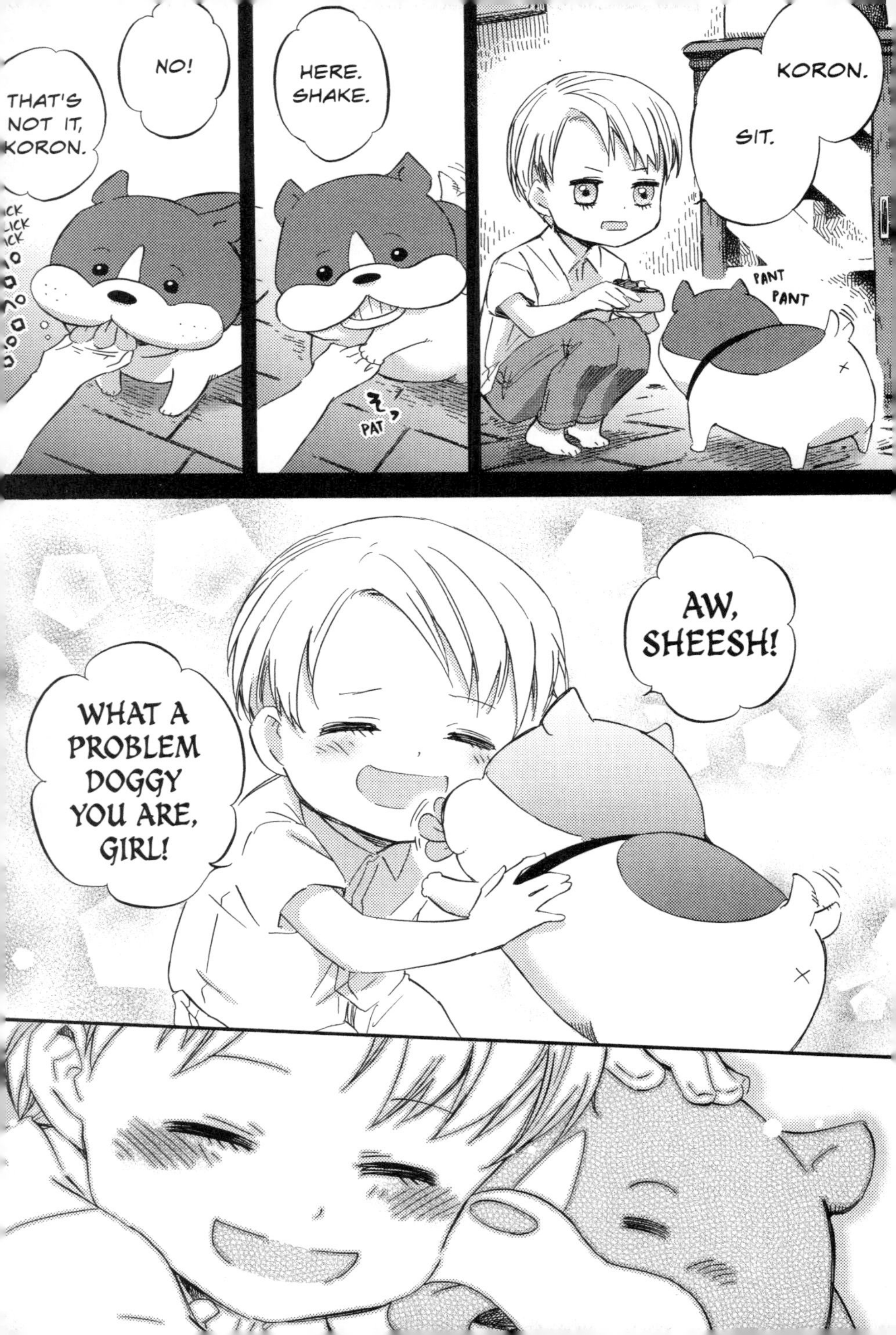
KORON.
SIT.
PANT PANT
HERE. SHAKE.
PAT
NO!
THAT'S NOT IT, KORON.
AW, SHEESH!
WHAT A PROBLEM DOGGY YOU ARE, GIRL!

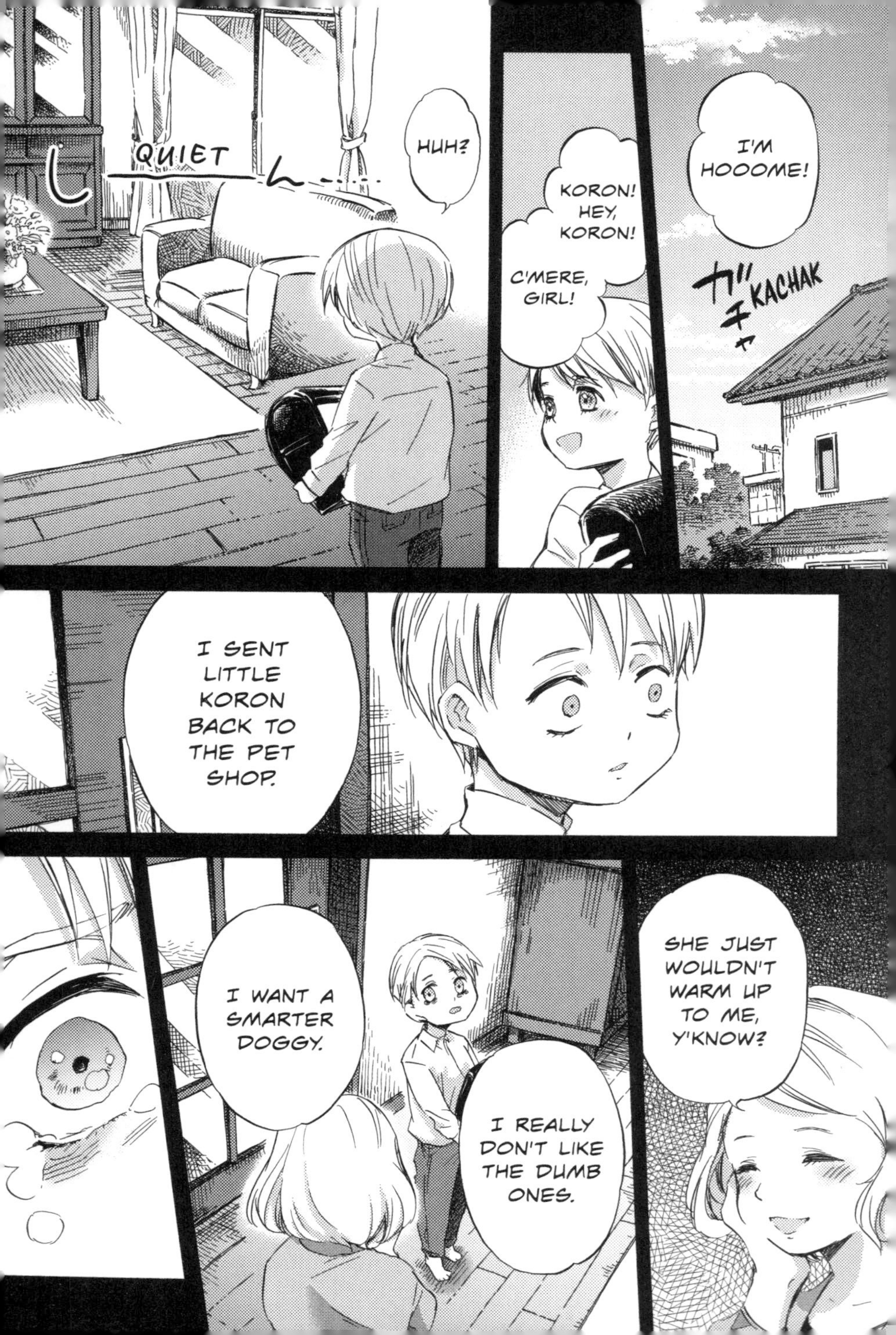
I'M HOOOME!
ガチャ KACHAK
KORON! HEY, KORON!
C'MERE, GIRL!
HUH?
QUIET
I SENT LITTLE KORON BACK TO THE PET SHOP.
SHE JUST WOULDN'T WARM UP TO ME, Y'KNOW?
I REALLY DON'T LIKE THE DUMB ONES.
I WANT A SMARTER DOGGY.

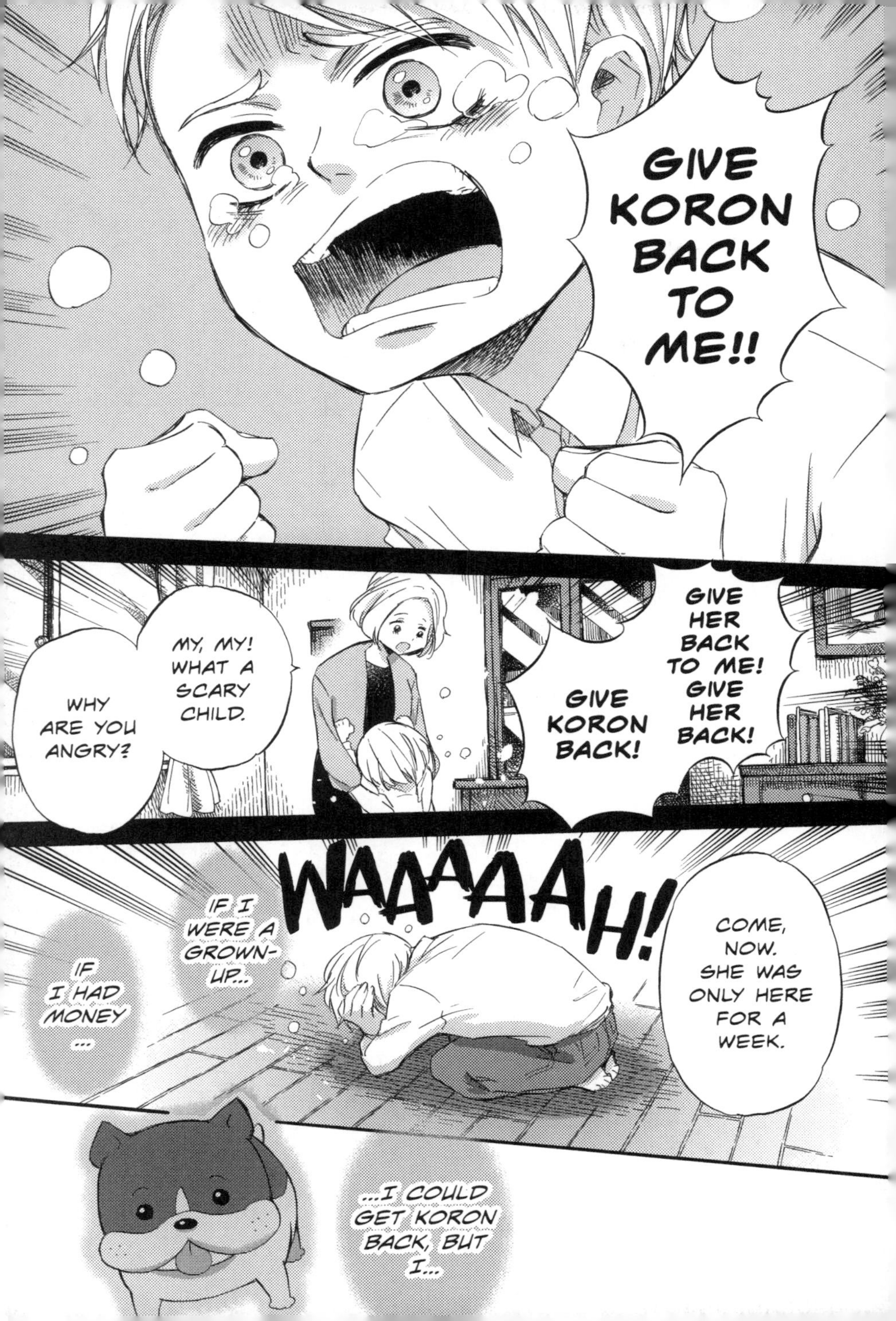
GIVE KORON BACK TO ME!!
GIVE HER BACK TO ME! GIVE HER BACK!
GIVE KORON BACK!
MY, MY! WHAT A SCARY CHILD.
WHY ARE YOU ANGRY?
COME, NOW. SHE WAS ONLY HERE FOR A WEEK.
WAAAAAH!
IF I WERE A GROWN-UP...
IF I HAD MONEY...
...I COULD GET KORON BACK, BUT I...

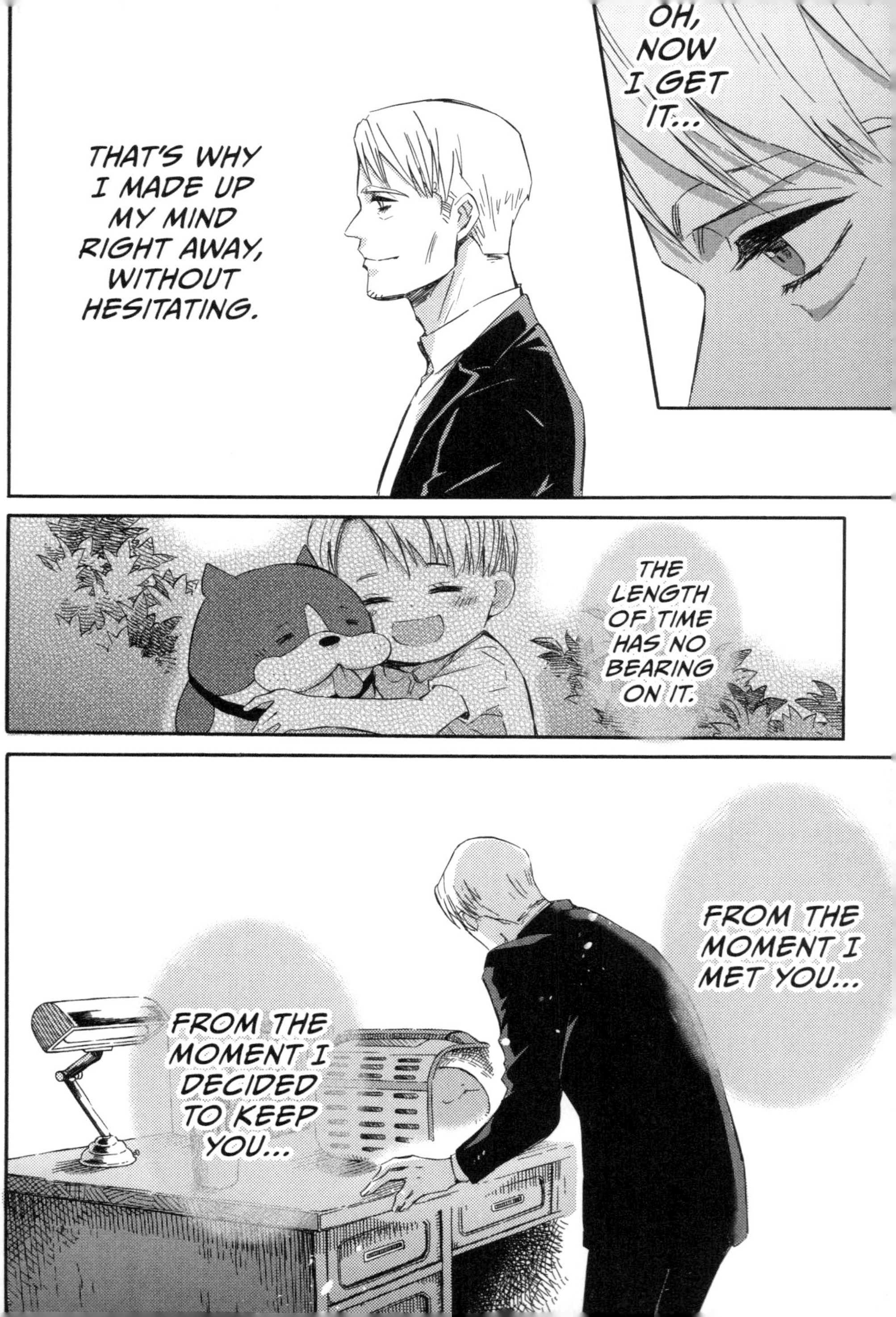
OH, NOW I GET IT...
THAT'S WHY I MADE UP MY MIND RIGHT AWAY, WITHOUT HESITATING.
THE LENGTH OF TIME HAS NO BEARING ON IT.
FROM THE MOMENT I MET YOU...
FROM THE MOMENT I DECIDED TO KEEP YOU...

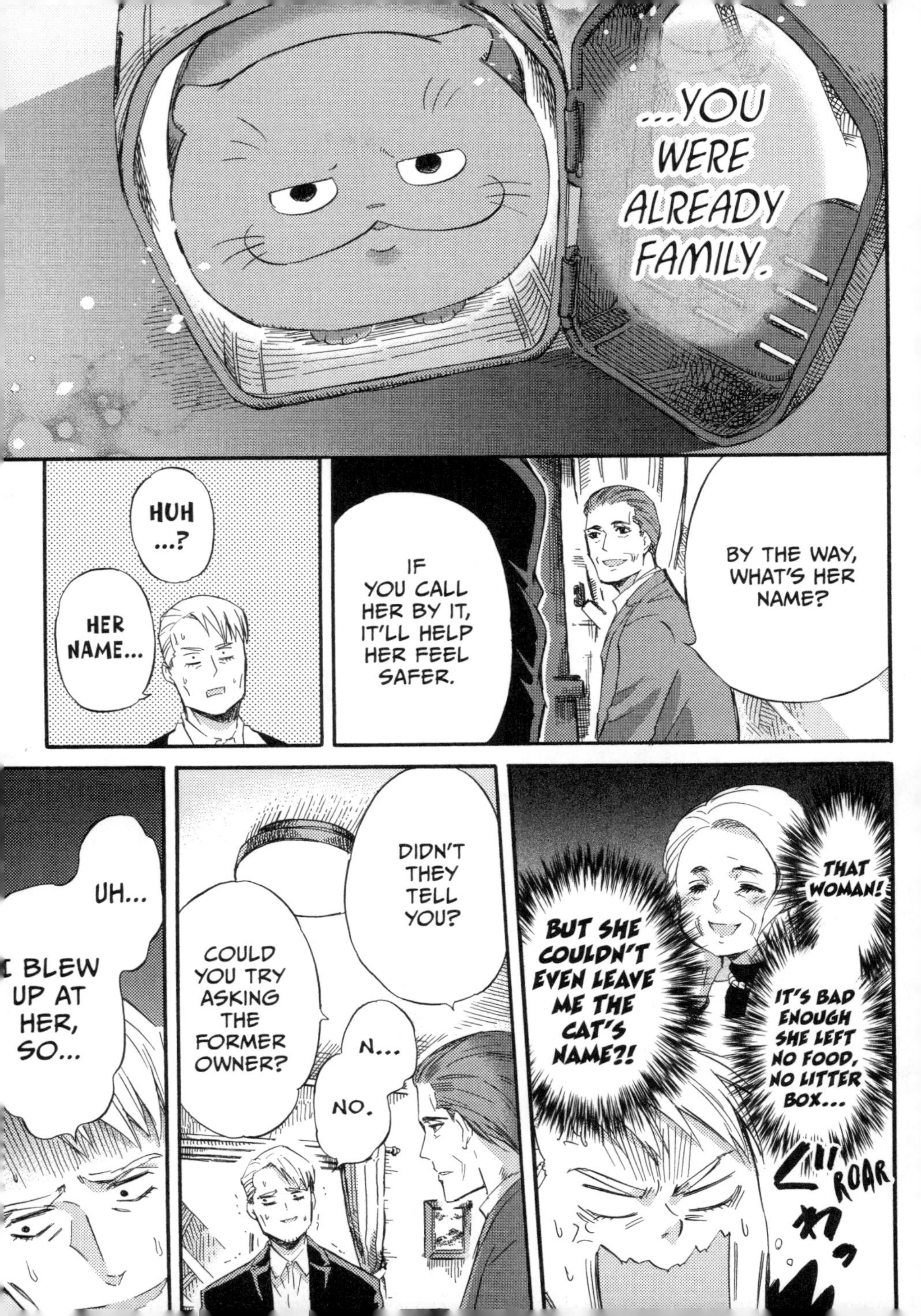
...YOU WERE ALREADY FAMILY.
BY THE WAY, WHAT'S HER NAME?
IF YOU CALL HER BY IT, IT'LL HELP HER FEEL SAFER.
HUH ...?
HER NAME...
THAT WOMAN!
IT'S BAD ENOUGH SHE LEFT NO FOOD, NO LITTER BOX...
BUT SHE COULDN'T EVEN LEAVE ME THE CAT'S NAME?!
ROAR
DIDN'T THEY TELL YOU?
COULD YOU TRY ASKING THE FORMER OWNER?
N...
NO.
UH...
I BLEW UP AT HER, SO...

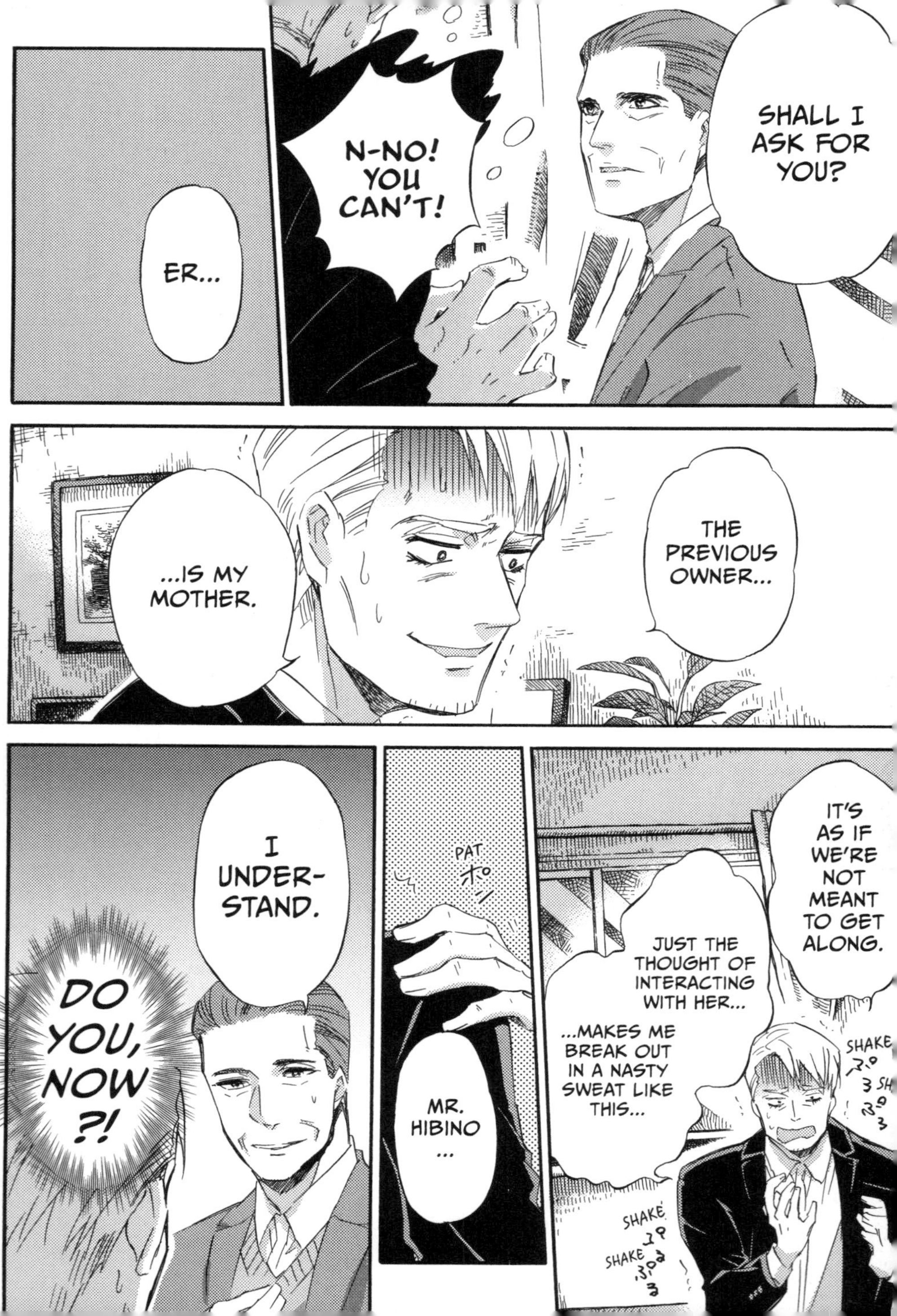
SHALL I ASK FOR YOU?
N-NO! YOU CAN'T!
ER...
THE PREVIOUS OWNER...
...IS MY MOTHER.
IT'S AS IF WE'RE NOT MEANT TO GET ALONG.
JUST THE THOUGHT OF INTERACTING WITH HER...
...MAKES ME BREAK OUT IN A NASTY SWEAT LIKE THIS...
SHAKE
SH
SHAKE
SHAKE
PAT
MR. HIBINO ...
I UNDER-STAND.
DO YOU, NOW?!

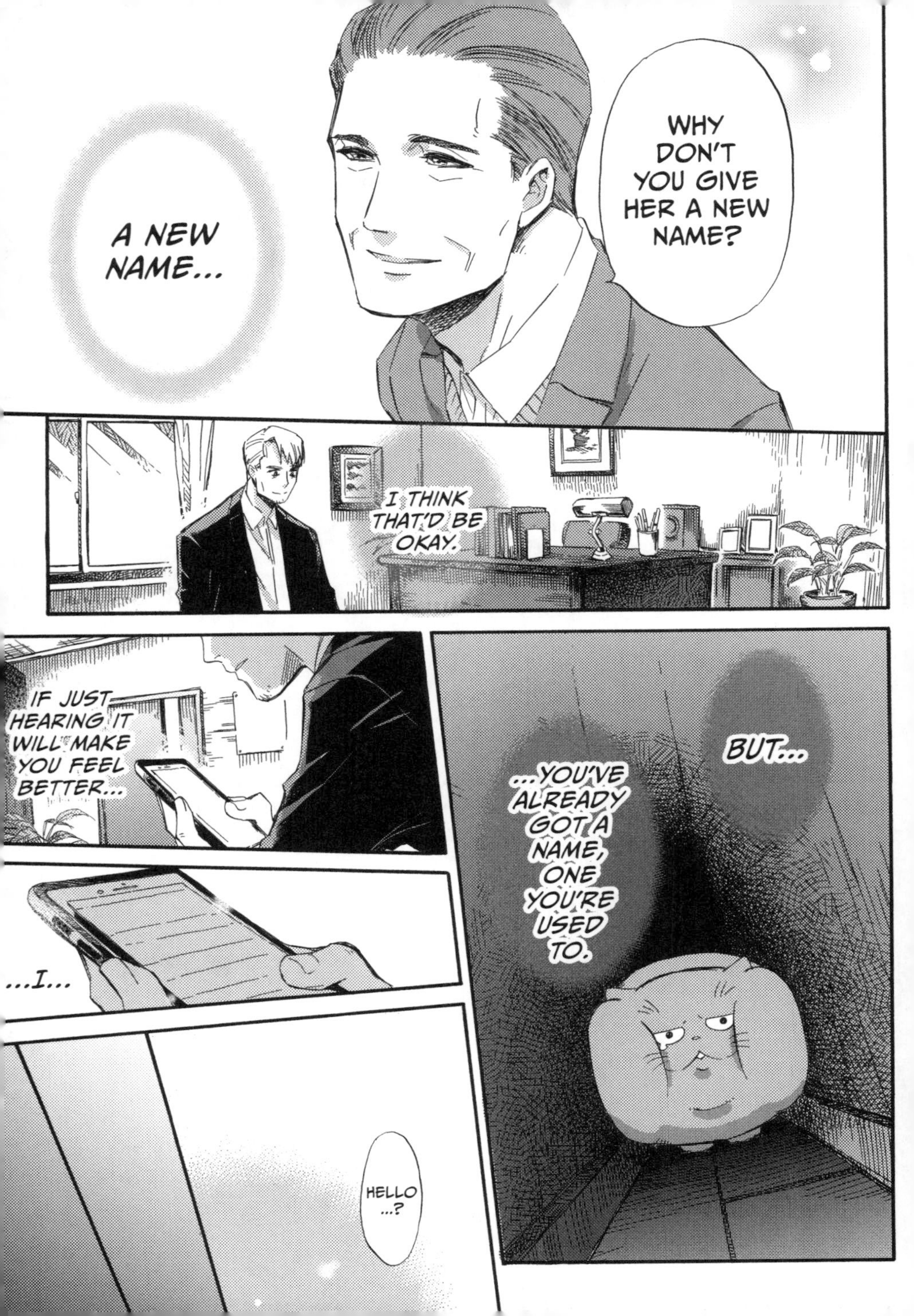
WHY DON'T YOU GIVE HER A NEW NAME?
A NEW NAME...
I THINK THAT'D BE OKAY.
BUT...
...YOU'VE ALREADY GOT A NAME, ONE YOU'RE USED TO.
IF JUST HEARING IT WILL MAKE YOU FEEL BETTER...
...I...
HELLO ...?

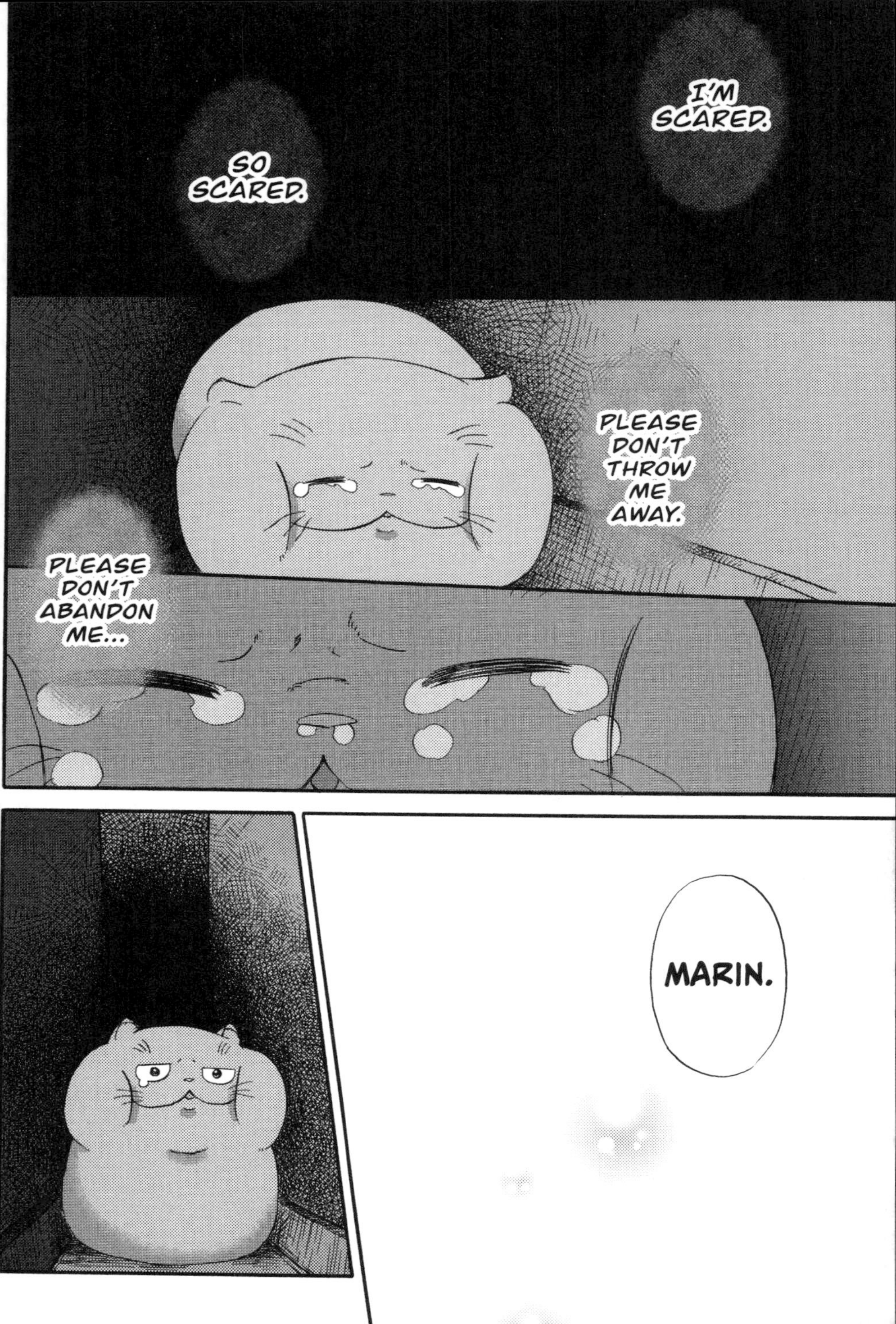
I'M SCARED.
SO SCARED.
PLEASE DON'T THROW ME AWAY.
PLEASE DON'T ABANDON ME...
MARIN.

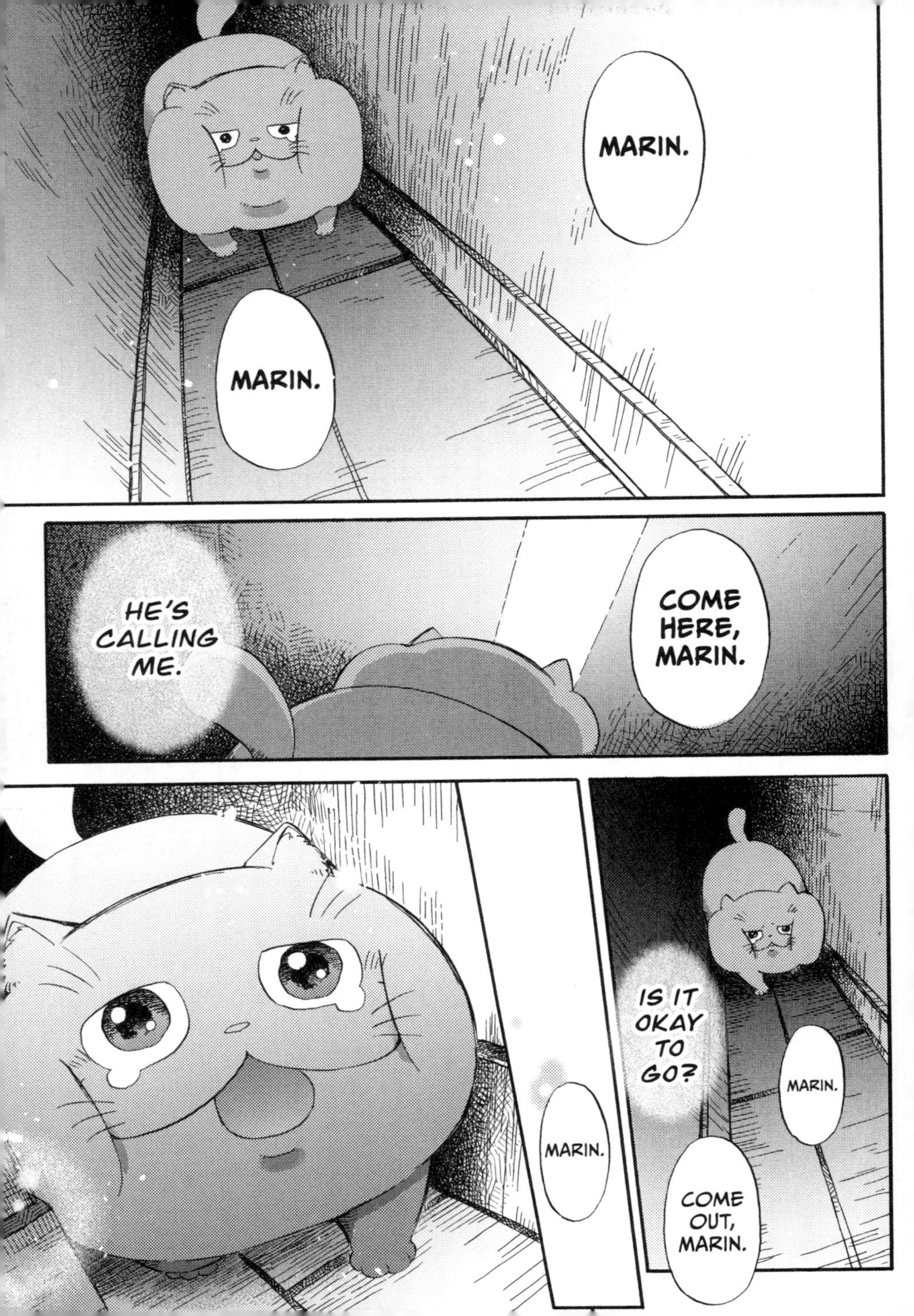
MARIN.
MARIN.
COME HERE, MARIN.
HE'S CALLING ME.
IS IT OKAY TO GO?
MARIN.
COME OUT, MARIN.
MARIN.

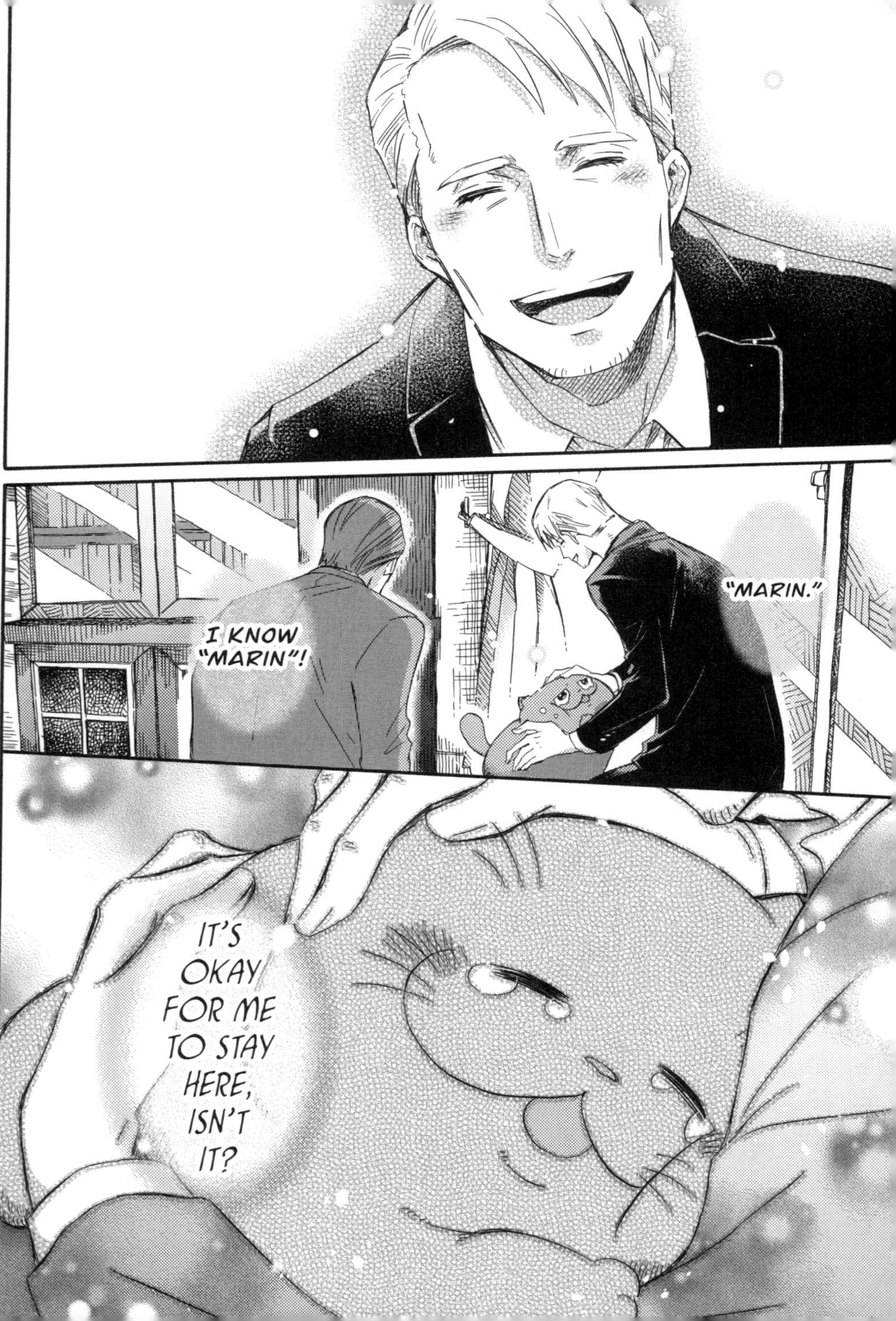
"MARIN."
I KNOW "MARIN"!
IT'S OKAY FOR ME TO STAY HERE, ISN'T IT?

The Man Is a Cat Guru

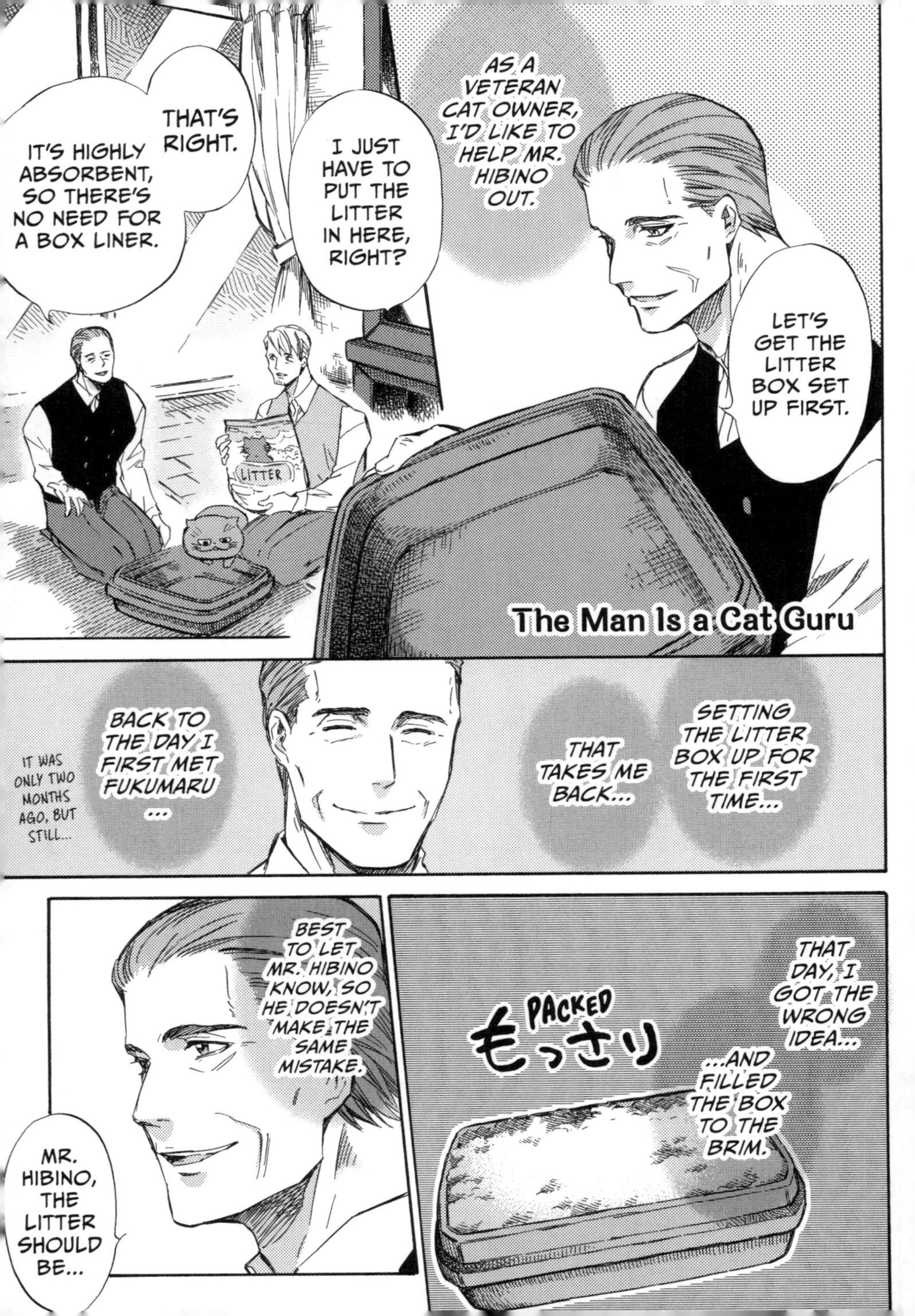

AS A VETERAN CAT OWNER, I'D LIKE TO HELP MR. HIBINO OUT.
LET'S GET THE LITTER BOX SET UP FIRST.
I JUST HAVE TO PUT THE LITTER IN HERE, RIGHT?
THAT'S RIGHT.
IT'S HIGHLY ABSORBENT, SO THERE'S NO NEED FOR A BOX LINER.
LITTER
SETTING THE LITTER BOX UP FOR THE FIRST TIME...
THAT TAKES ME BACK...
BACK TO THE DAY I FIRST MET FUKUMARU ...
IT WAS ONLY TWO MONTHS AGO, BUT STILL...
THAT DAY, I GOT THE WRONG IDEA...
...AND FILLED THE BOX TO THE BRIM.
もっさり PACKED
BEST TO LET MR. HIBINO KNOW, SO HE DOESN'T MAKE THE SAME MISTAKE.
MR. HIBINO, THE LITTER SHOULD BE...

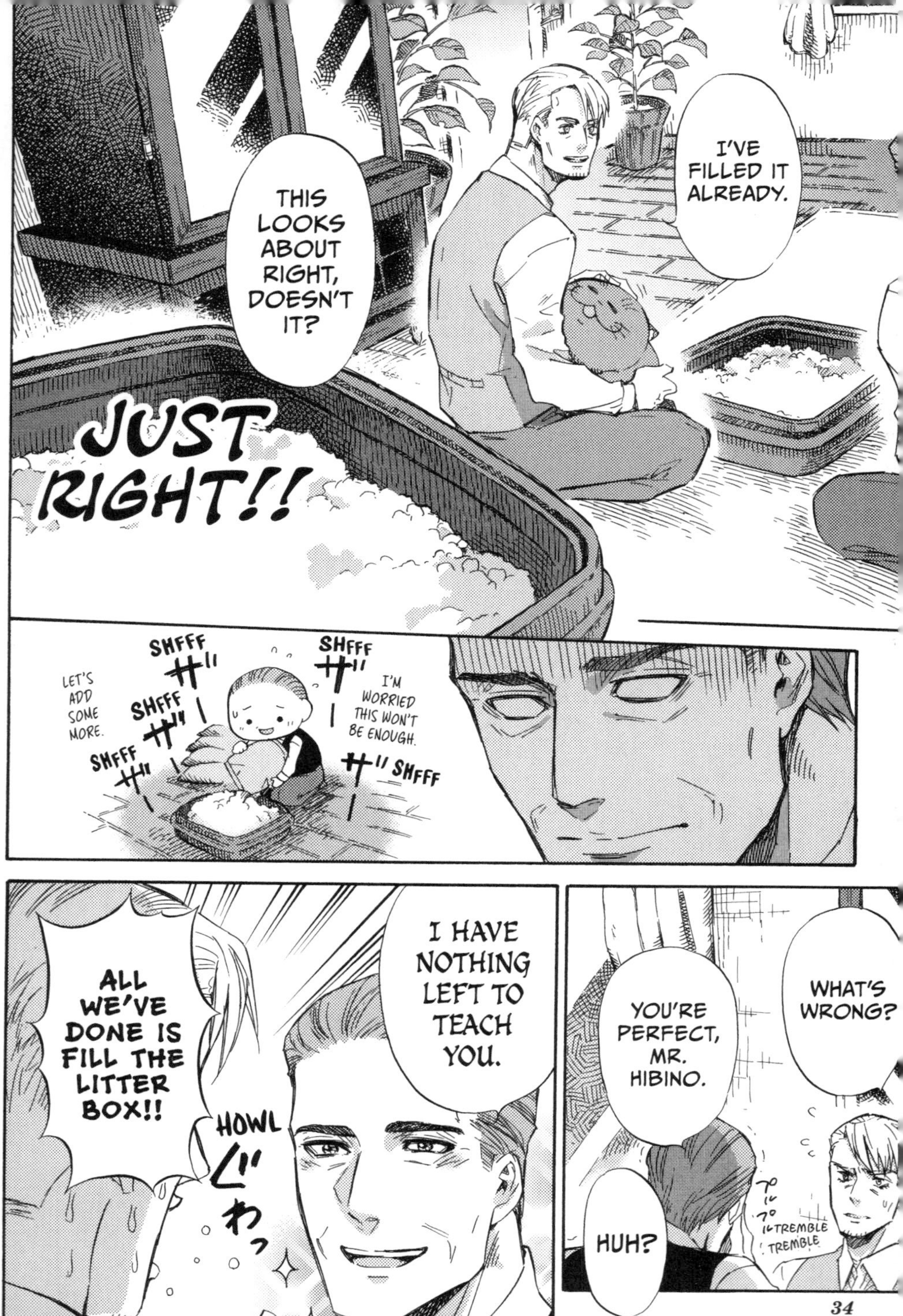
I'VE FILLED IT ALREADY.
THIS LOOKS ABOUT RIGHT, DOESN'T IT?
JUST RIGHT!!
SHFFF
I'M WORRIED THIS WON'T BE ENOUGH.
SHFFF
SHFFF
LET'S ADD SOME MORE.
SHFFF
SHFFF
WHAT'S WRONG?
YOU'RE PERFECT, MR. HIBINO.
HUH?
TREMBLE TREMBLE
I HAVE NOTHING LEFT TO TEACH YOU.
ALL WE'VE DONE IS FILL THE LITTER BOX!!
HOWL

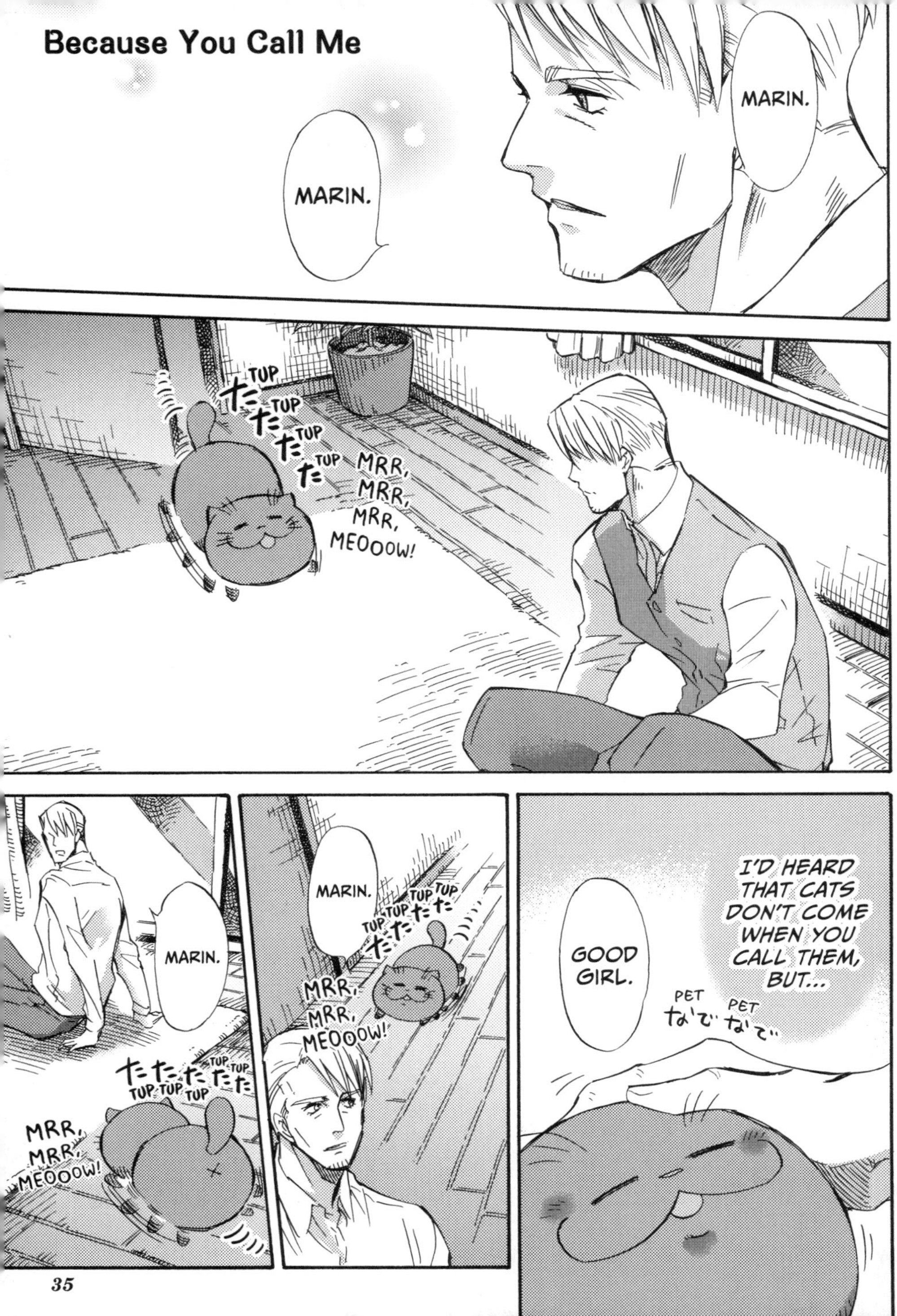
MARIN.
MARIN.
TUP TUP TUP TUP
MRR, MRR, MRR, MEOOOW!
I'D HEARD THAT CATS DON'T COME WHEN YOU CALL THEM, BUT...
GOOD GIRL.
PET PET
MARIN.
TUP TUP TUP TUP
MRR, MRR, MEOOOW!
MARIN.
TUP TUP TUP TUP TUP TUP
MRR, MRR, MEOOOW!

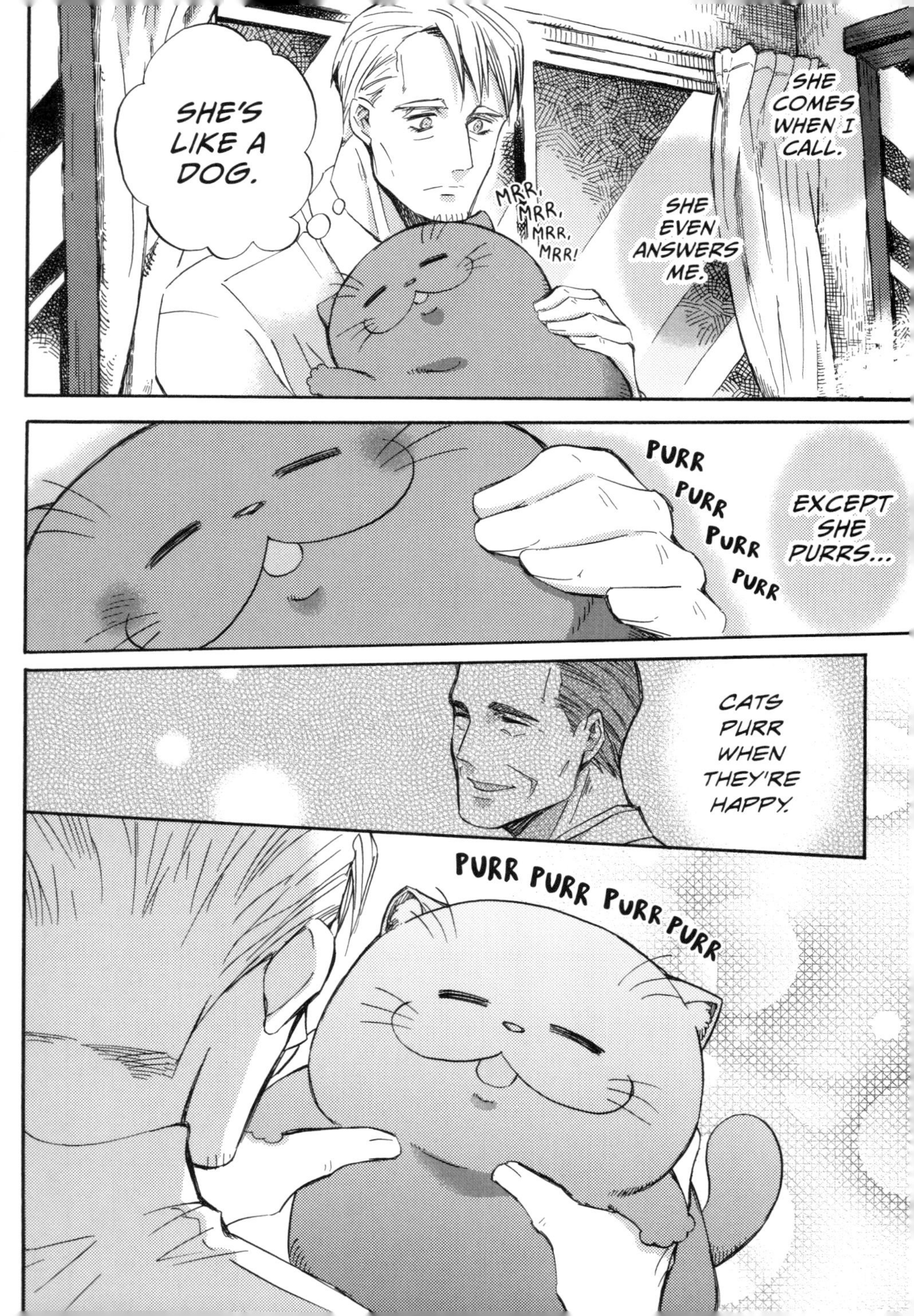
SHE COMES WHEN I CALL.
SHE EVEN ANSWERS ME.
MRR, MRR, MRR, MRR!
SHE'S LIKE A DOG.
EXCEPT SHE PURRS...
PURR PURR PURR PURR
CATS PURR WHEN THEY'RE HAPPY.
PURR PURR PURR PURR

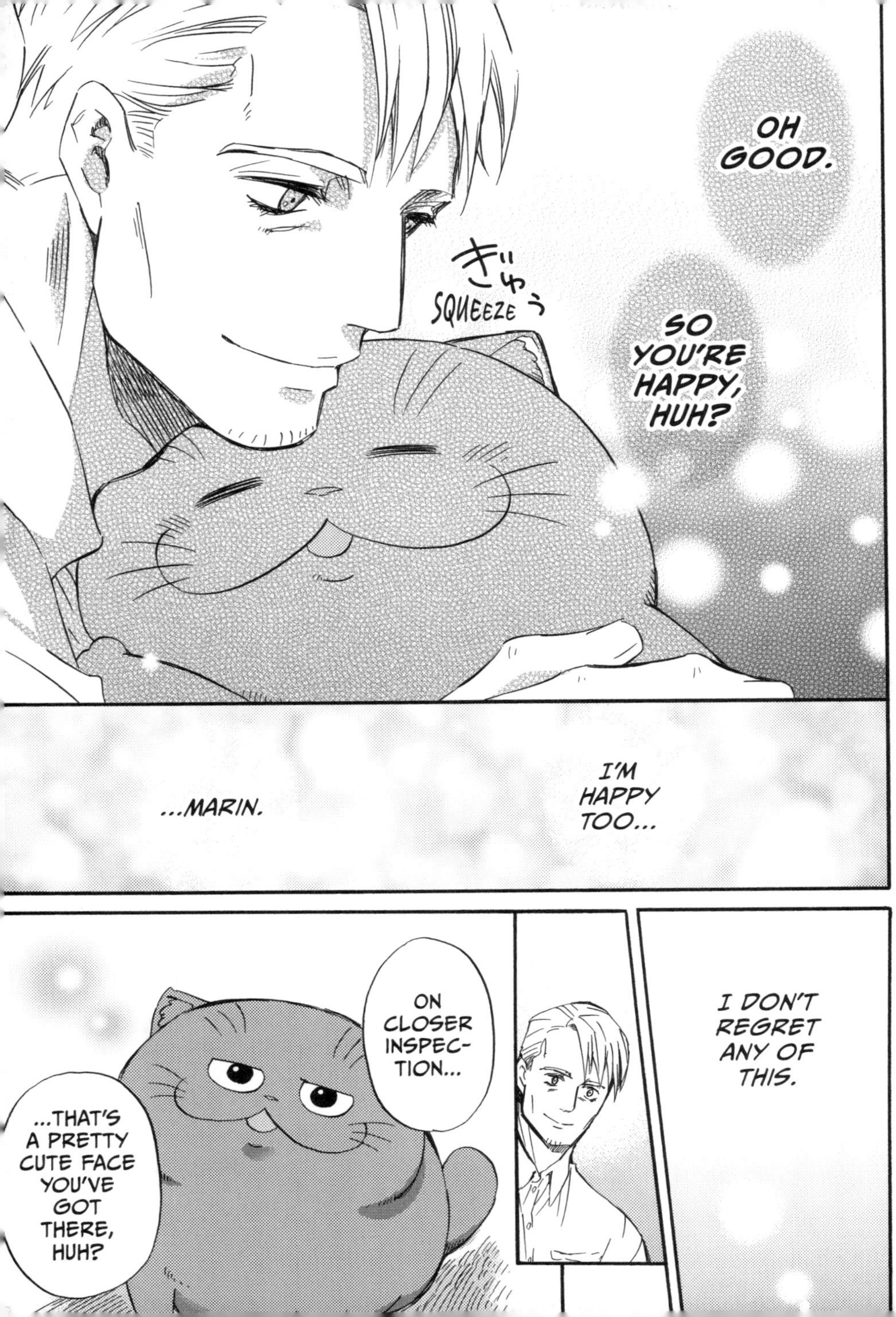
OH GOOD.
SO YOU'RE HAPPY, HUH?
ぎゅう
SQUEEZE
I'M HAPPY TOO...
...MARIN.
I DON'T REGRET ANY OF THIS.
ON CLOSER INSPEC-TION...
...THAT'S A PRETTY CUTE FACE YOU'VE GOT THERE, HUH?

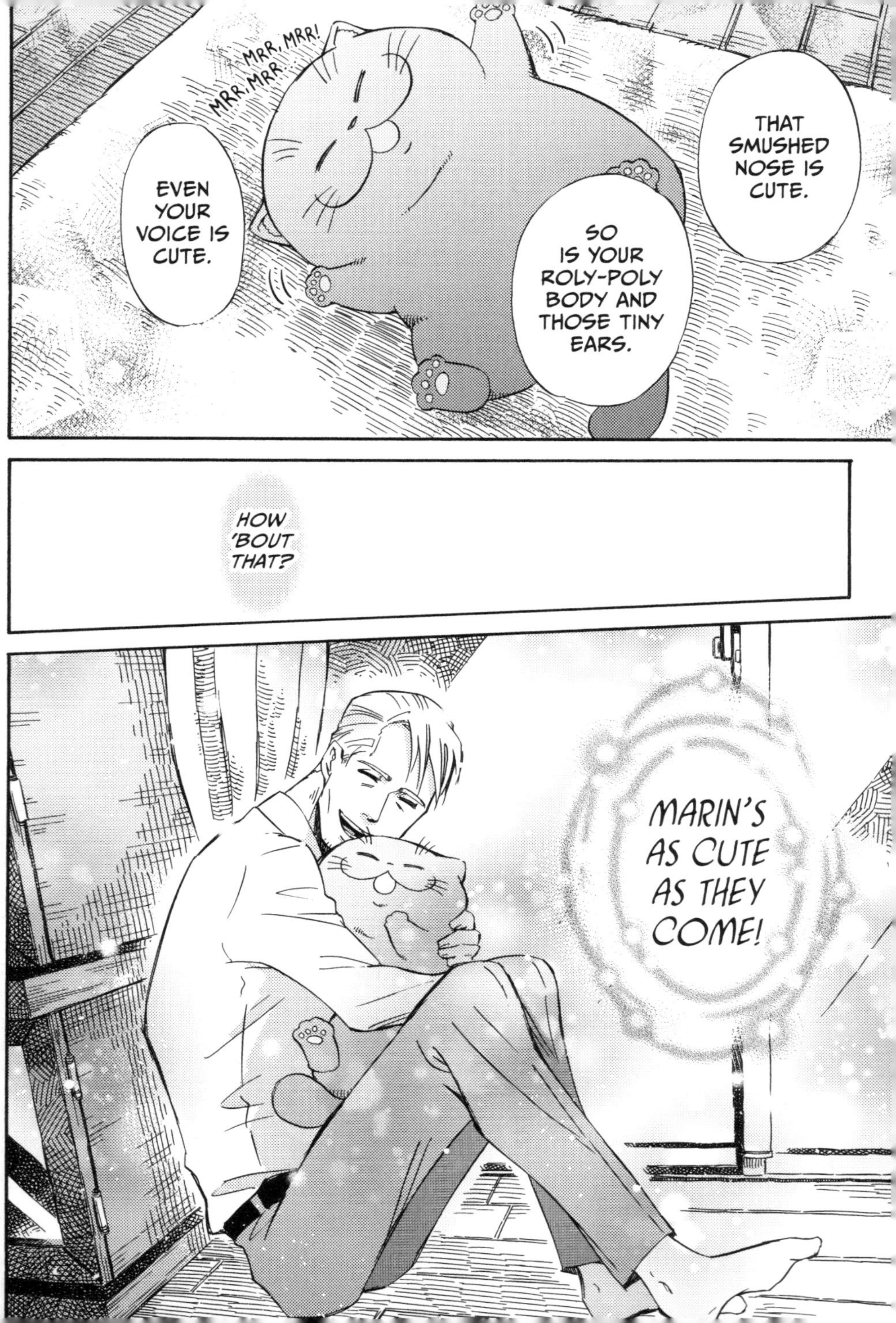
THAT SMUSHED NOSE IS CUTE.
MRR, MRR! MRR, MRR...
SO IS YOUR ROLY-POLY BODY AND THOSE TINY EARS.
EVEN YOUR VOICE IS CUTE.
HOW 'BOUT THAT?
MARIN'S AS CUTE AS THEY COME!

THE MAN'S LIMIT

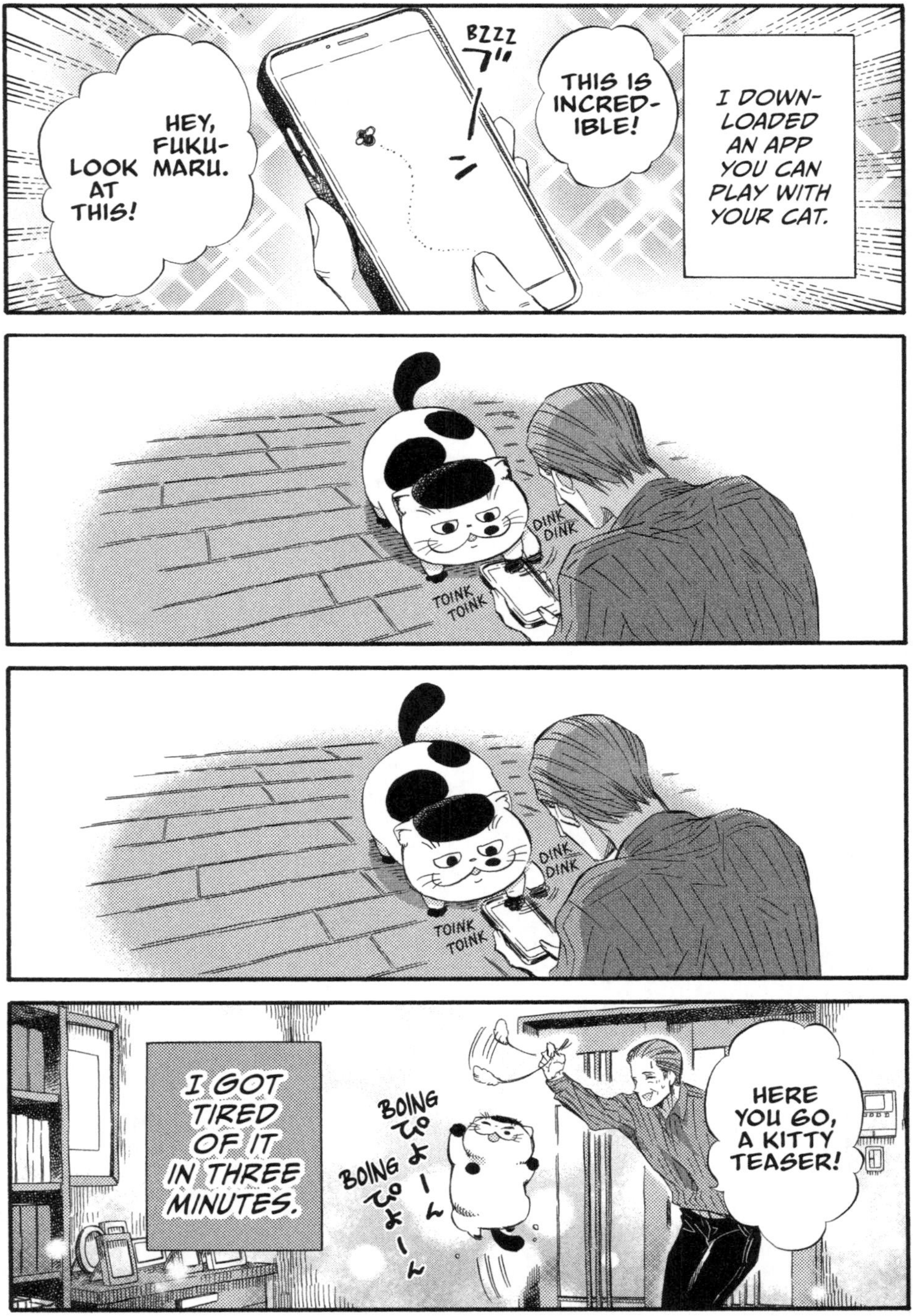

I DOWNLOADED AN APP YOU CAN PLAY WITH YOUR CAT.
THIS IS INCREDIBLE!
BZZZ
ブ"
HEY, FUKUMARU. LOOK AT THIS!
DINK DINK
TOINK TOINK
DINK DINK
TOINK TOINK
HERE YOU GO, A KITTY TEASER!
BOING
ぴょーん
BOING
ぴょーん
I GOT TIRED OF IT IN THREE MINUTES.

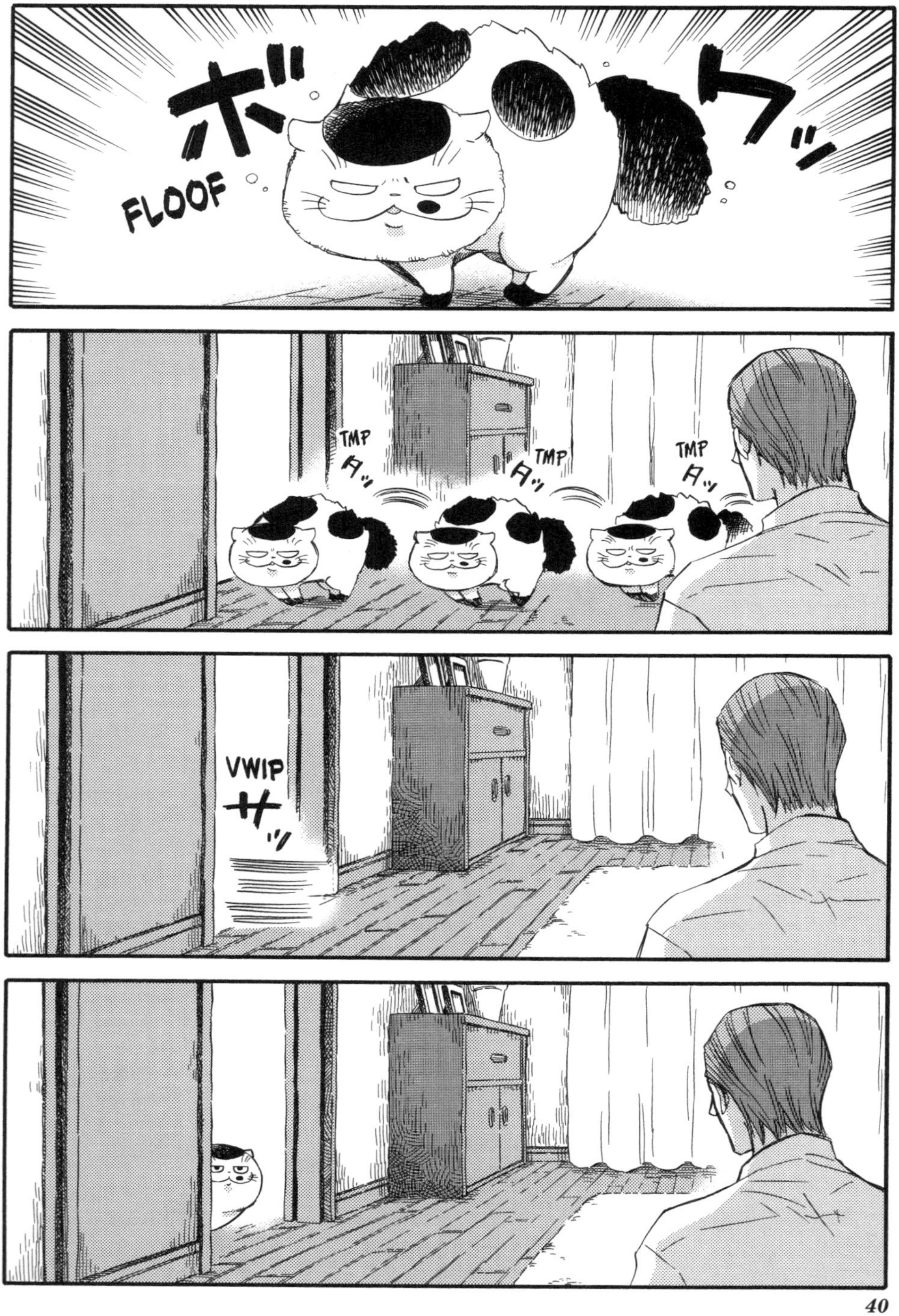
ボワッ
FLOOF
TMP
タッ
TMP
タッ
TMP
タッ
VWIP
サッ

THE MAN'S CHALLENGE

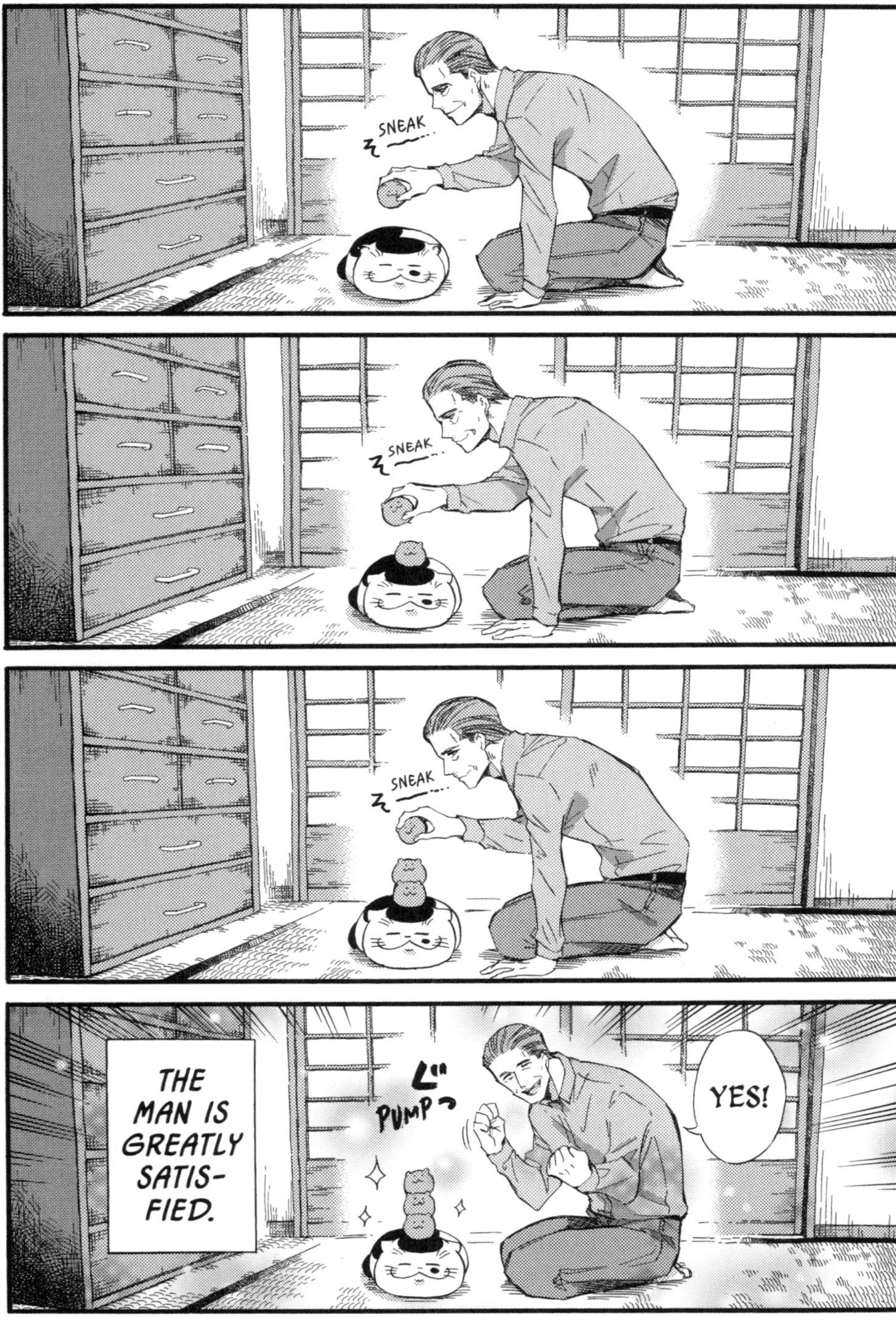
SNEAK
SNEAK
SNEAK
YES!
PUMP
THE MAN IS GREATLY SATIS-FIED.

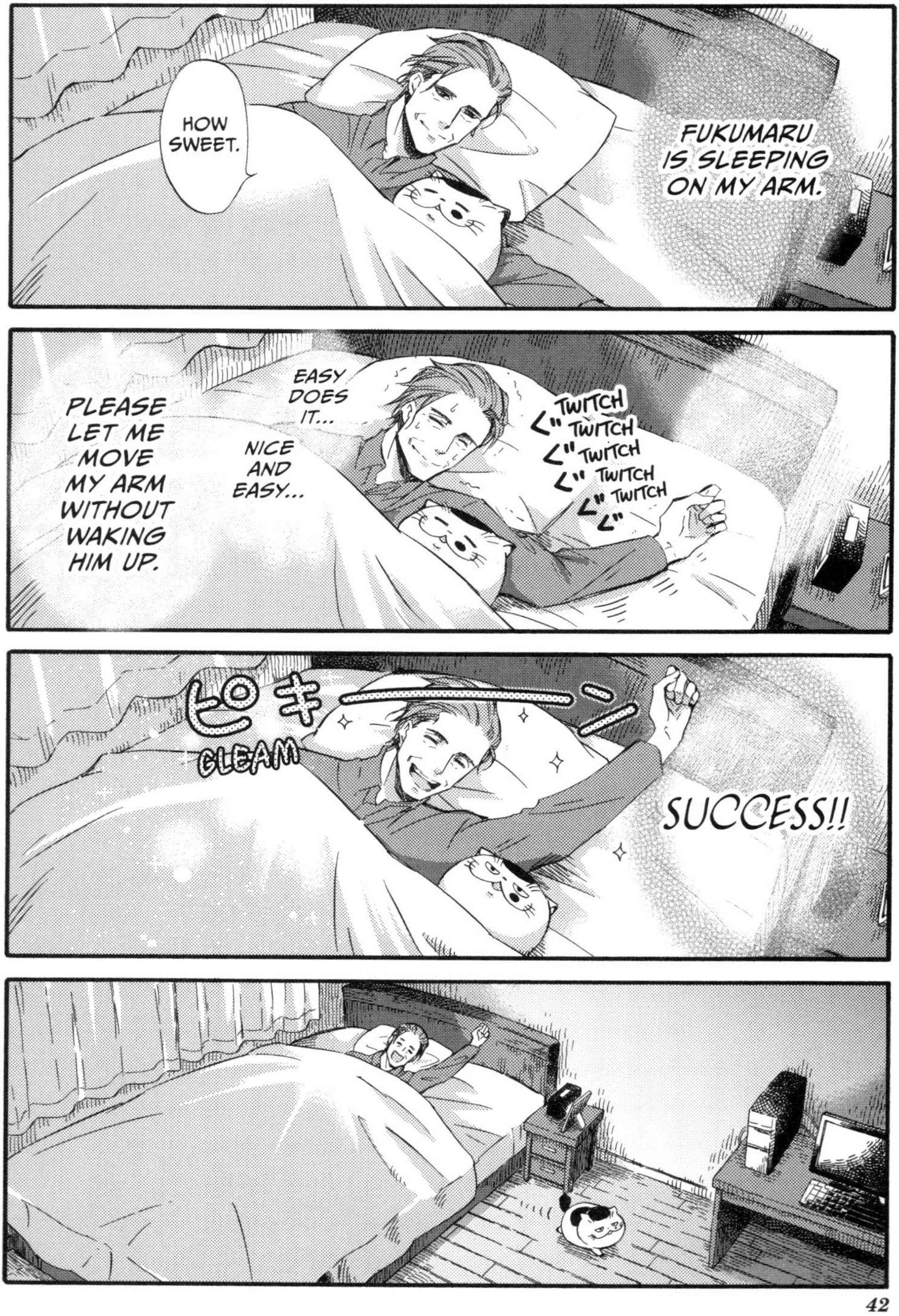
FUKUMARU IS SLEEPING ON MY ARM.
HOW SWEET.
TWITCH TWITCH TWITCH TWITCH TWITCH
EASY DOES IT...
NICE AND EASY...
PLEASE LET ME MOVE MY ARM WITHOUT WAKING HIM UP.
SUCCESS!!
ピキーン
GLEAM

GOOD AT CLEANING UP

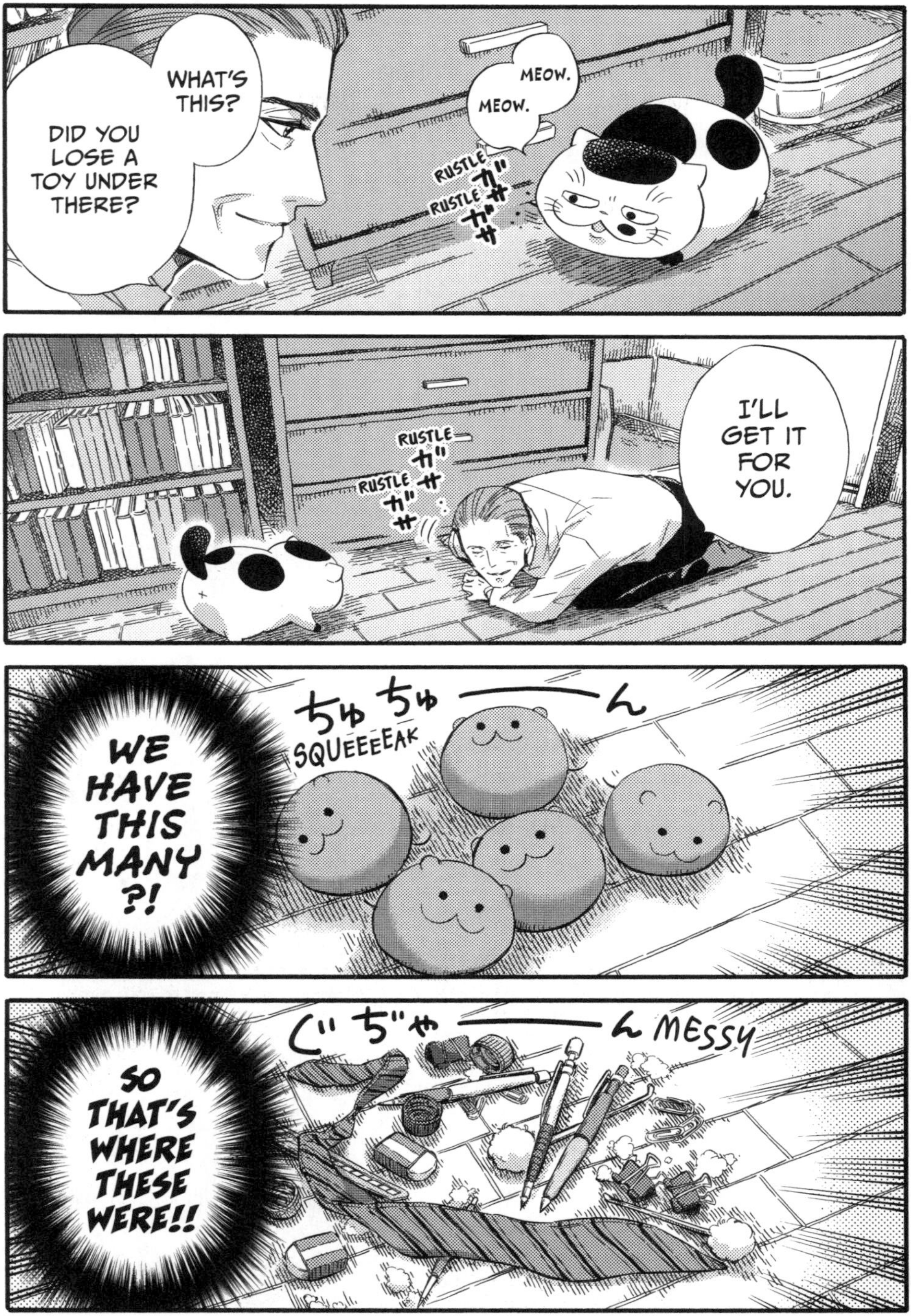
MEOW.
MEOW.
RUSTLE ガサ
RUSTLE ガサ
WHAT'S THIS?
DID YOU LOSE A TOY UNDER THERE?
I'LL GET IT FOR YOU.
RUSTLE ガサ
RUSTLE ガサ
ちゅちゅーーん
SQUEEEEAK
WE HAVE THIS MANY?!
ぐちゃーーん MESSY
SO THAT'S WHERE THESE WERE!!

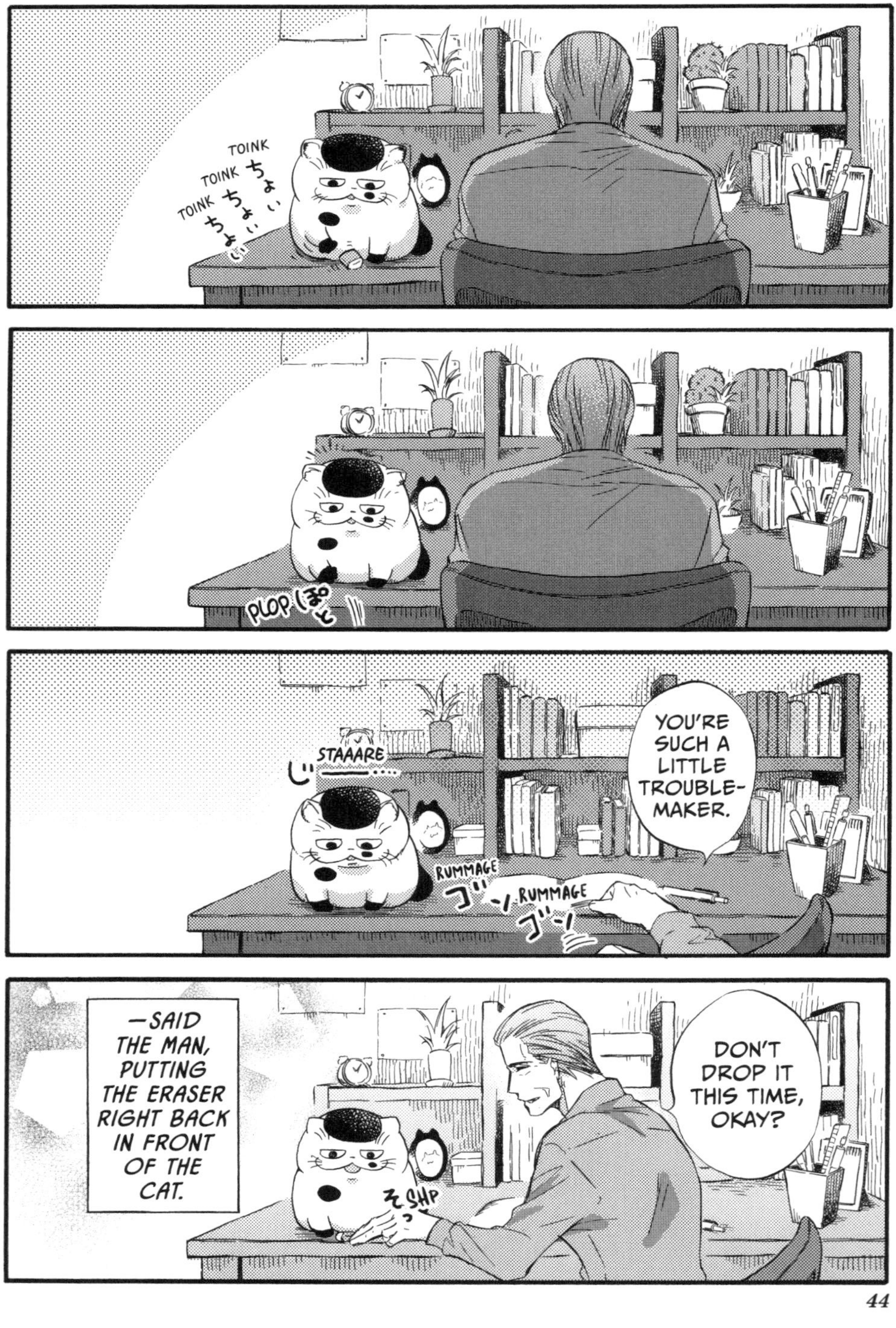
TOINK
TOINK
TOINK
ちょい
ちょい
ちょい
PLOP
ぽと
STAAARE
じ——……
YOU'RE SUCH A LITTLE TROUBLE-MAKER.
RUMMAGE
RUMMAGE
DON'T DROP IT THIS TIME, OKAY?
—SAID THE MAN, PUTTING THE ERASER RIGHT BACK IN FRONT OF THE CAT.
そっ
SHP

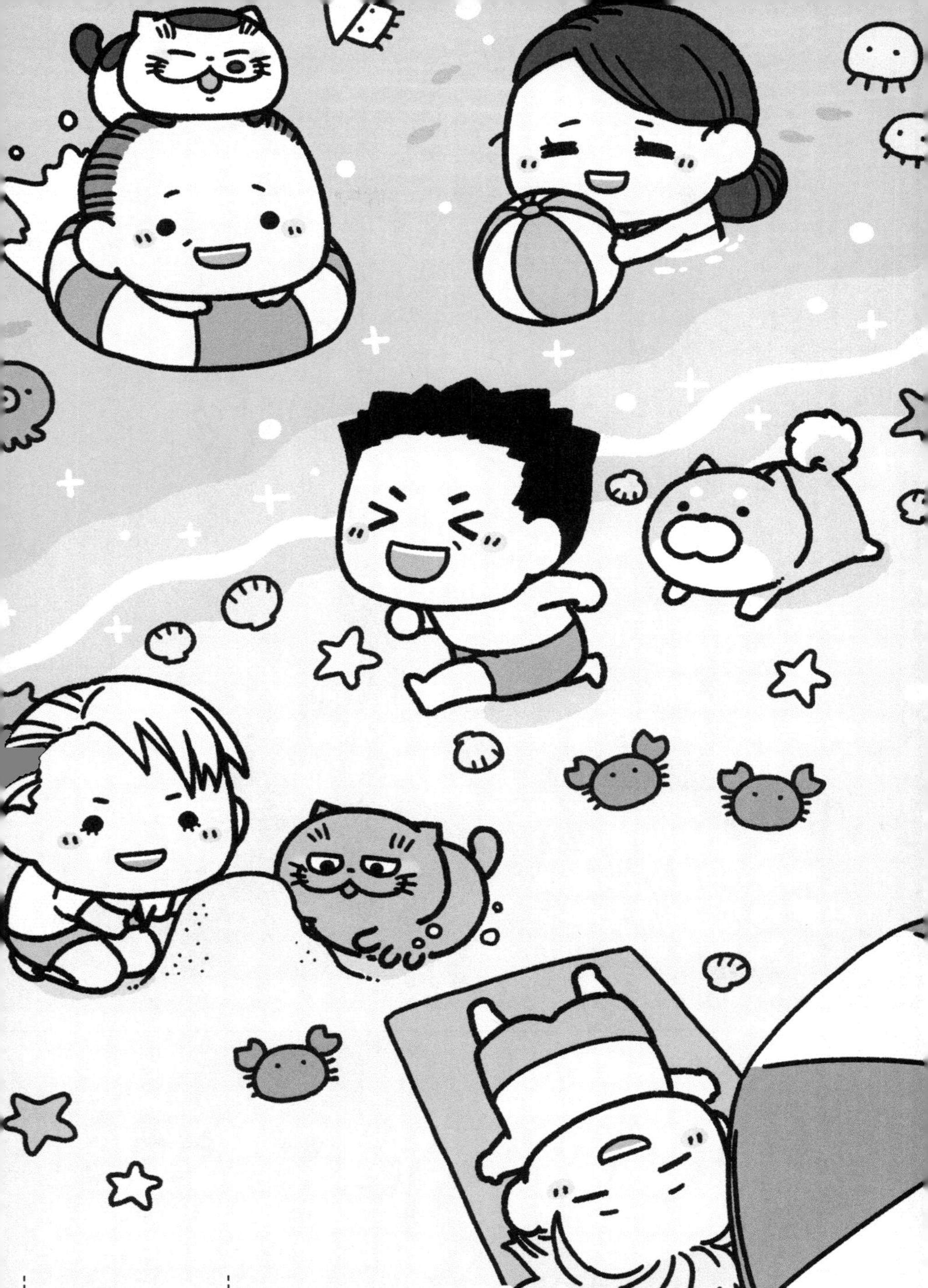

Chapter 41 | **Welcome, Cat Friend**

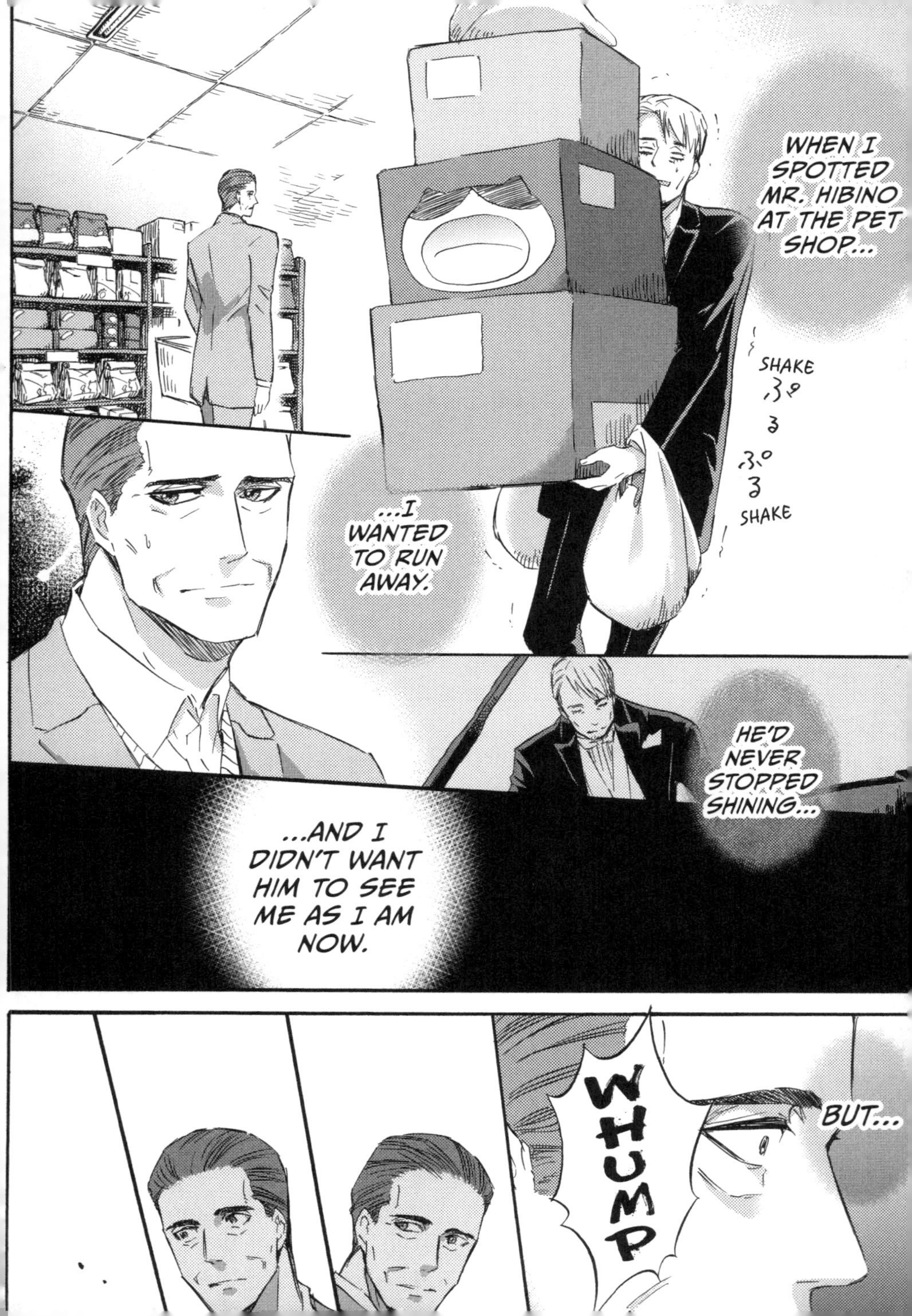
WHEN I SPOTTED MR. HIBINO AT THE PET SHOP...
SHAKE
ぷるぷる
SHAKE
...I WANTED TO RUN AWAY.
HE'D NEVER STOPPED SHINING...
...AND I DIDN'T WANT HIM TO SEE ME AS I AM NOW.
BUT...
WHUMP

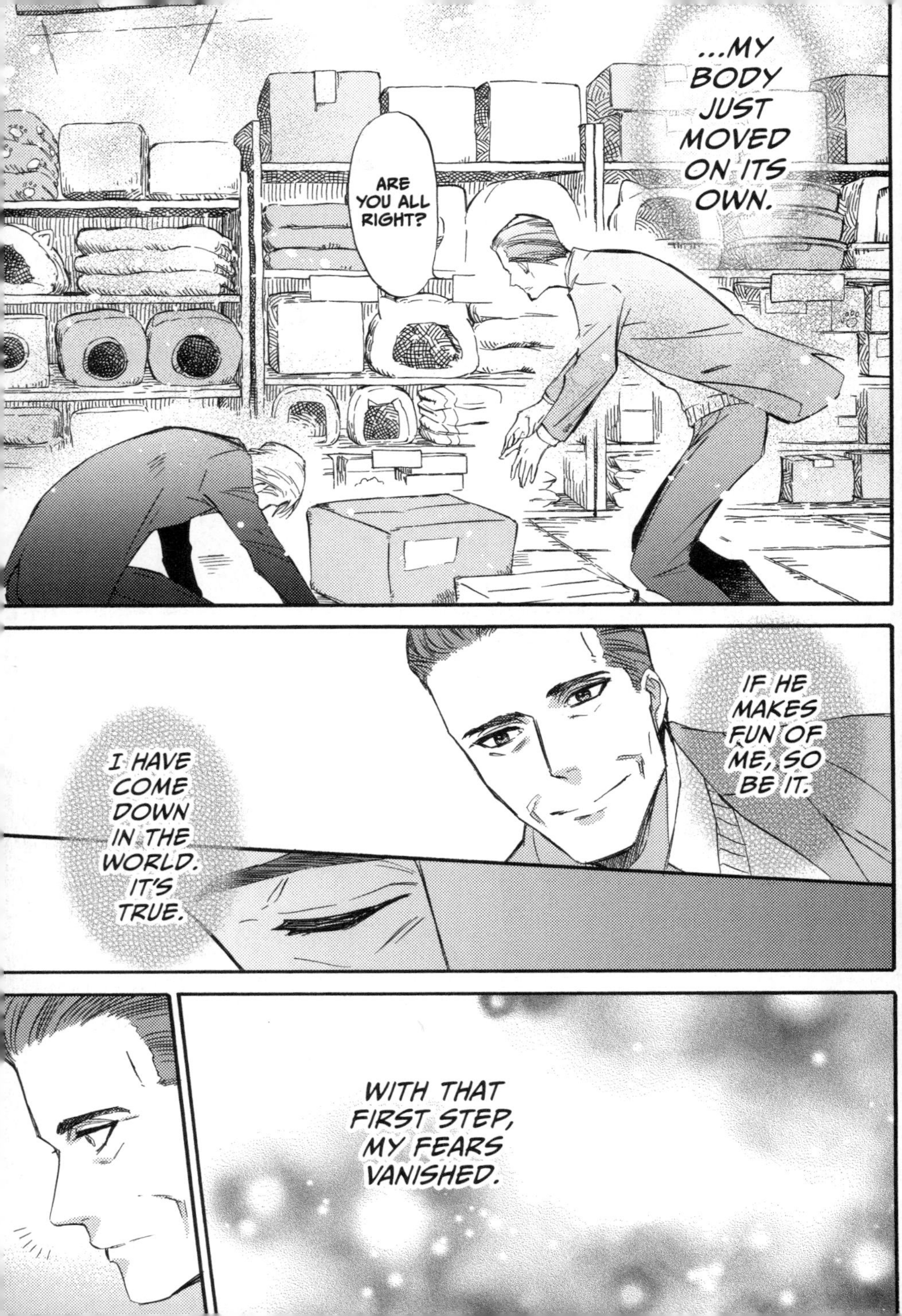
...MY BODY JUST MOVED ON ITS OWN.
ARE YOU ALL RIGHT?
IF HE MAKES FUN OF ME, SO BE IT.
I HAVE COME DOWN IN THE WORLD. IT'S TRUE.
WITH THAT FIRST STEP, MY FEARS VANISHED.

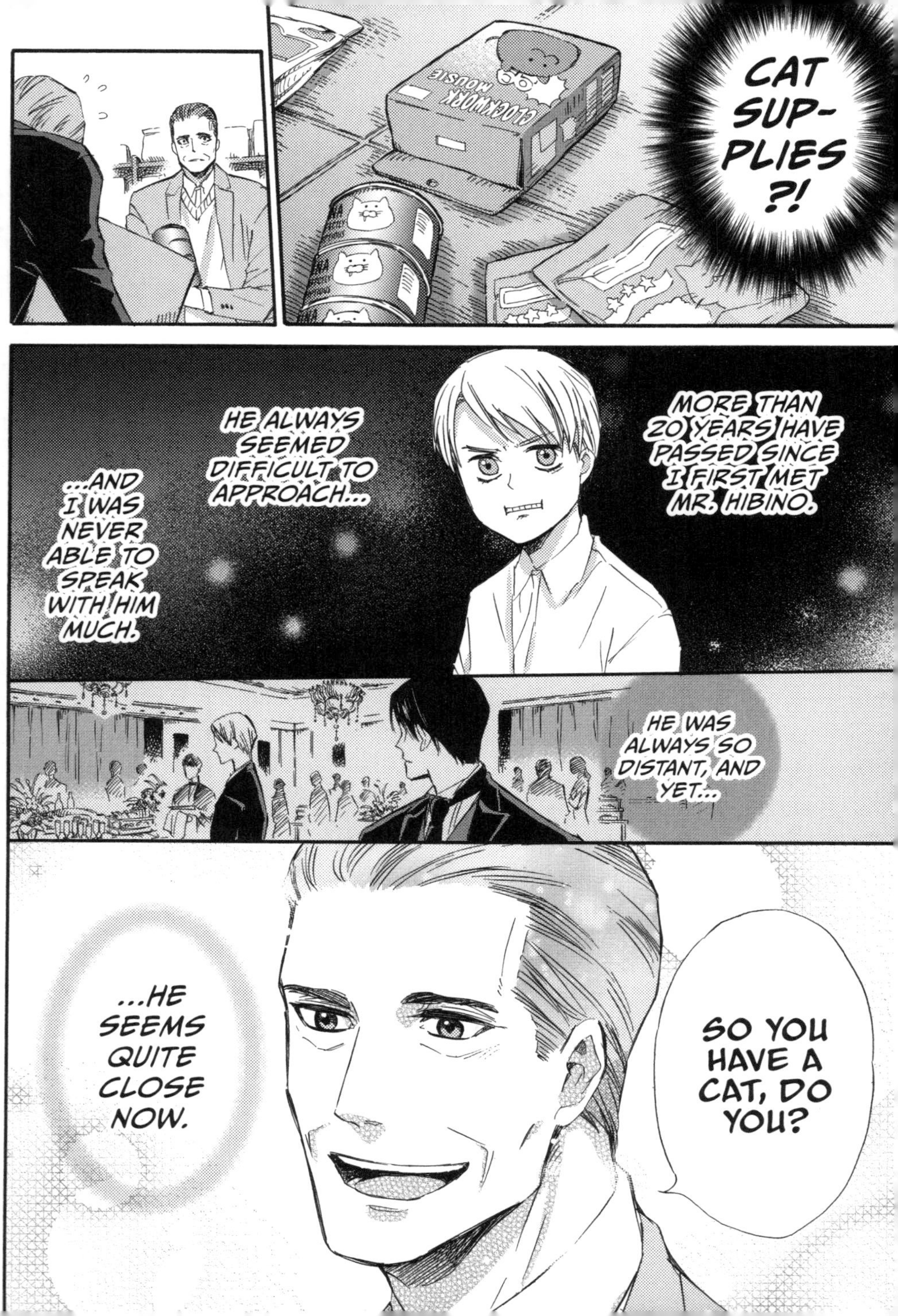
CLOCKWORK MOUSIE
CAT SUP-PLIES?!
MORE THAN 20 YEARS HAVE PASSED SINCE I FIRST MET MR. HIBINO.
HE ALWAYS SEEMED DIFFICULT TO APPROACH...
...AND I WAS NEVER ABLE TO SPEAK WITH HIM MUCH.
HE WAS ALWAYS SO DISTANT, AND YET...
SO YOU HAVE A CAT, DO YOU?
...HE SEEMS QUITE CLOSE NOW.

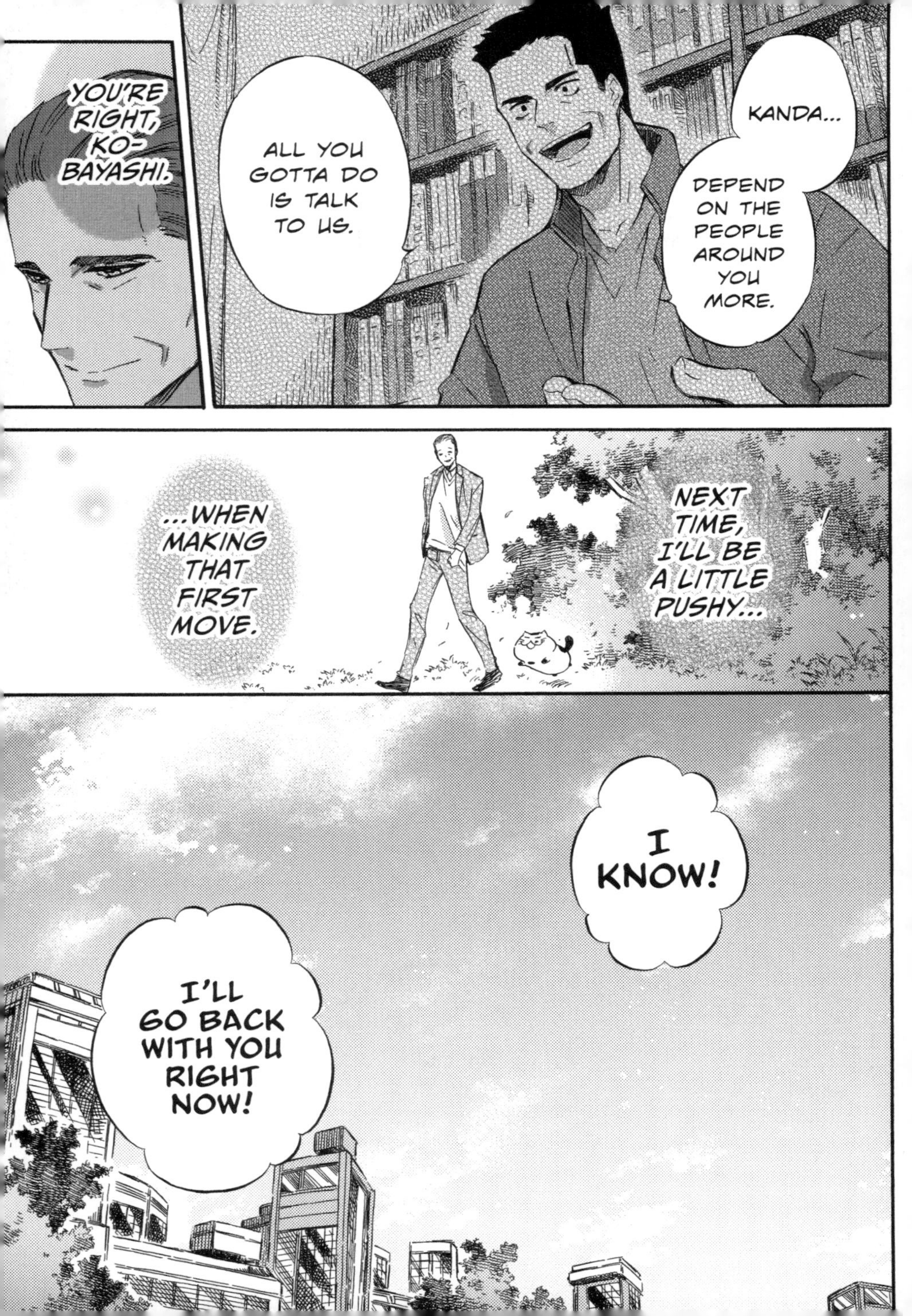
KANDA...
DEPEND ON THE PEOPLE AROUND YOU MORE.
ALL YOU GOTTA DO IS TALK TO US.
YOU'RE RIGHT, KO-BAYASHI.
NEXT TIME, I'LL BE A LITTLE PUSHY...
...WHEN MAKING THAT FIRST MOVE.
I KNOW!
I'LL GO BACK WITH YOU RIGHT NOW!

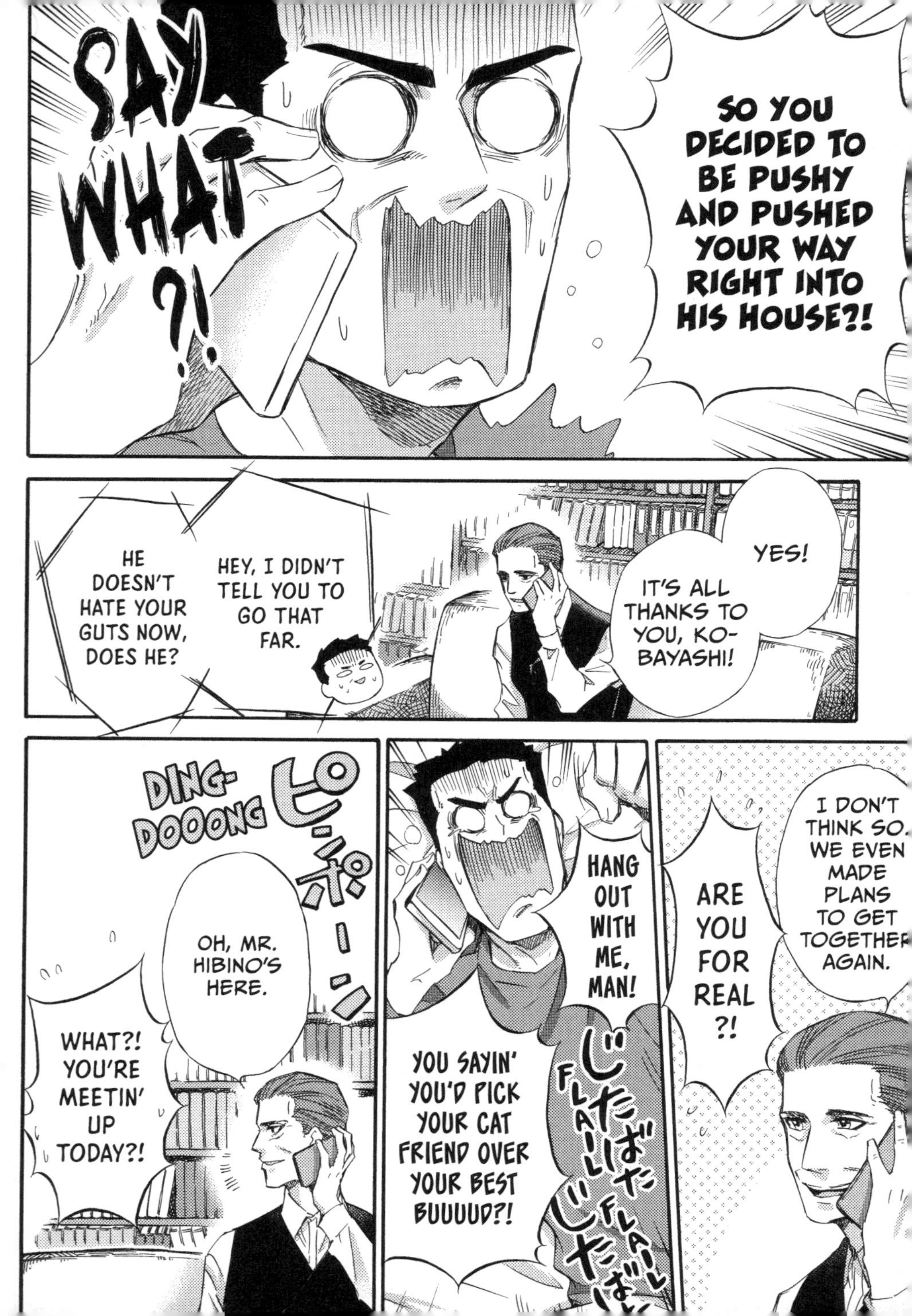
SO YOU DECIDED TO BE PUSHY AND PUSHED YOUR WAY RIGHT INTO HIS HOUSE?!
SAY WHAT?!
YES!
IT'S ALL THANKS TO YOU, KO-BAYASHI!
HEY, I DIDN'T TELL YOU TO GO THAT FAR.
HE DOESN'T HATE YOUR GUTS NOW, DOES HE?
I DON'T THINK SO. WE EVEN MADE PLANS TO GET TOGETHER AGAIN.
ARE YOU FOR REAL?!
HANG OUT WITH ME, MAN!
YOU SAYIN' YOU'D PICK YOUR CAT FRIEND OVER YOUR BEST BUUUUD?!
じたばた
FLAIL FLAIL
DING-DOOONG
ピーンポーン
OH, MR. HIBINO'S HERE.
WHAT?! YOU'RE MEETIN' UP TODAY?!

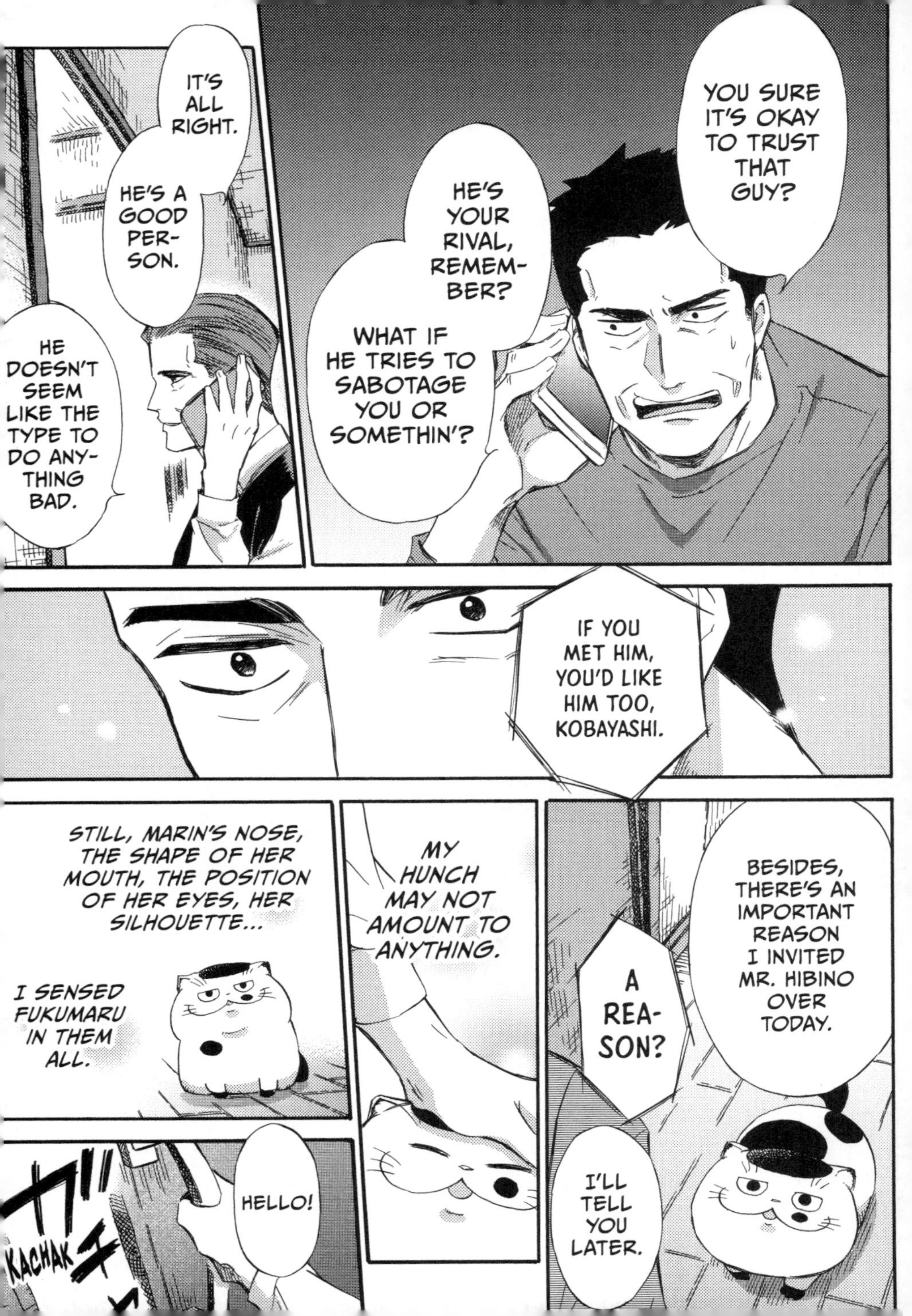
YOU SURE IT'S OKAY TO TRUST THAT GUY?
HE'S YOUR RIVAL, REMEMBER?
WHAT IF HE TRIES TO SABOTAGE YOU OR SOMETHIN'?
IT'S ALL RIGHT.
HE'S A GOOD PERSON.
HE DOESN'T SEEM LIKE THE TYPE TO DO ANYTHING BAD.
IF YOU MET HIM, YOU'D LIKE HIM TOO, KOBAYASHI.
BESIDES, THERE'S AN IMPORTANT REASON I INVITED MR. HIBINO OVER TODAY.
A REASON?
I'LL TELL YOU LATER.
MY HUNCH MAY NOT AMOUNT TO ANYTHING.
STILL, MARIN'S NOSE, THE SHAPE OF HER MOUTH, THE POSITION OF HER EYES, HER SILHOUETTE...
I SENSED FUKUMARU IN THEM ALL.
HELLO!
KACHAK

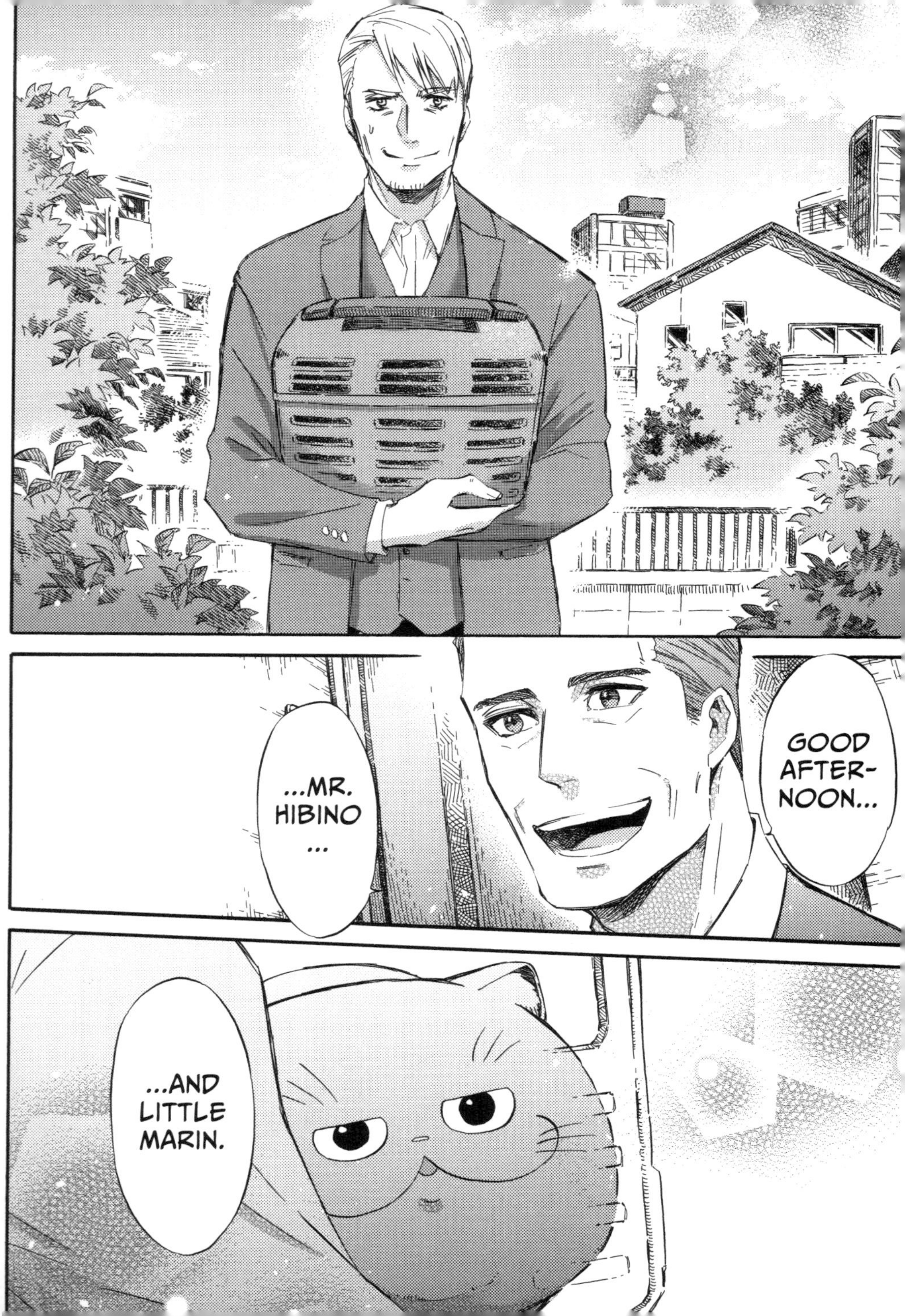
GOOD AFTER-NOON...
...MR. HIBINO ...
...AND LITTLE MARIN.

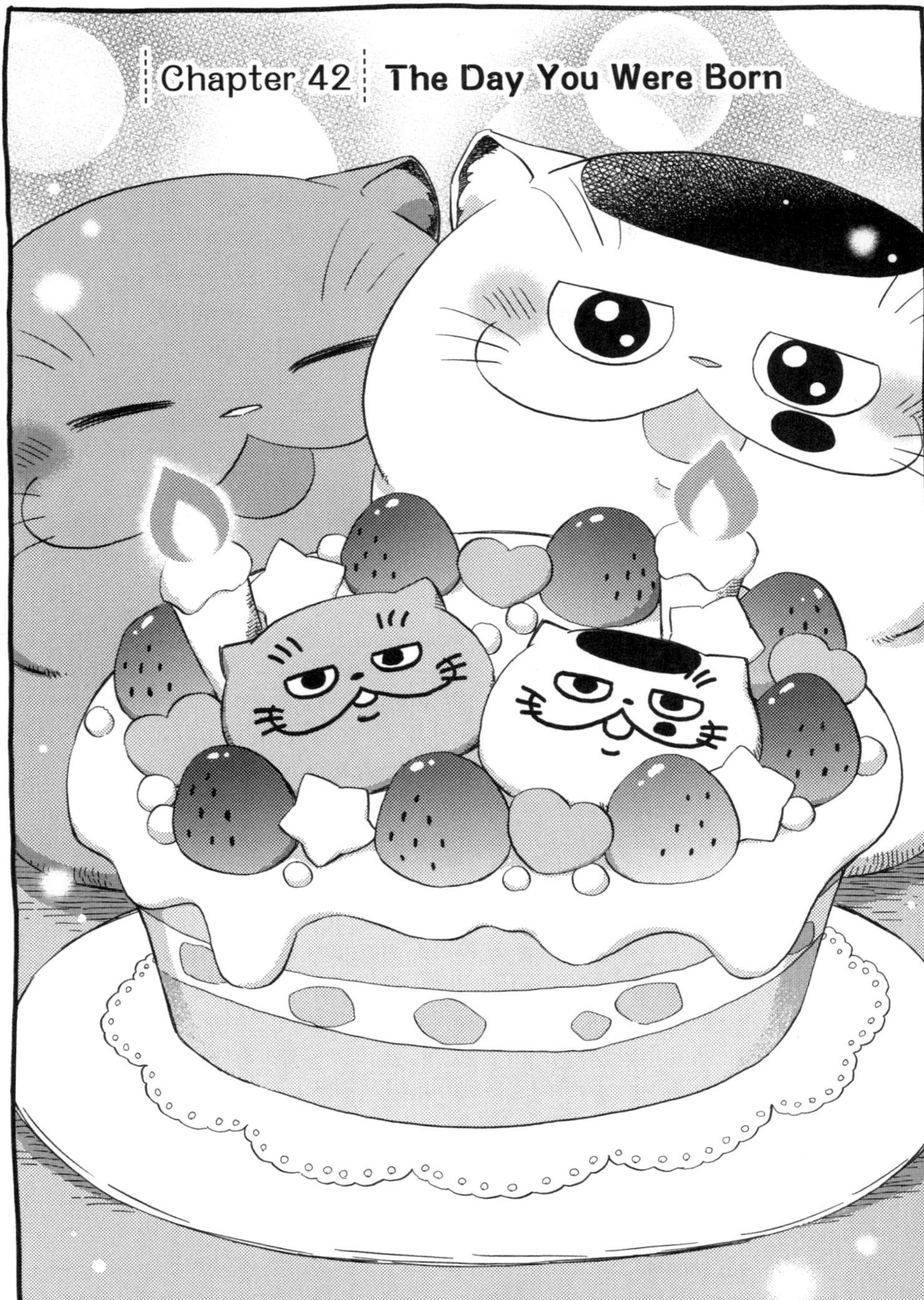
Chapter 42 The Day You Were Born

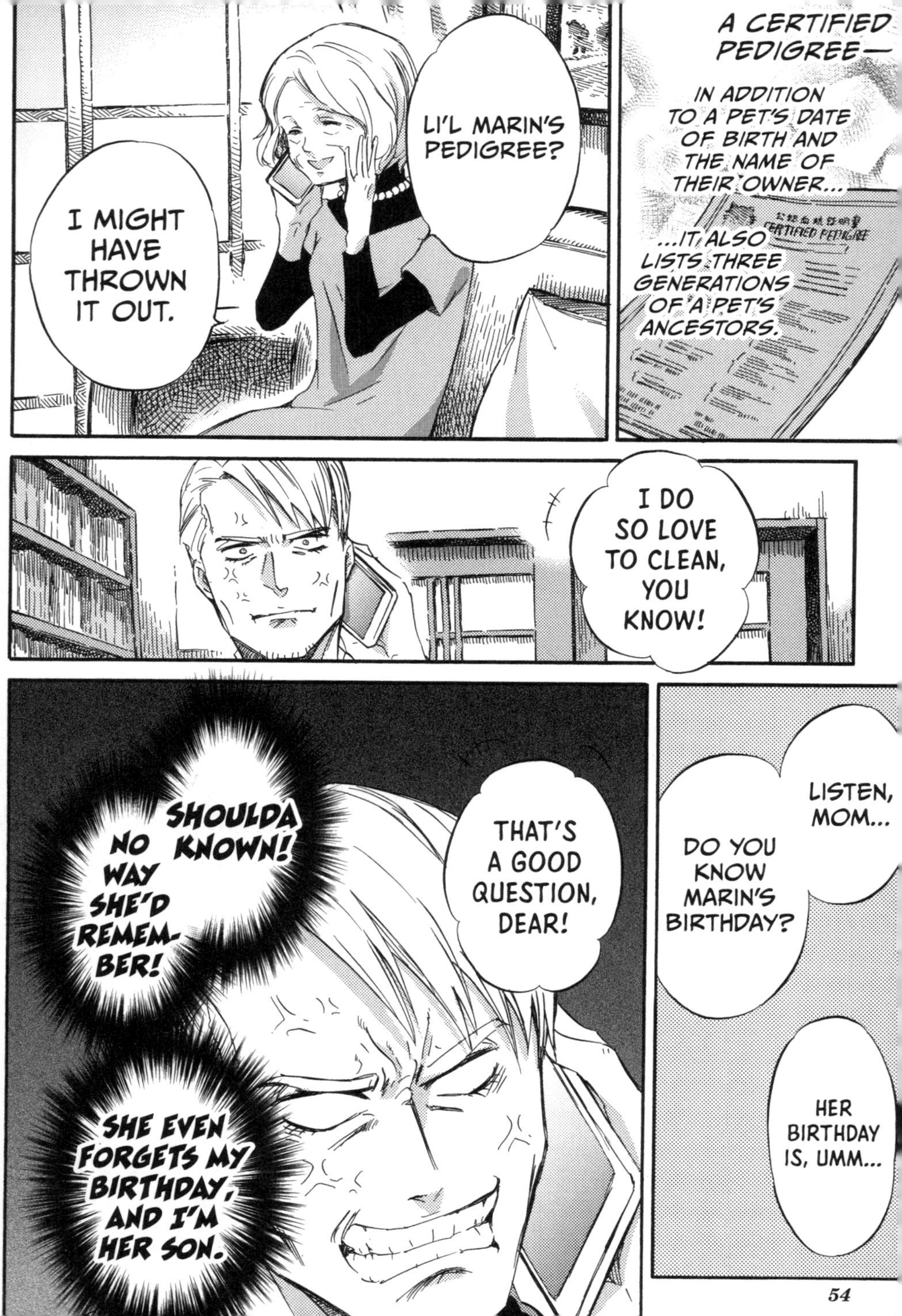
A CERTIFIED PEDIGREE—
IN ADDITION TO A PET'S DATE OF BIRTH AND THE NAME OF THEIR OWNER...
CERTIFIED PEDIGREE
...IT ALSO LISTS THREE GENERATIONS OF A PET'S ANCESTORS.
LI'L MARIN'S PEDIGREE?
I MIGHT HAVE THROWN IT OUT.
I DO SO LOVE TO CLEAN, YOU KNOW!
LISTEN, MOM...
DO YOU KNOW MARIN'S BIRTHDAY?
HER BIRTHDAY IS, UMM...
THAT'S A GOOD QUESTION, DEAR!
SHOULDA KNOWN! NO WAY SHE'D REMEMBER!
SHE EVEN FORGETS MY BIRTHDAY, AND I'M HER SON.

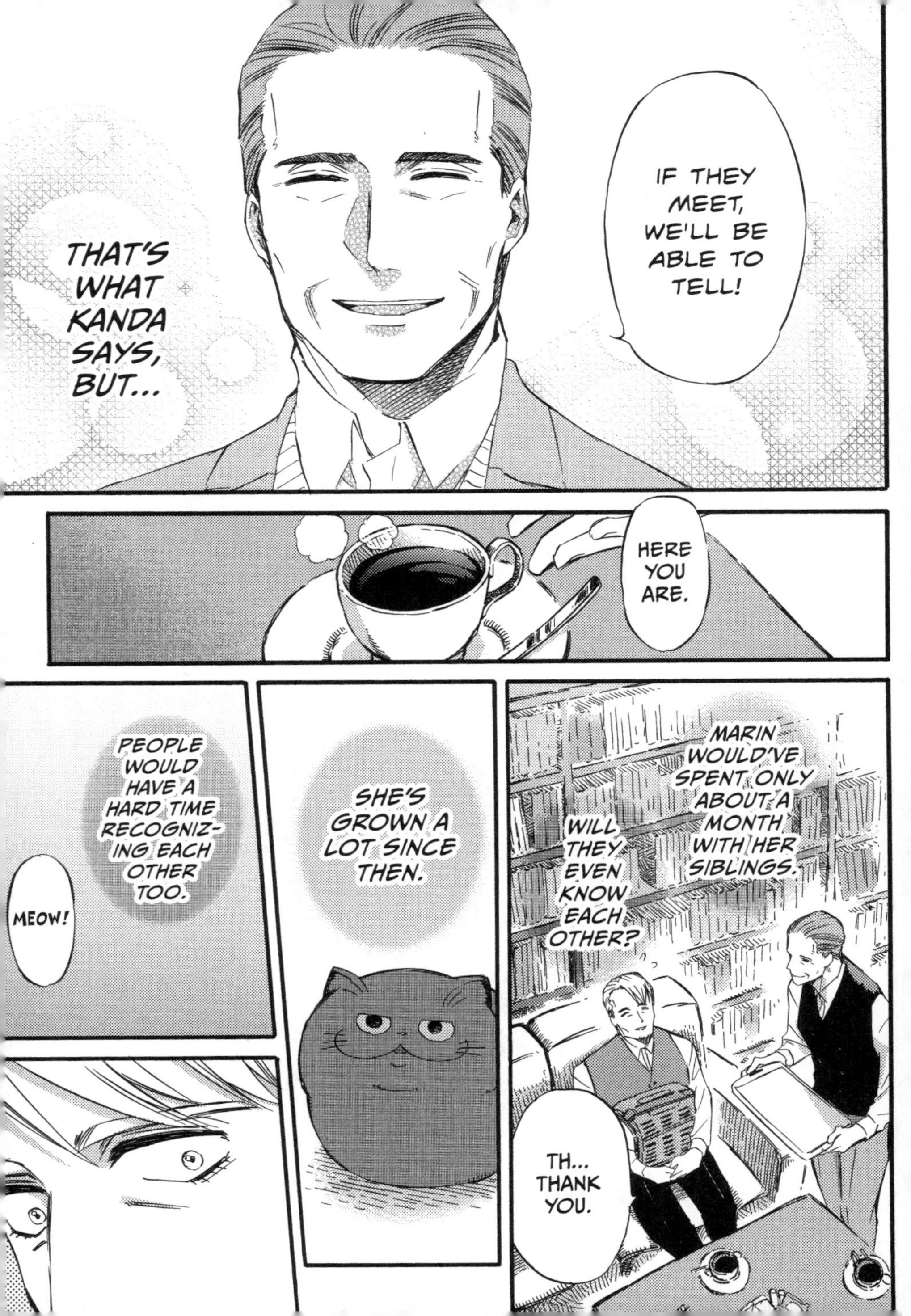
IF THEY MEET, WE'LL BE ABLE TO TELL!
THAT'S WHAT KANDA SAYS, BUT...
HERE YOU ARE.
MARIN WOULD'VE SPENT ONLY ABOUT A MONTH WITH HER SIBLINGS.
WILL THEY EVEN KNOW EACH OTHER?
TH... THANK YOU.
SHE'S GROWN A LOT SINCE THEN.
PEOPLE WOULD HAVE A HARD TIME RECOGNIZING EACH OTHER TOO.
MEOW!

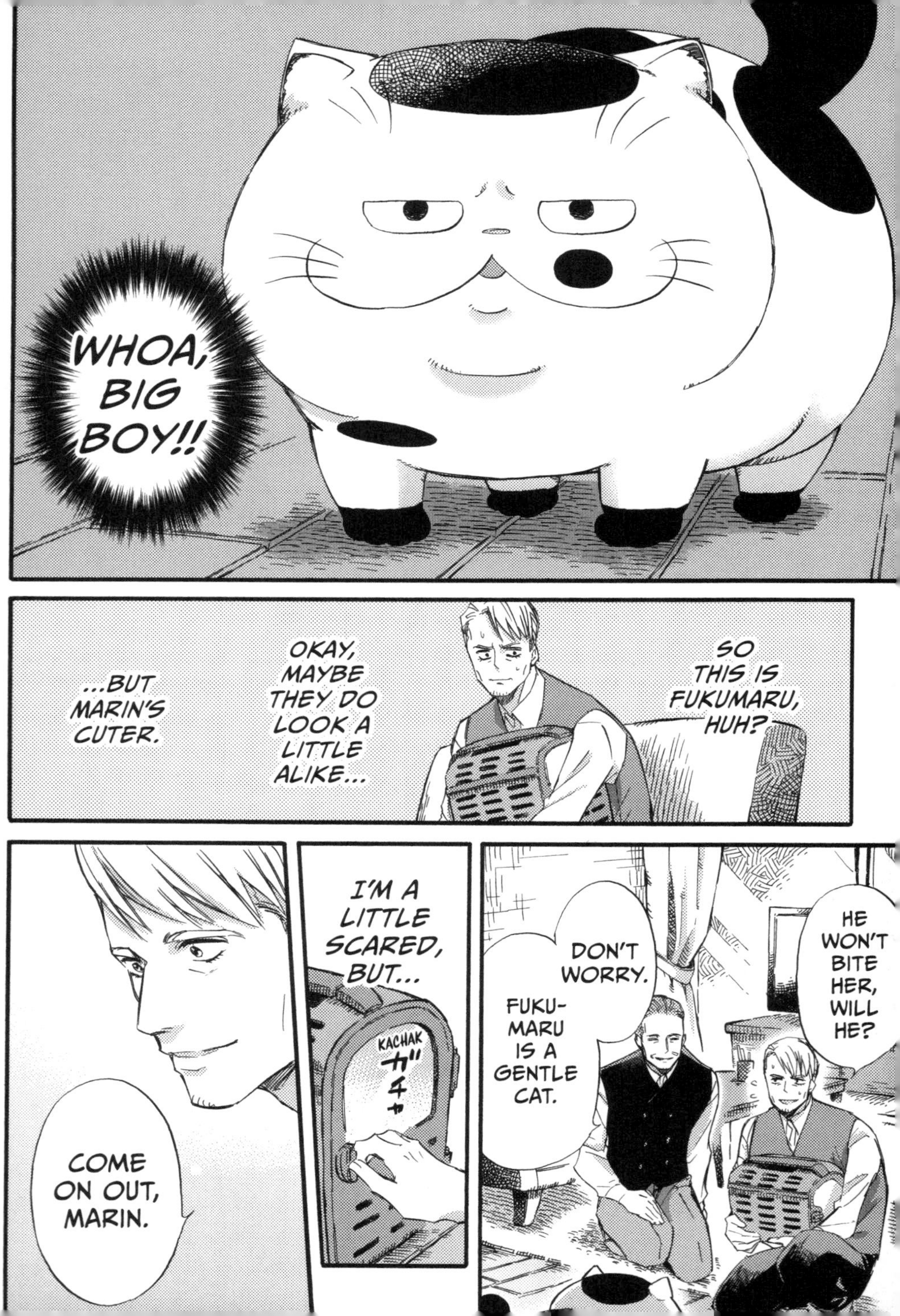
WHOA, BIG BOY!!
SO THIS IS FUKUMARU, HUH?
OKAY, MAYBE THEY DO LOOK A LITTLE ALIKE...
...BUT MARIN'S CUTER.
HE WON'T BITE HER, WILL HE?
DON'T WORRY.
FUKU-MARU IS A GENTLE CAT.
I'M A LITTLE SCARED, BUT...
KACHAK
ガチャ
COME ON OUT, MARIN.

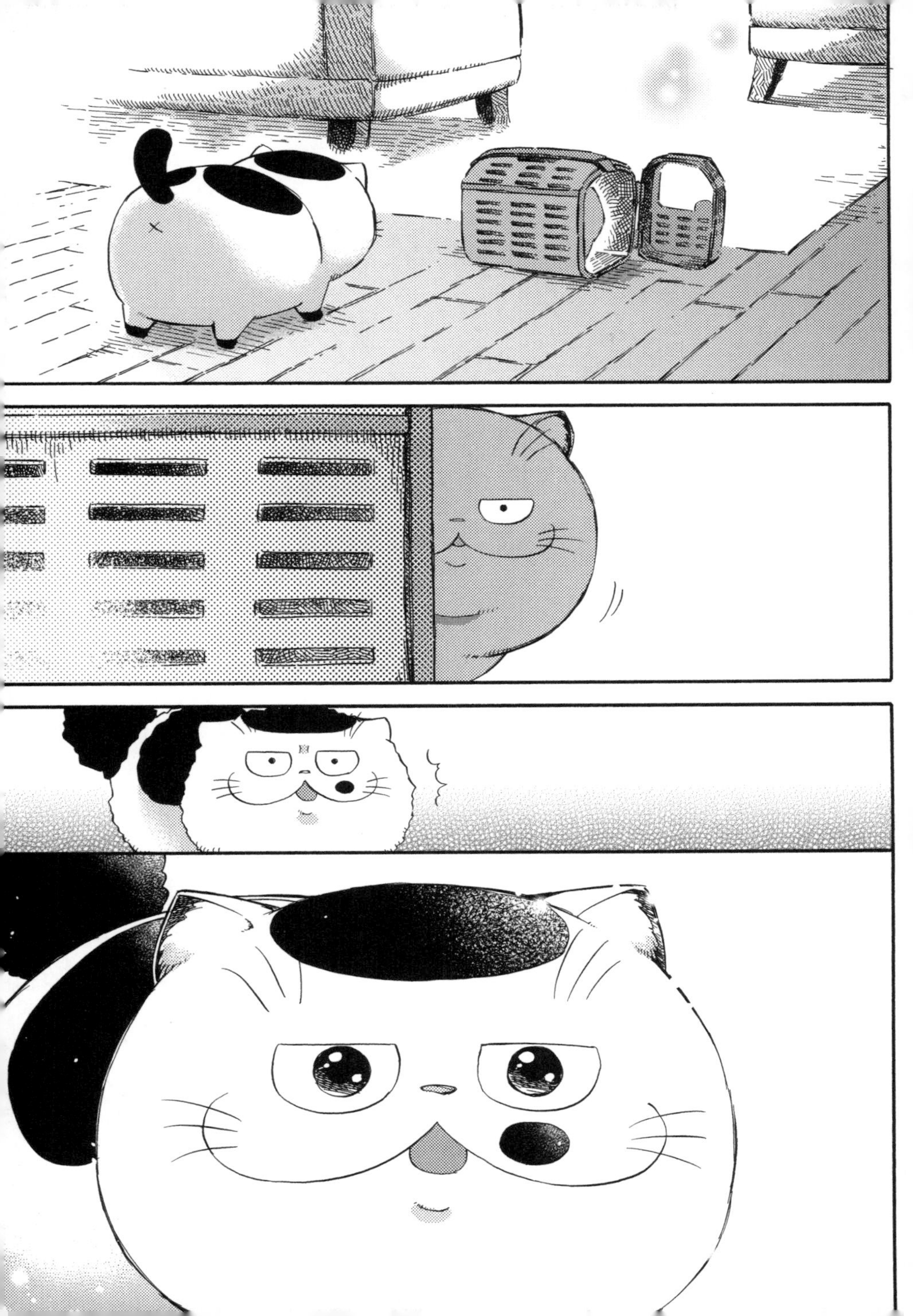

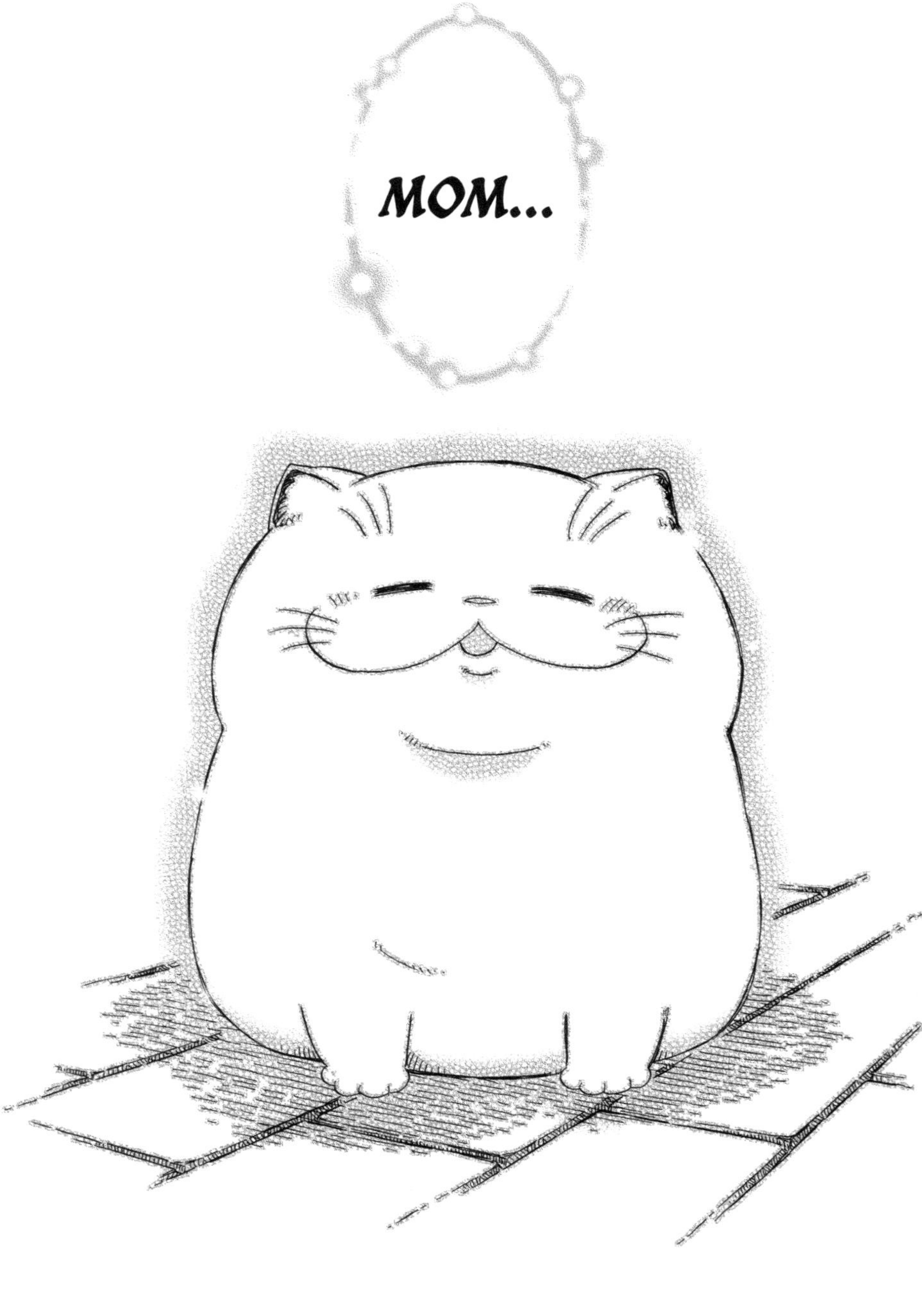
MOM...

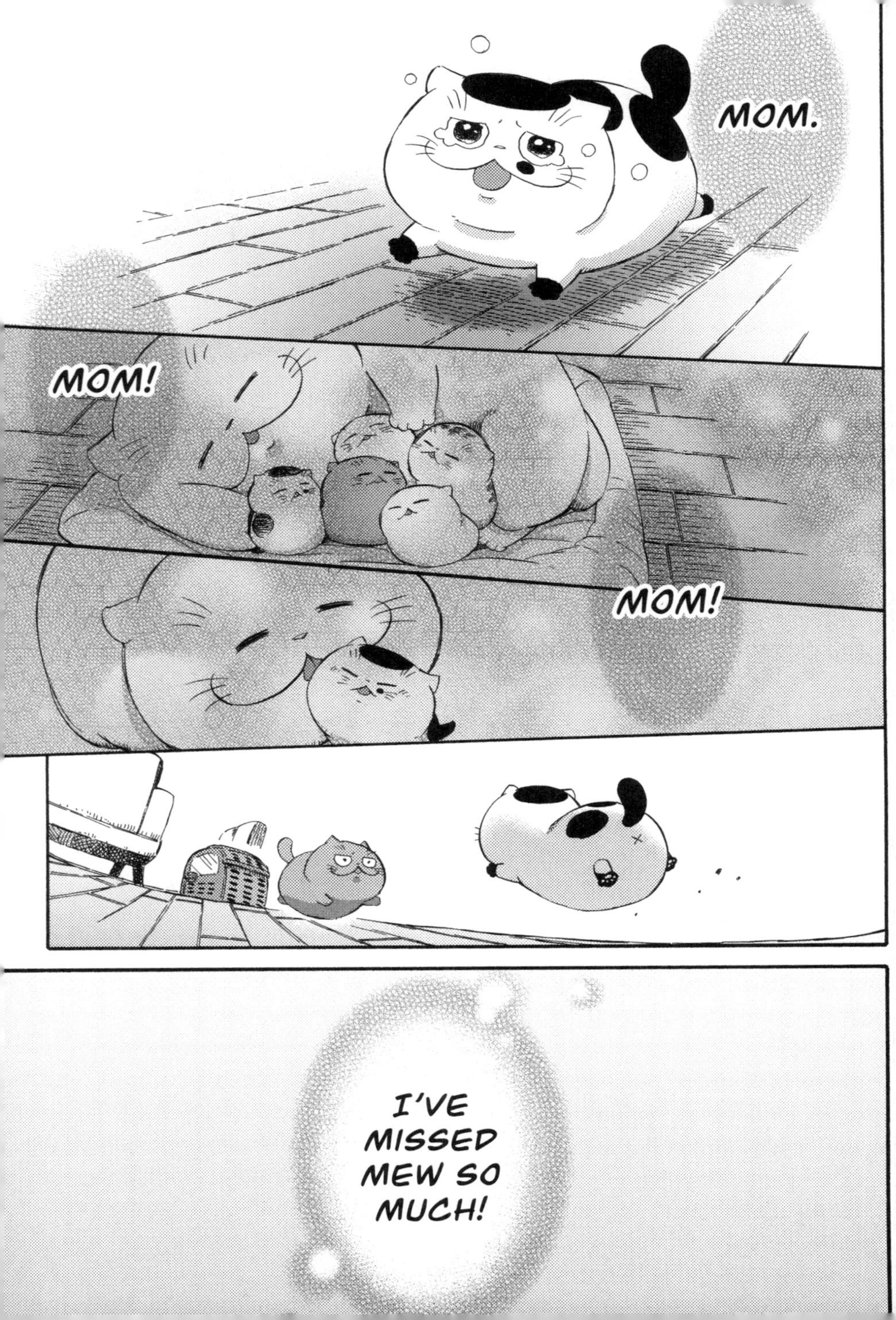
MOM.
MOM!
MOM!
I'VE MISSED MEW SO MUCH!

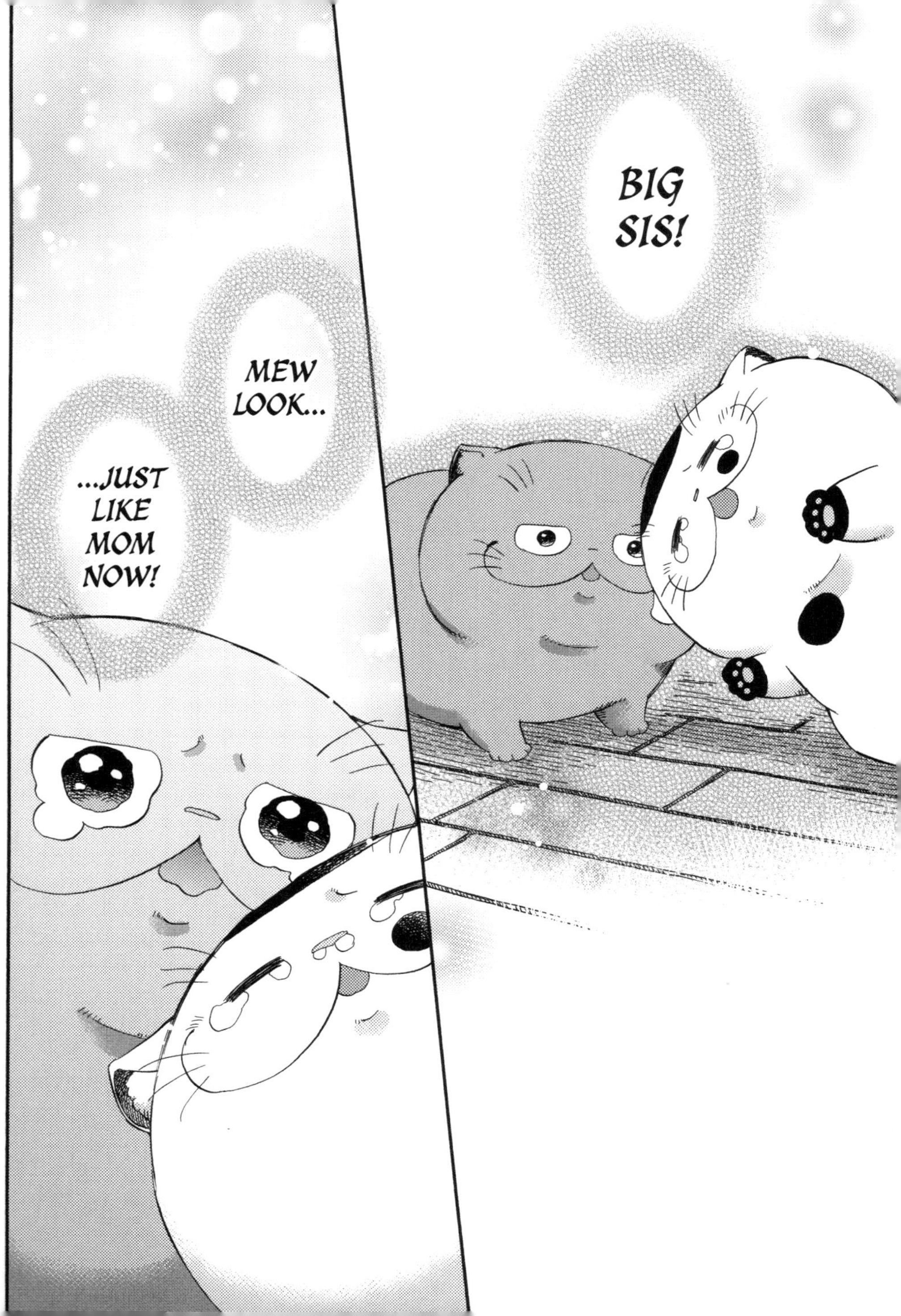
BIG SIS!
MEW LOOK...
...JUST LIKE MOM NOW!

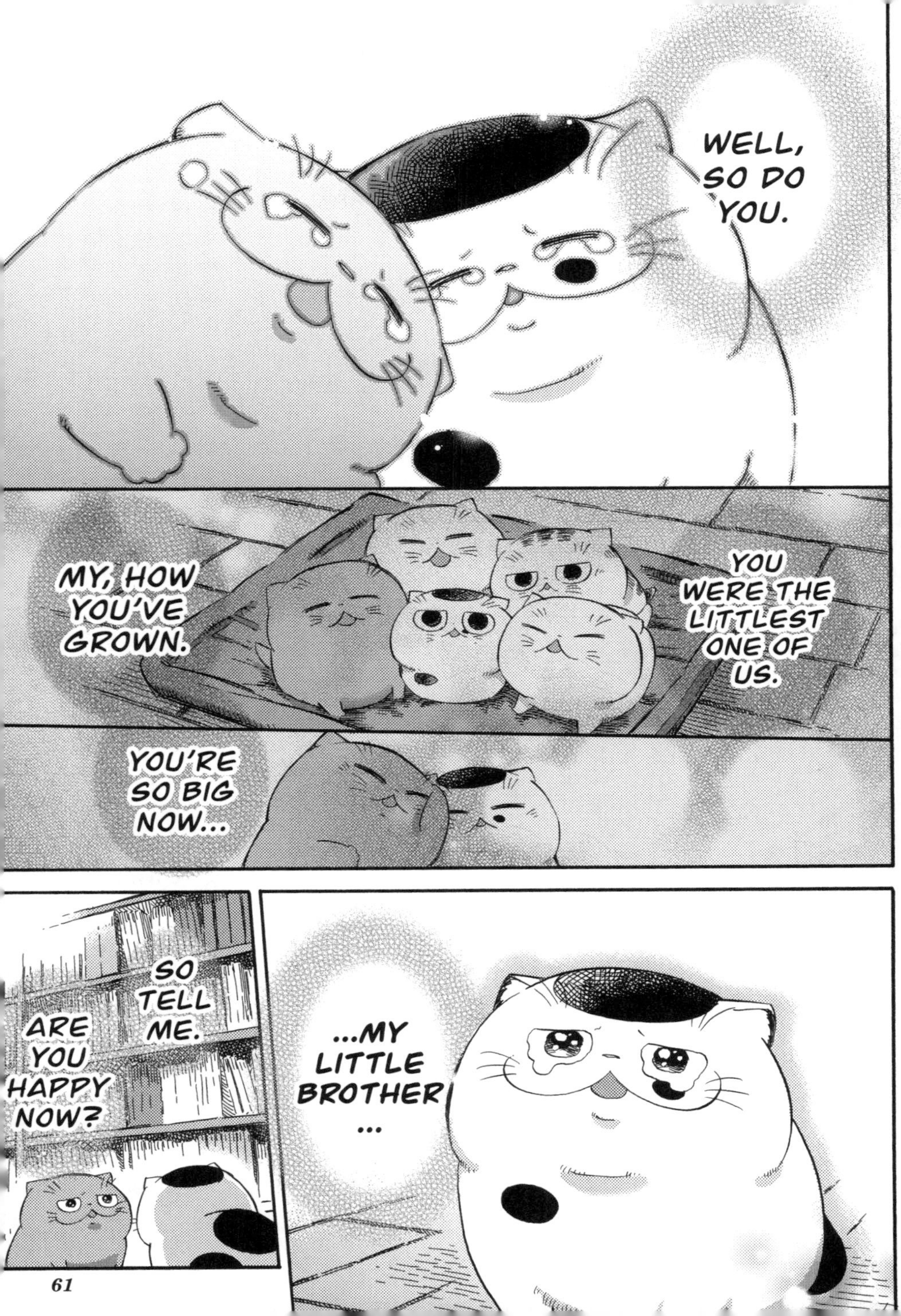
WELL, SO DO YOU.
YOU WERE THE LITTLEST ONE OF US.
MY, HOW YOU'VE GROWN.
YOU'RE SO BIG NOW...
...MY LITTLE BROTHER...
SO TELL ME.
ARE YOU HAPPY NOW?

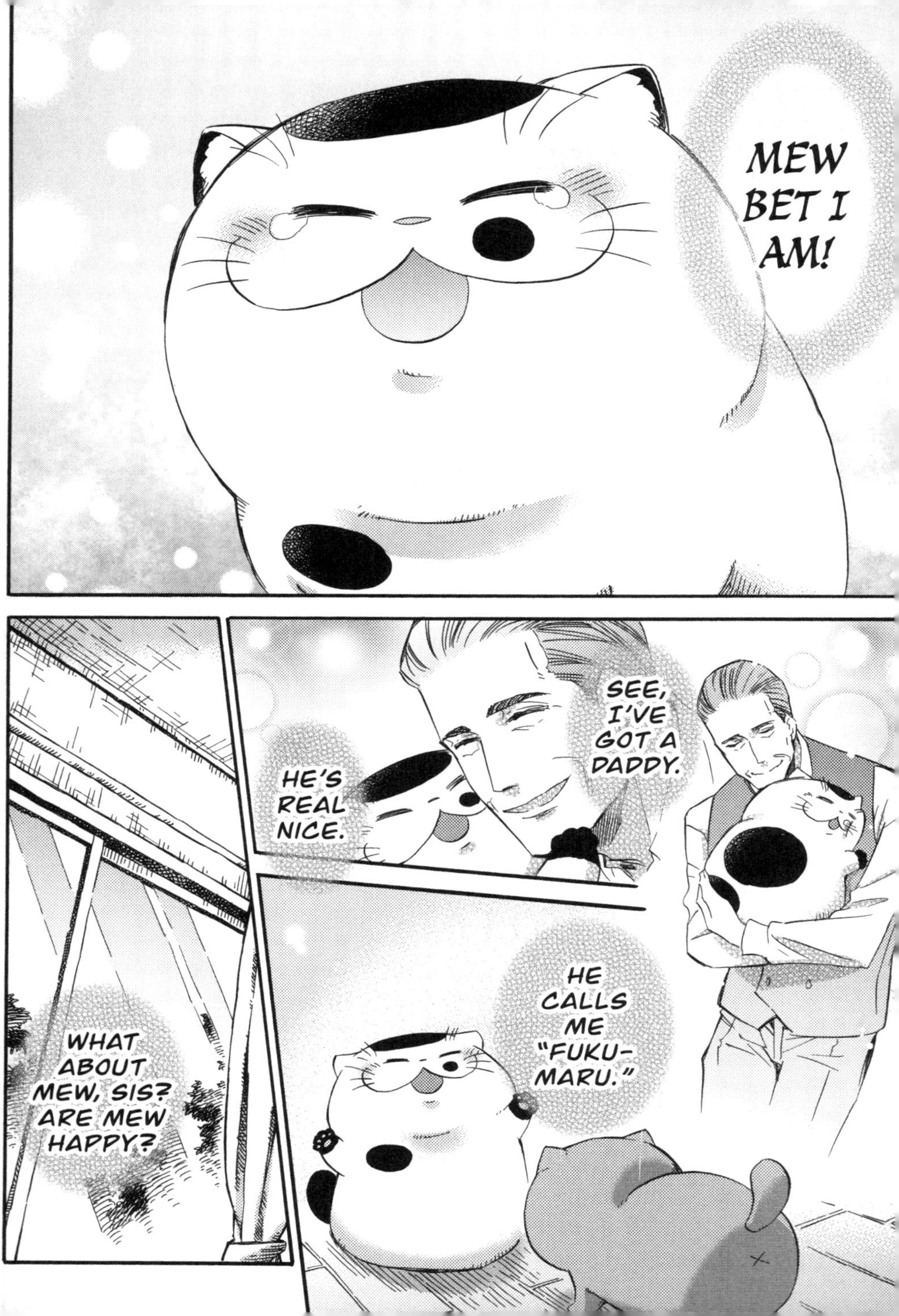
MEW BET I AM!
SEE, I'VE GOT A DADDY.
HE'S REAL NICE.
HE CALLS ME "FUKU-MARU."
WHAT ABOUT MEW, SIS? ARE MEW HAPPY?

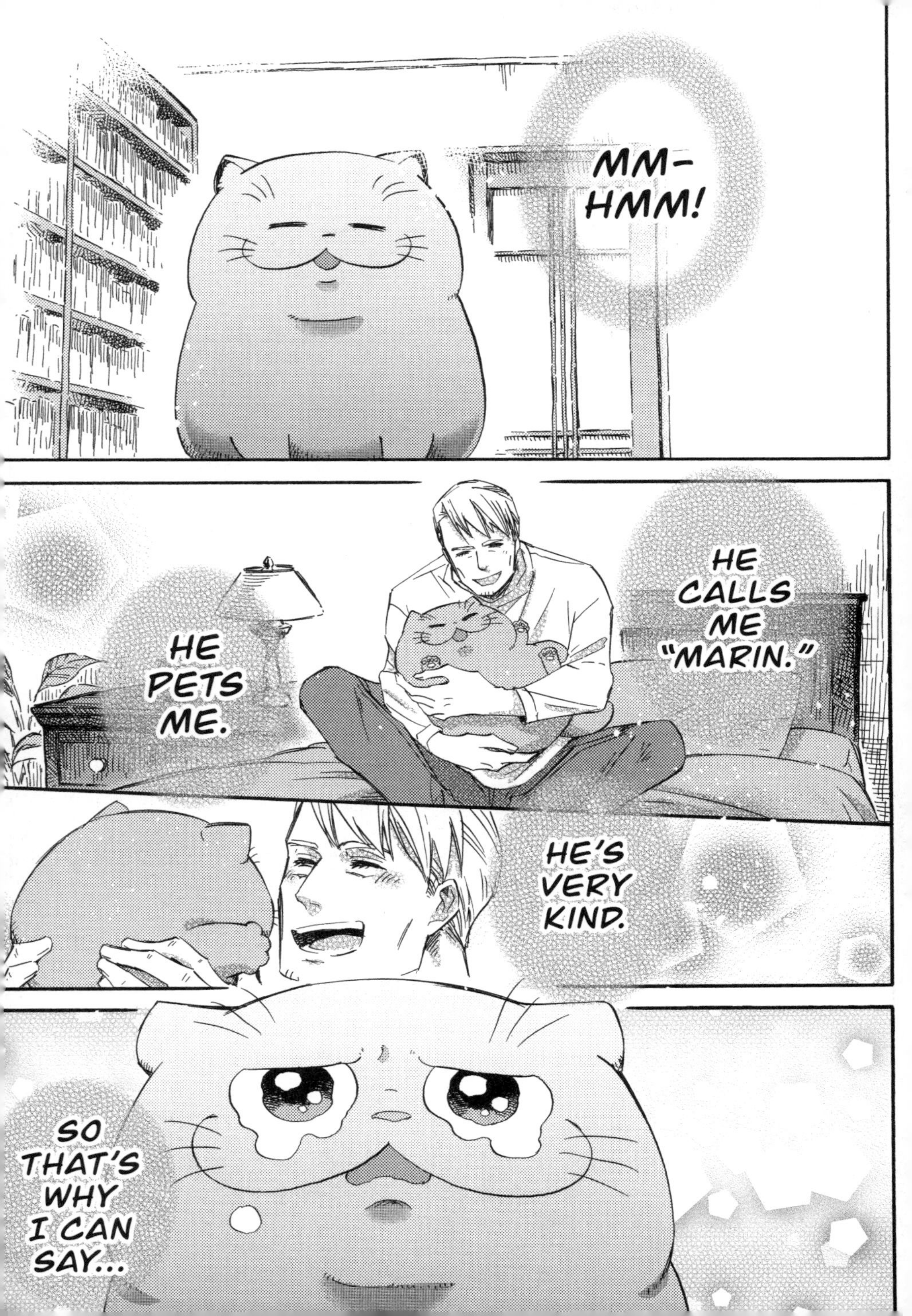
MM-HMM!
HE CALLS ME "MARIN."
HE PETS ME.
HE'S VERY KIND.
SO THAT'S WHY I CAN SAY...

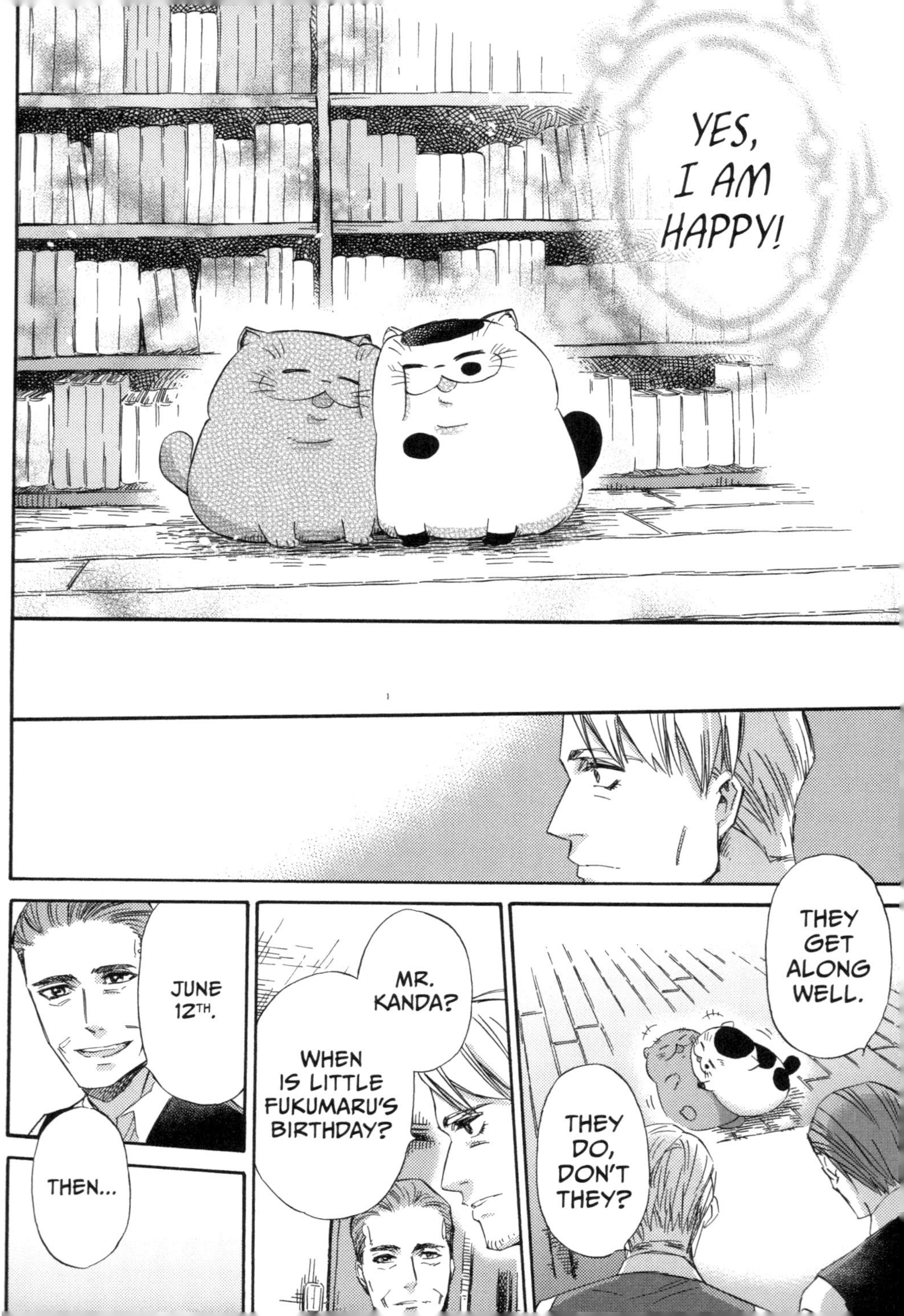
YES, I AM HAPPY!
THEY GET ALONG WELL.
THEY DO, DON'T THEY?
MR. KANDA?
WHEN IS LITTLE FUKUMARU'S BIRTHDAY?
JUNE 12TH.
THEN...

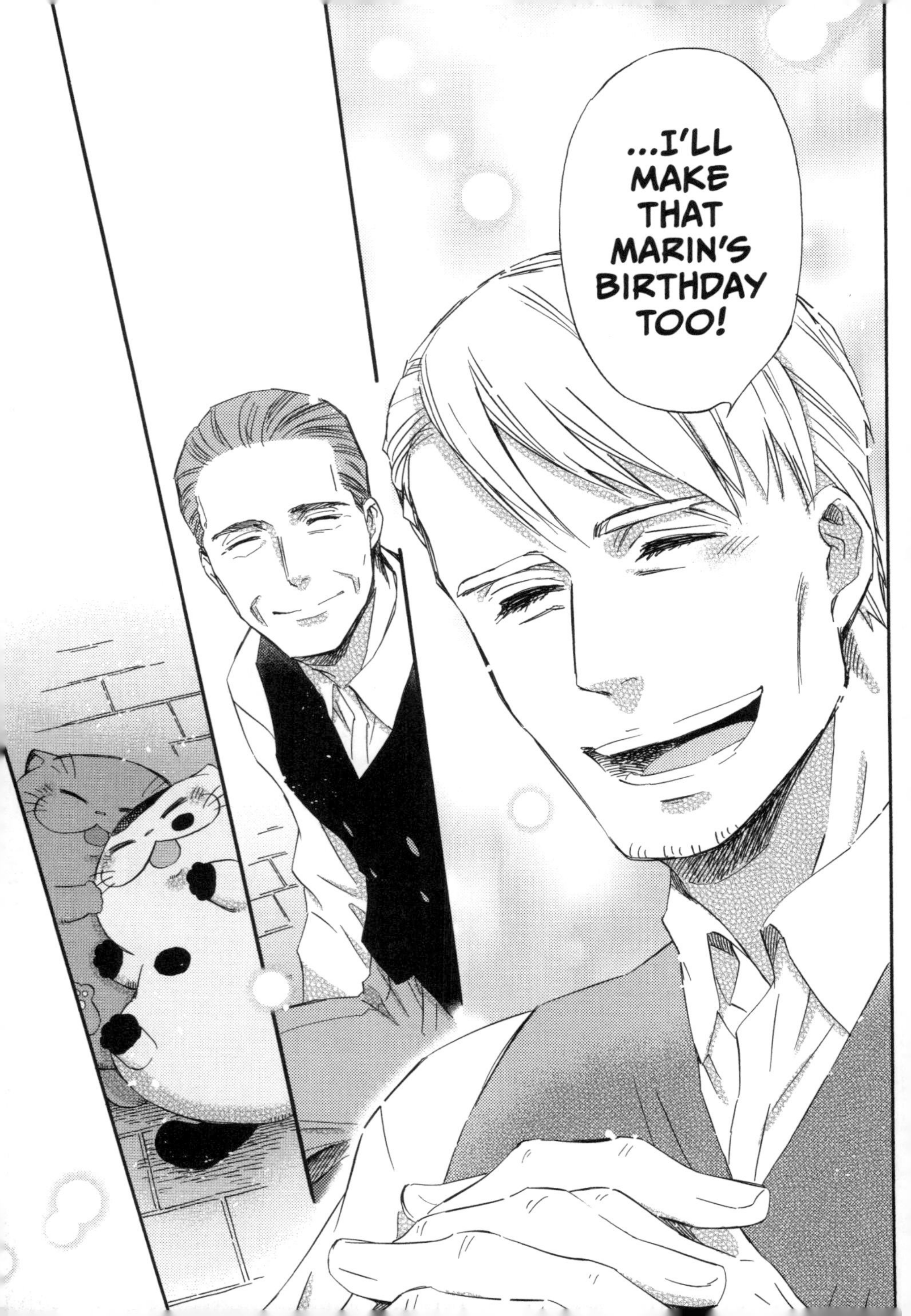
...I'LL MAKE THAT MARIN'S BIRTHDAY TOO!

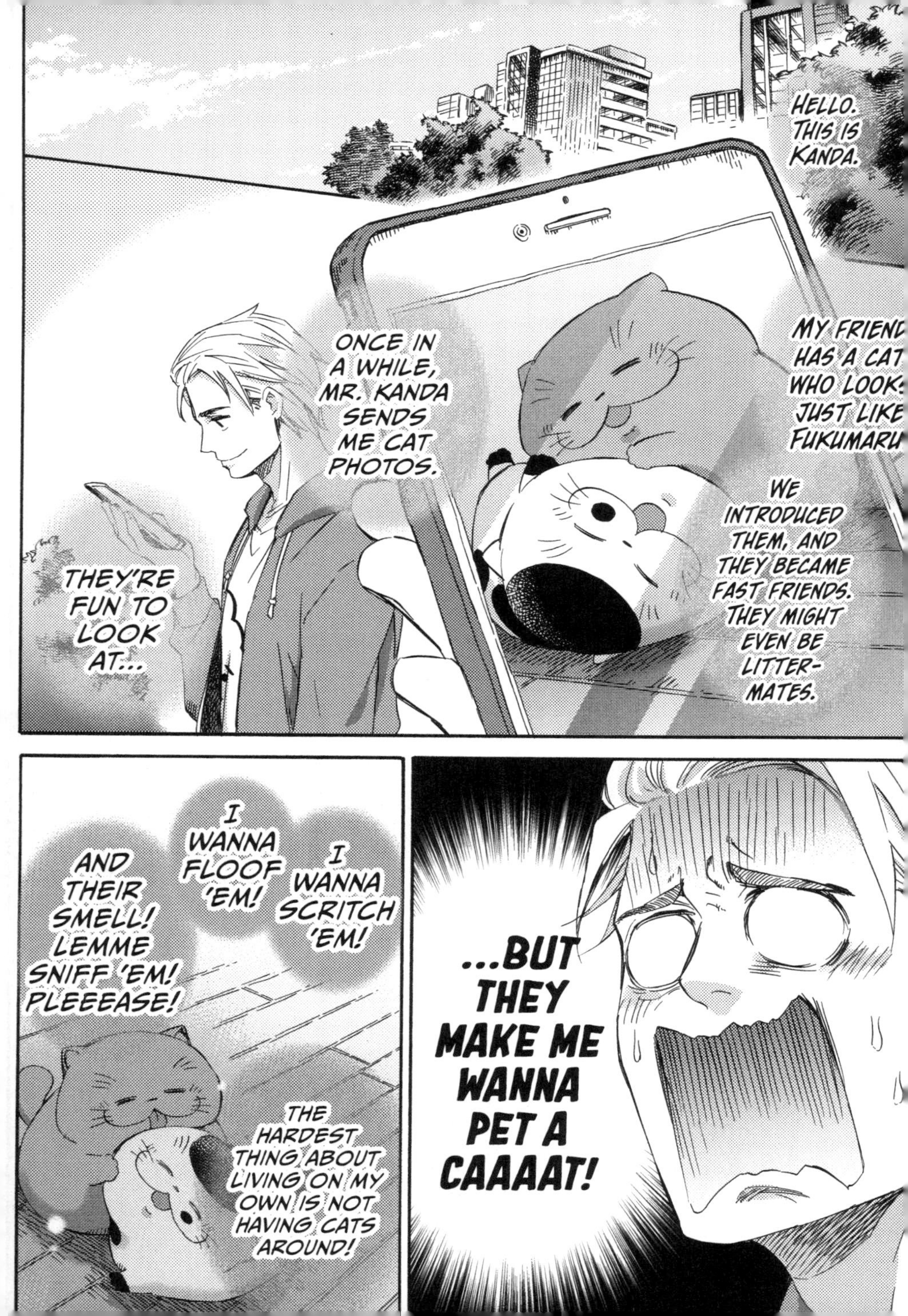
HELLO. THIS IS KANDA.
MY FRIEND HAS A CAT WHO LOOKS JUST LIKE FUKUMARU.
WE INTRODUCED THEM, AND THEY BECAME FAST FRIENDS. THEY MIGHT EVEN BE LITTER-MATES.
ONCE IN A WHILE, MR. KANDA SENDS ME CAT PHOTOS.
THEY'RE FUN TO LOOK AT...
...BUT THEY MAKE ME WANNA PET A CAAAAT!
I WANNA SCRITCH 'EM!
I WANNA FLOOF 'EM!
AND THEIR SMELL! LEMME SNIFF 'EM! PLEEEASE!
THE HARDEST THING ABOUT LIVING ON MY OWN IS NOT HAVING CATS AROUND!

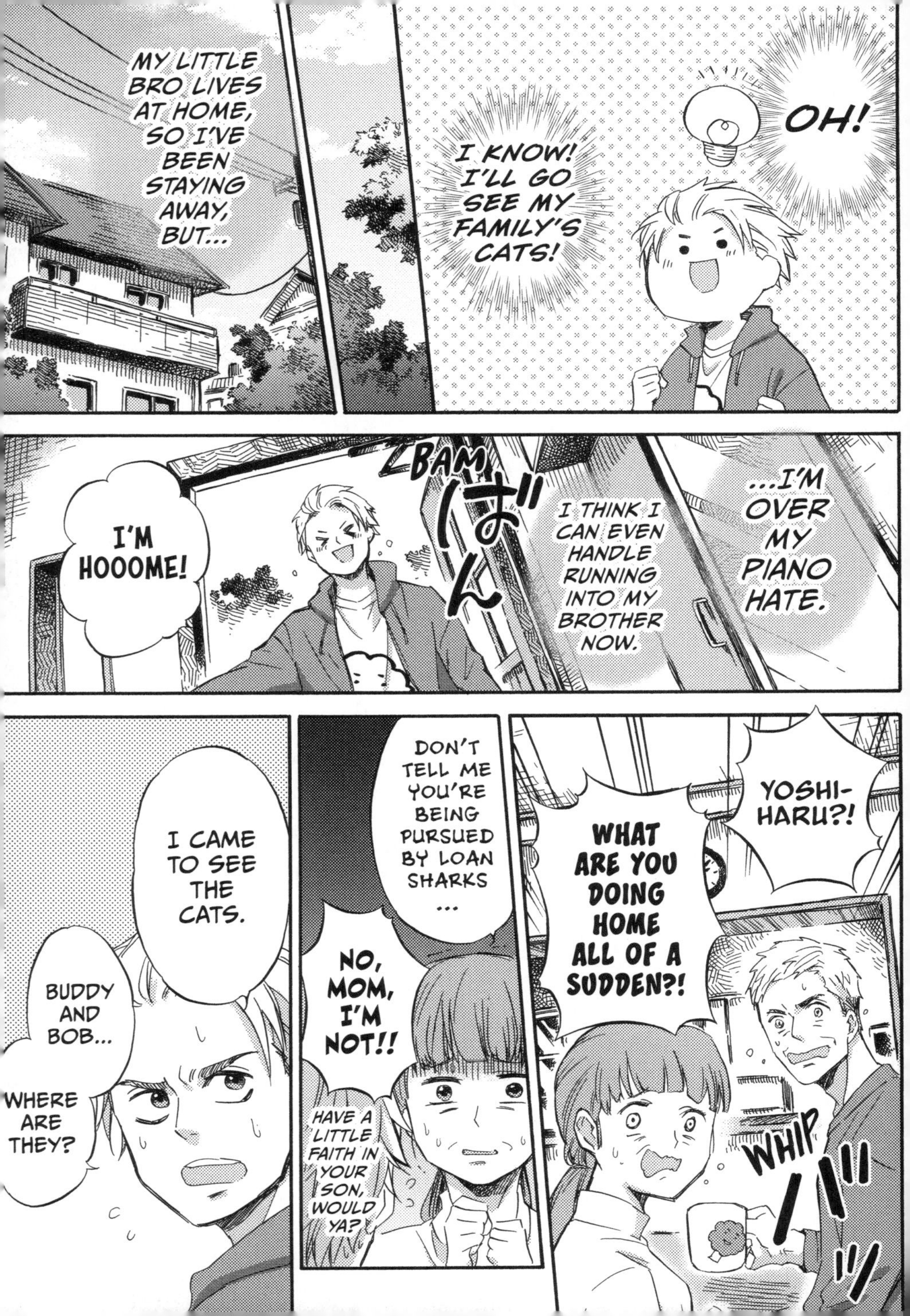
OH!
I KNOW! I'LL GO SEE MY FAMILY'S CATS!
MY LITTLE BRO LIVES AT HOME, SO I'VE BEEN STAYING AWAY, BUT...
...I'M OVER MY PIANO HATE.
I THINK I CAN EVEN HANDLE RUNNING INTO MY BROTHER NOW.
BAM
ばん
I'M HOOOME!
YOSHI-HARU?!
WHAT ARE YOU DOING HOME ALL OF A SUDDEN?!
WHIP
DON'T TELL ME YOU'RE BEING PURSUED BY LOAN SHARKS...
NO, MOM, I'M NOT!!
HAVE A LITTLE FAITH IN YOUR SON, WOULD YA?
I CAME TO SEE THE CATS.
BUDDY AND BOB...
WHERE ARE THEY?

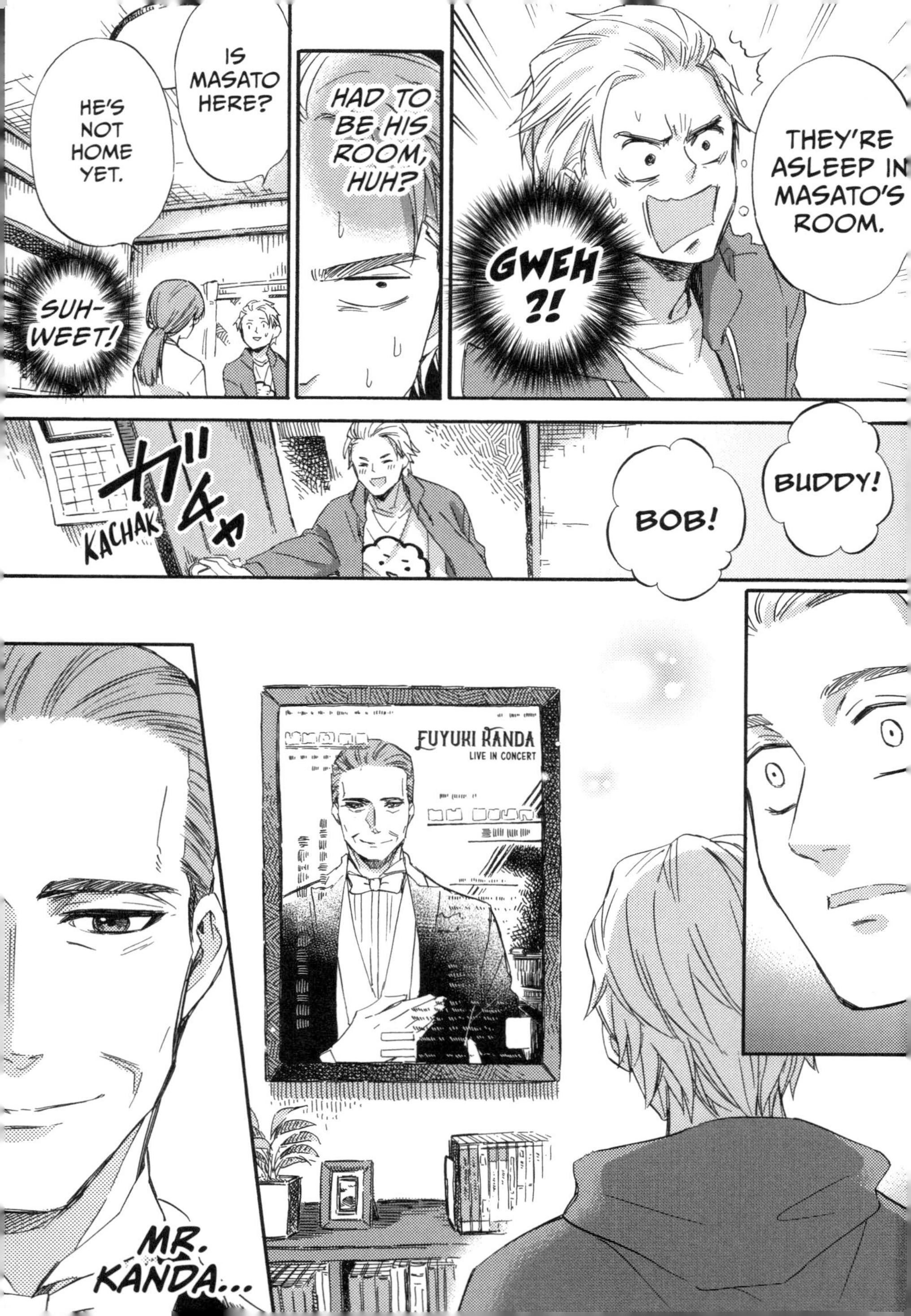
THEY'RE ASLEEP IN MASATO'S ROOM.
GWEH ?!
HAD TO BE HIS ROOM, HUH?
IS MASATO HERE?
HE'S NOT HOME YET.
SUH-WEET!
BUDDY!
BOB!
ガチャ
KACHAK
FUYUKI KANDA
LIVE IN CONCERT
MR. KANDA...

Hoarding Happiness

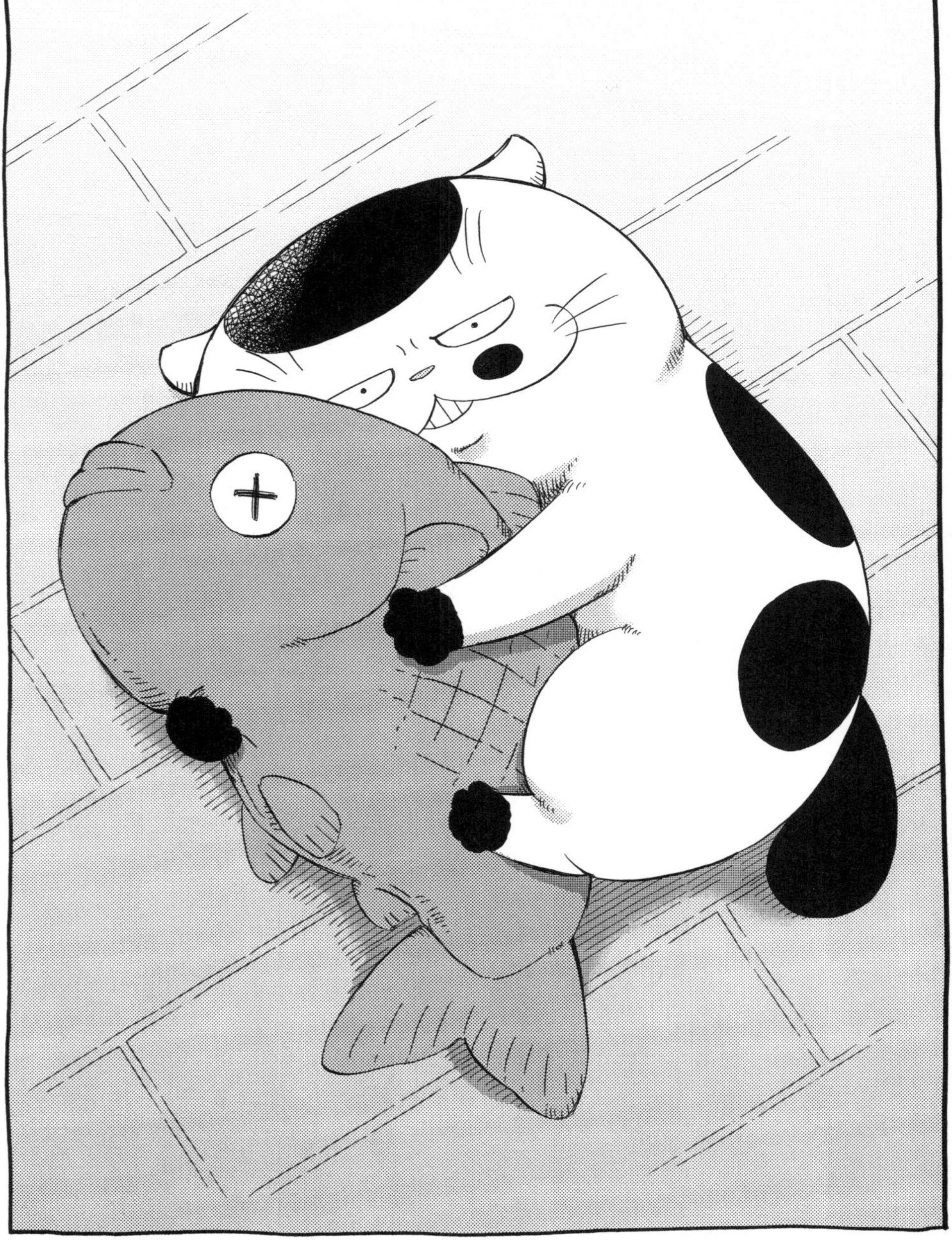

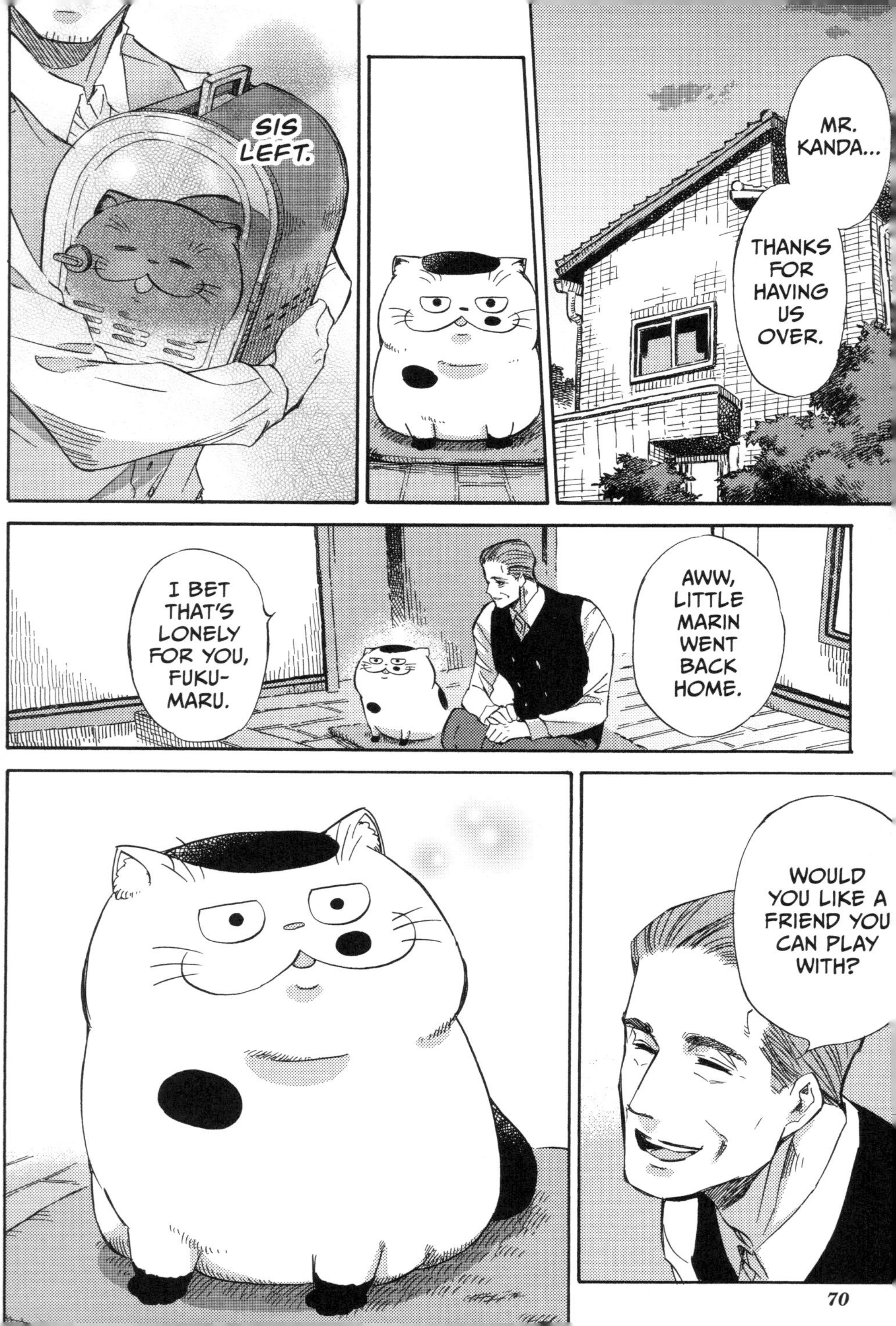
MR. KANDA...
THANKS FOR HAVING US OVER.
SIS LEFT.
AWW, LITTLE MARIN WENT BACK HOME.
I BET THAT'S LONELY FOR YOU, FUKU-MARU.
WOULD YOU LIKE A FRIEND YOU CAN PLAY WITH?

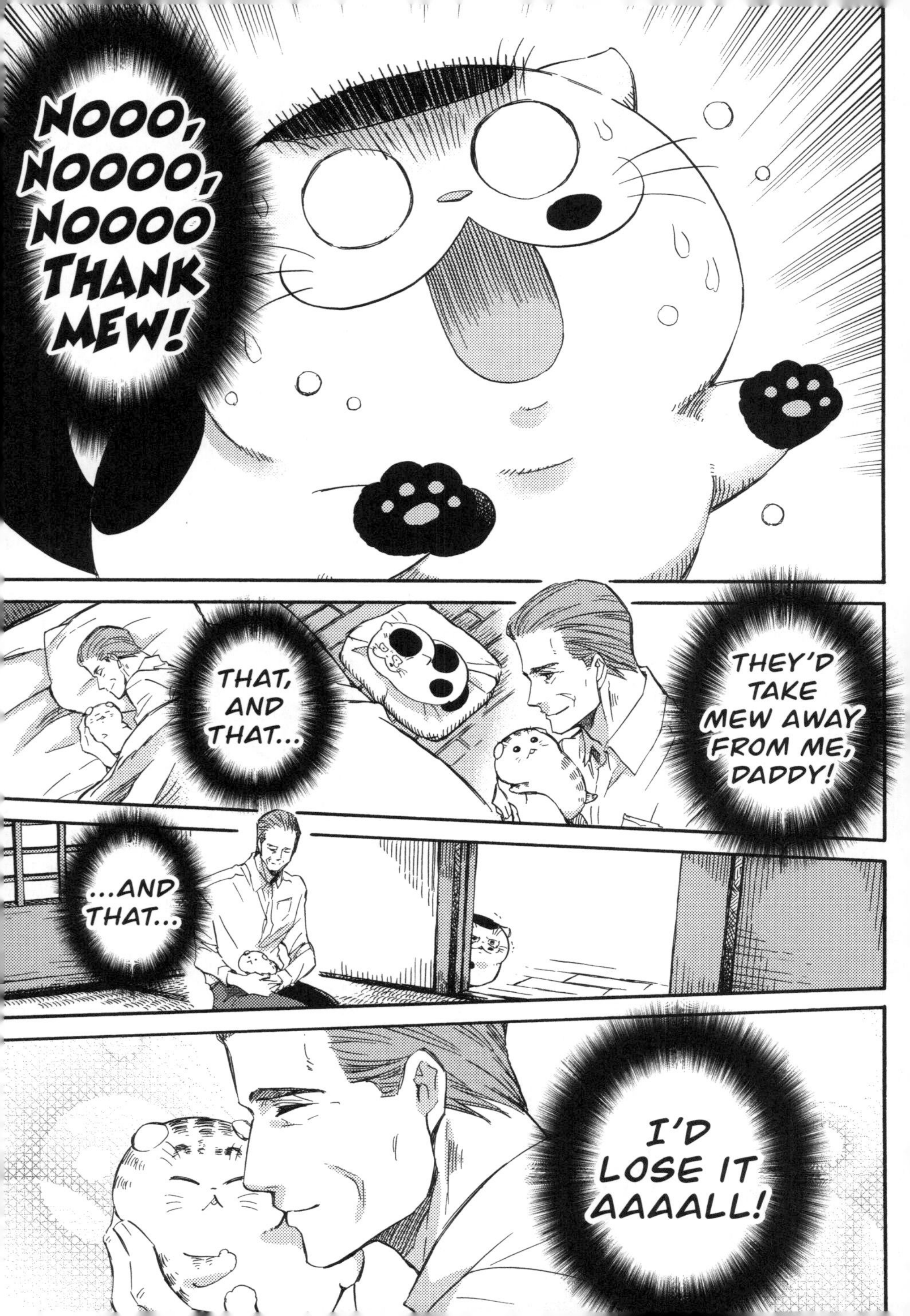
NOOO, NOOOO, NOOOO THANK MEW!
THEY'D TAKE MEW AWAY FROM ME, DADDY!
THAT, AND THAT...
...AND THAT...
I'D LOSE IT AAAALL!

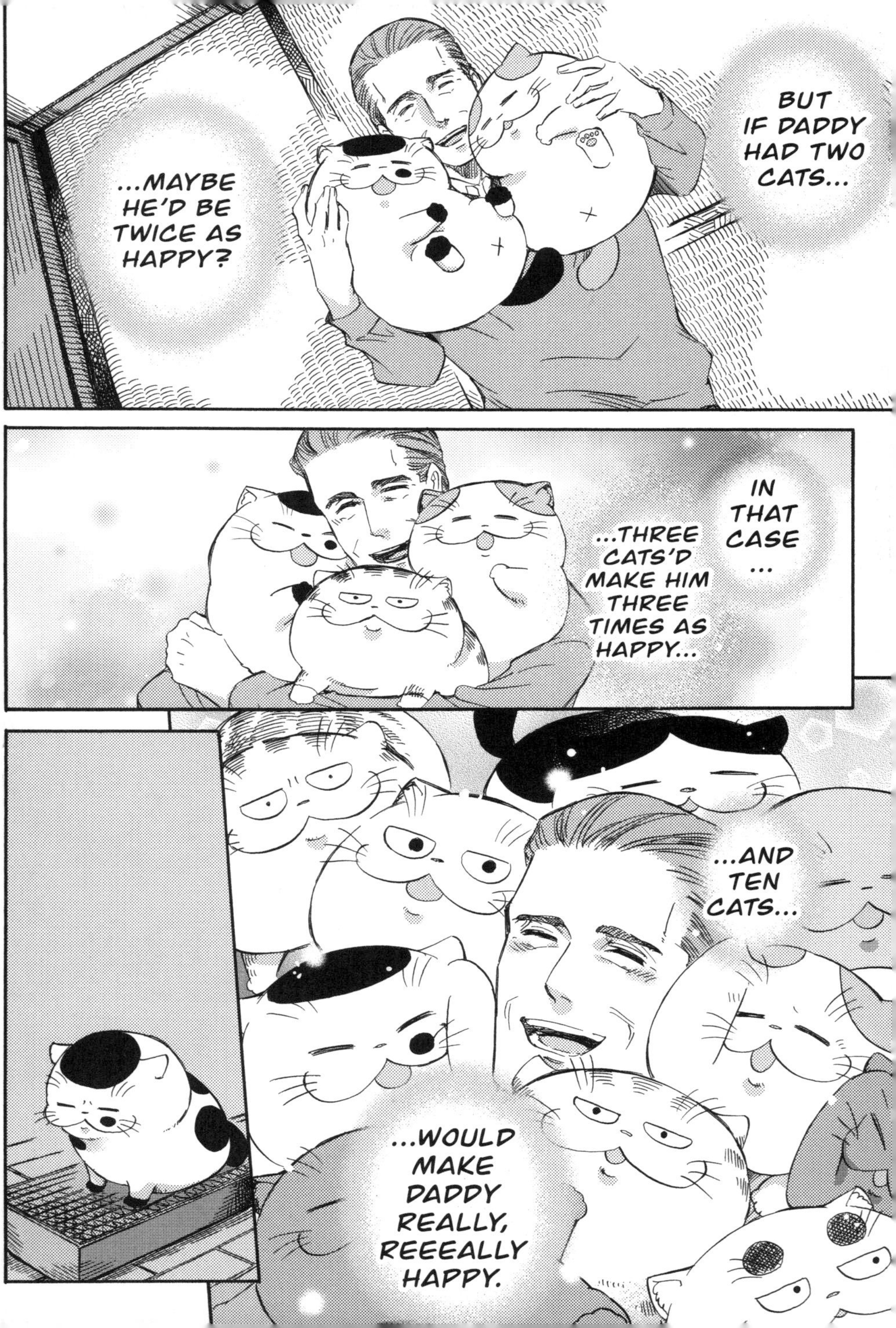
BUT IF DADDY HAD TWO CATS...
...MAYBE HE'D BE TWICE AS HAPPY?
IN THAT CASE ...
...THREE CATS'D MAKE HIM THREE TIMES AS HAPPY...
...AND TEN CATS...
...WOULD MAKE DADDY REALLY, REEEALLY HAPPY.

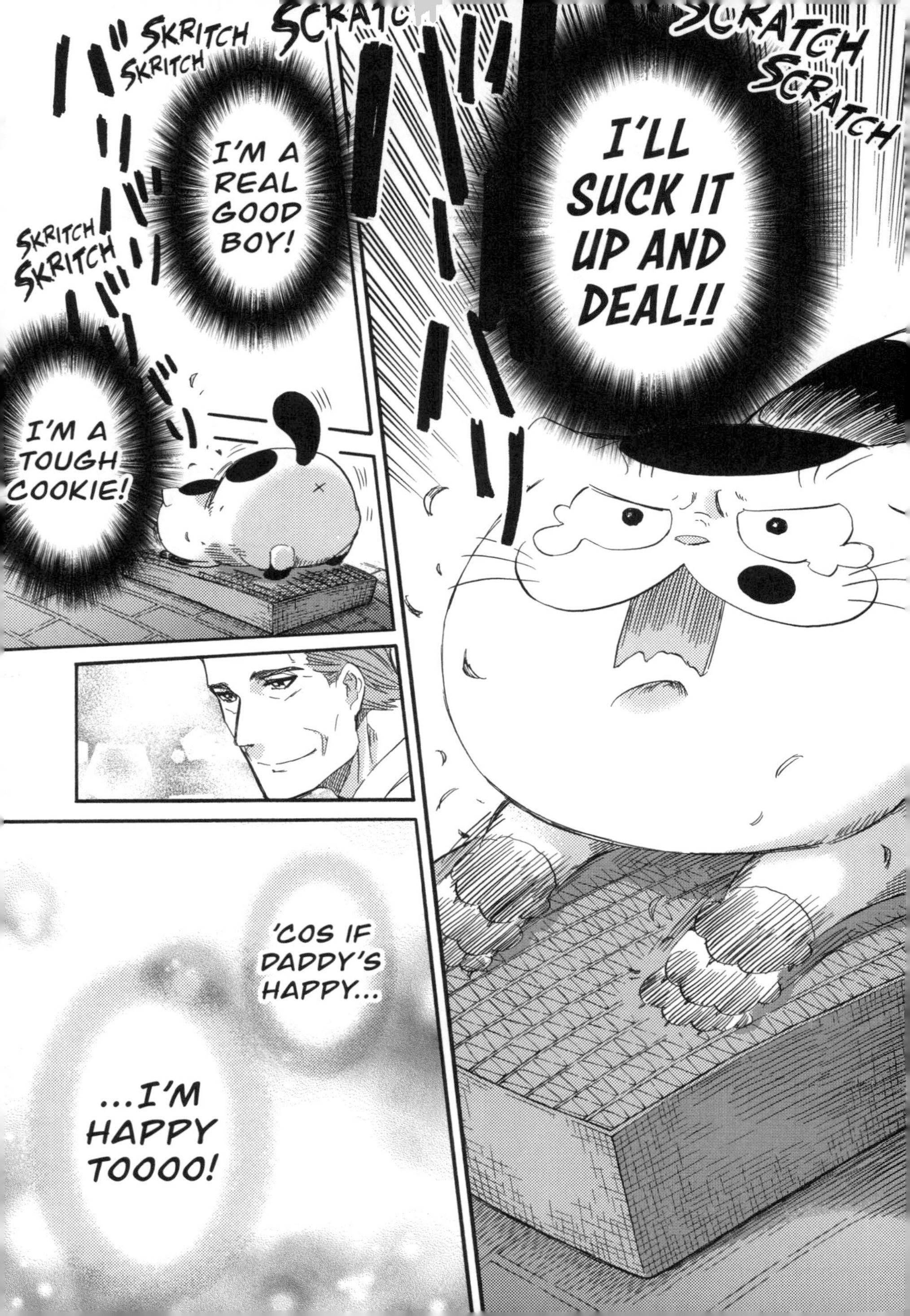
SCRATCH
SCRATCH
SCRATCH
I'LL SUCK IT UP AND DEAL!!
SKRITCH
SKRITCH
I'M A REAL GOOD BOY!
SKRITCH
SKRITCH
I'M A TOUGH COOKIE!
'COS IF DADDY'S HAPPY...
...I'M HAPPY TOOOO!

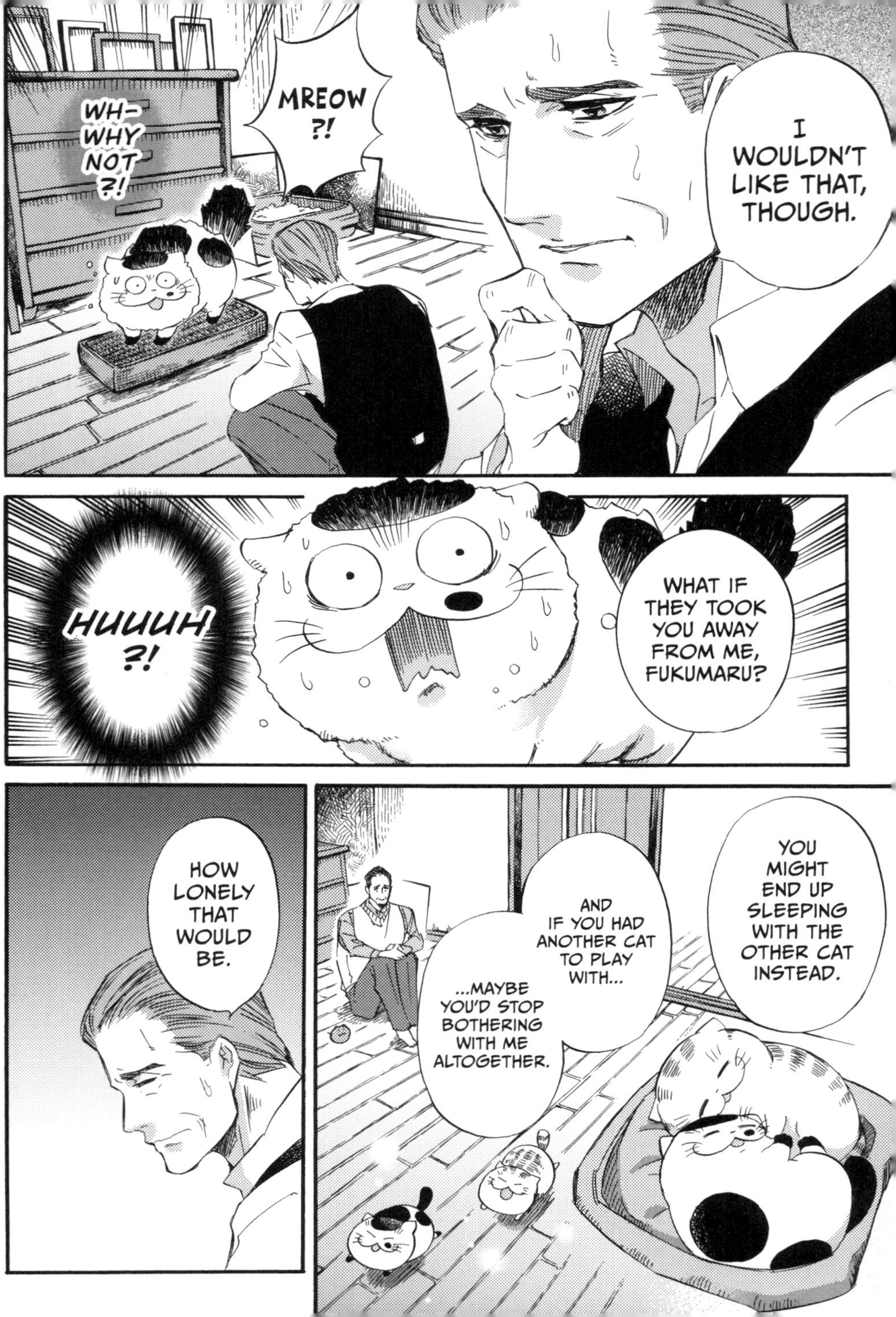
I WOULDN'T LIKE THAT, THOUGH.
MREOW ?!
WH- WHY NOT ?!
WHAT IF THEY TOOK YOU AWAY FROM ME, FUKUMARU?
HUUUH ?!
YOU MIGHT END UP SLEEPING WITH THE OTHER CAT INSTEAD.
AND IF YOU HAD ANOTHER CAT TO PLAY WITH...
...MAYBE YOU'D STOP BOTHERING WITH ME ALTOGETHER.
HOW LONELY THAT WOULD BE.

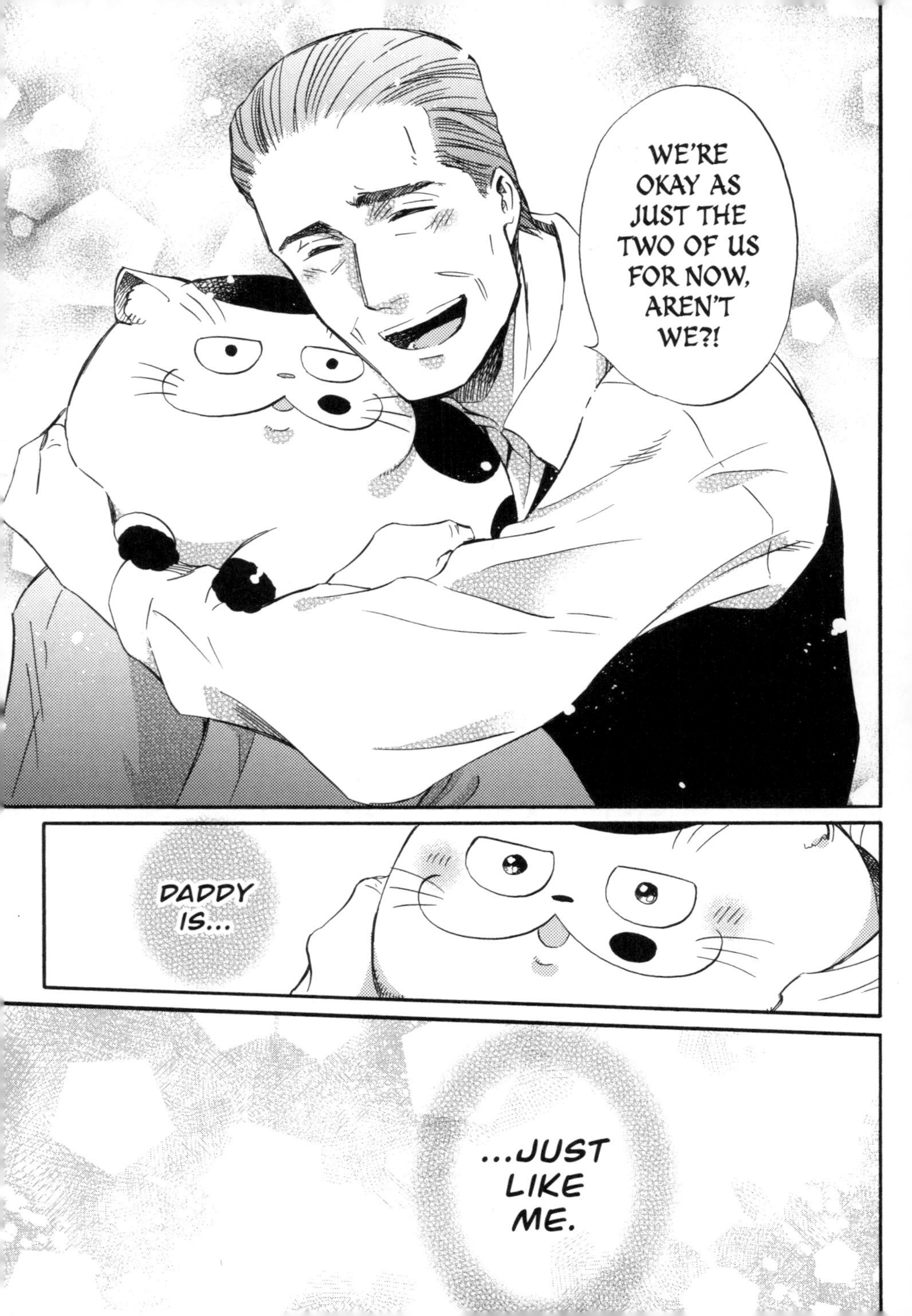
WE'RE OKAY AS JUST THE TWO OF US FOR NOW, AREN'T WE?!
DADDY IS...
...JUST LIKE ME.

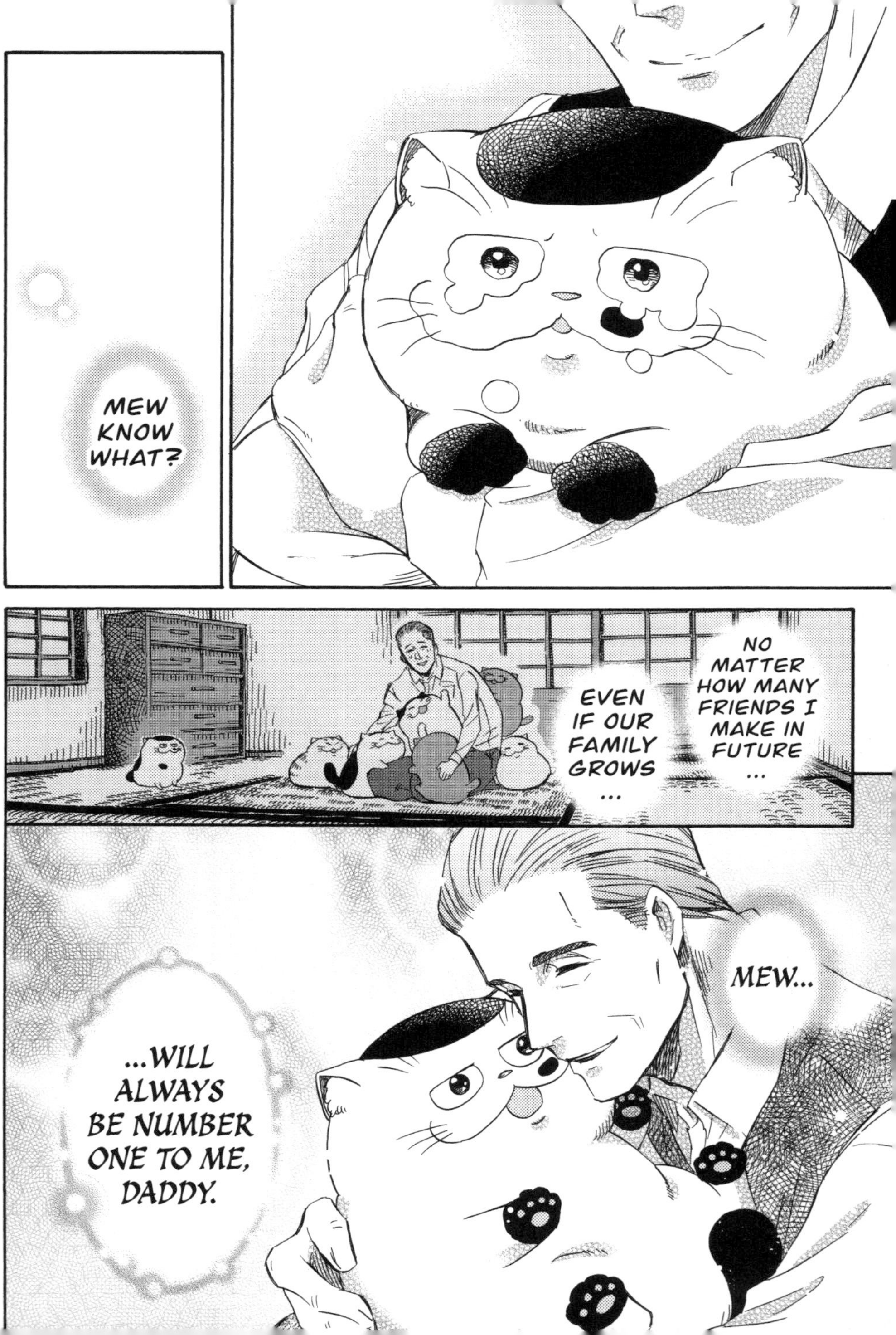
MEW KNOW WHAT?
NO MATTER HOW MANY FRIENDS I MAKE IN FUTURE ...
EVEN IF OUR FAMILY GROWS ...
MEW...
...WILL ALWAYS BE NUMBER ONE TO ME, DADDY.

Fuku v Kanda Fish Fight

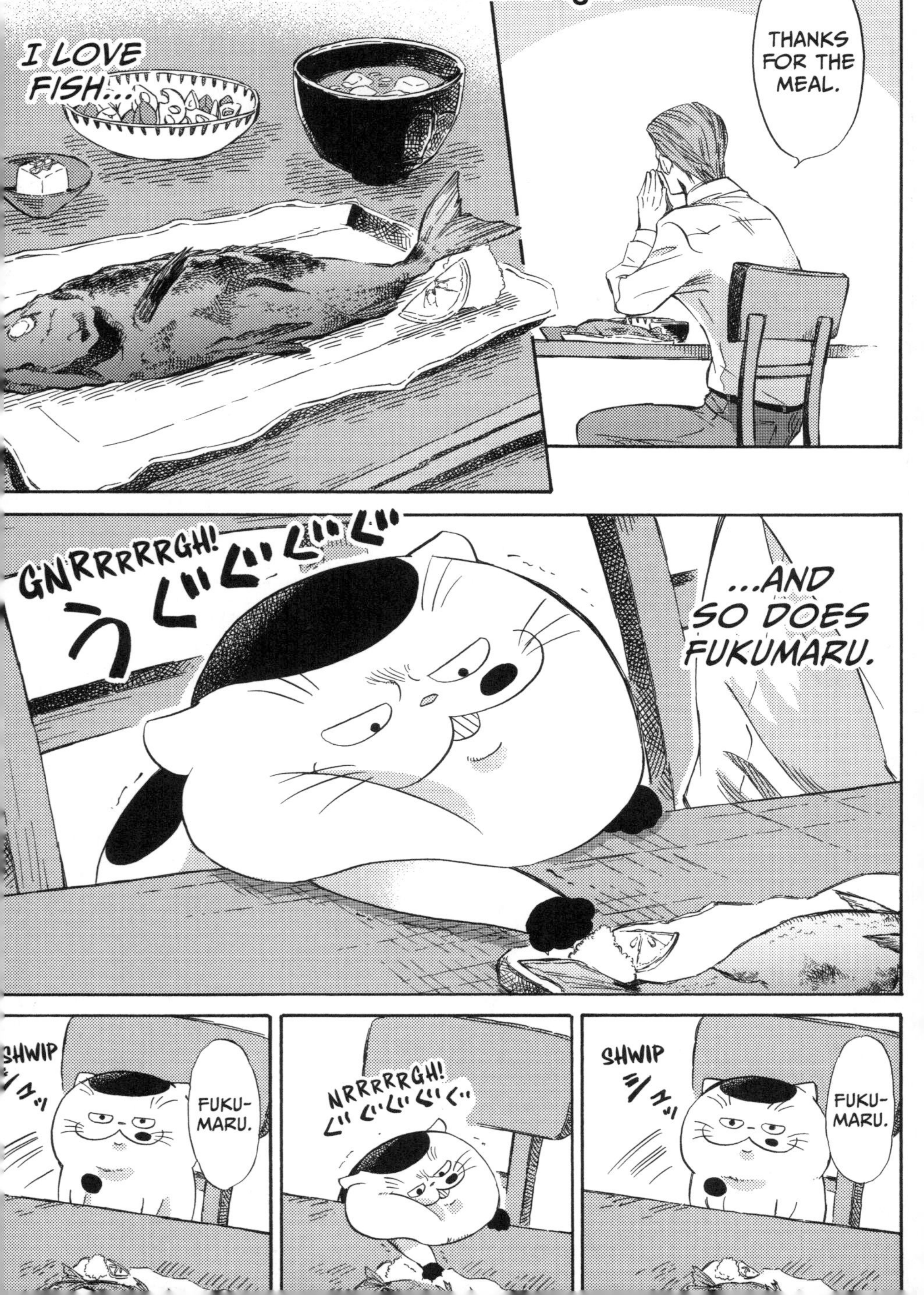
THANKS FOR THE MEAL.
I LOVE FISH...
...AND SO DOES FUKUMARU.
GNRRRRRGH!
うぐぐぐぐ
SHWIP
FUKU-MARU.
NRRRRRGH!
SHWIP
FUKU-MARU.

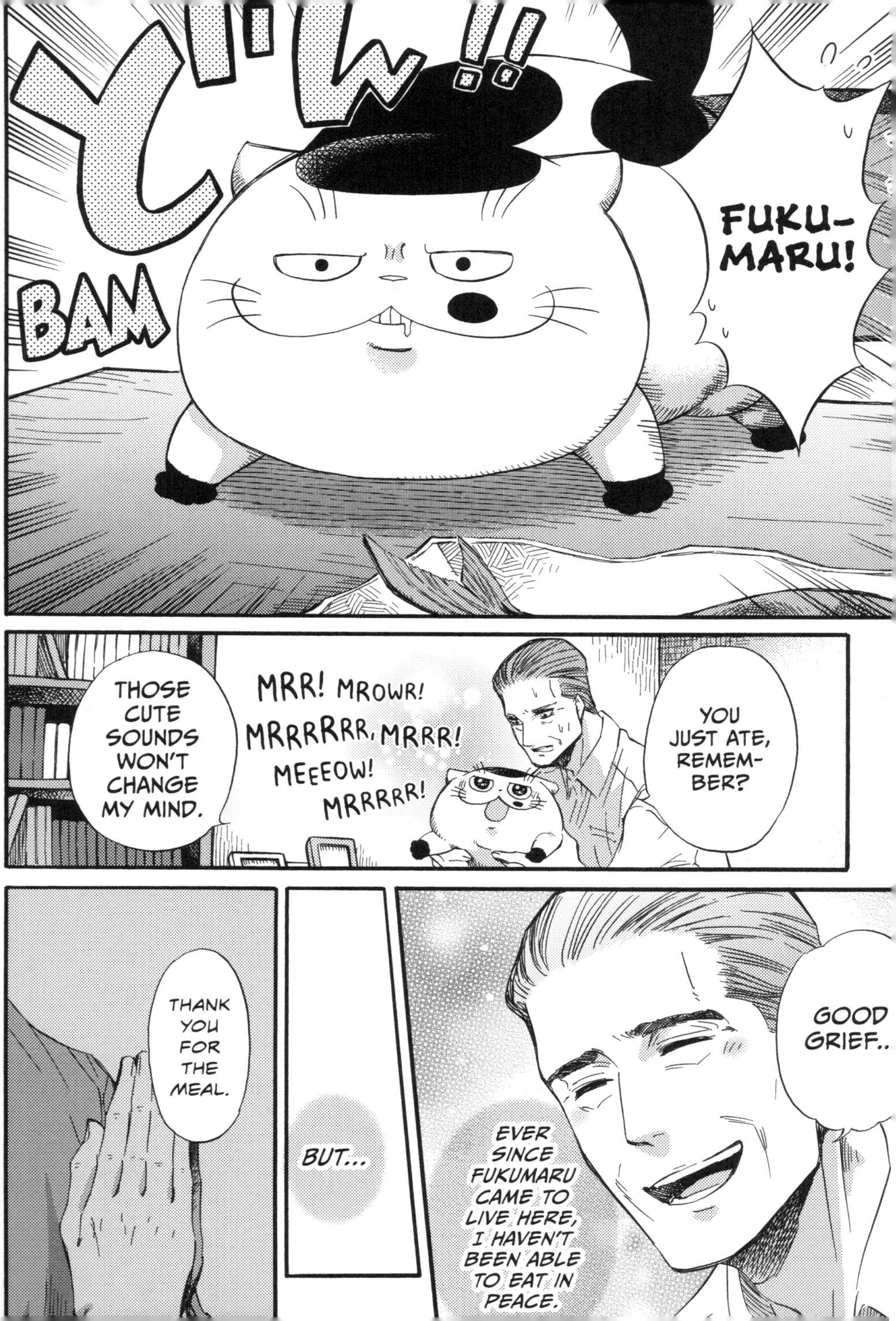
FUKU-MARU!
BAM
YOU JUST ATE, REMEMBER?
MRR! MROWR!
MRRRRRR, MRRR!
MEEEOW!
MRRRRR!
THOSE CUTE SOUNDS WON'T CHANGE MY MIND.
GOOD GRIEF...
EVER SINCE FUKUMARU CAME TO LIVE HERE, I HAVEN'T BEEN ABLE TO EAT IN PEACE.
BUT...
THANK YOU FOR THE MEAL.

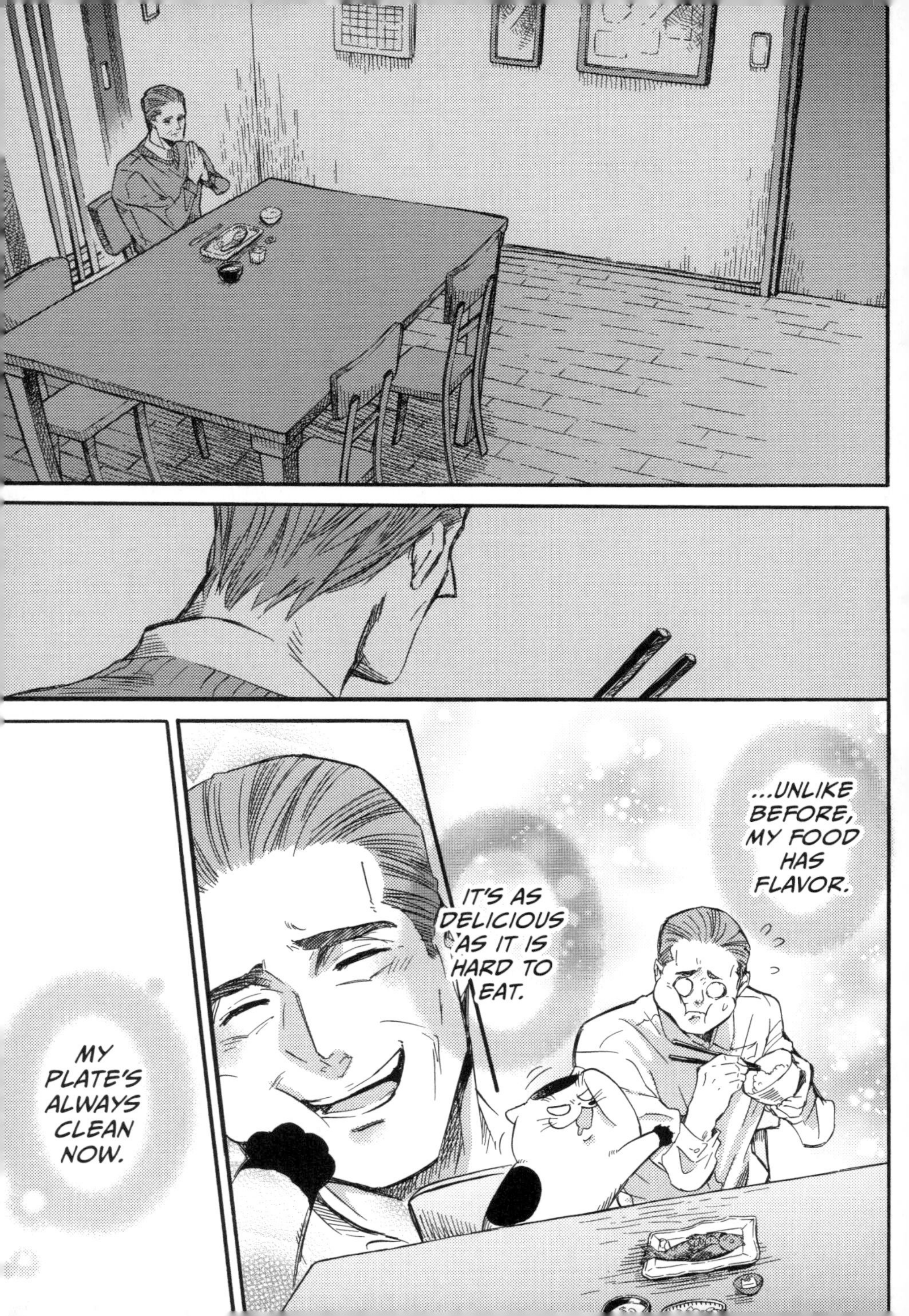
...UNLIKE BEFORE, MY FOOD HAS FLAVOR.
IT'S AS DELICIOUS AS IT IS HARD TO EAT.
MY PLATE'S ALWAYS CLEAN NOW.

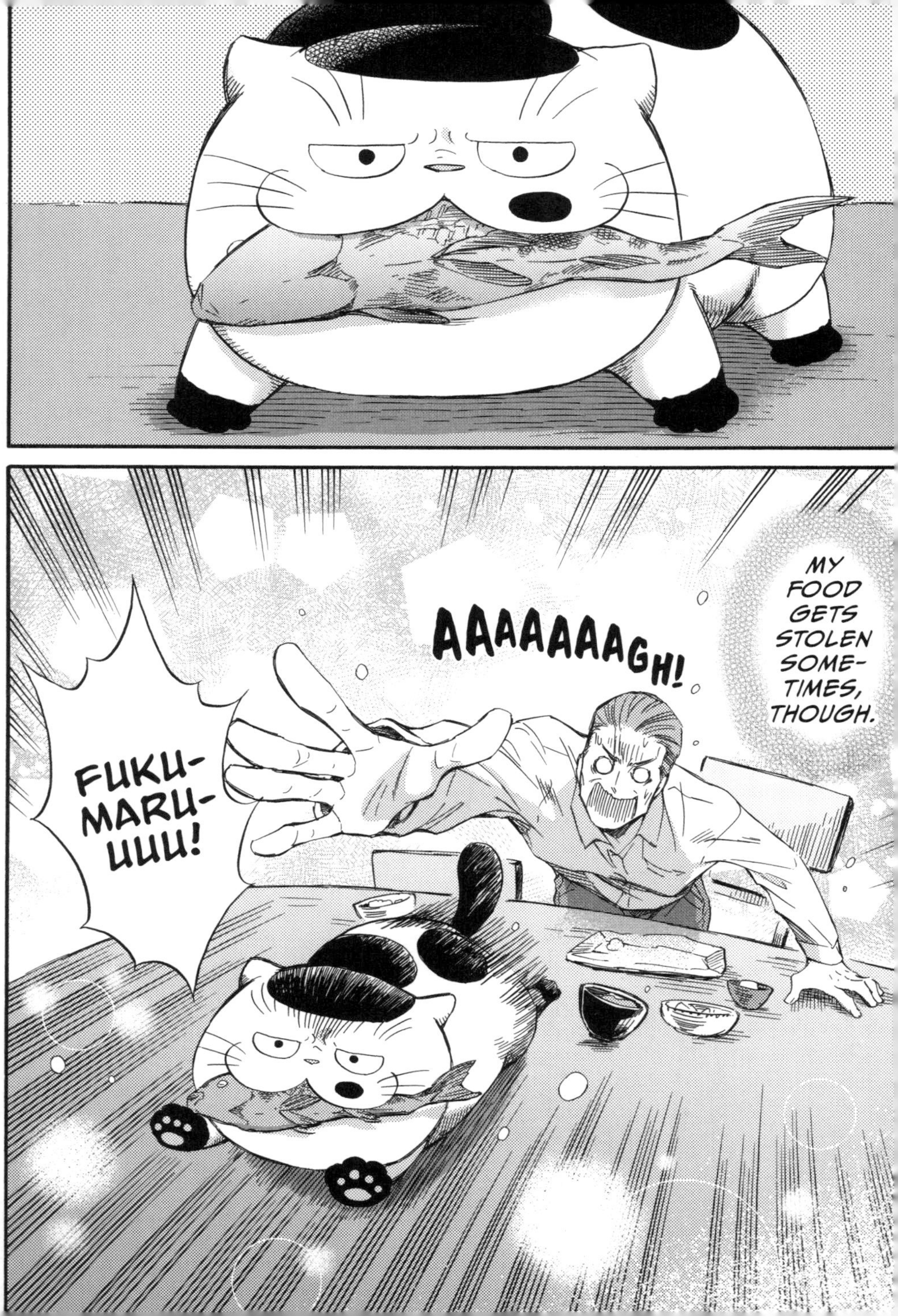
MY FOOD GETS STOLEN SOME-TIMES, THOUGH.
AAAAAAAGH!
FUKU-MARU-UUUU!

THE MAN WANTS TO SHARE HIS KNOWLEDGE

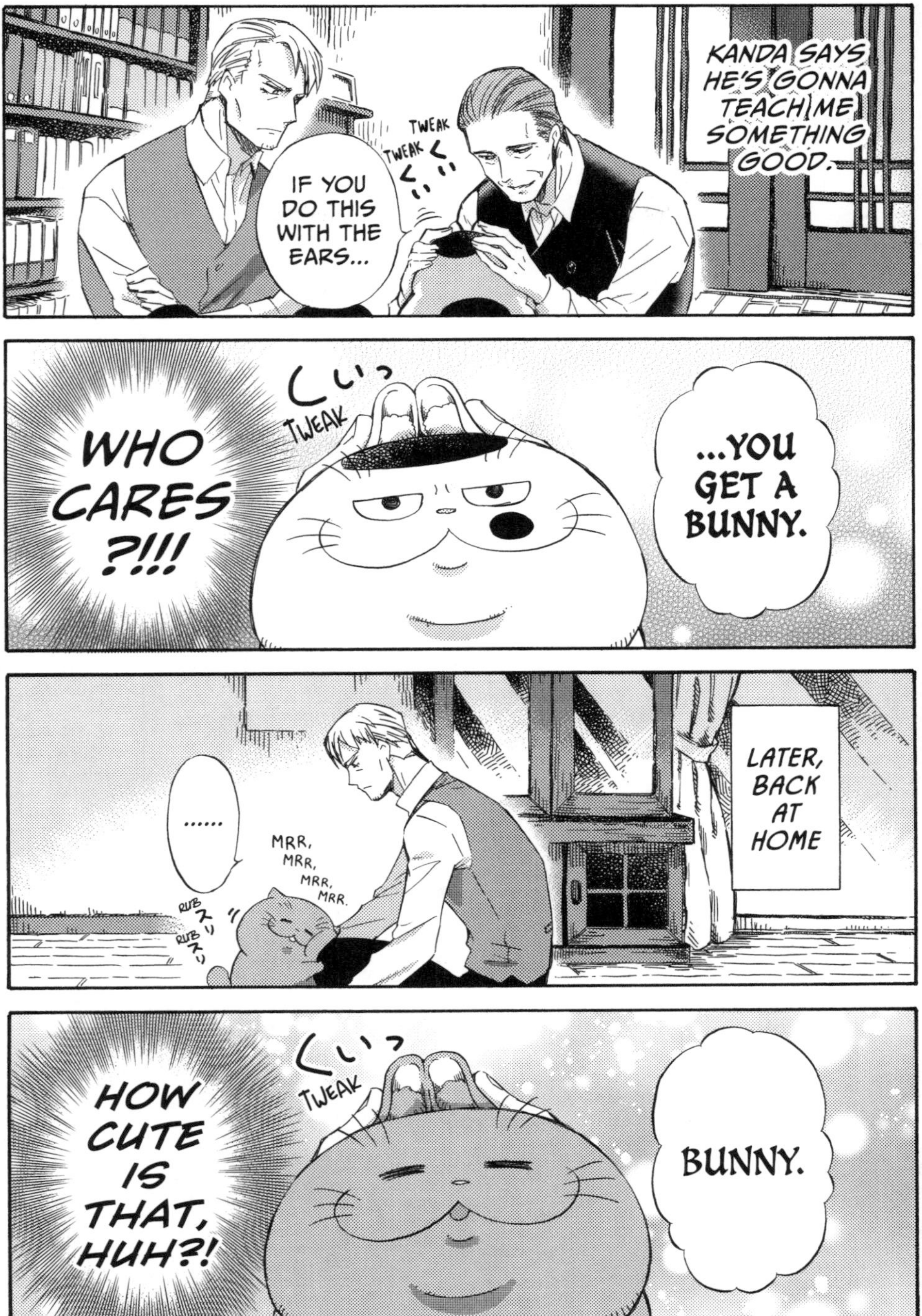
KANDA SAYS HE'S GONNA TEACH ME SOMETHING GOOD.
TWEAK
TWEAK
IF YOU DO THIS WITH THE EARS...
...YOU GET A BUNNY.
くいっ
TWEAK
WHO CARES ?!!!
LATER, BACK AT HOME
MRR, MRR, MRR, MRR.
......
RUB スリ
RUB スリ
BUNNY.
くいっ
TWEAK
HOW CUTE IS THAT, HUH?!

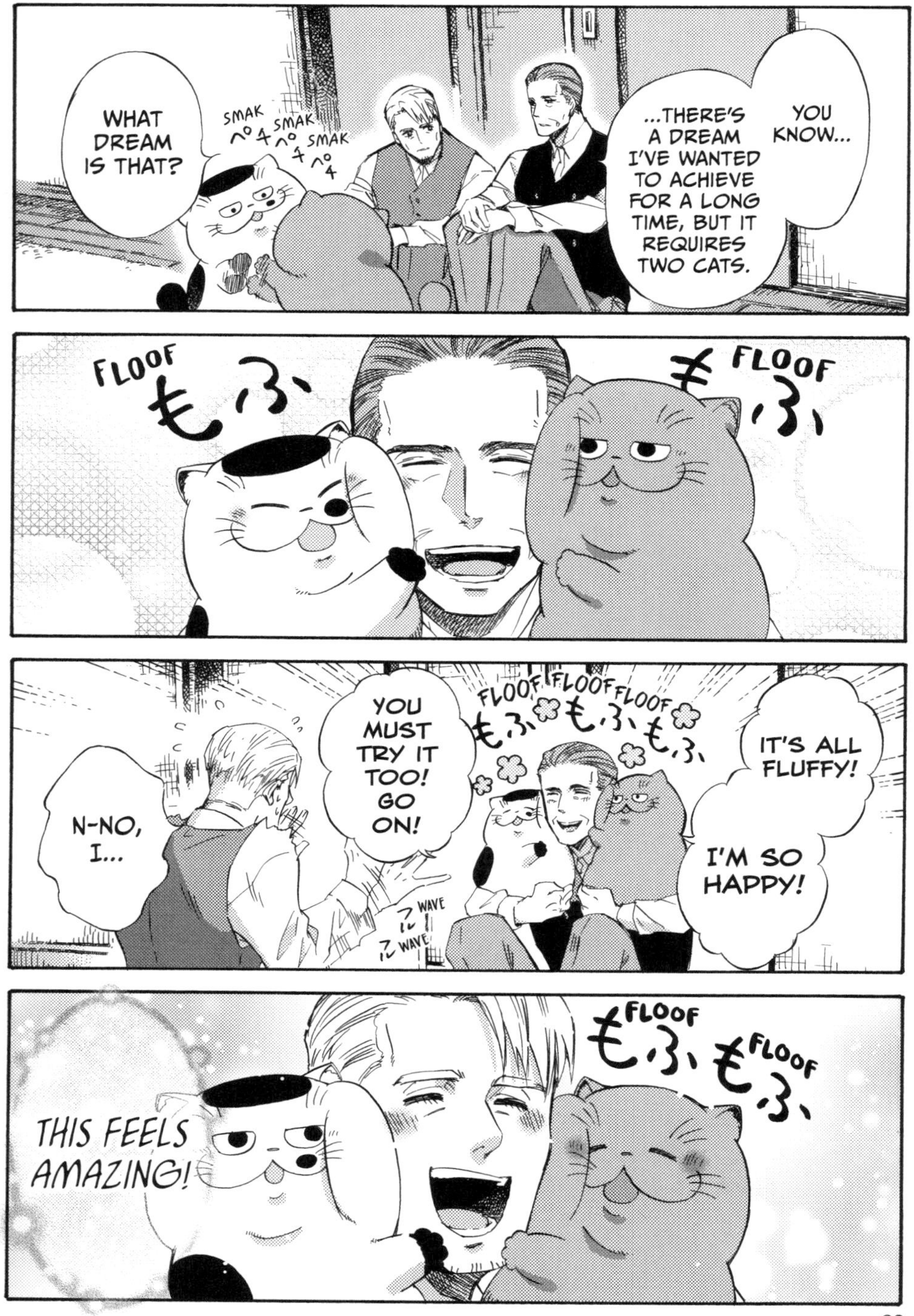
YOU KNOW...
...THERE'S A DREAM I'VE WANTED TO ACHIEVE FOR A LONG TIME, BUT IT REQUIRES TWO CATS.
SMAK SMAK SMAK
WHAT DREAM IS THAT?
FLOOF
FLOOF
IT'S ALL FLUFFY!
I'M SO HAPPY!
FLOOF FLOOF FLOOF
YOU MUST TRY IT TOO! GO ON!
WAVE WAVE
N-NO, I...
FLOOF FLOOF
THIS FEELS AMAZING!

SCRITCH, SCRITCH, LICK, LICK

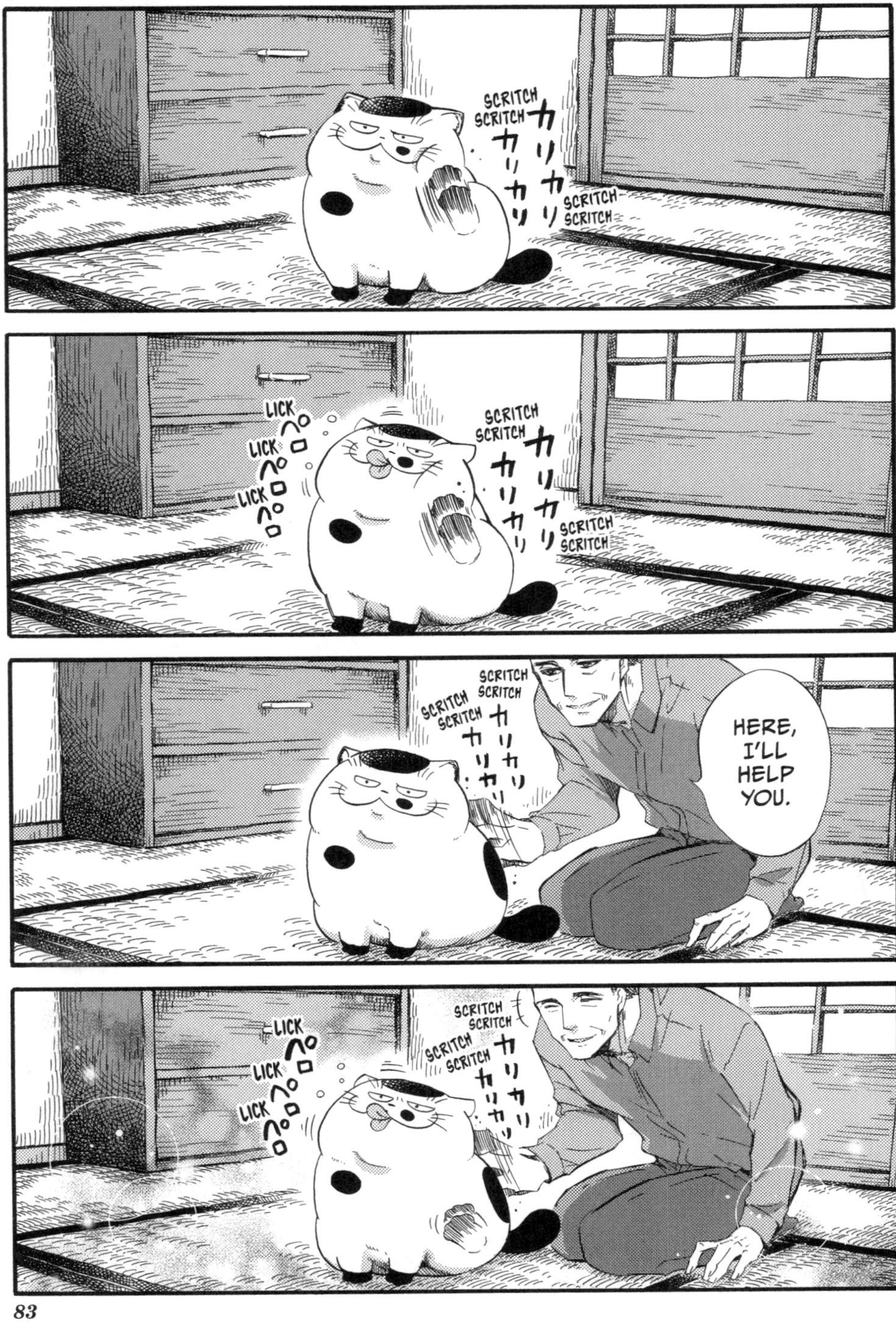
SCRITCH SCRITCH
カリカリ
カリカリ
SCRITCH SCRITCH
SCRITCH SCRITCH
カリカリ
カリカリ
SCRITCH SCRITCH
LICK ペロ
LICK ペロ
LICK ペロ
HERE, I'LL HELP YOU.
SCRITCH SCRITCH
カリカリ
SCRITCH SCRITCH
カリカリ
SCRITCH SCRITCH
カリカリ
SCRITCH SCRITCH
カリカッ
LICK ペロ
LICK ペロ
LICK ペロ

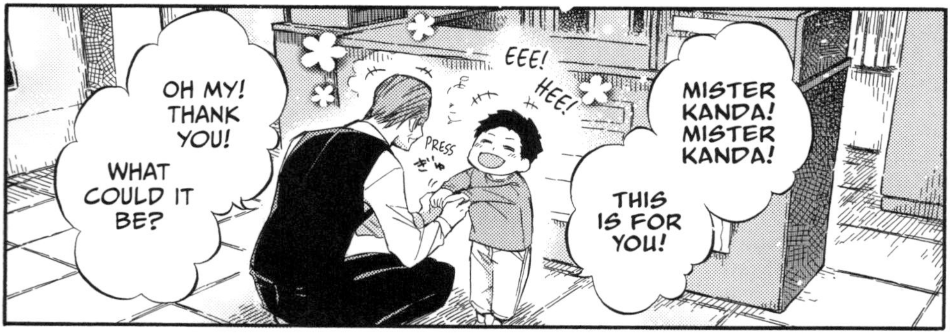
MISTER KANDA! MISTER KANDA!
THIS IS FOR YOU!
EEE!
HEE!
PRESS
ぎゅ
OH MY! THANK YOU!
WHAT COULD IT BE?

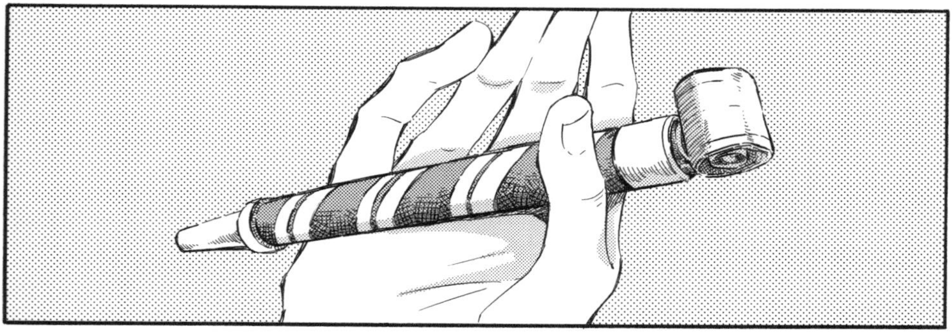

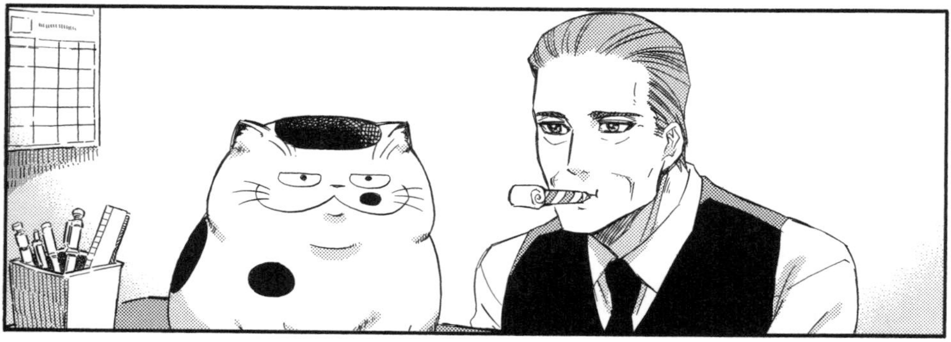

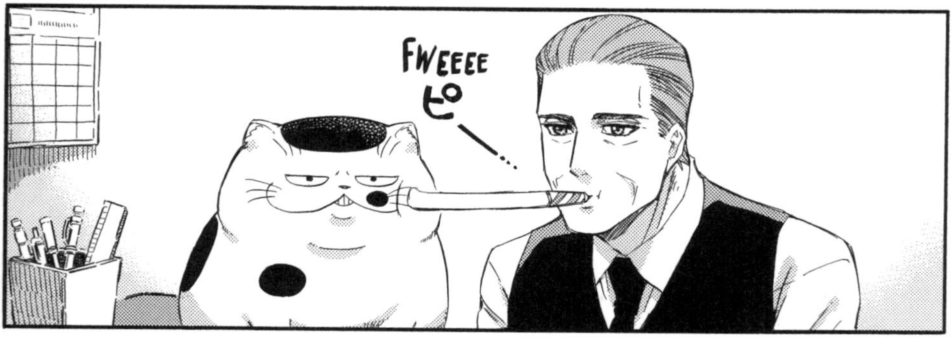
FWEEEE
ピー

UNIDENTIFIED OBJECT

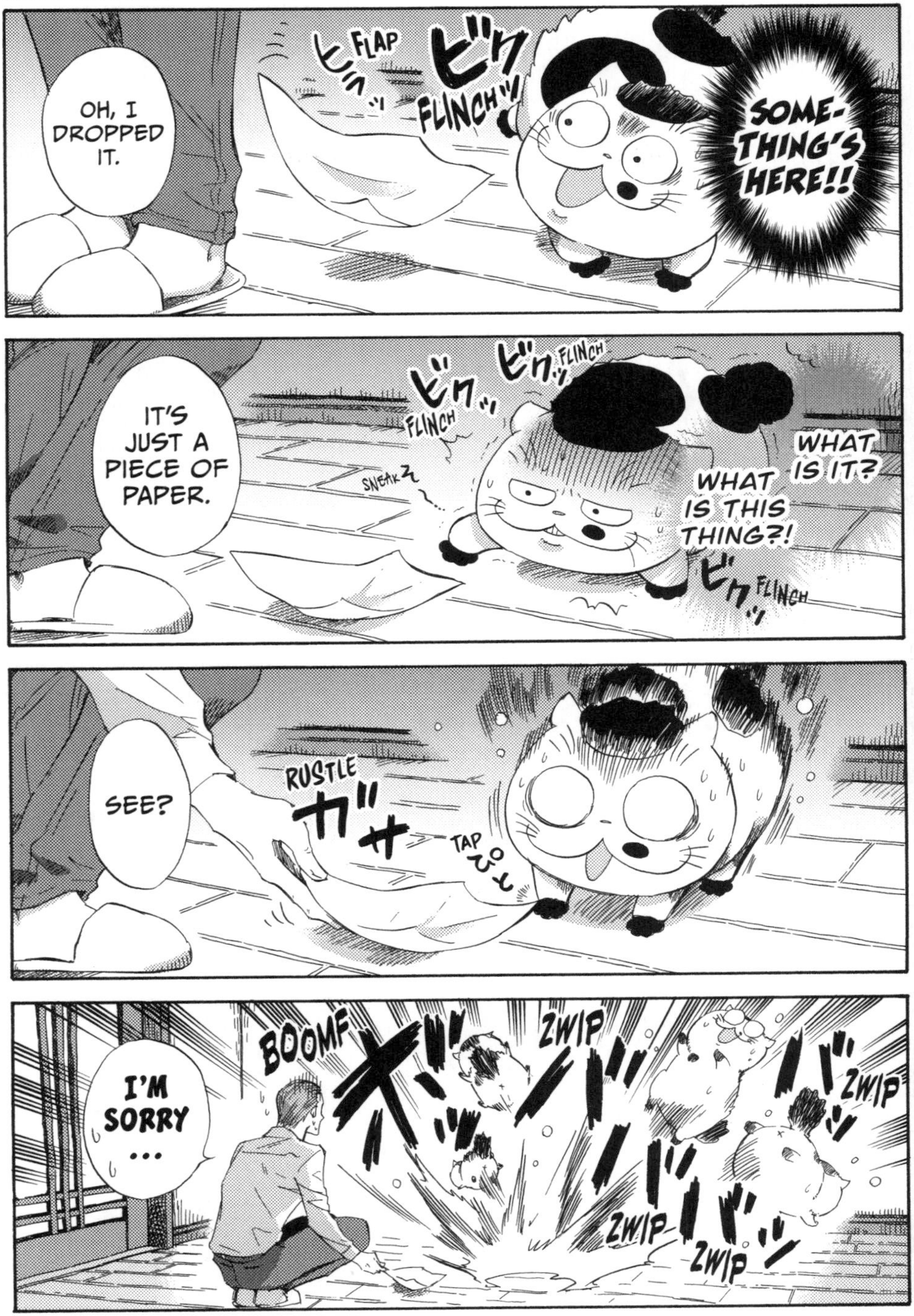
SOME-THING'S HERE!!
ビクッ FLINCH
ヒラッ FLAP
OH, I DROPPED IT.
WHAT IS IT?
WHAT IS THIS THING?!
ビクッ FLINCH
ビクッ FLINCH
ビクッ FLINCH
SNEAK
IT'S JUST A PIECE OF PAPER.
TAP ぴと
RUSTLE ガサ
SEE?
ZWIP
ZWIP
BOOMF
ZWIP
ZWIP
I'M SORRY...

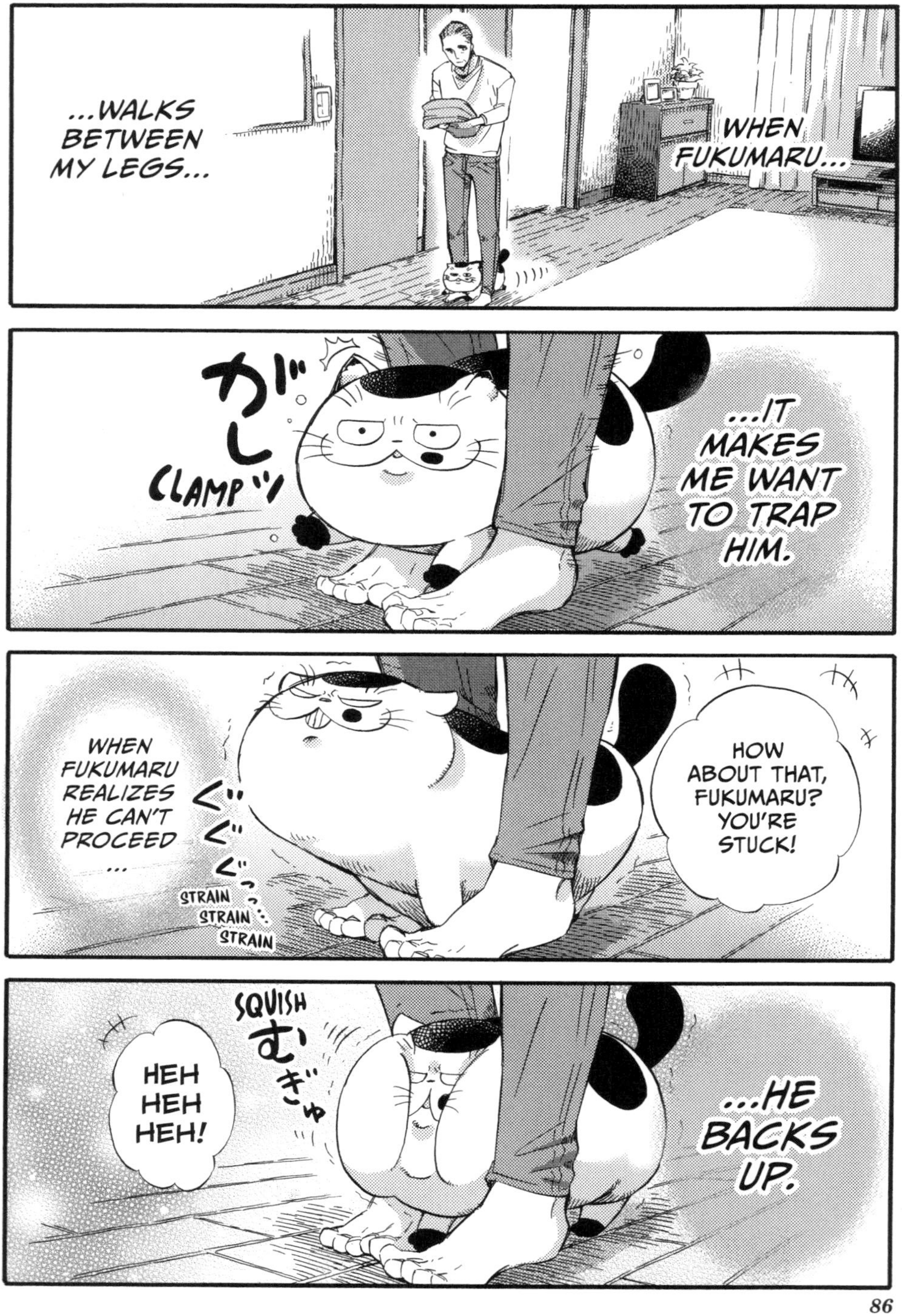
WHEN FUKUMARU...
...WALKS BETWEEN MY LEGS...
...IT MAKES ME WANT TO TRAP HIM.
がし
CLAMP ッ
HOW ABOUT THAT, FUKUMARU? YOU'RE STUCK!
ぐぐぐっっ...
STRAIN STRAIN STRAIN
WHEN FUKUMARU REALIZES HE CAN'T PROCEED...
...HE BACKS UP.
SQUISH
むぎゅ
HEH HEH HEH!

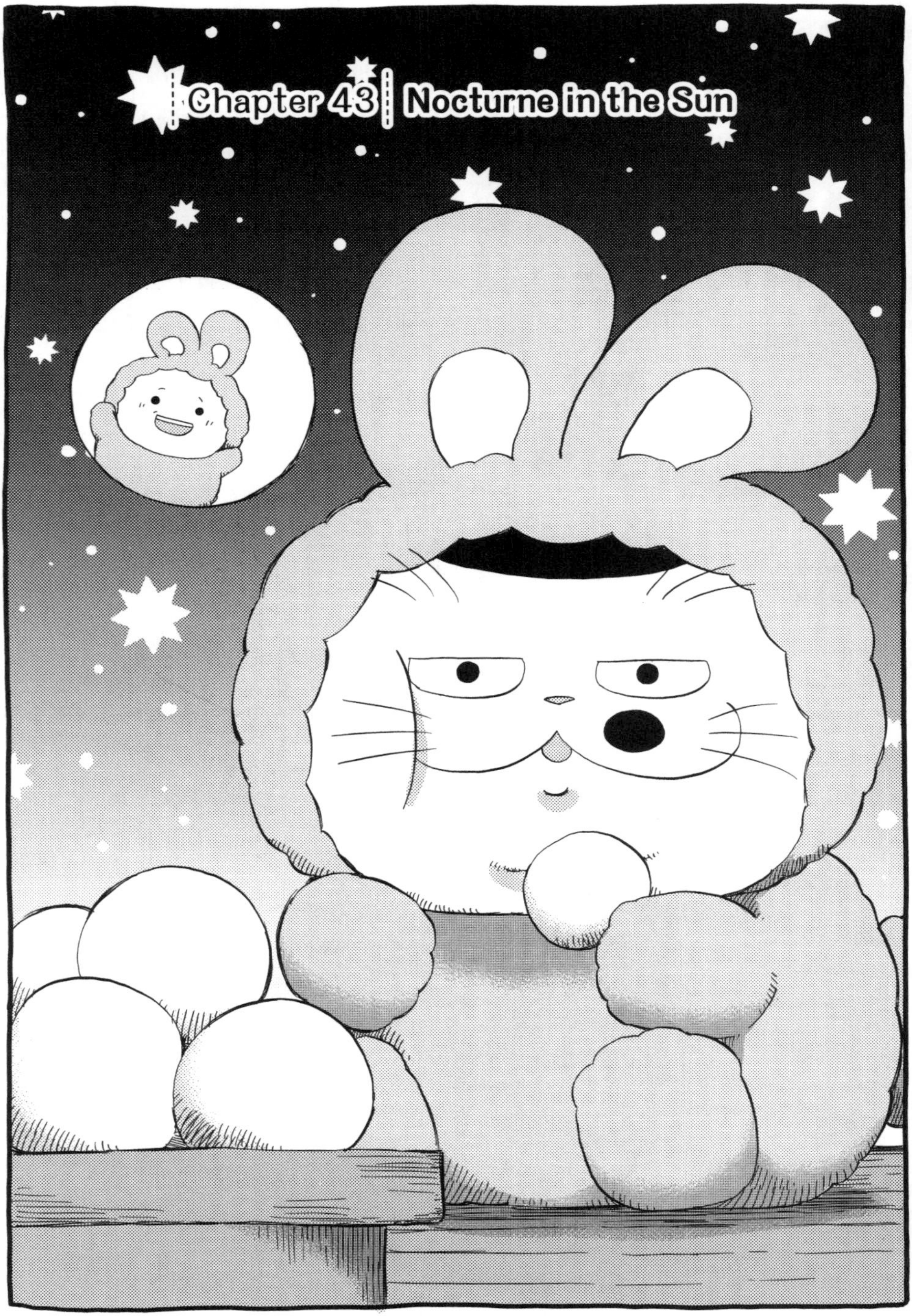
Chapter 43 Nocturne in the Sun

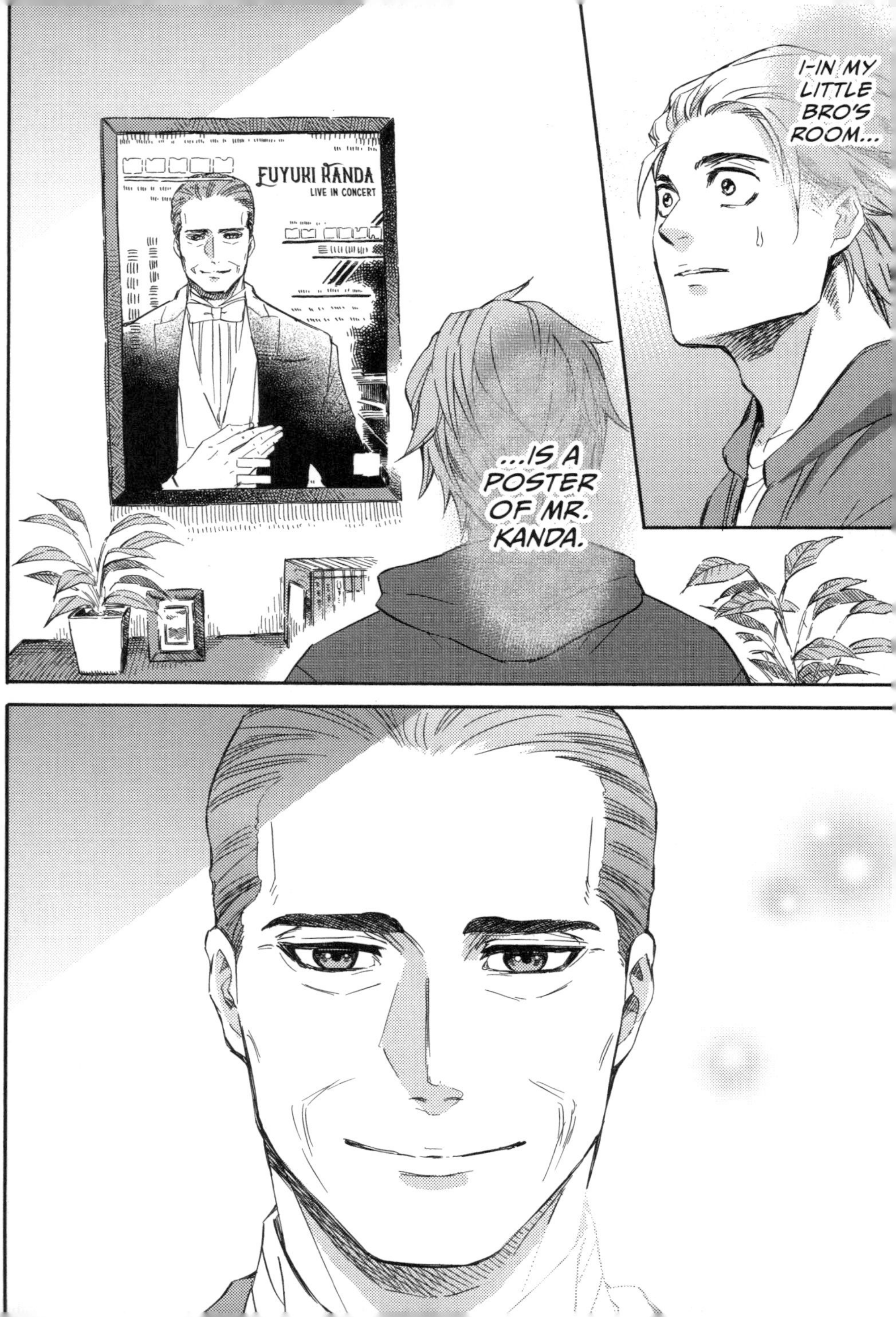
I-IN MY LITTLE BRO'S ROOM...
FUYUKI KANDA
LIVE IN CONCERT
...IS A POSTER OF MR. KANDA.

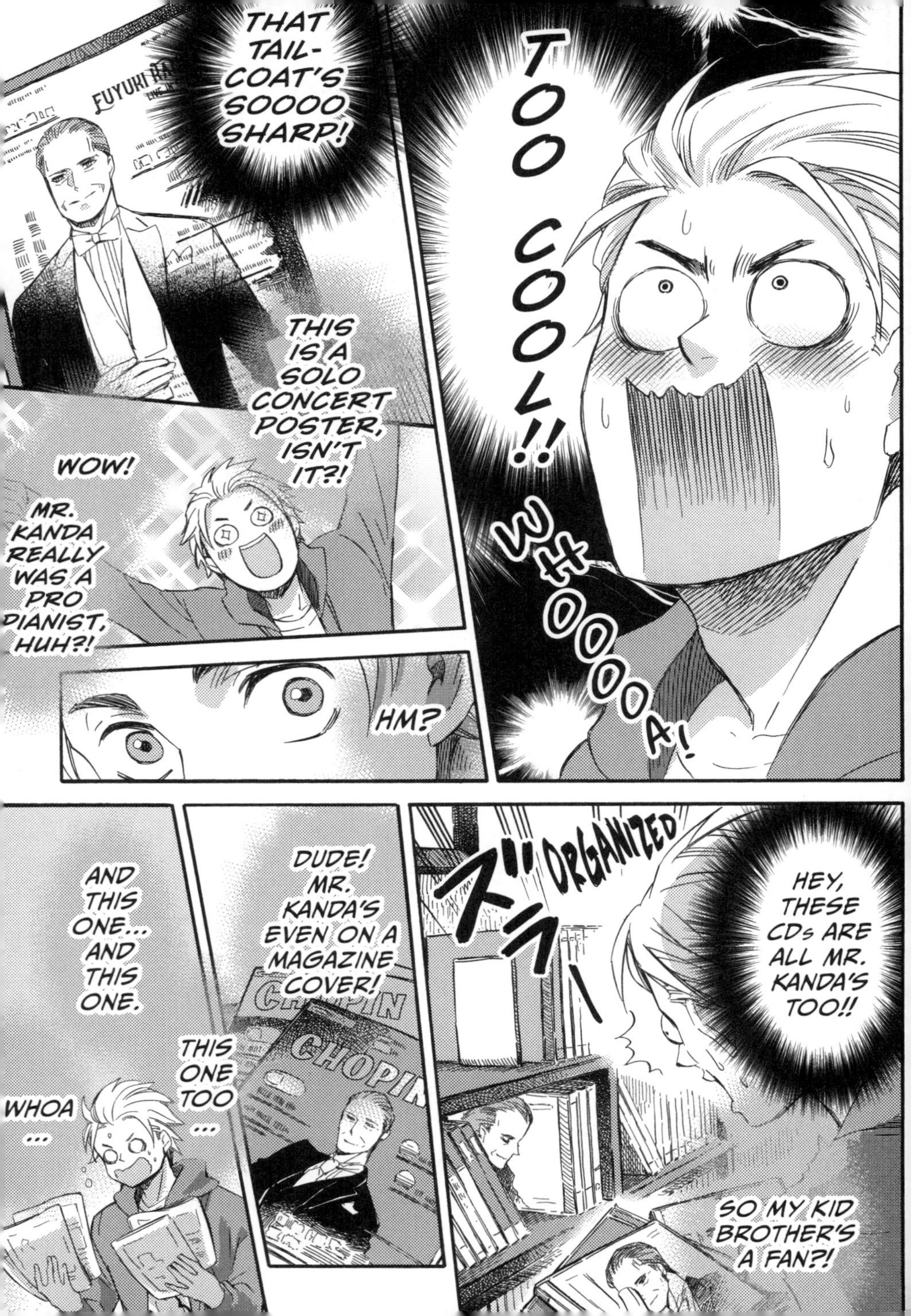
TOO COOL!!
WHOOOOA!
THAT TAIL-COAT'S SOOOO SHARP!
THIS IS A SOLO CONCERT POSTER, ISN'T IT?!
WOW!
MR. KANDA REALLY WAS A PRO PIANIST, HUH?!
HM?
ズラ
ORGANIZED
HEY, THESE CDs ARE ALL MR. KANDA'S TOO!!
SO MY KID BROTHER'S A FAN?!
DUDE! MR. KANDA'S EVEN ON A MAGAZINE COVER!
CHOPIN
CHOPIN
AND THIS ONE... AND THIS ONE.
THIS ONE TOO...
WHOA...

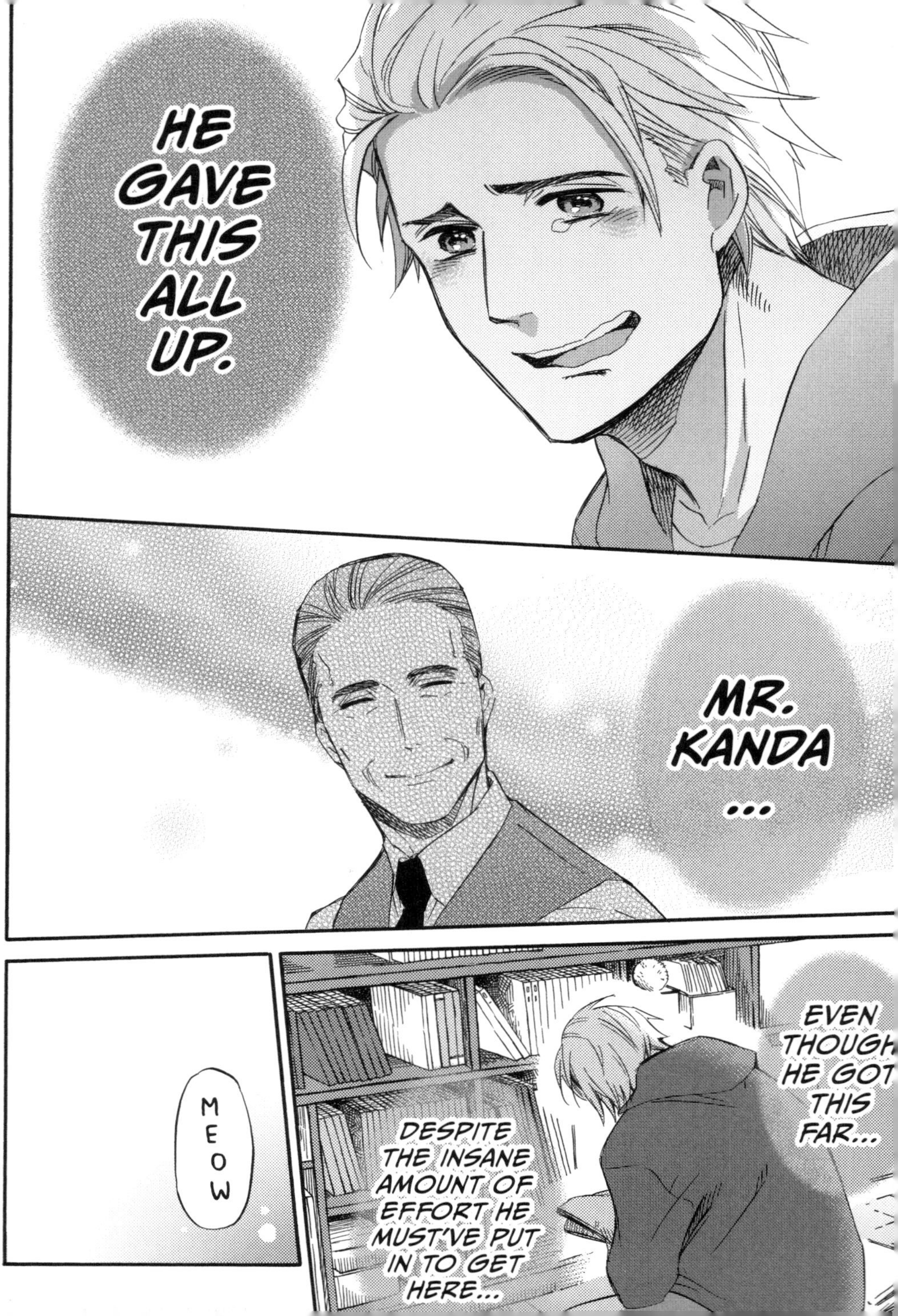
HE GAVE THIS ALL UP.
MR. KANDA ...
EVEN THOUGH HE GOT THIS FAR...
DESPITE THE INSANE AMOUNT OF EFFORT HE MUST'VE PUT IN TO GET HERE...
MEOW

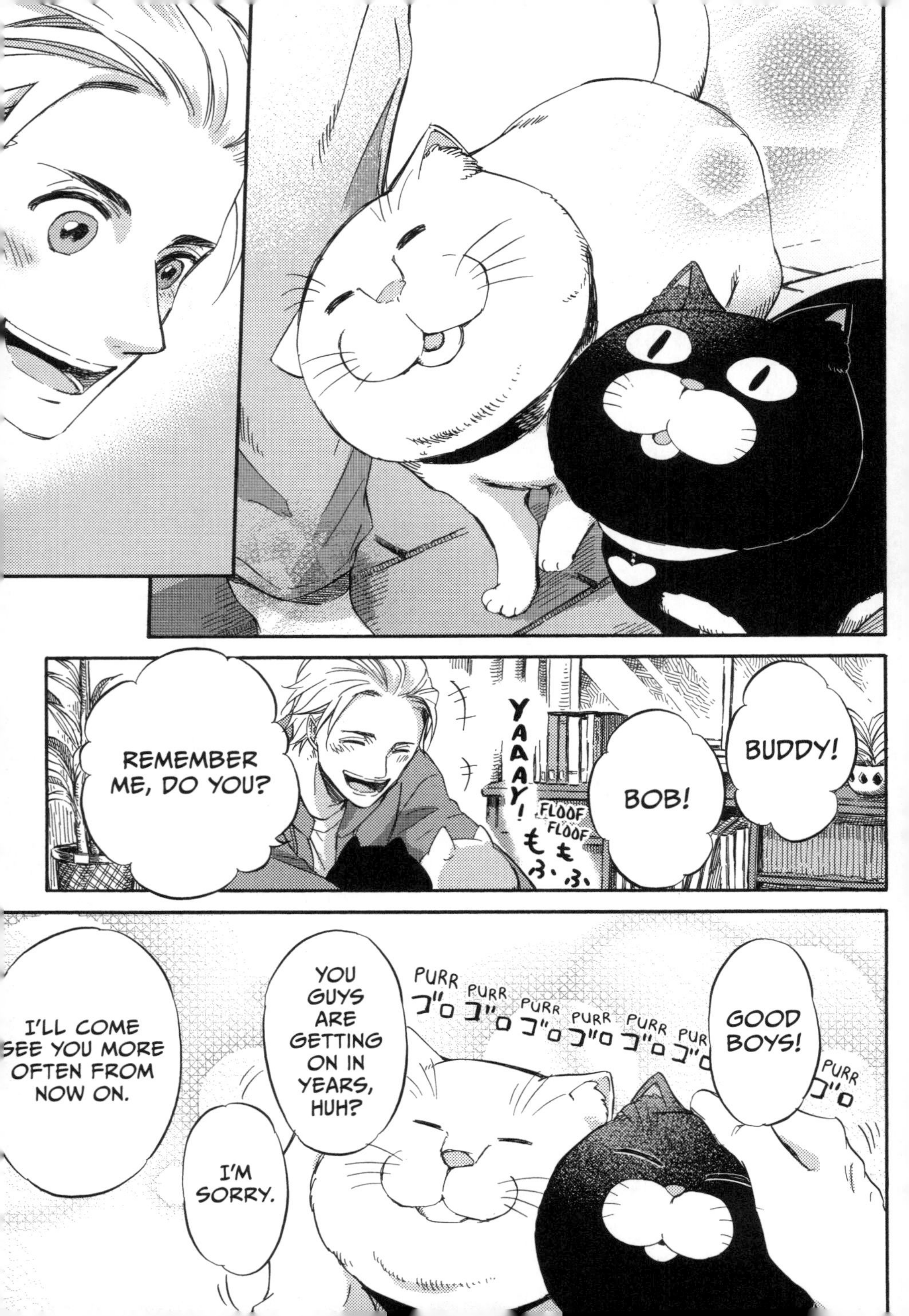
BUDDY!
BOB!
YAAAY!
FLOOF FLOOF
もふもふ
REMEMBER ME, DO YOU?
PURR
ゴロ
GOOD BOYS!
PURR PURR PURR PURR PURR PUR
ゴロゴロゴロゴロゴロゴロ
YOU GUYS ARE GETTING ON IN YEARS, HUH?
I'M SORRY.
I'LL COME SEE YOU MORE OFTEN FROM NOW ON.

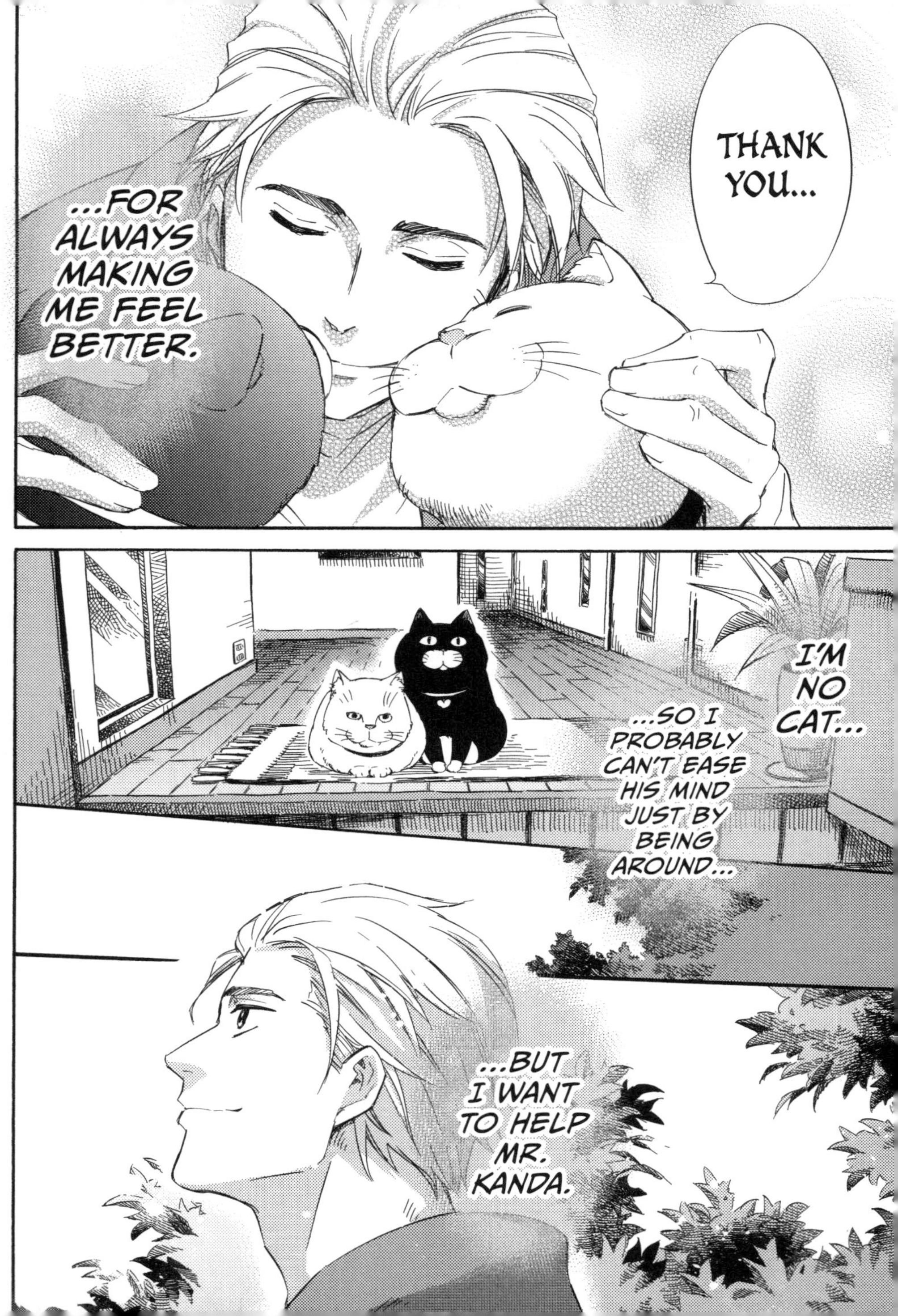
THANK YOU...
...FOR ALWAYS MAKING ME FEEL BETTER.
I'M NO CAT...
...SO I PROBABLY CAN'T EASE HIS MIND JUST BY BEING AROUND...
...BUT I WANT TO HELP MR. KANDA.

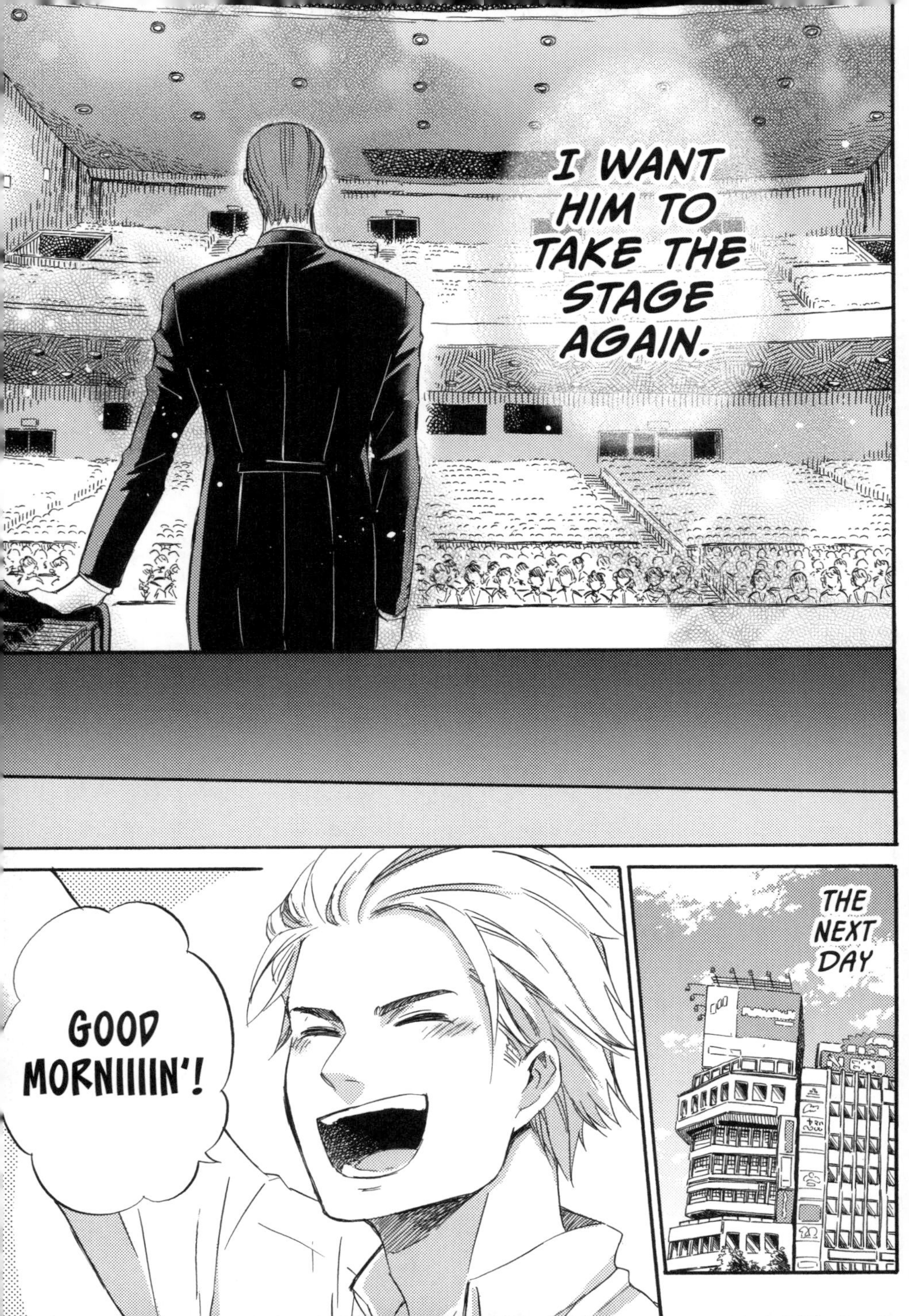
I WANT HIM TO TAKE THE STAGE AGAIN.
THE NEXT DAY
GOOD MORNIIIIN'!

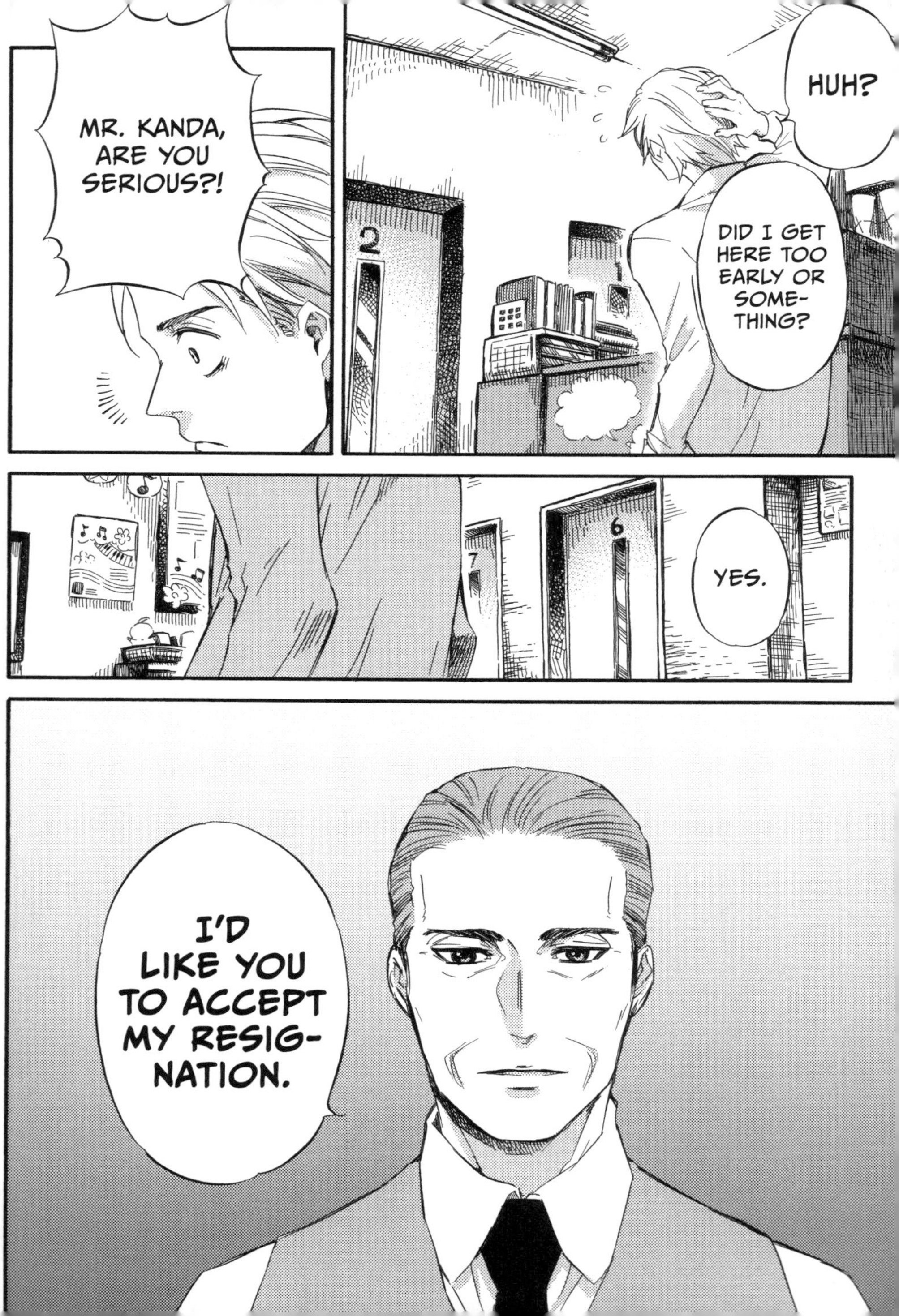
HUH?
DID I GET HERE TOO EARLY OR SOME-THING?
MR. KANDA, ARE YOU SERIOUS?!
YES.
I'D LIKE YOU TO ACCEPT MY RESIG-NATION.

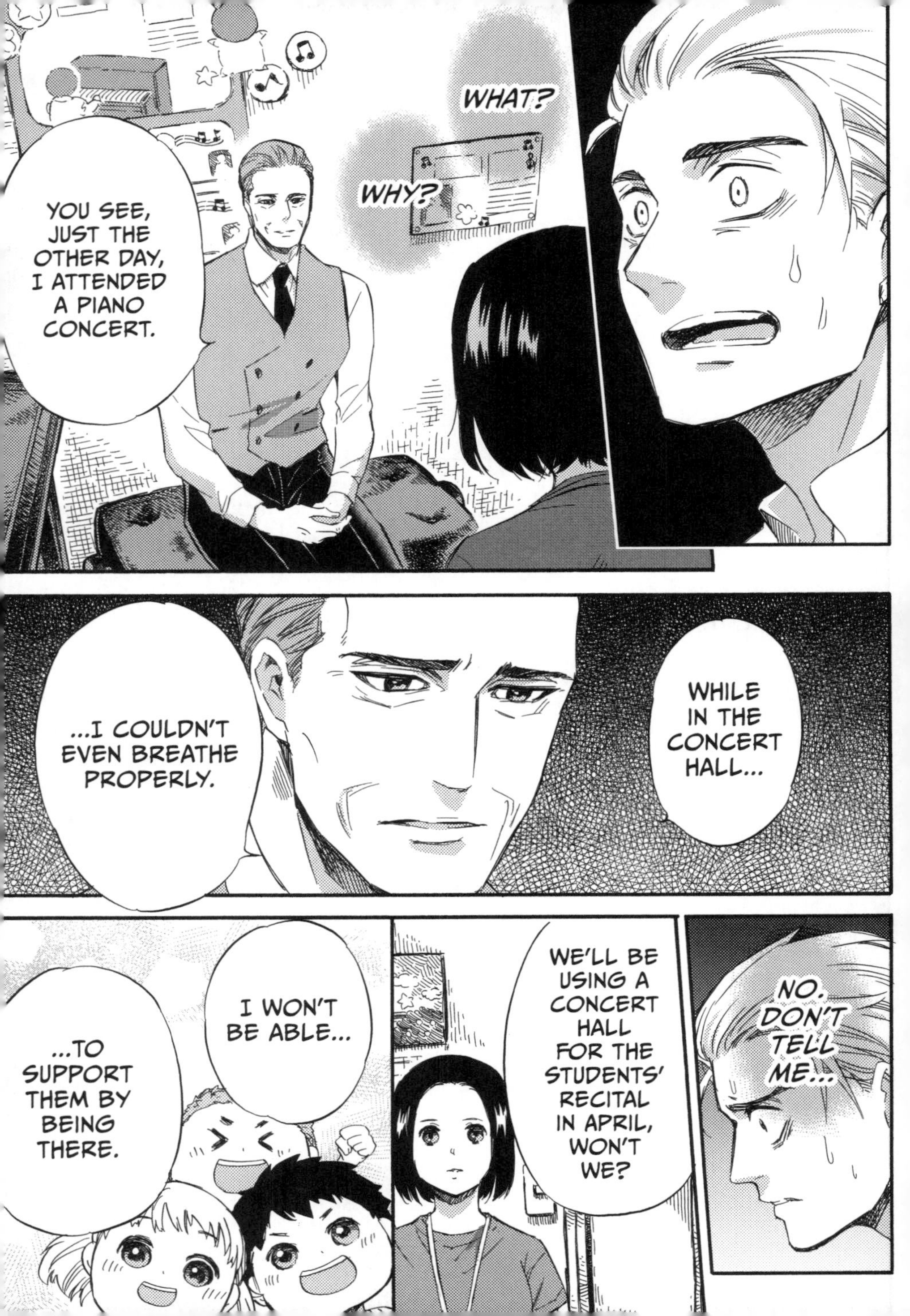
WHAT?
WHY?
YOU SEE, JUST THE OTHER DAY, I ATTENDED A PIANO CONCERT.
WHILE IN THE CONCERT HALL...
...I COULDN'T EVEN BREATHE PROPERLY.
NO. DON'T TELL ME...
WE'LL BE USING A CONCERT HALL FOR THE STUDENTS' RECITAL IN APRIL, WON'T WE?
I WON'T BE ABLE...
...TO SUPPORT THEM BY BEING THERE.

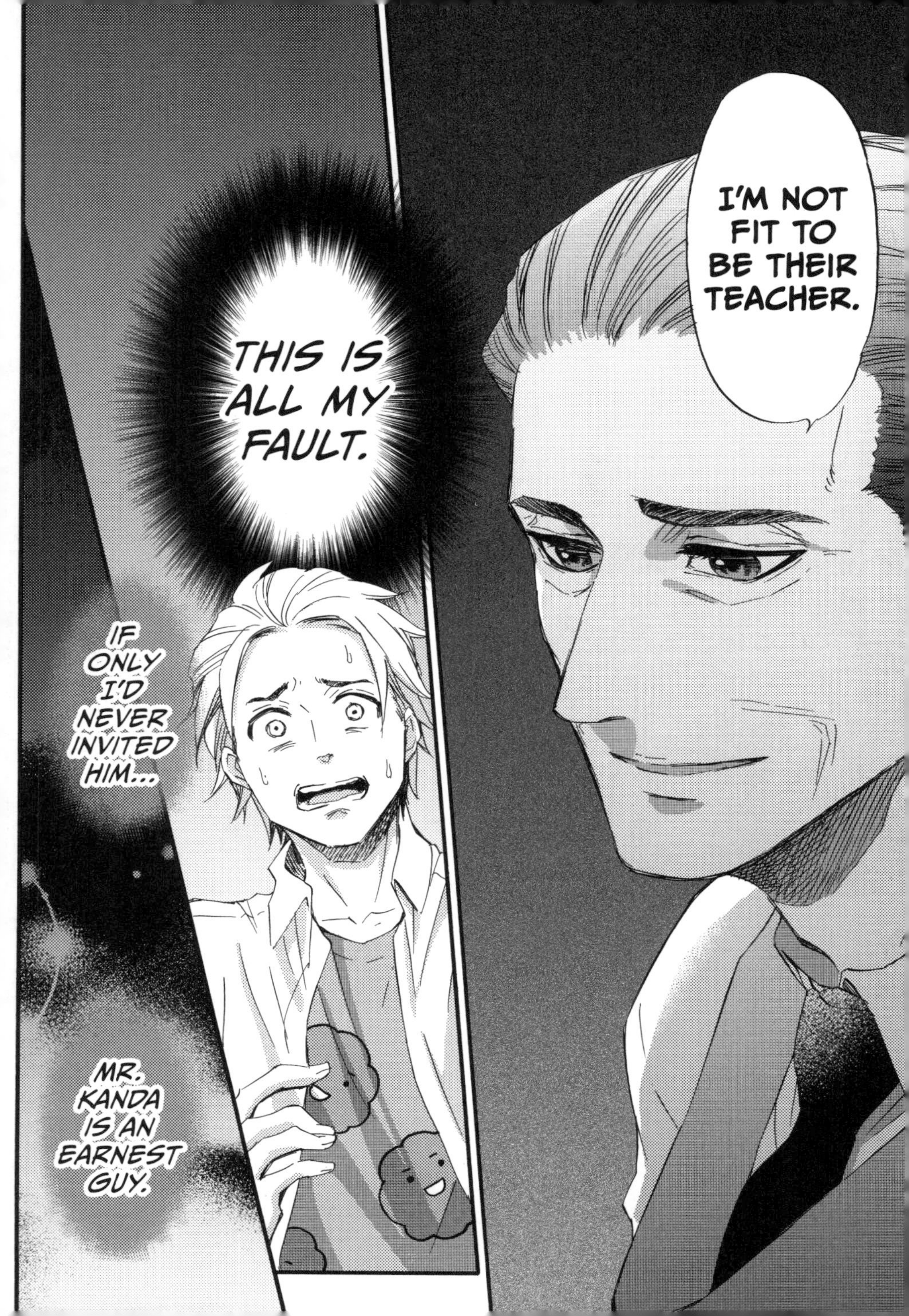
I'M NOT FIT TO BE THEIR TEACHER.
THIS IS ALL MY FAULT.
IF ONLY I'D NEVER INVITED HIM...
MR. KANDA IS AN EARNEST GUY.

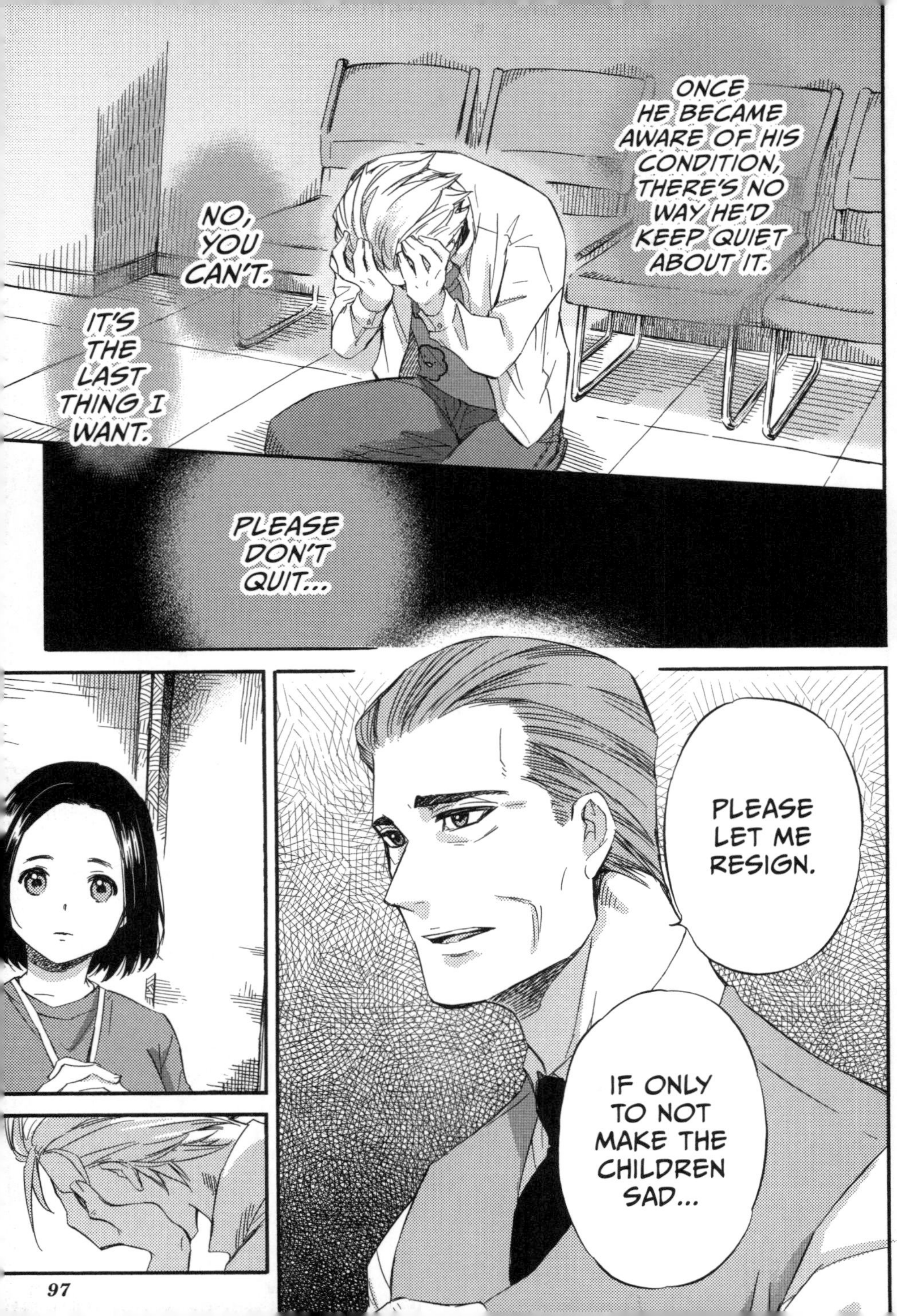
ONCE HE BECAME AWARE OF HIS CONDITION, THERE'S NO WAY HE'D KEEP QUIET ABOUT IT.
NO, YOU CAN'T.
IT'S THE LAST THING I WANT.
PLEASE DON'T QUIT...
PLEASE LET ME RESIGN.
IF ONLY TO NOT MAKE THE CHILDREN SAD...

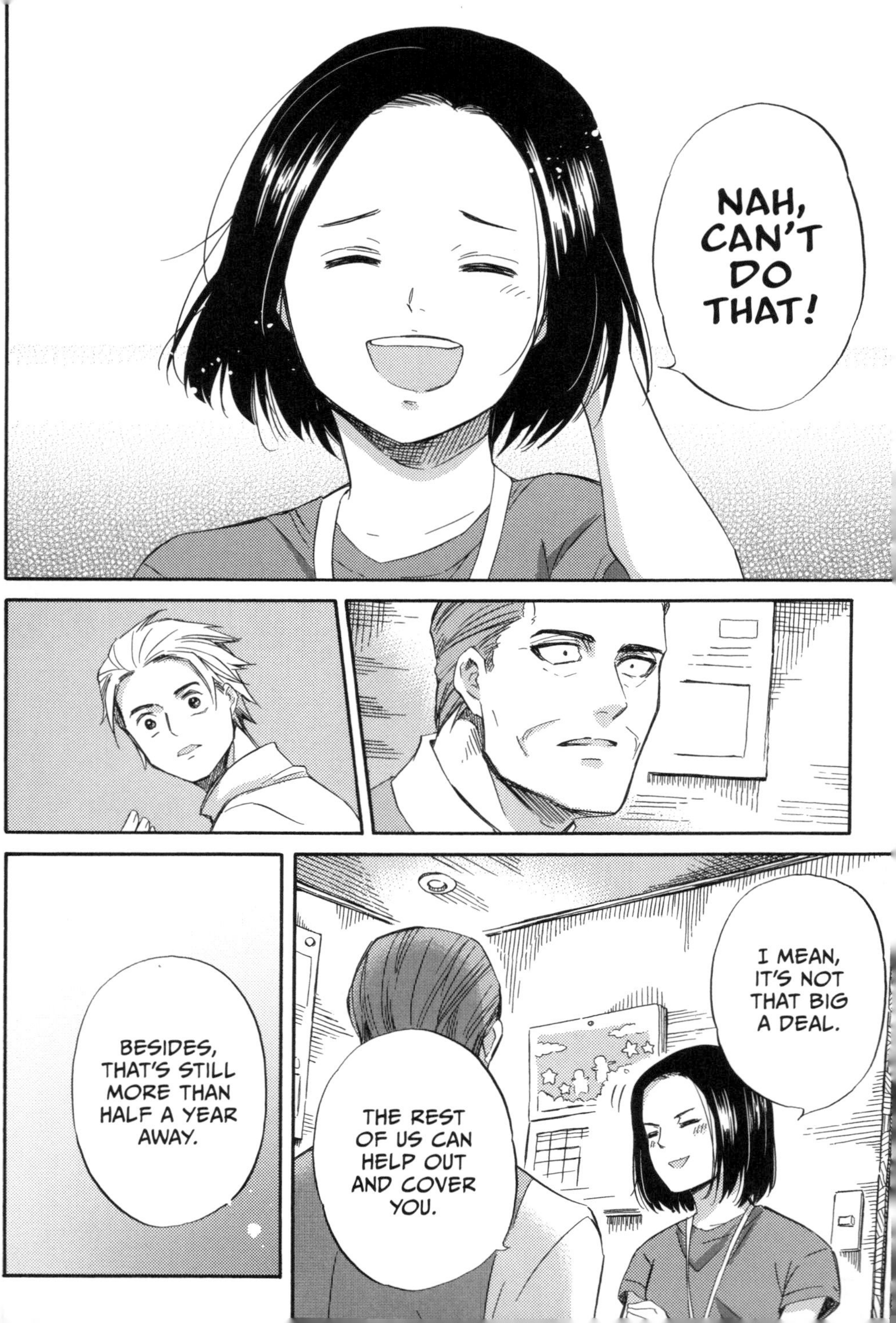
NAH, CAN'T DO THAT!
I MEAN, IT'S NOT THAT BIG A DEAL.
THE REST OF US CAN HELP OUT AND COVER YOU.
BESIDES, THAT'S STILL MORE THAN HALF A YEAR AWAY.

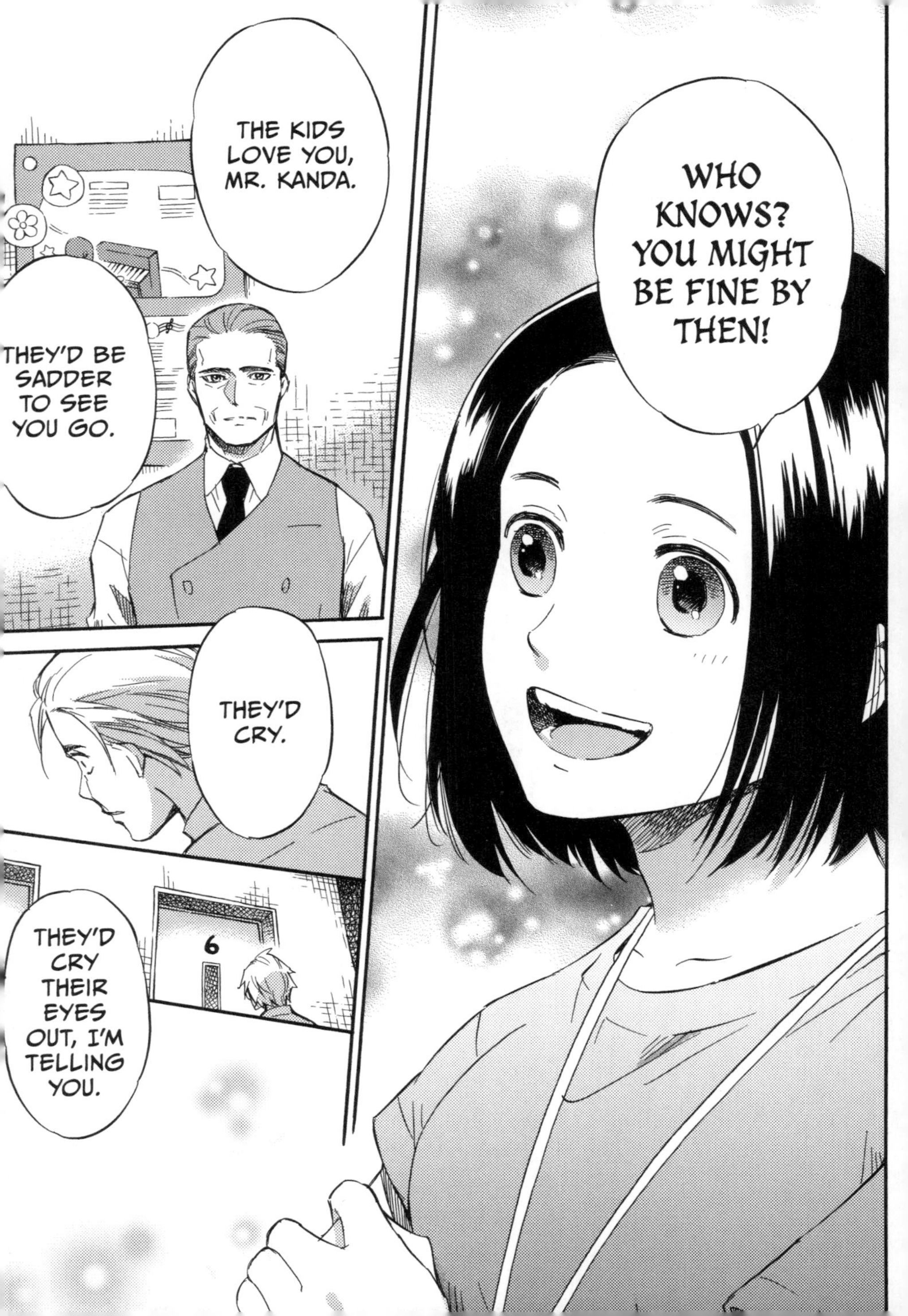
WHO KNOWS? YOU MIGHT BE FINE BY THEN!
THE KIDS LOVE YOU, MR. KANDA.
THEY'D BE SADDER TO SEE YOU GO.
THEY'D CRY.
6
THEY'D CRY THEIR EYES OUT, I'M TELLING YOU.

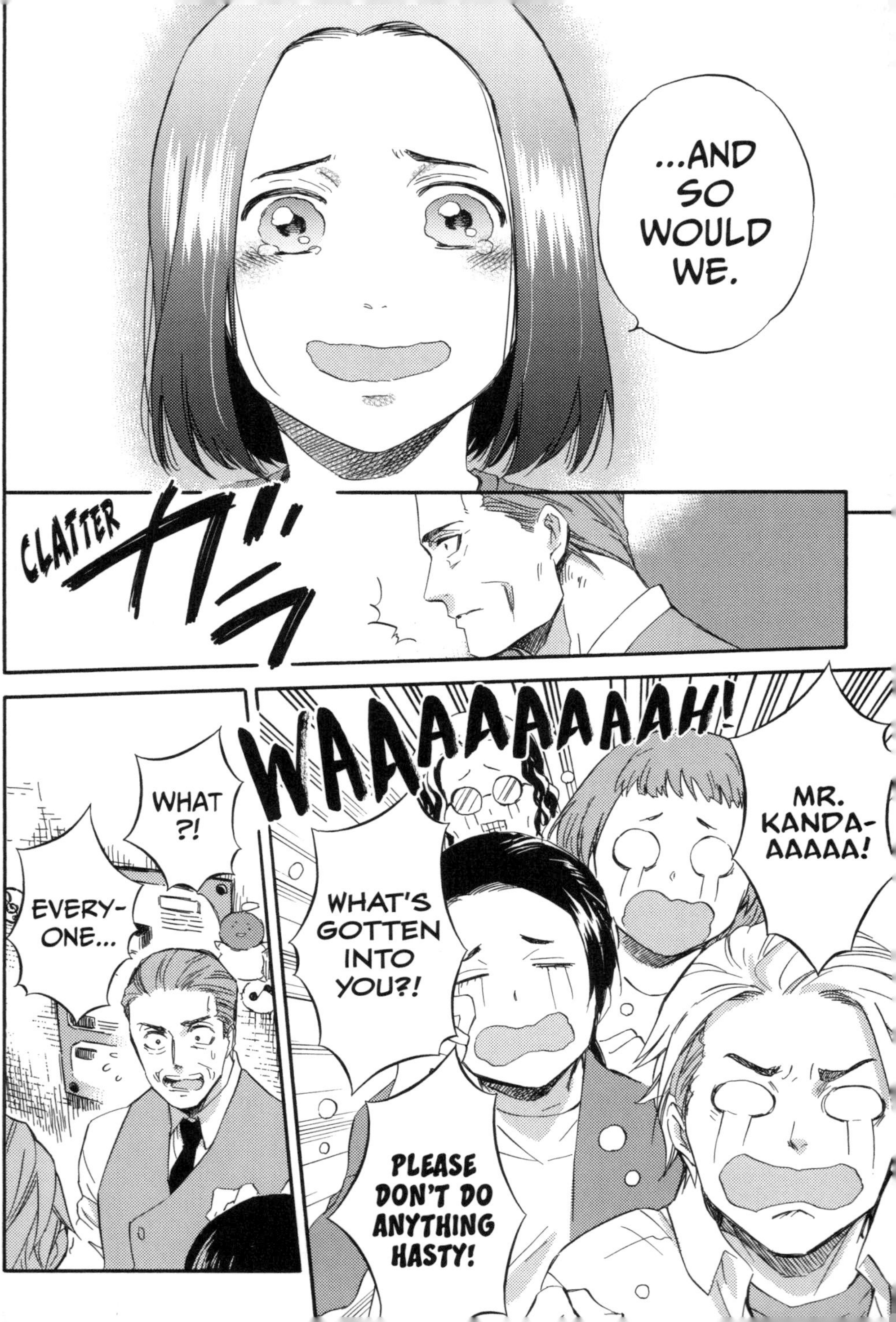
...AND SO WOULD WE.
CLATTER
WAAAAAAAAAH!
MR. KANDA-AAAAA!
WHAT'S GOTTEN INTO YOU?!
PLEASE DON'T DO ANYTHING HASTY!
WHAT?!
EVERY-ONE...

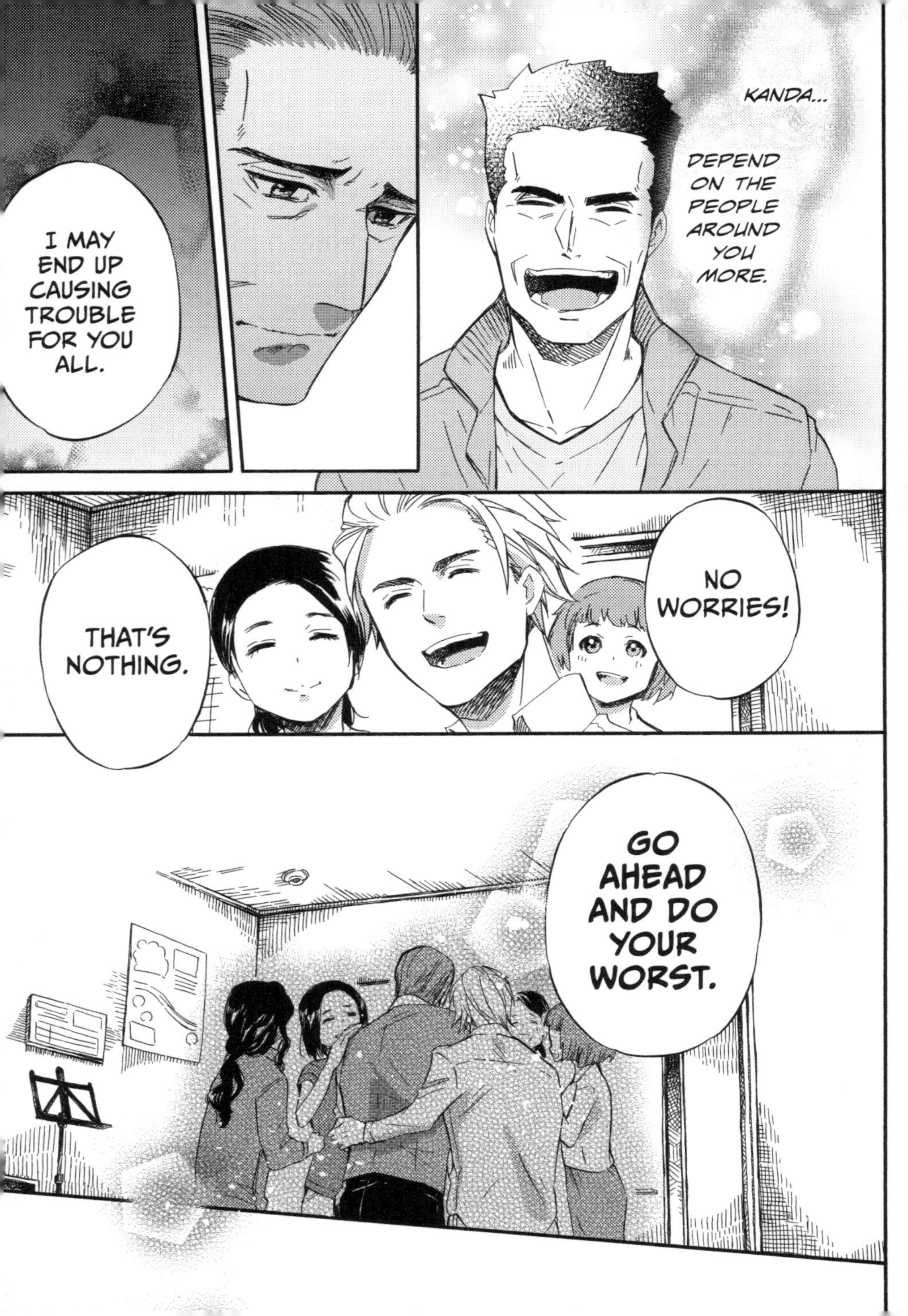
KANDA...
DEPEND ON THE PEOPLE AROUND YOU MORE.
I MAY END UP CAUSING TROUBLE FOR YOU ALL.
NO WORRIES!
THAT'S NOTHING.
GO AHEAD AND DO YOUR WORST.

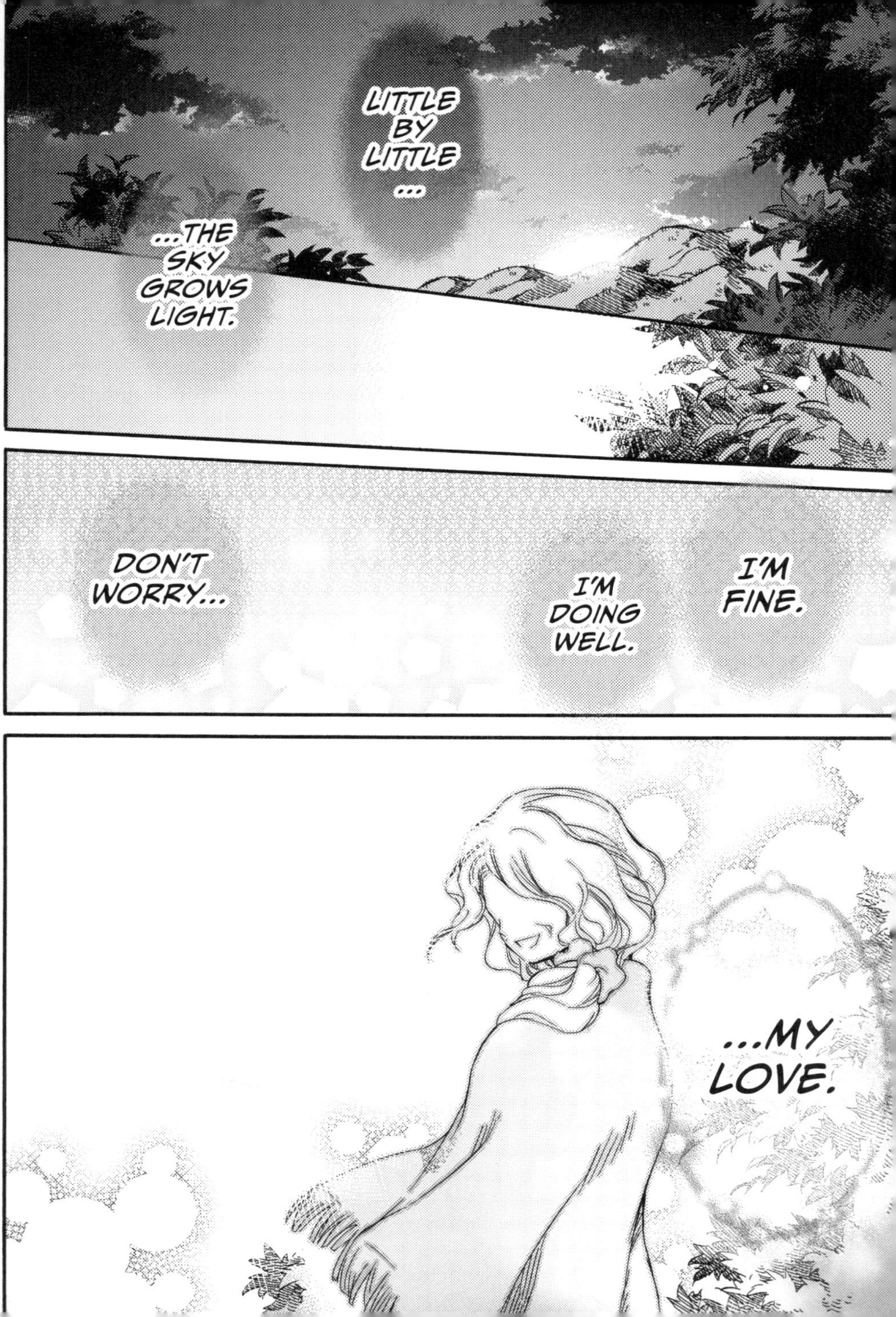
LITTLE BY LITTLE...
...THE SKY GROWS LIGHT.
I'M FINE.
I'M DOING WELL.
DON'T WORRY...
...MY LOVE.

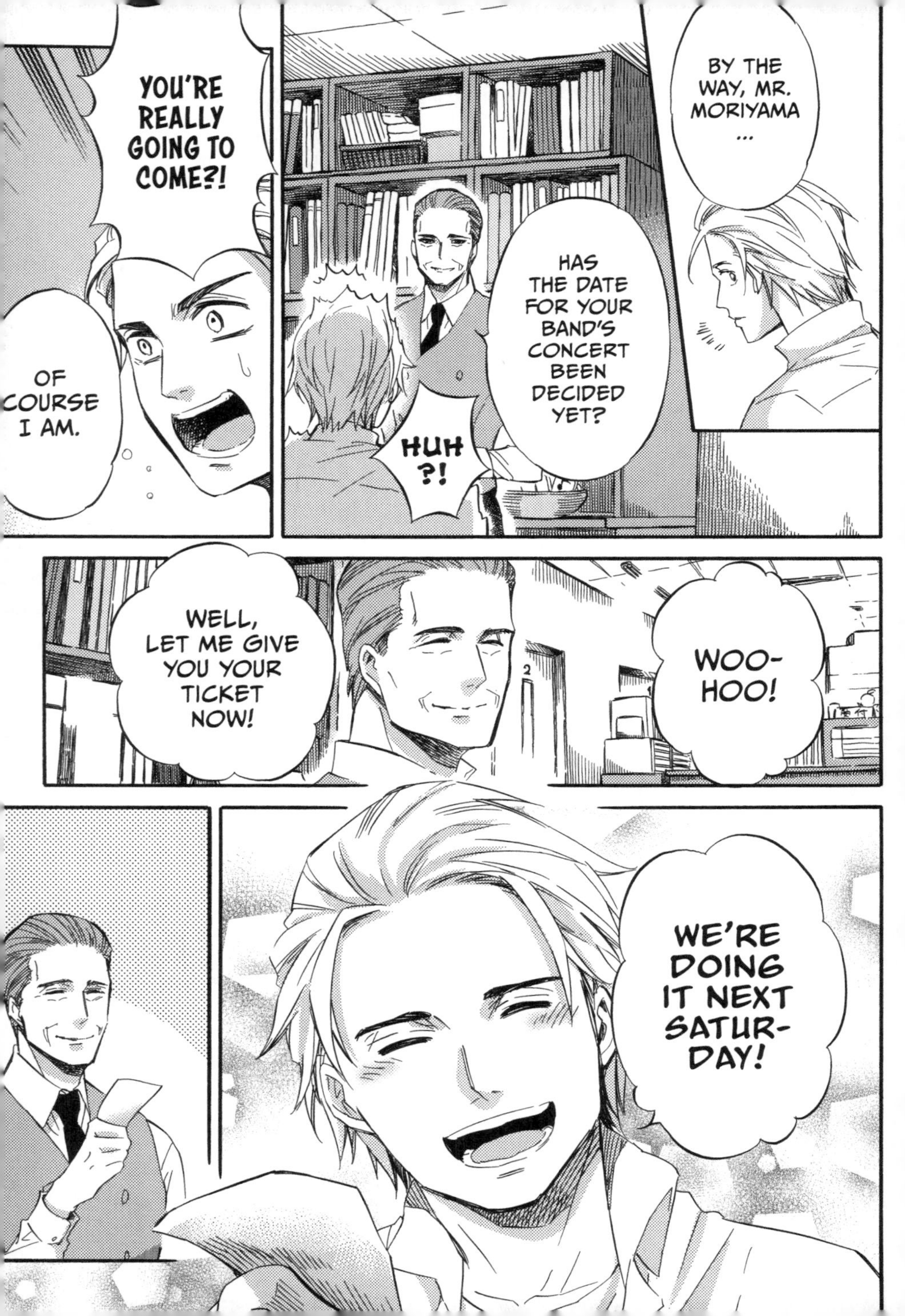
BY THE WAY, MR. MORIYAMA ...
HAS THE DATE FOR YOUR BAND'S CONCERT BEEN DECIDED YET?
HUH ?!
YOU'RE REALLY GOING TO COME?!
OF COURSE I AM.
WOO-HOO!
WELL, LET ME GIVE YOU YOUR TICKET NOW!
WE'RE DOING IT NEXT SATUR-DAY!

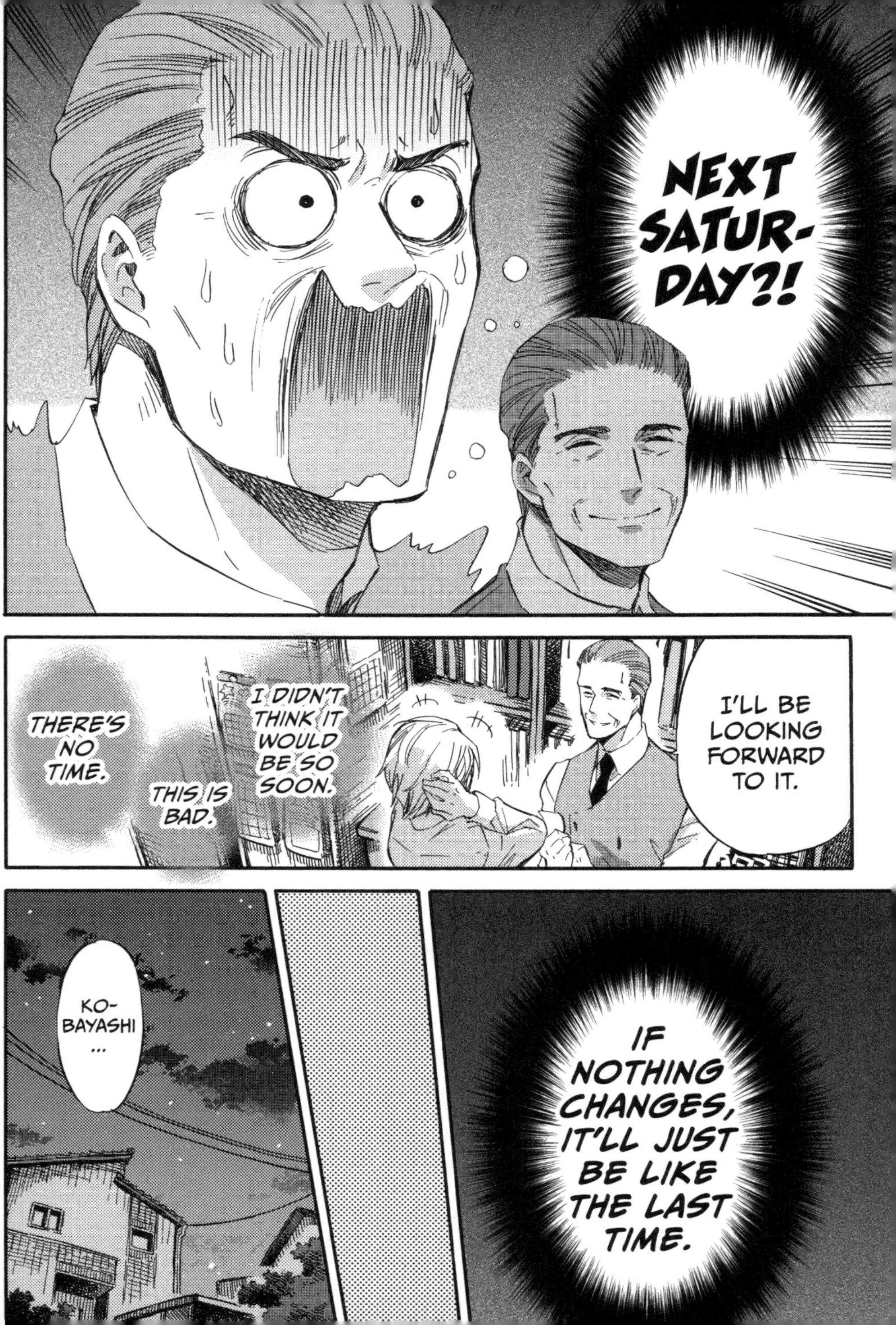
NEXT SATUR-DAY?!
I'LL BE LOOKING FORWARD TO IT.
I DIDN'T THINK IT WOULD BE SO SOON.
THIS IS BAD.
THERE'S NO TIME.
IF NOTHING CHANGES, IT'LL JUST BE LIKE THE LAST TIME.
KO-BAYASHI...

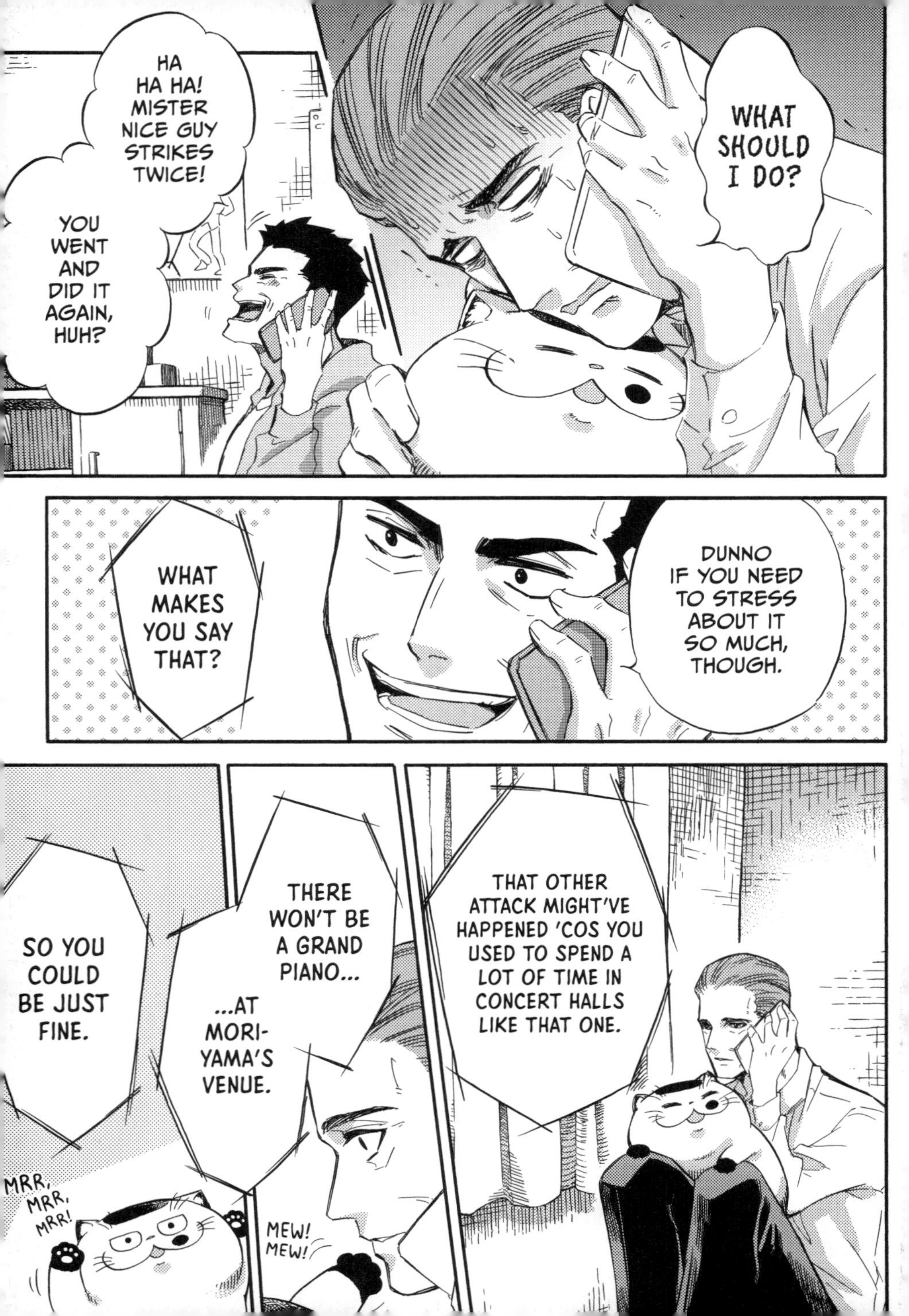
WHAT SHOULD I DO?
HA HA HA! MISTER NICE GUY STRIKES TWICE!
YOU WENT AND DID IT AGAIN, HUH?
DUNNO IF YOU NEED TO STRESS ABOUT IT SO MUCH, THOUGH.
WHAT MAKES YOU SAY THAT?
THAT OTHER ATTACK MIGHT'VE HAPPENED 'COS YOU USED TO SPEND A LOT OF TIME IN CONCERT HALLS LIKE THAT ONE.
THERE WON'T BE A GRAND PIANO...
...AT MORI-YAMA'S VENUE.
MEW! MEW!
SO YOU COULD BE JUST FINE.
MRR, MRR, MRR!

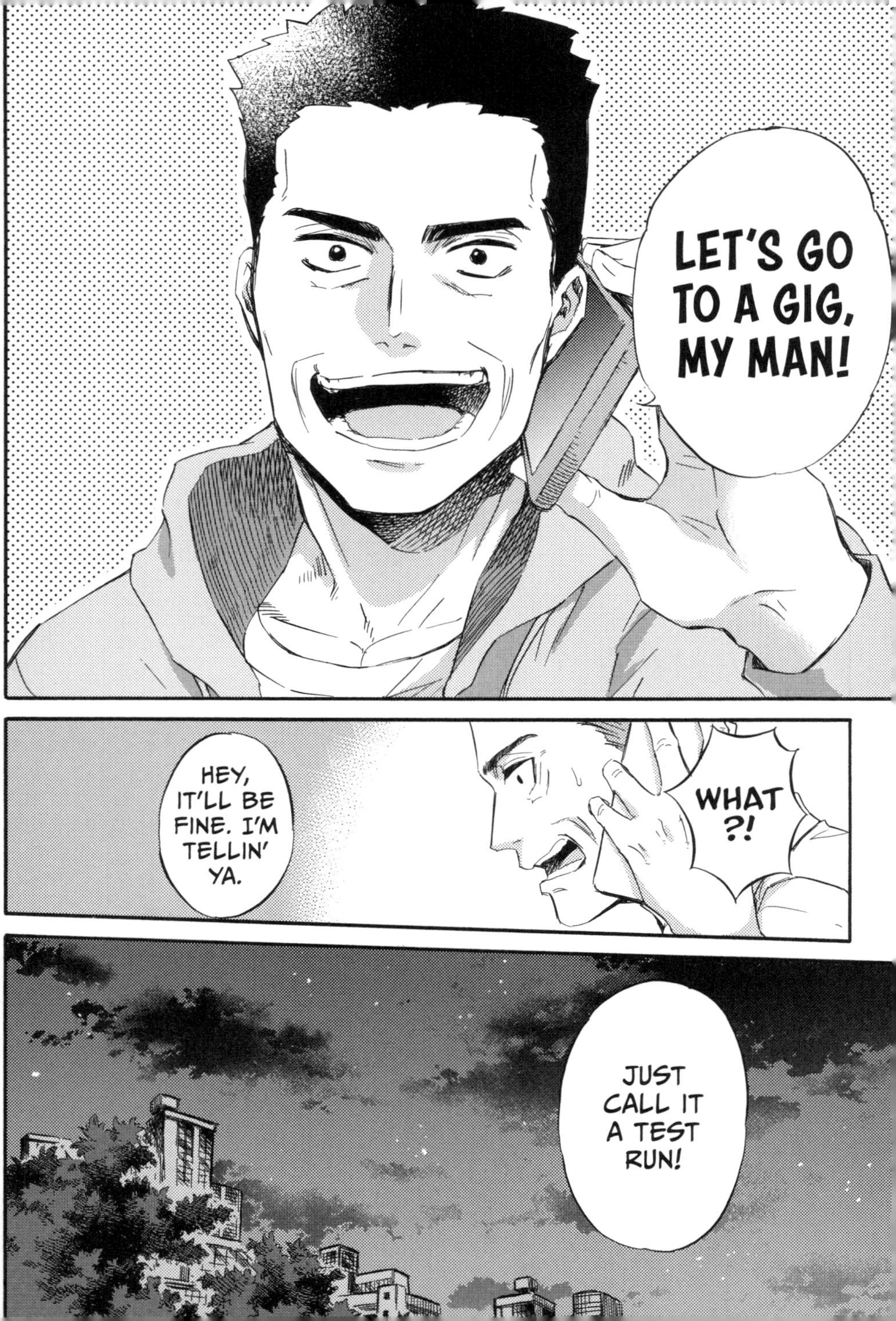
LET'S GO TO A GIG, MY MAN!
WHAT ?!
HEY, IT'LL BE FINE. I'M TELLIN' YA.
JUST CALL IT A TEST RUN!

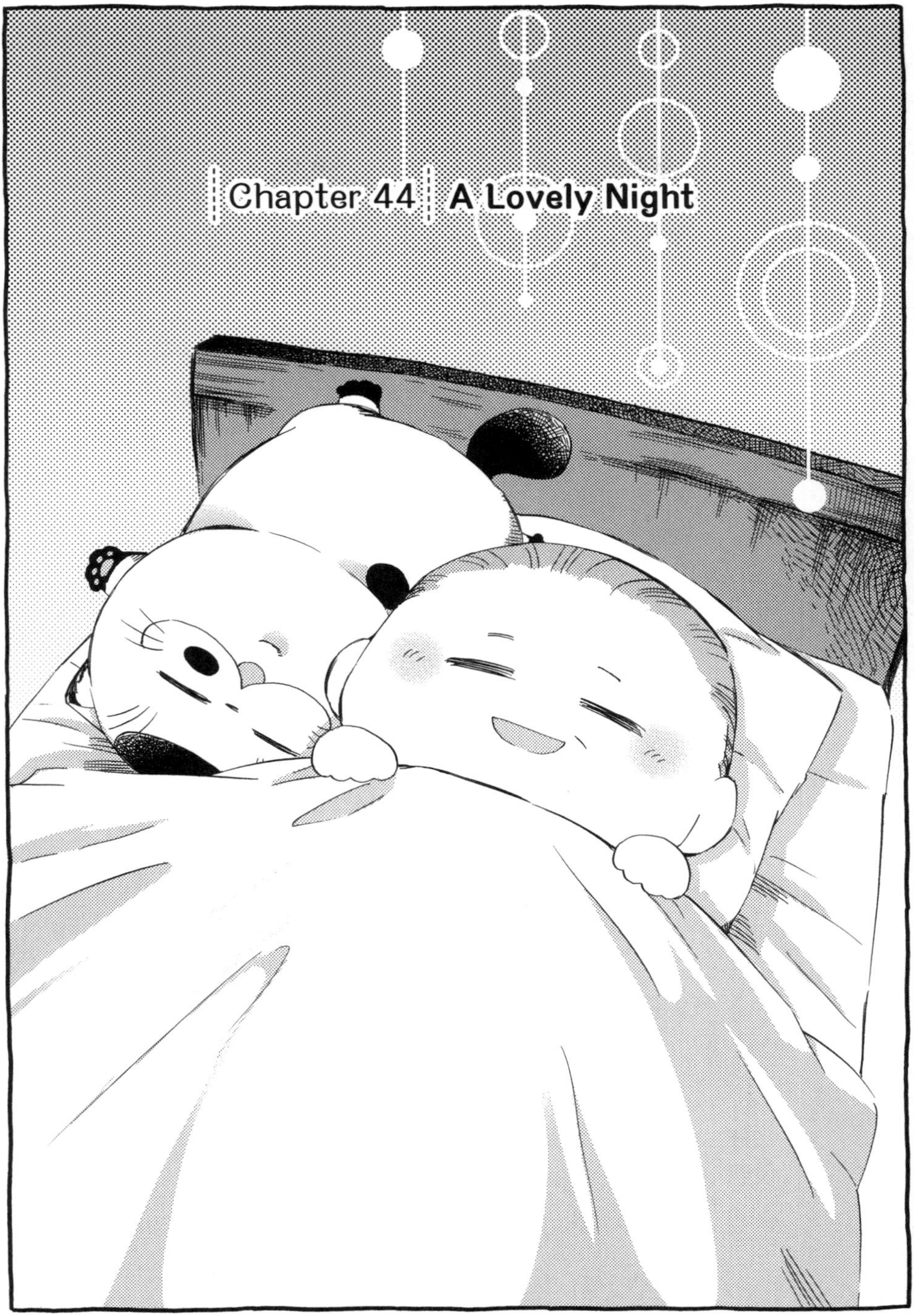
Chapter 44 A Lovely Night

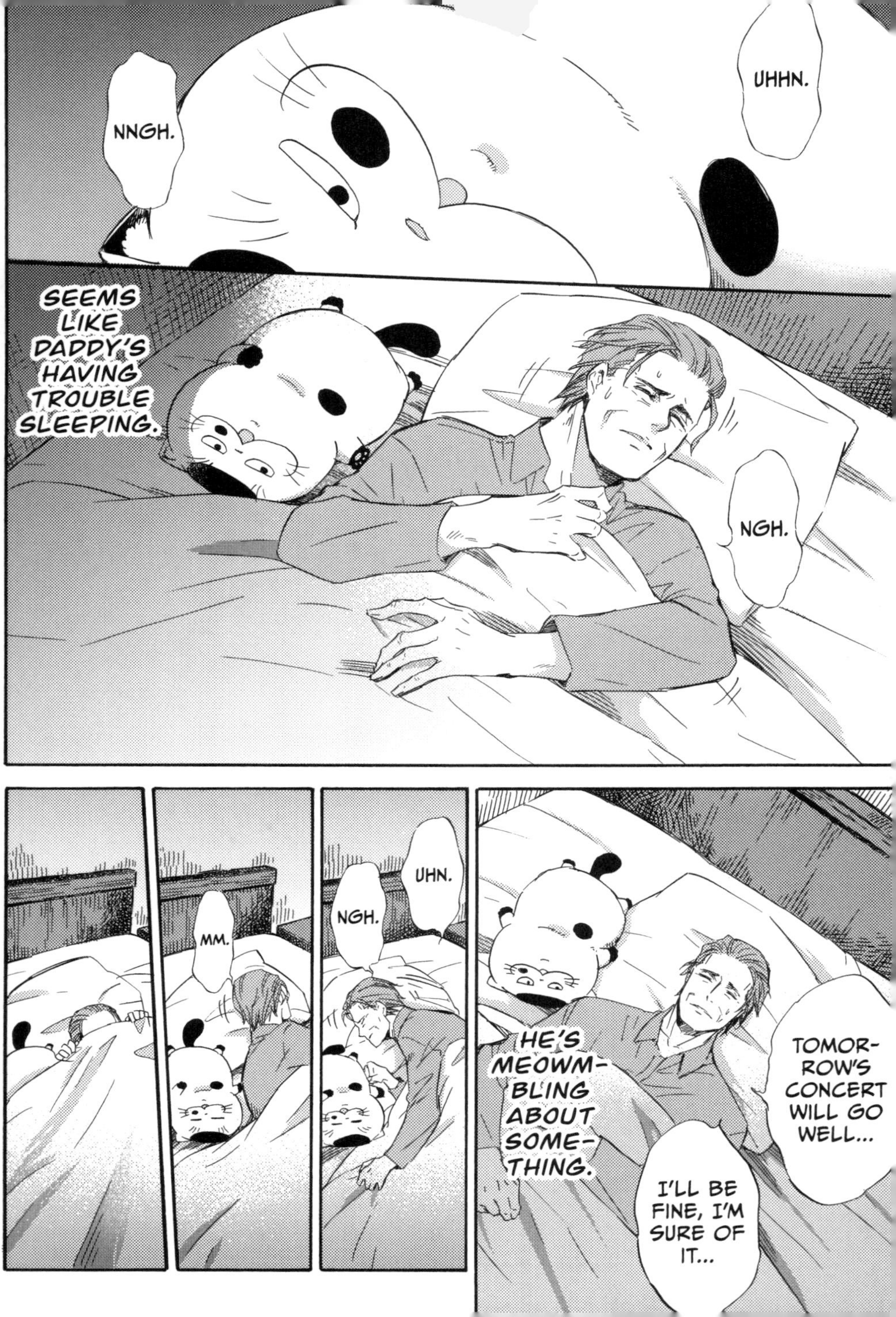
UHHN.
NNGH.
SEEMS LIKE DADDY'S HAVING TROUBLE SLEEPING.
NGH.
TOMOR-ROW'S CONCERT WILL GO WELL...
HE'S MEOWM-BLING ABOUT SOME-THING.
I'LL BE FINE, I'M SURE OF IT...
UHN.
NGH.
MM.

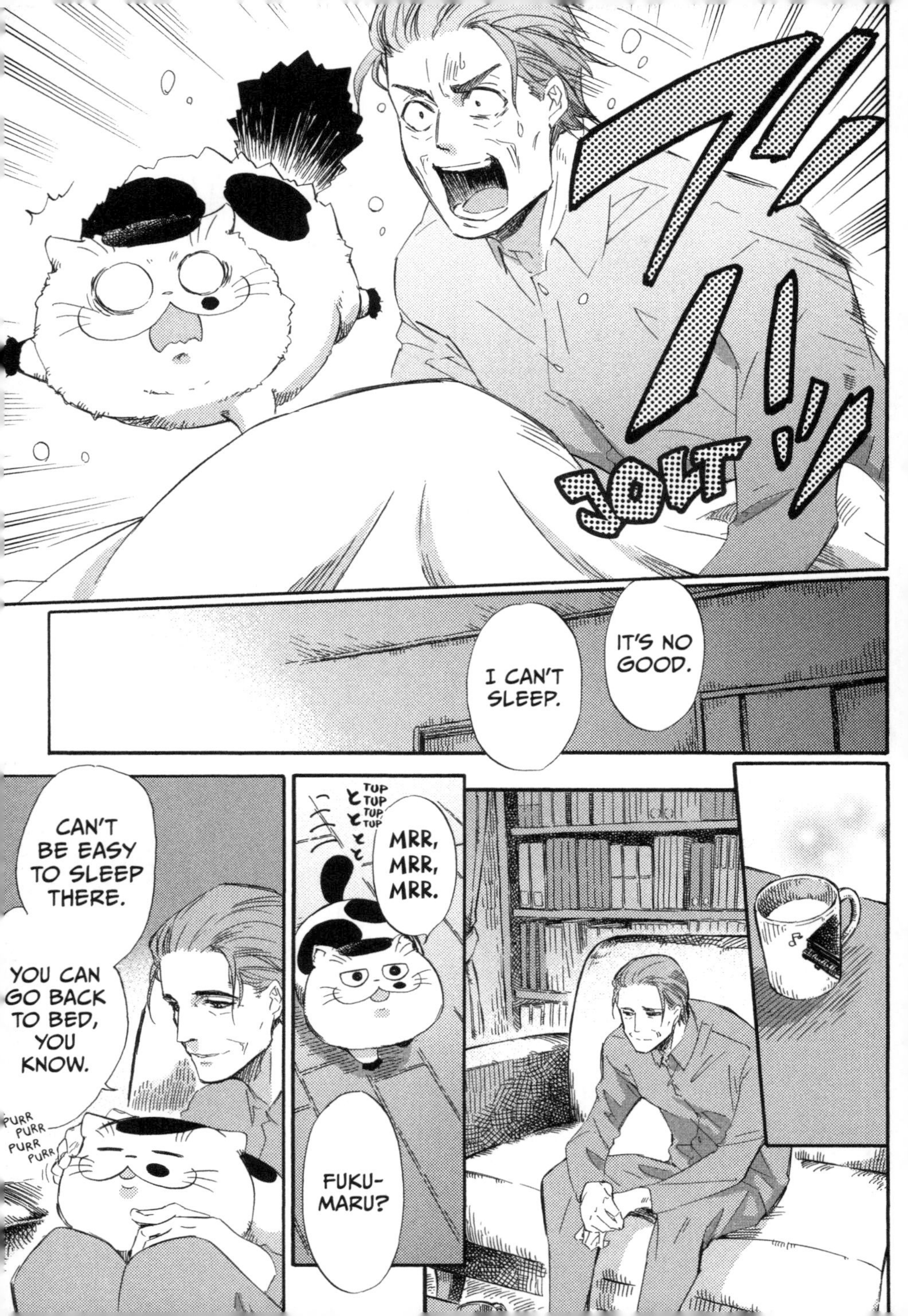
JOLT
IT'S NO GOOD.
I CAN'T SLEEP.
TUP TUP TUP TUP
MRR, MRR, MRR.
FUKU-MARU?
CAN'T BE EASY TO SLEEP THERE.
YOU CAN GO BACK TO BED, YOU KNOW.
PURR PURR PURR PURR

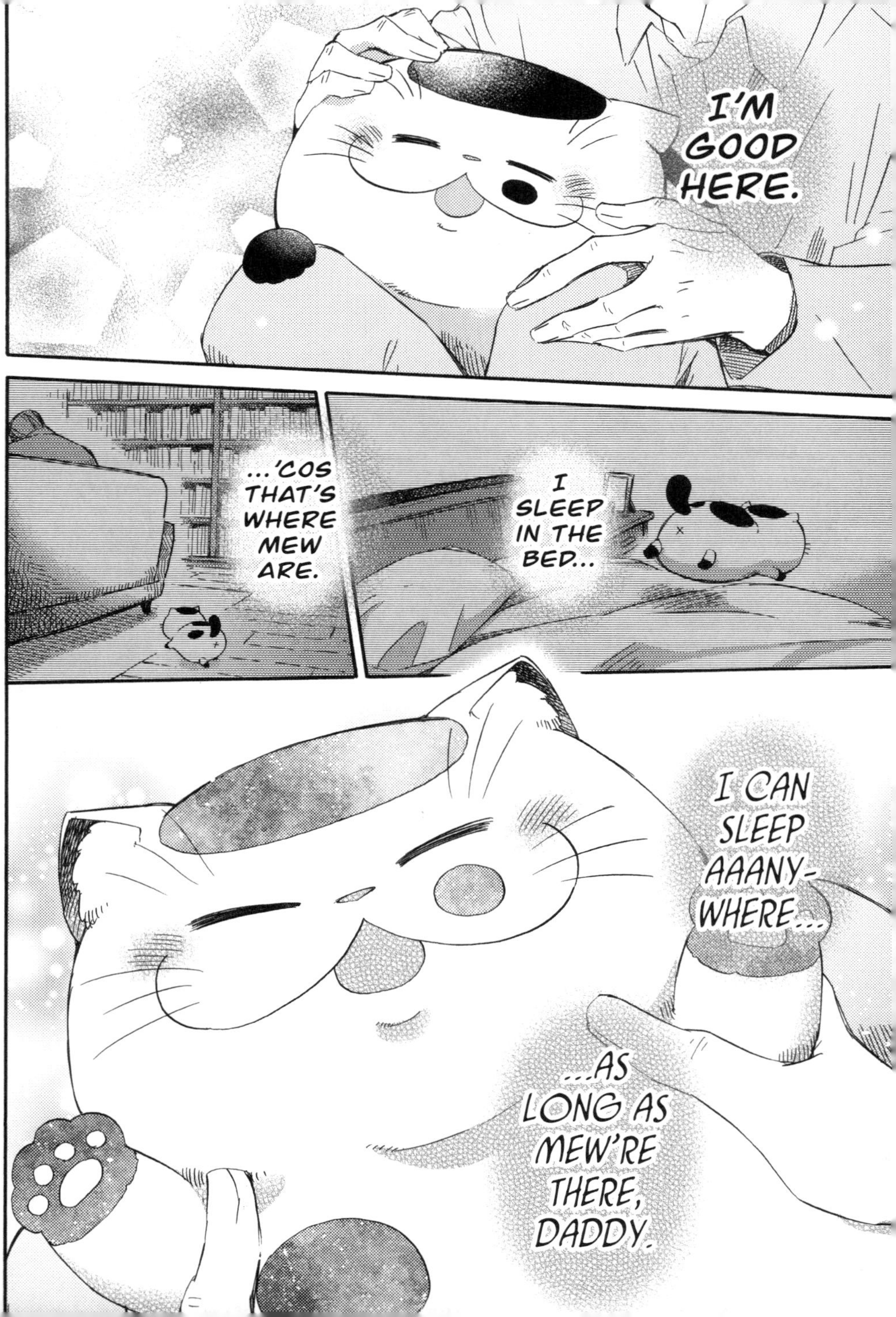
I'M GOOD HERE.
I SLEEP IN THE BED...
...'COS THAT'S WHERE MEW ARE.
I CAN SLEEP AAANY-WHERE...
...AS LONG AS MEW'RE THERE, DADDY.

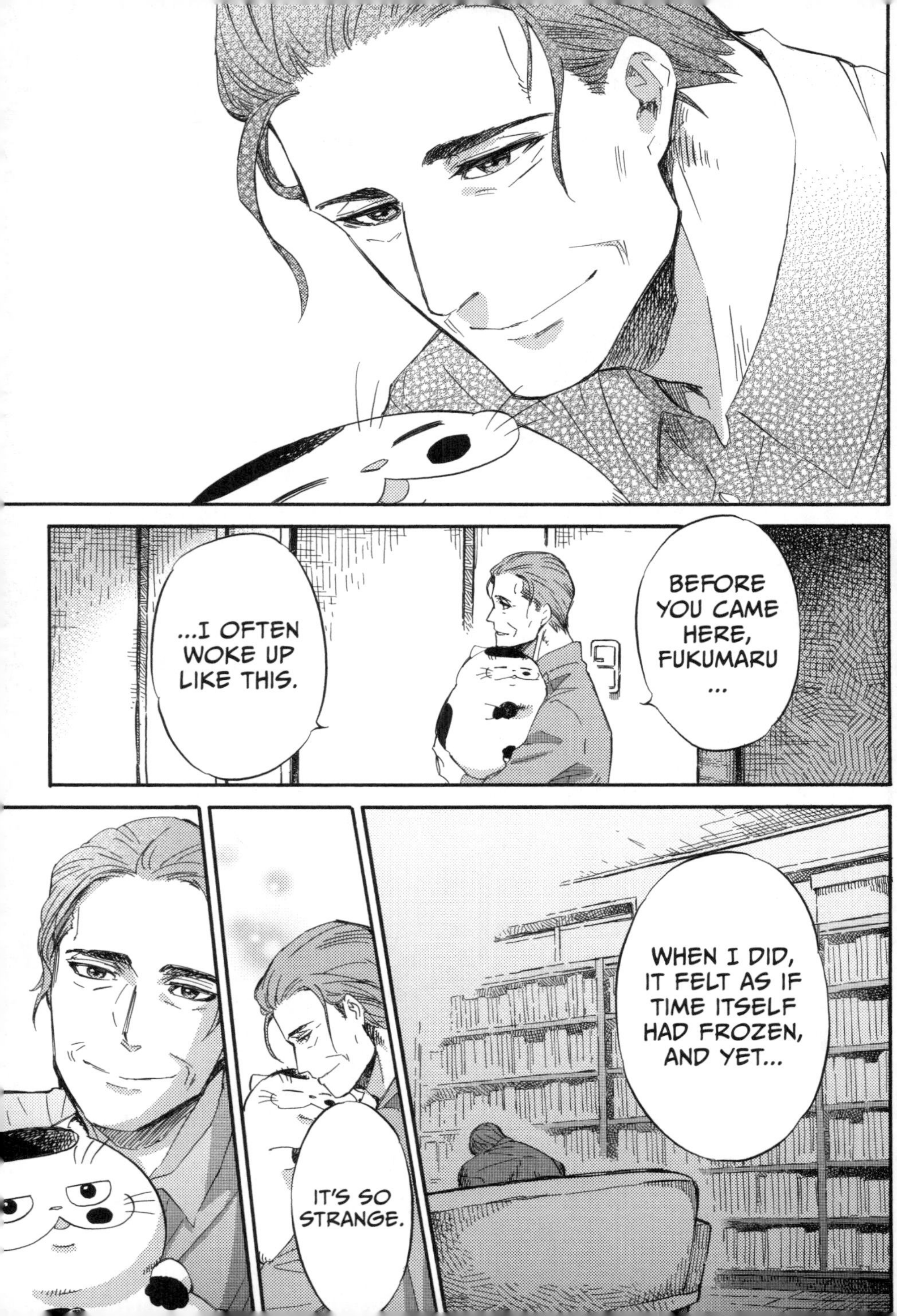
BEFORE YOU CAME HERE, FUKUMARU ...
...I OFTEN WOKE UP LIKE THIS.
WHEN I DID, IT FELT AS IF TIME ITSELF HAD FROZEN, AND YET...
IT'S SO STRANGE.

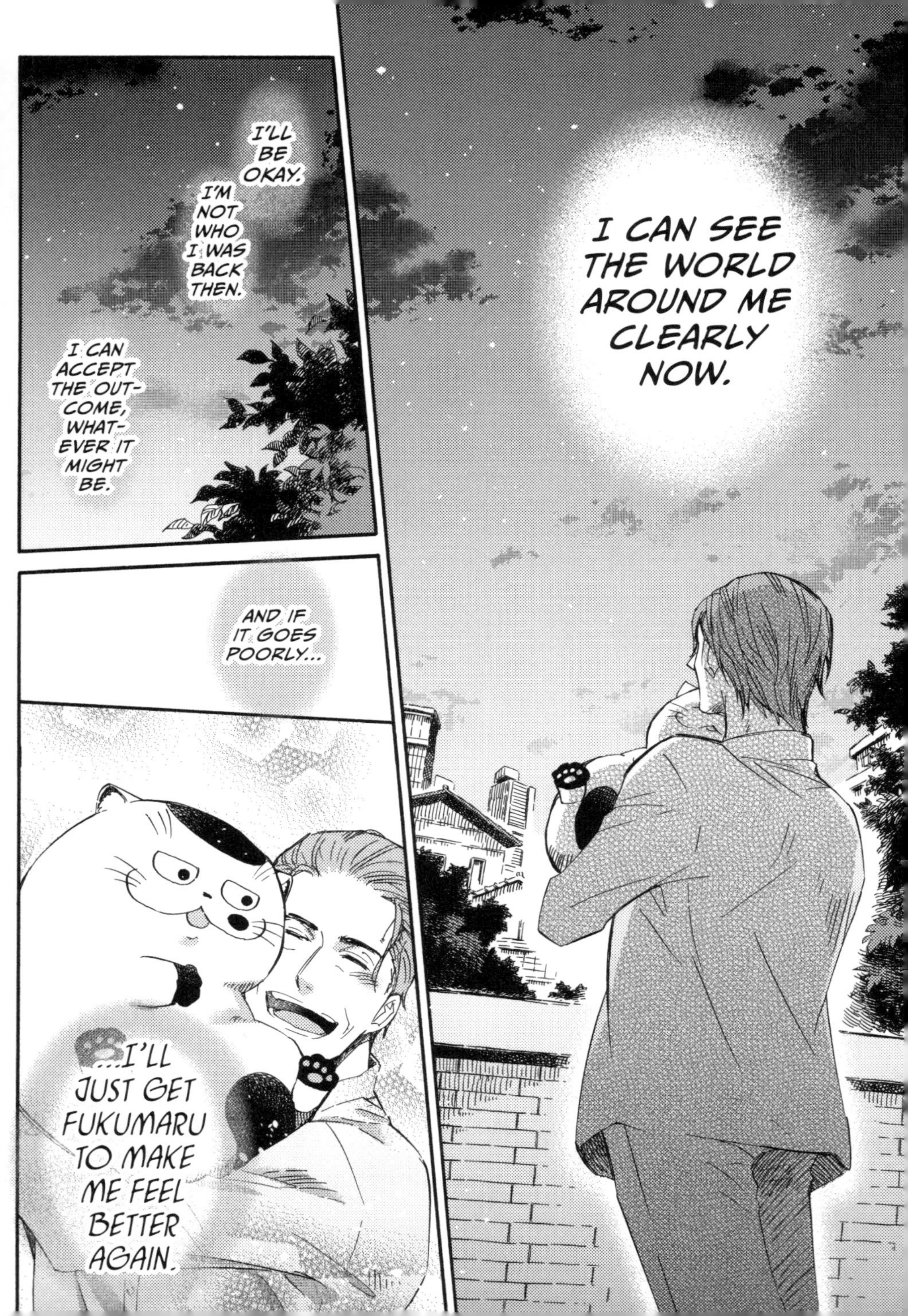
I CAN SEE THE WORLD AROUND ME CLEARLY NOW.
I'LL BE OKAY.
I'M NOT WHO I WAS BACK THEN.
I CAN ACCEPT THE OUT-COME, WHAT-EVER IT MIGHT BE.
AND IF IT GOES POORLY...
...I'LL JUST GET FUKUMARU TO MAKE ME FEEL BETTER AGAIN.

MEW CAN'T TELL, BUT I'M FLUSTERED

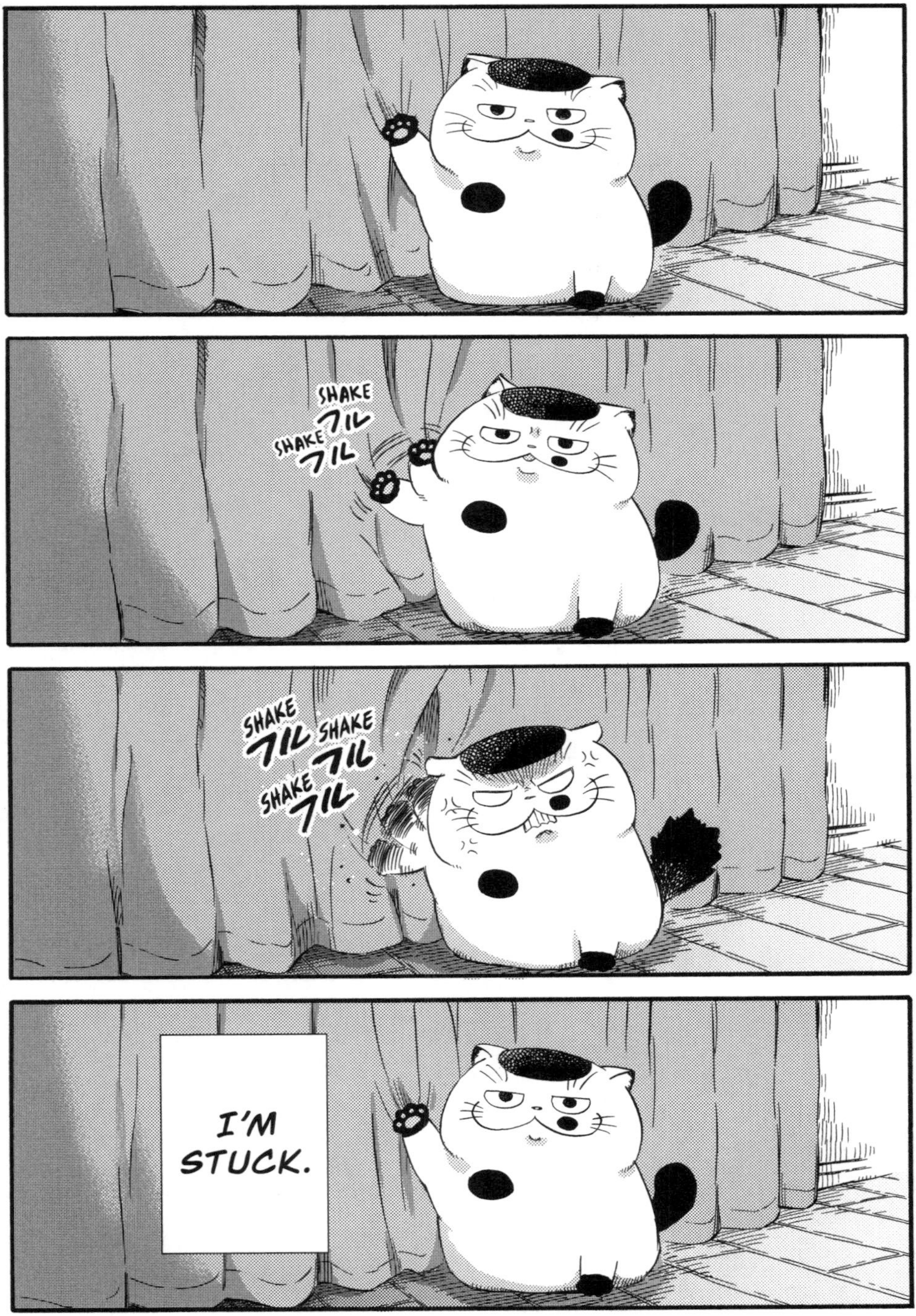
SHAKE フル
SHAKE フル
SHAKE フル
SHAKE フル
SHAKE フル
I'M STUCK.

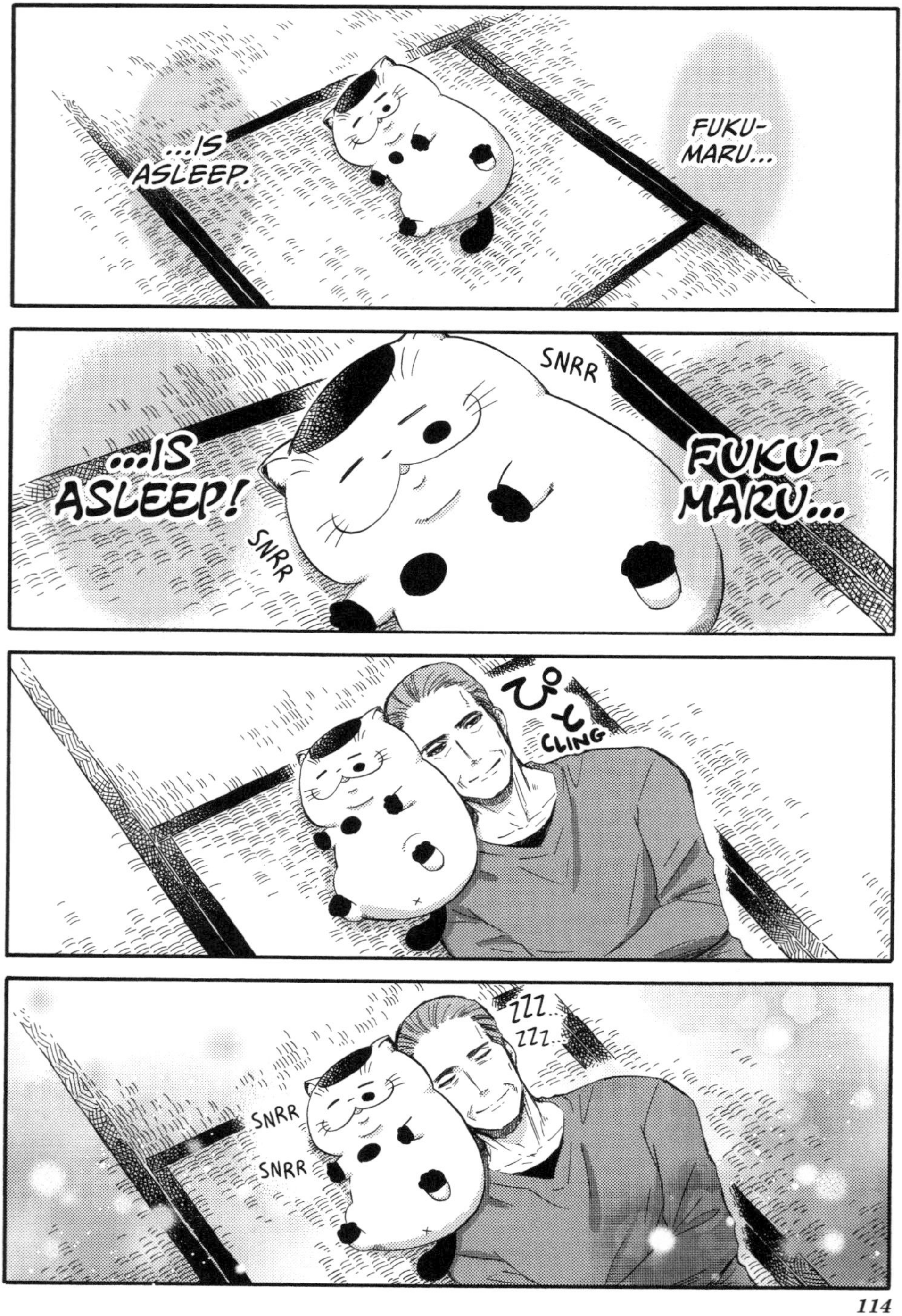
FUKU-
MARU...
...IS
ASLEEP.
SNRR
FUKU-
MARU...
...IS
ASLEEP!
SNRR
ぴと
CLING
ZZZ...
ZZZ...
SNRR
SNRR

FUKUMARU'S HIDDEN CLOUD TECHNIQUE

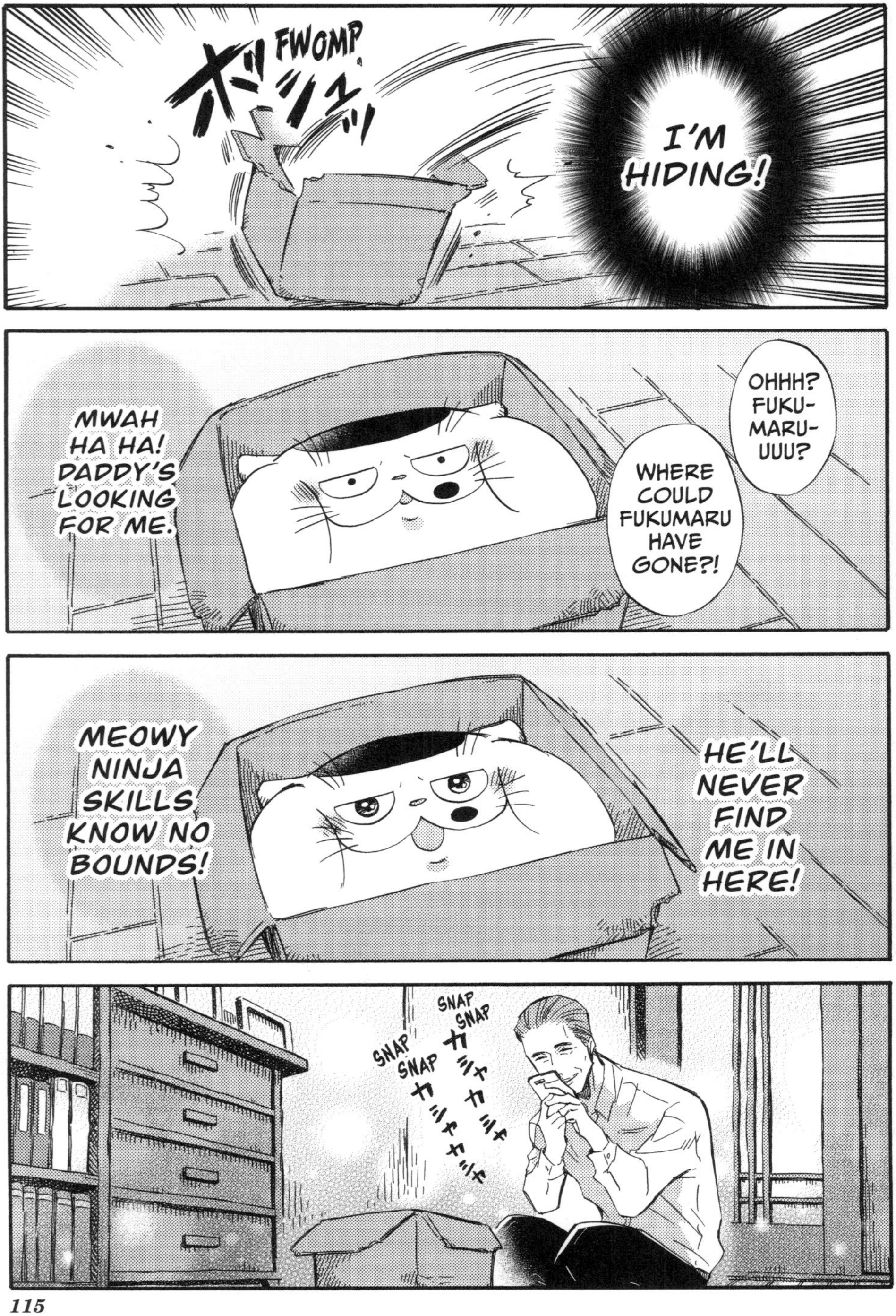
I'M HIDING!
FWOMP
OHHH? FUKU-MARU-UUU?
WHERE COULD FUKUMARU HAVE GONE?!
MWAH HA HA! DADDY'S LOOKING FOR ME.
HE'LL NEVER FIND ME IN HERE!
MEOWY NINJA SKILLS KNOW NO BOUNDS!
SNAP SNAP
SNAP SNAP

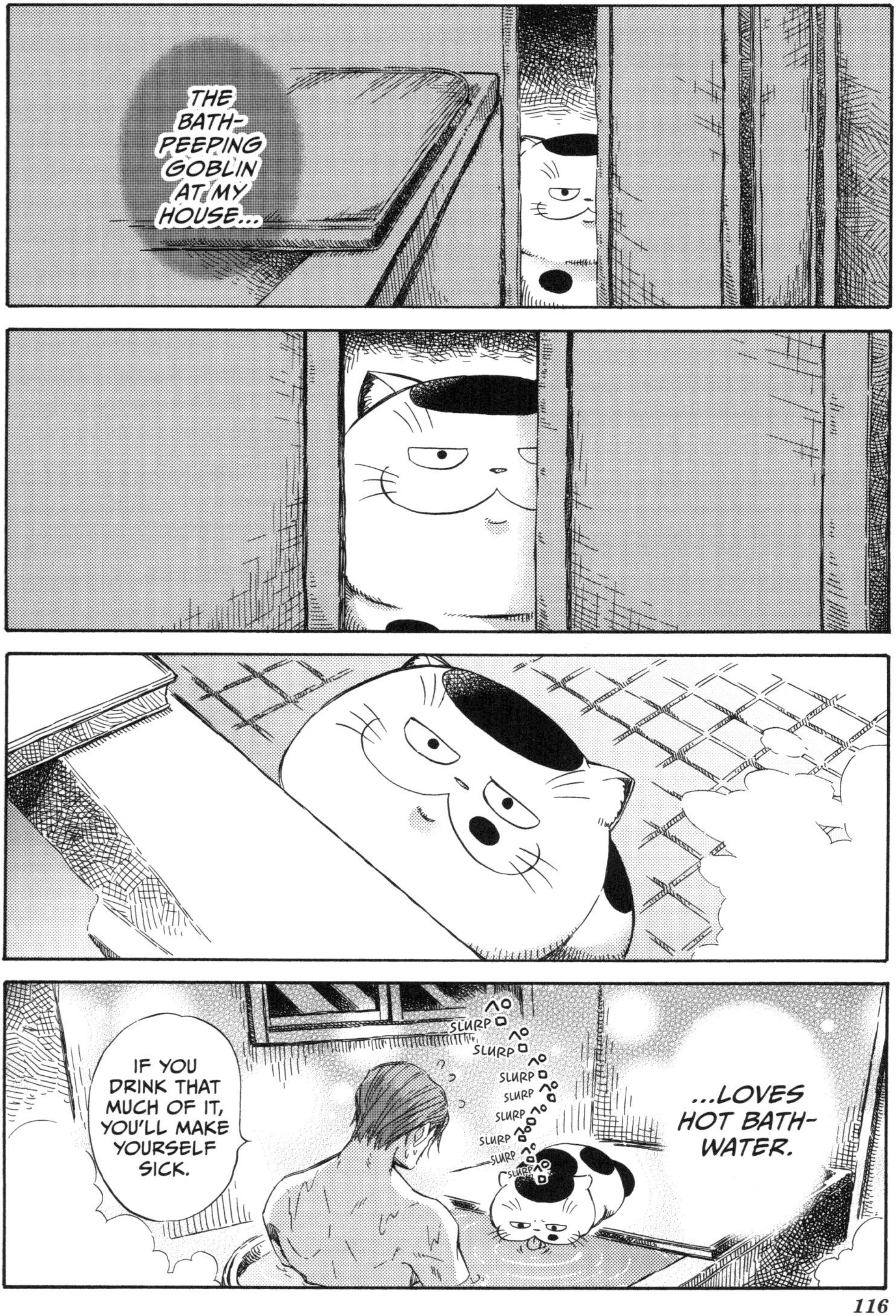
THE BATH-PEEPING GOBLIN AT MY HOUSE...
...LOVES HOT BATH-WATER.
SLURP
SLURP
SLURP
SLURP
SLURP
SLURP
SLURP
SLURP
IF YOU DRINK THAT MUCH OF IT, YOU'LL MAKE YOURSELF SICK.

THE MAN LOVES CATS

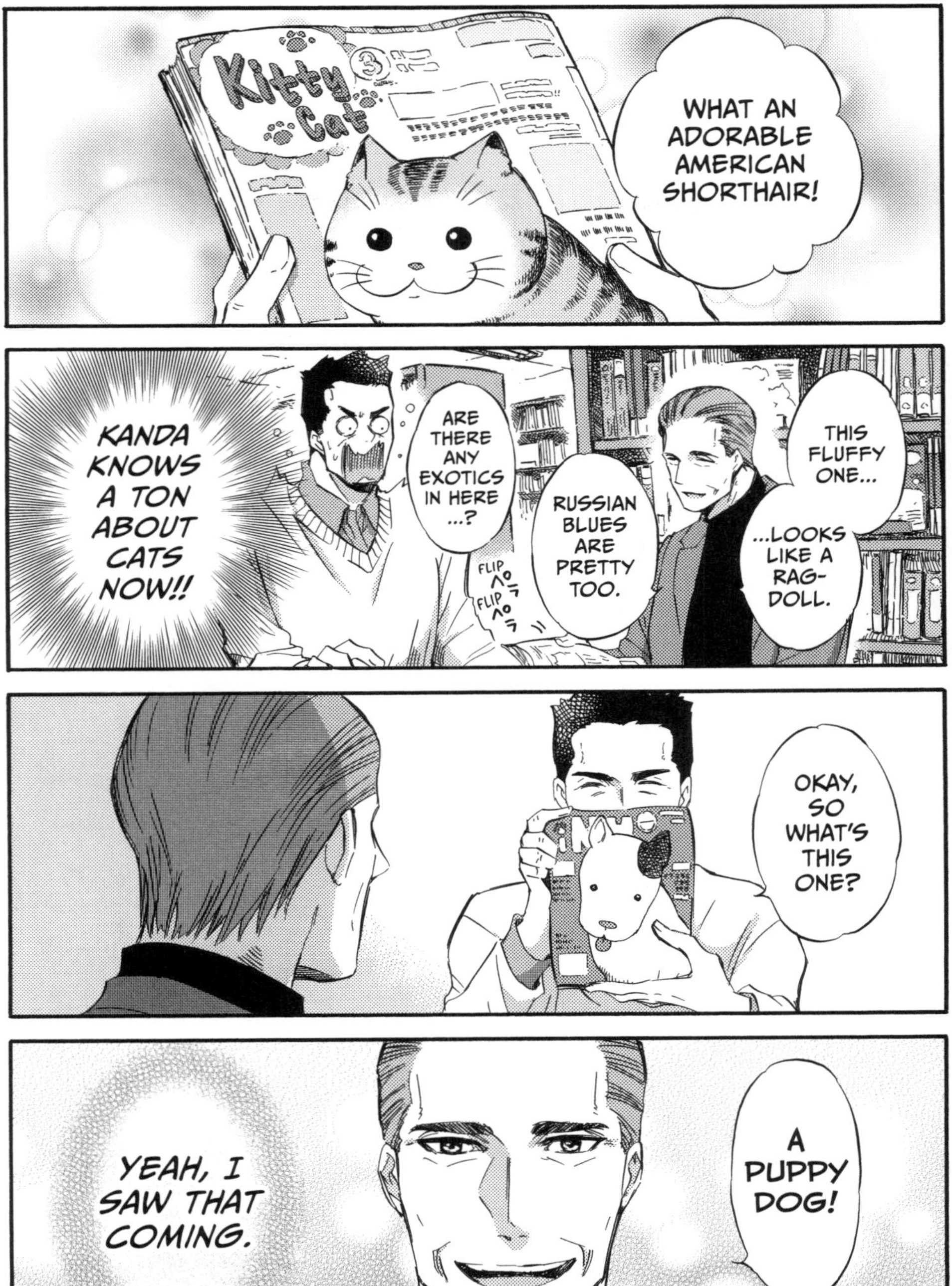
Kitty Cat
WHAT AN ADORABLE AMERICAN SHORTHAIR!
THIS FLUFFY ONE...
...LOOKS LIKE A RAG-DOLL.
RUSSIAN BLUES ARE PRETTY TOO.
ARE THERE ANY EXOTICS IN HERE ...?
FLIP FLIP
KANDA KNOWS A TON ABOUT CATS NOW!!
OKAY, SO WHAT'S THIS ONE?
A PUPPY DOG!
YEAH, I SAW THAT COMING.

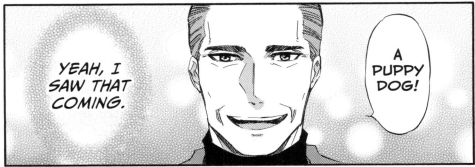

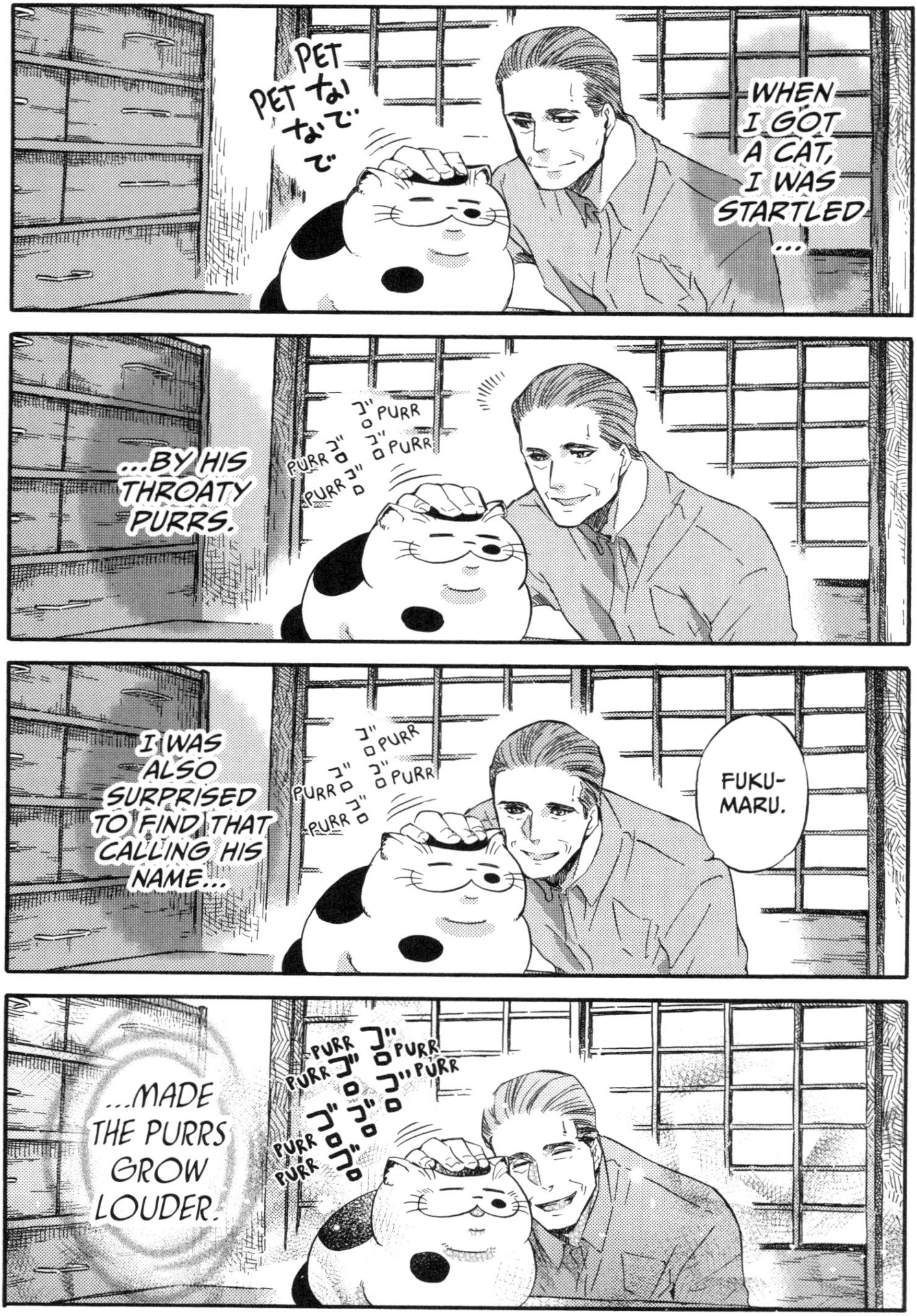
WHEN I GOT A CAT, I WAS STARTLED...
PET PET
なでなで
ゴロゴロ PURR PURR
PURR PURR
...BY HIS THROATY PURRS.
FUKU-MARU.
ゴロゴロ PURR PURR
PURR PURR
I WAS ALSO SURPRISED TO FIND THAT CALLING HIS NAME...
ゴロゴロ PURR PURR
PURR PURR
PURR PURR
...MADE THE PURRS GROW LOUDER.

Chapter 45 My Best Friend

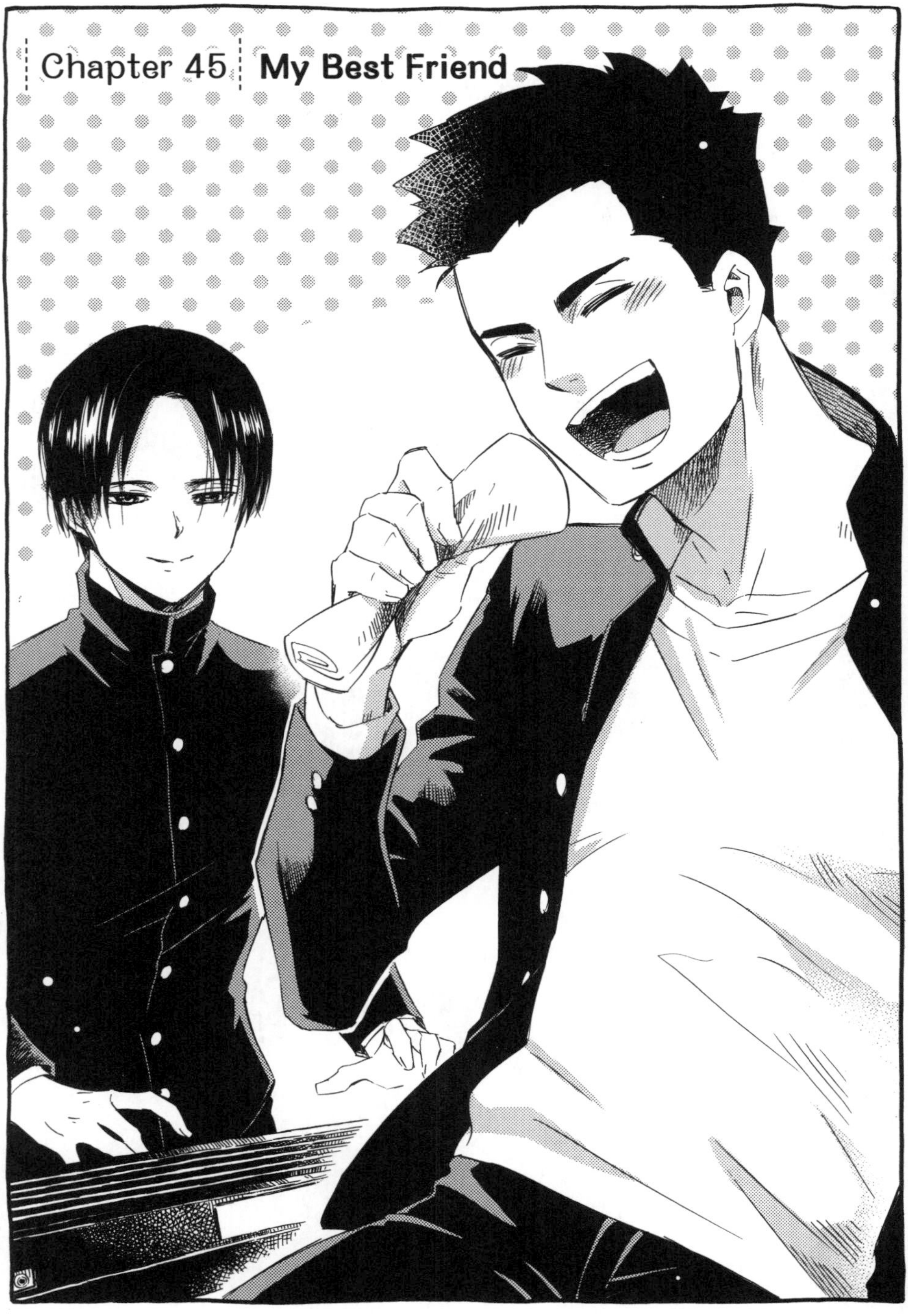

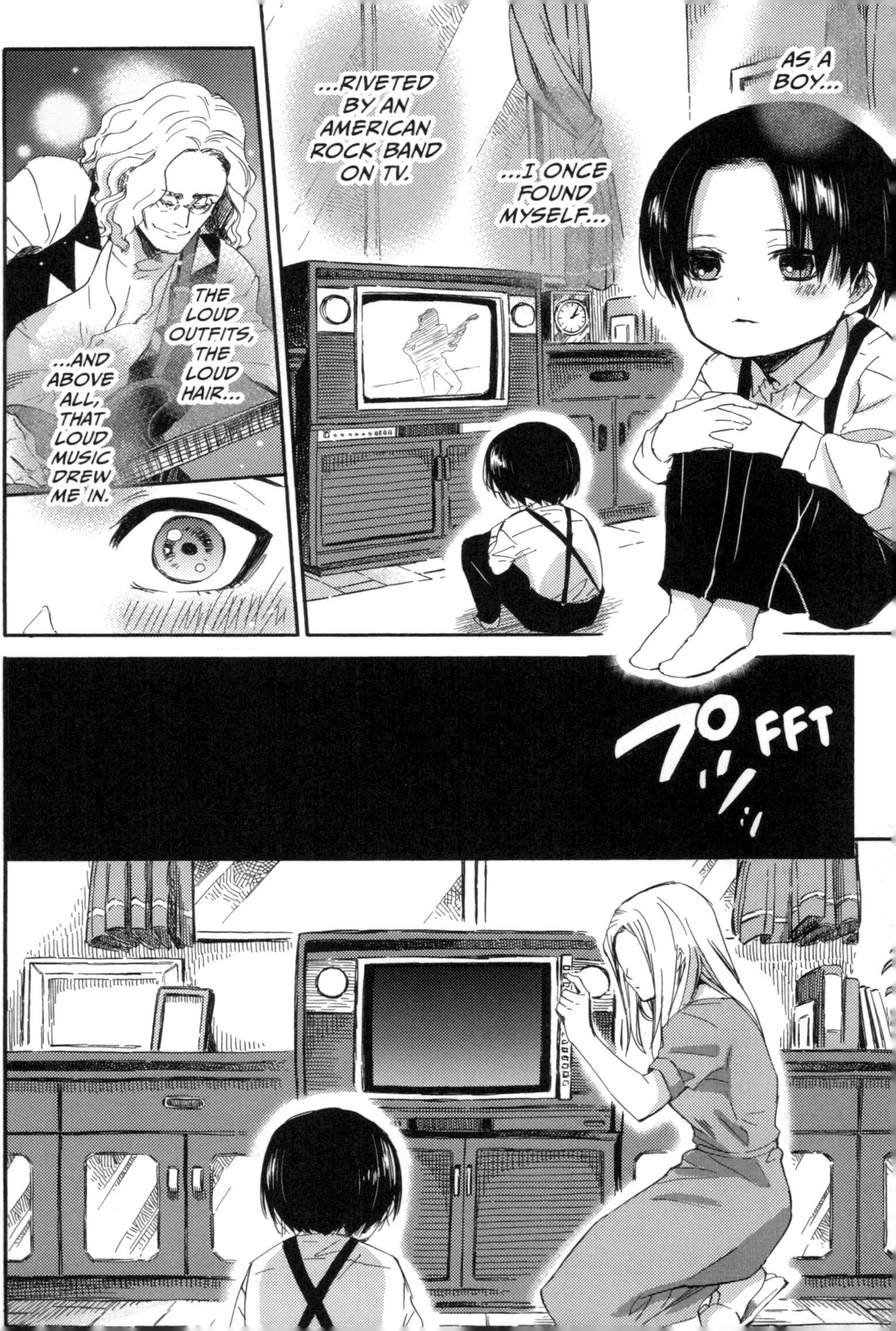

AS A BOY...
...I ONCE FOUND MYSELF...
...RIVETED BY AN AMERICAN ROCK BAND ON TV.
THE LOUD OUTFITS, THE LOUD HAIR...
...AND ABOVE ALL, THAT LOUD MUSIC DREW ME IN.
FFT

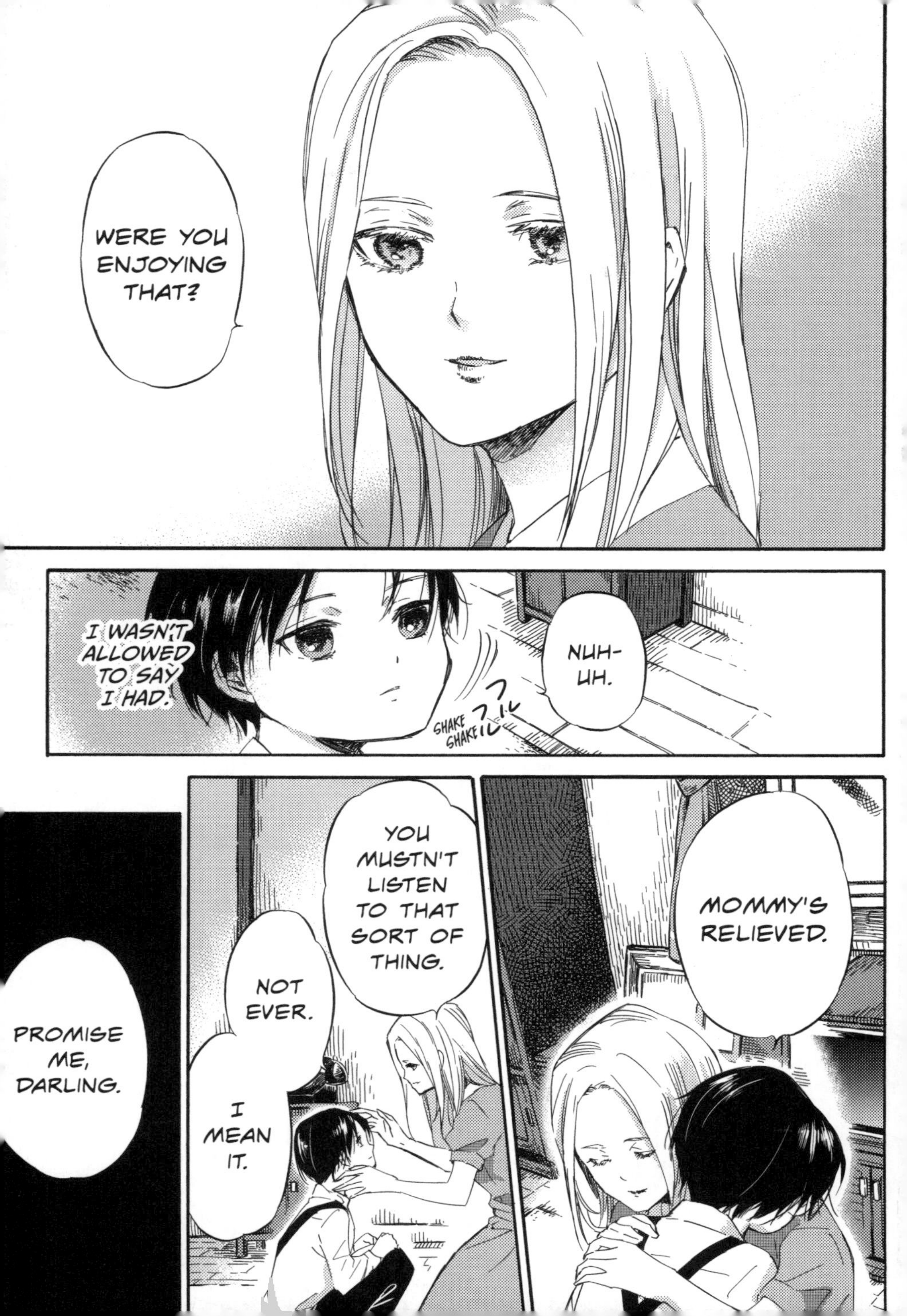
WERE YOU ENJOYING THAT?
NUH-UH.
SHAKE SHAKE
I WASN'T ALLOWED TO SAY I HAD.
MOMMY'S RELIEVED.
YOU MUSTN'T LISTEN TO THAT SORT OF THING.
NOT EVER.
I MEAN IT.
PROMISE ME, DARLING.

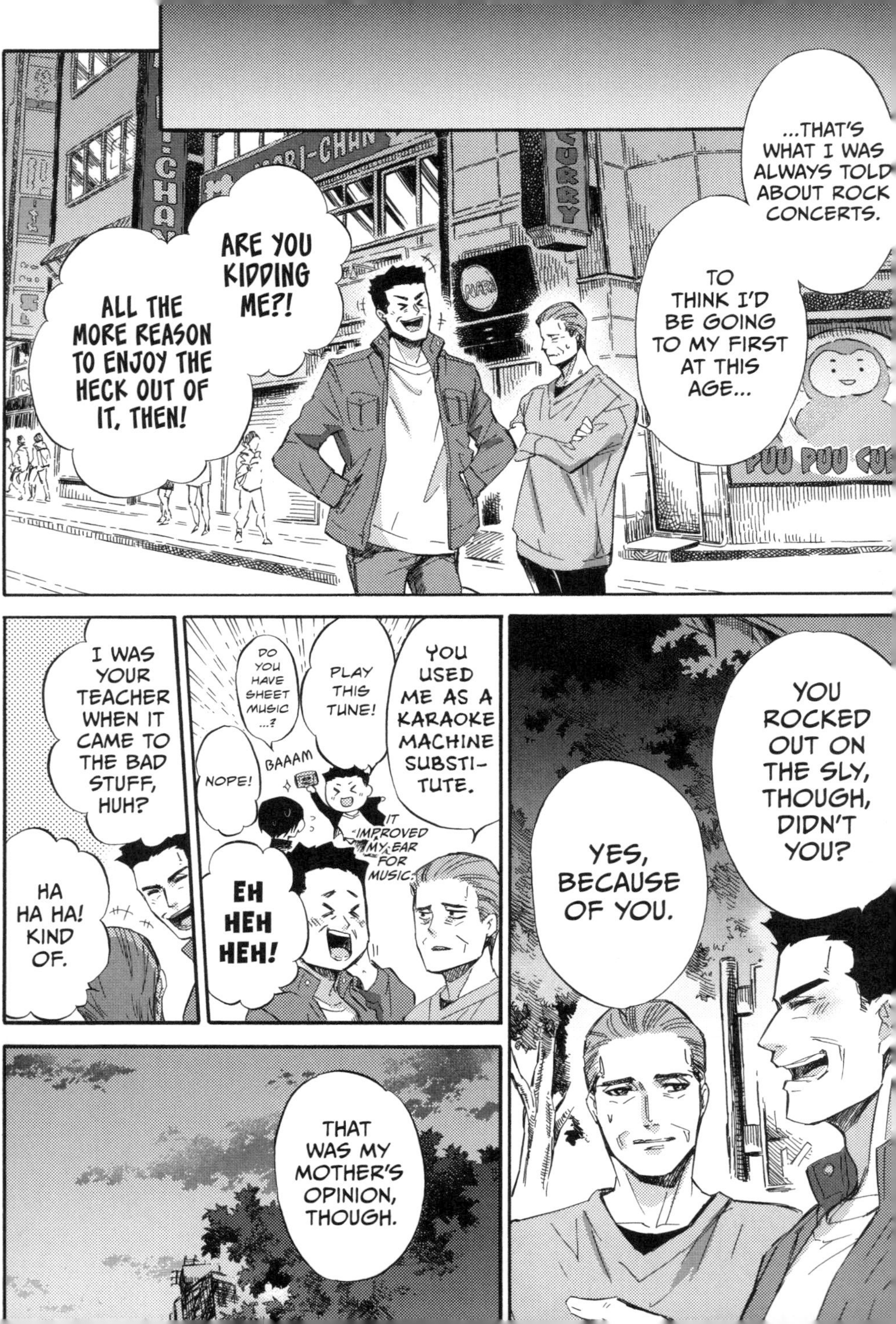
...THAT'S WHAT I WAS ALWAYS TOLD ABOUT ROCK CONCERTS.
TO THINK I'D BE GOING TO MY FIRST AT THIS AGE...
ARE YOU KIDDING ME?!
ALL THE MORE REASON TO ENJOY THE HECK OUT OF IT, THEN!
CURRY
YOU ROCKED OUT ON THE SLY, THOUGH, DIDN'T YOU?
YES, BECAUSE OF YOU.
YOU USED ME AS A KARAOKE MACHINE SUBSTITUTE.
PLAY THIS TUNE!
DO YOU HAVE SHEET MUSIC...?
BAAAM
NOPE!
IT IMPROVED MY EAR FOR MUSIC.
EH HEH HEH!
I WAS YOUR TEACHER WHEN IT CAME TO THE BAD STUFF, HUH?
HA HA HA! KIND OF.
THAT WAS MY MOTHER'S OPINION, THOUGH.

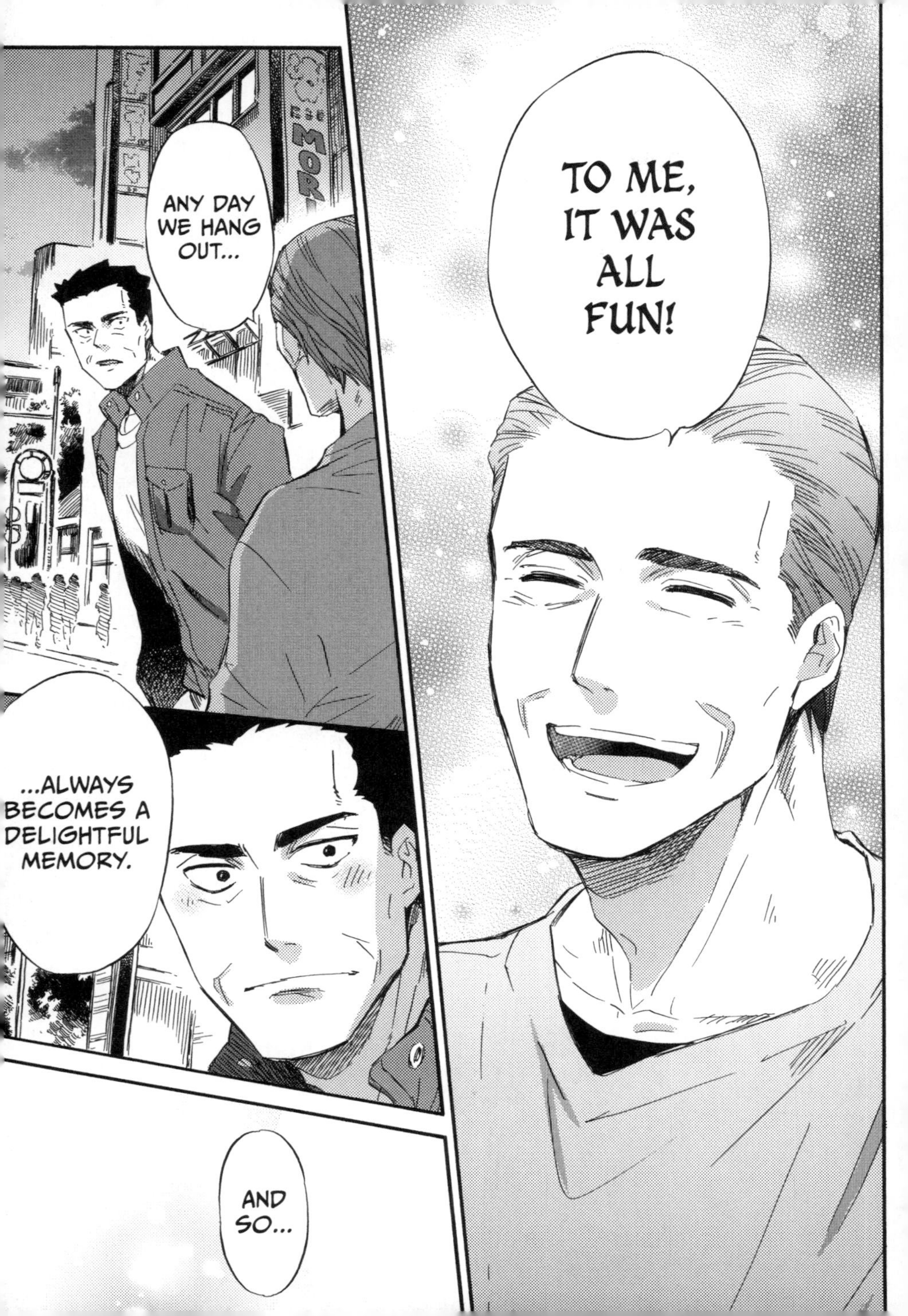
TO ME, IT WAS ALL FUN!
ANY DAY WE HANG OUT...
...ALWAYS BECOMES A DELIGHTFUL MEMORY.
AND SO...

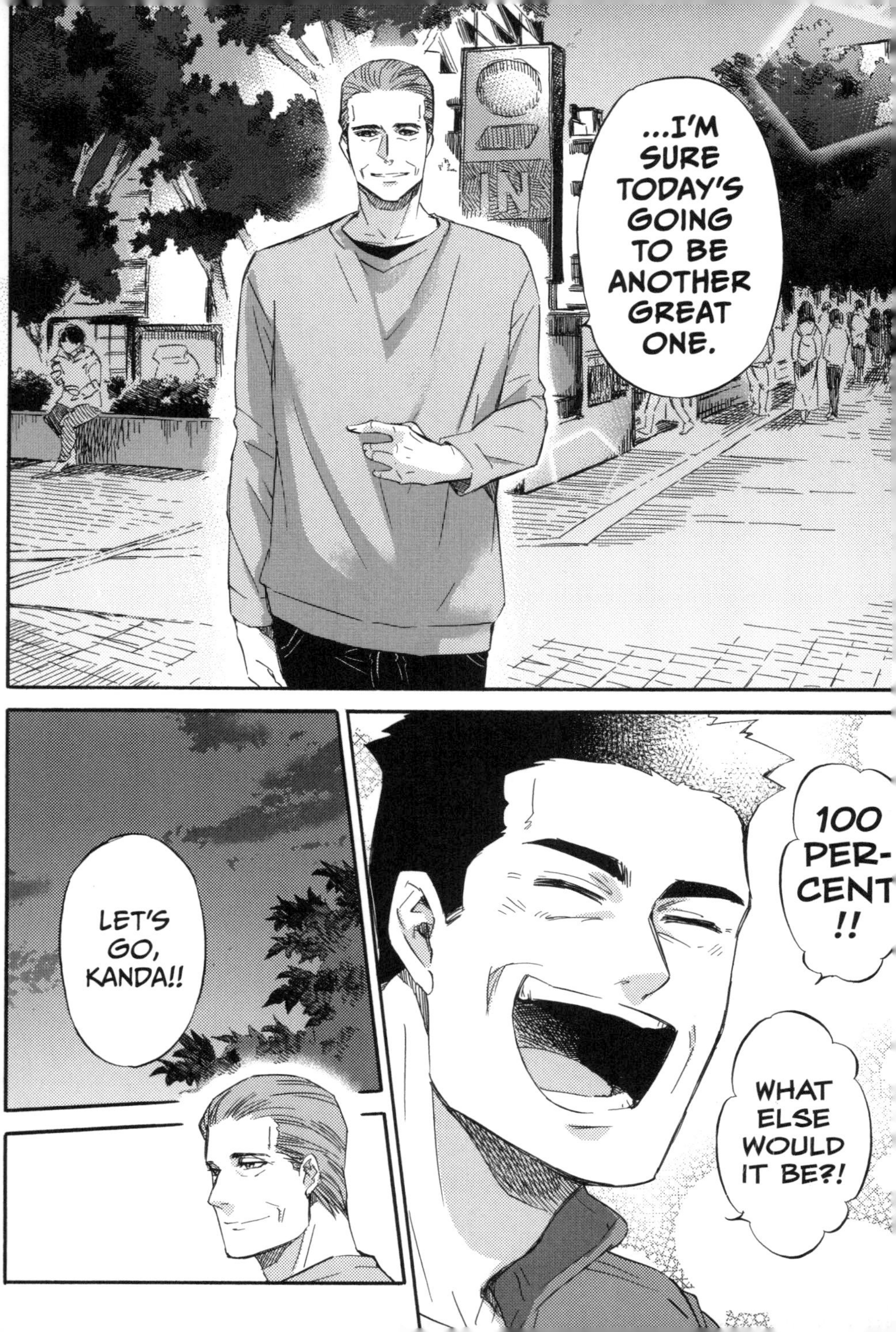
...I'M SURE TODAY'S GOING TO BE ANOTHER GREAT ONE.
100 PERCENT!!
WHAT ELSE WOULD IT BE?!
LET'S GO, KANDA!!

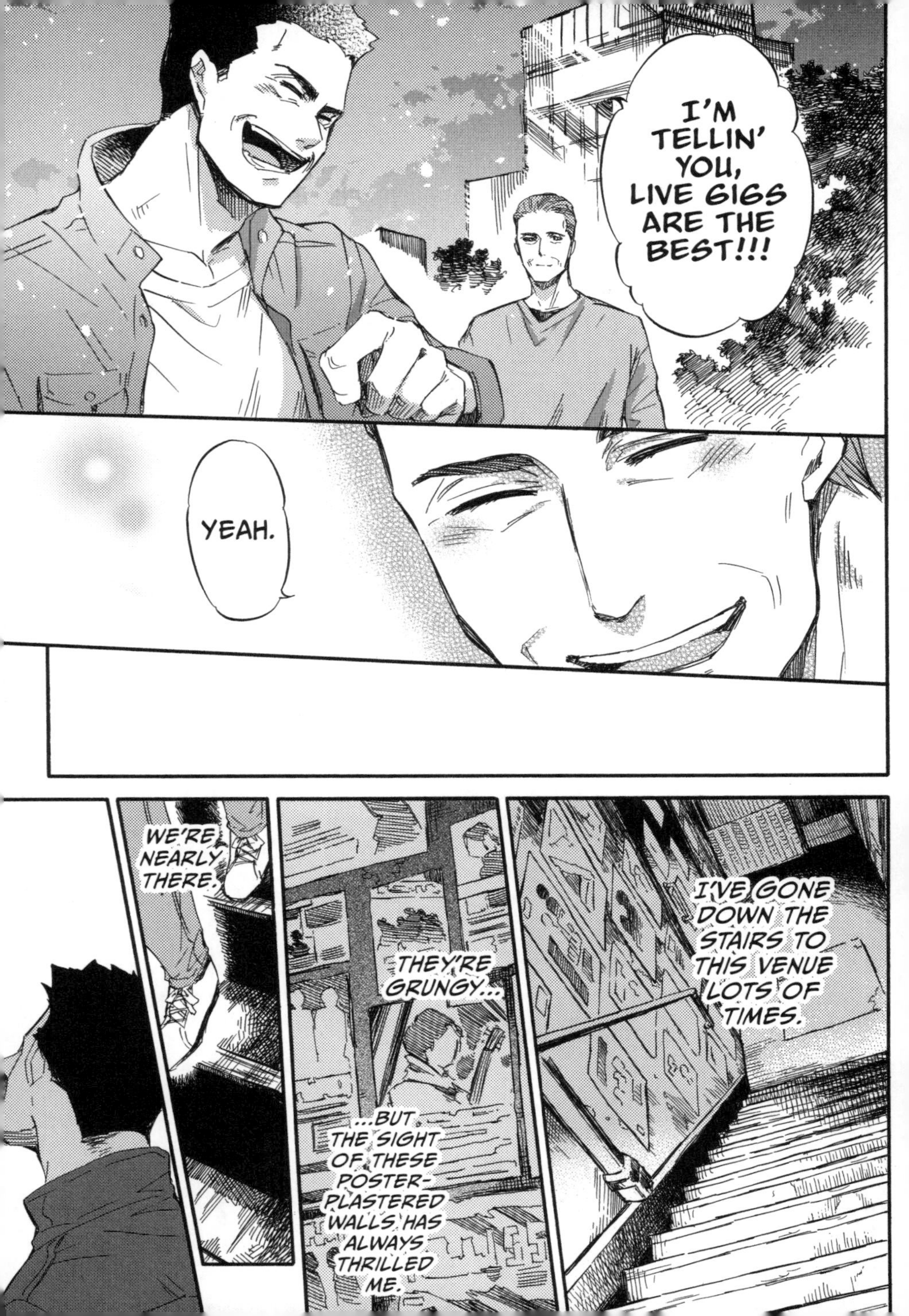
I'M TELLIN' YOU, LIVE GIGS ARE THE BEST!!!
YEAH.
I'VE GONE DOWN THE STAIRS TO THIS VENUE LOTS OF TIMES.
THEY'RE GRUNGY...
...BUT THE SIGHT OF THESE POSTER-PLASTERED WALLS HAS ALWAYS THRILLED ME.
WE'RE NEARLY THERE.

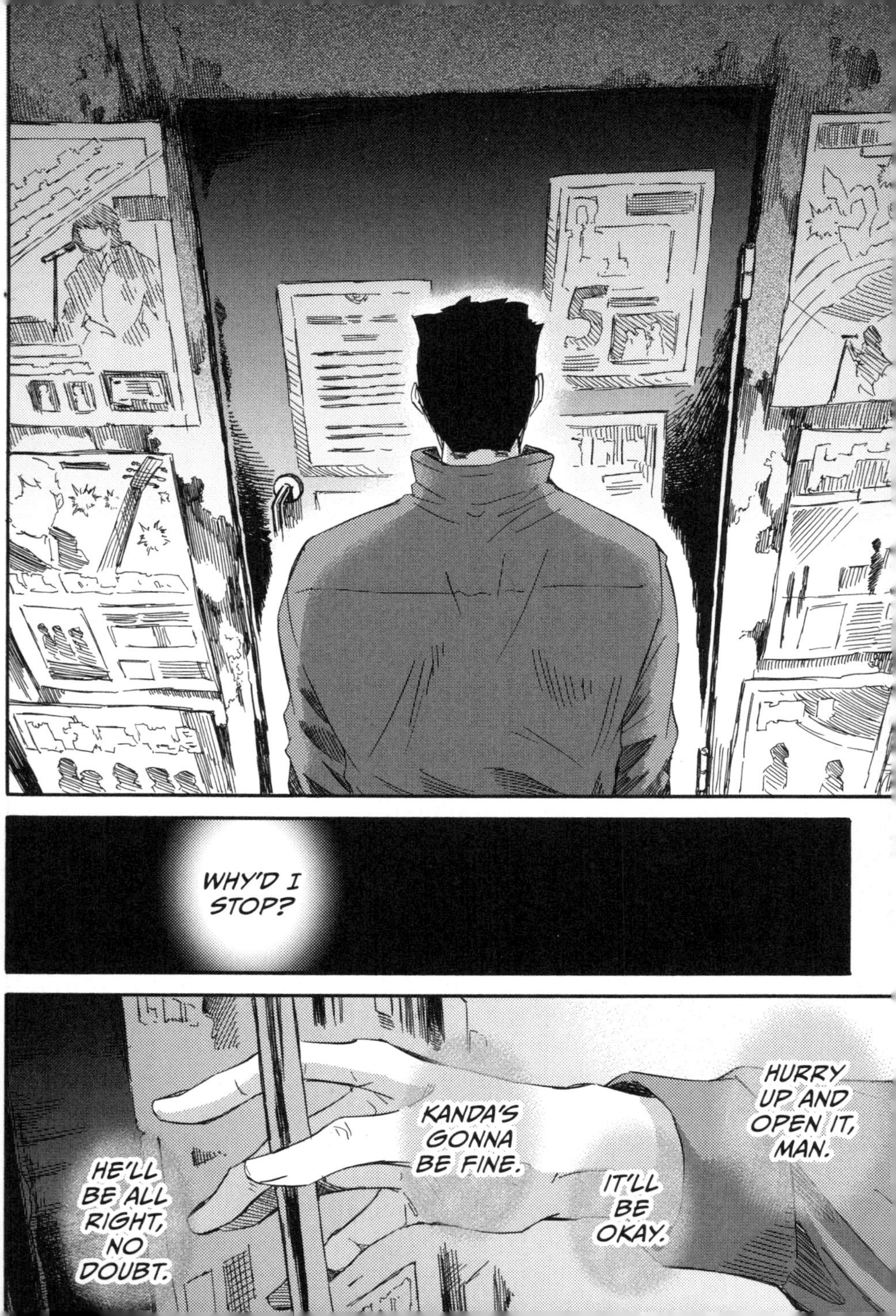
WHY'D I STOP?
HURRY UP AND OPEN IT, MAN.
IT'LL BE OKAY.
KANDA'S GONNA BE FINE.
HE'LL BE ALL RIGHT, NO DOUBT.

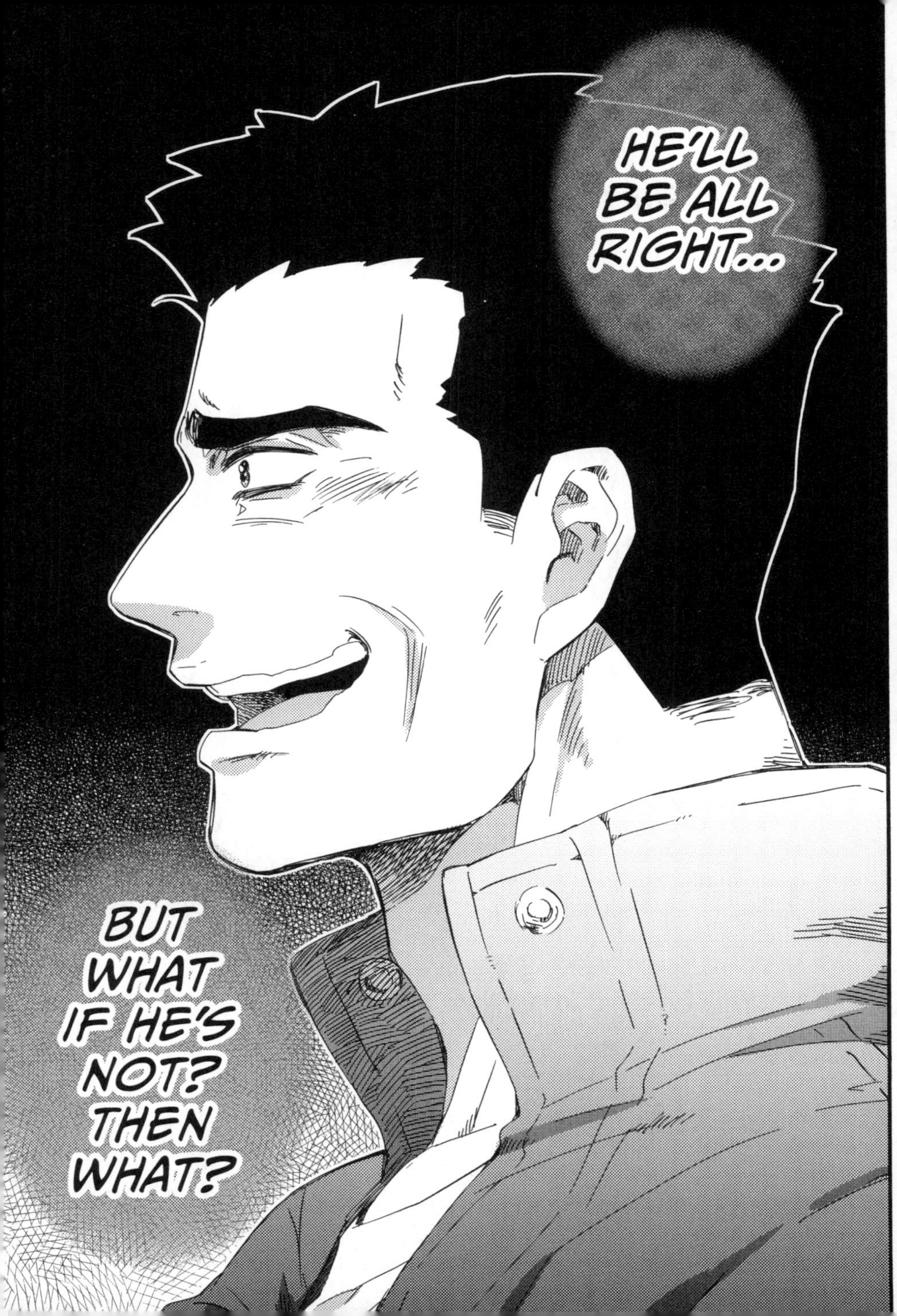
HE'LL BE ALL RIGHT...
BUT WHAT IF HE'S NOT? THEN WHAT?

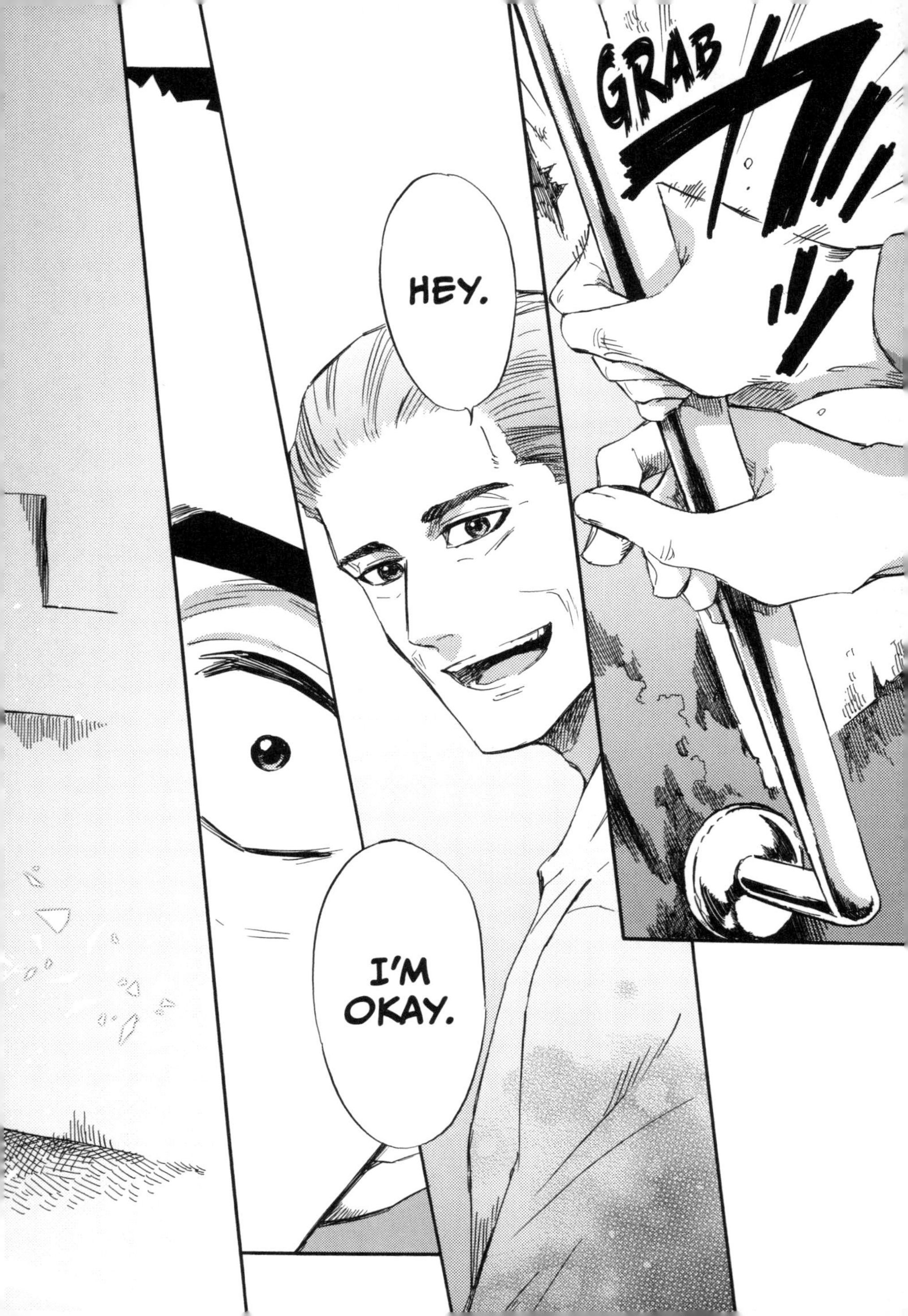
GRAB
HEY.
I'M OKAY.

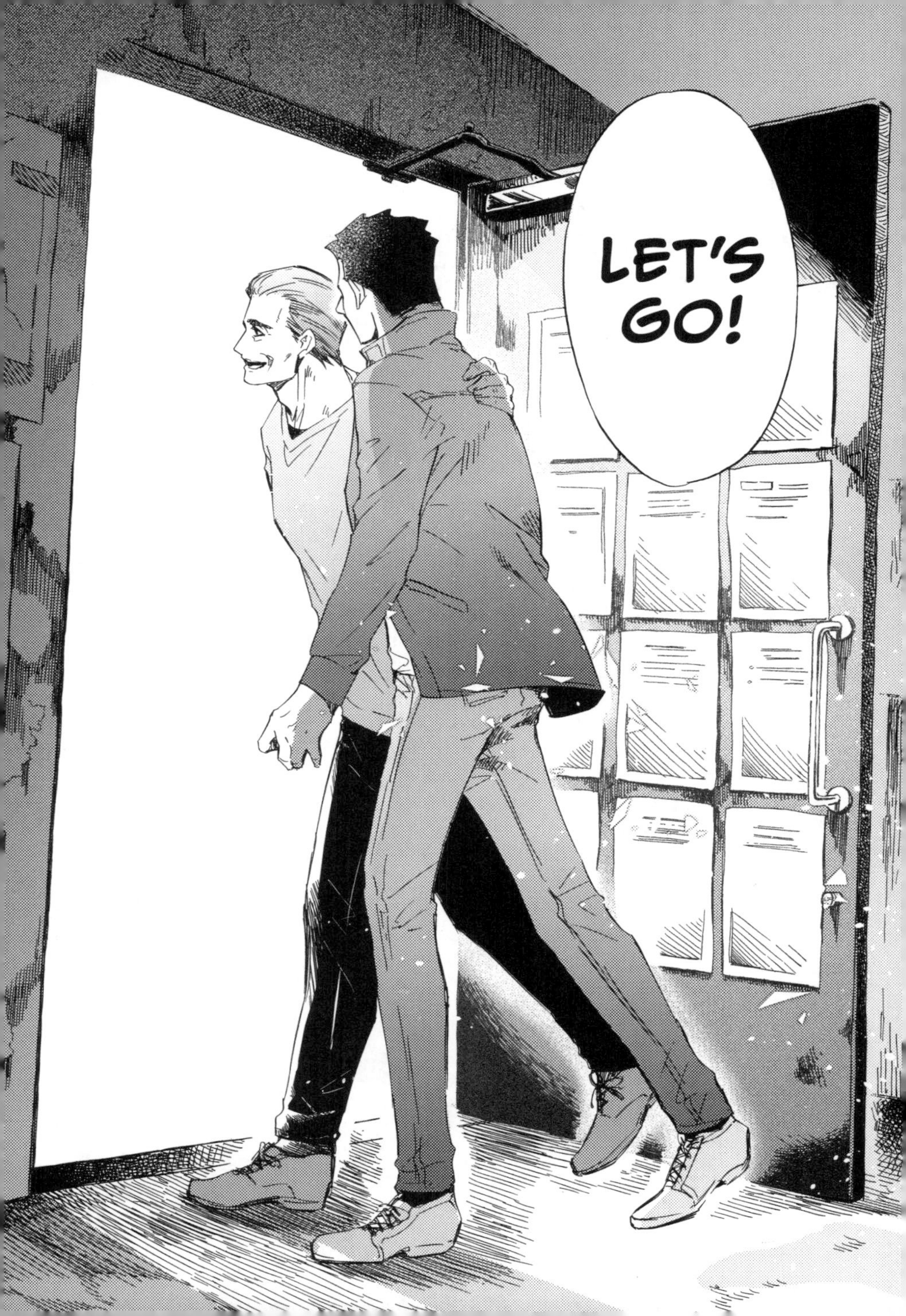
LET'S GO!

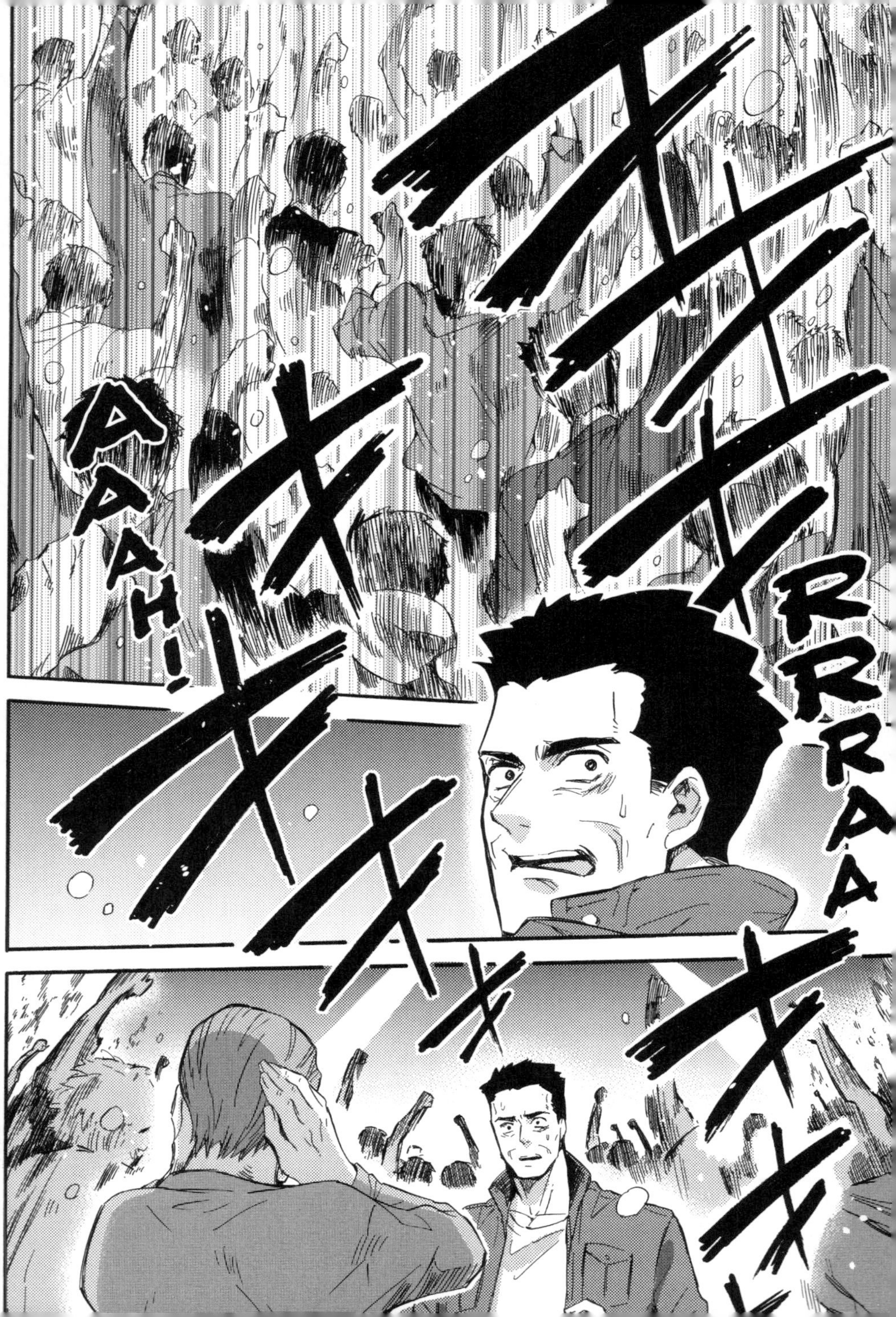
RRRAA
AAAH!

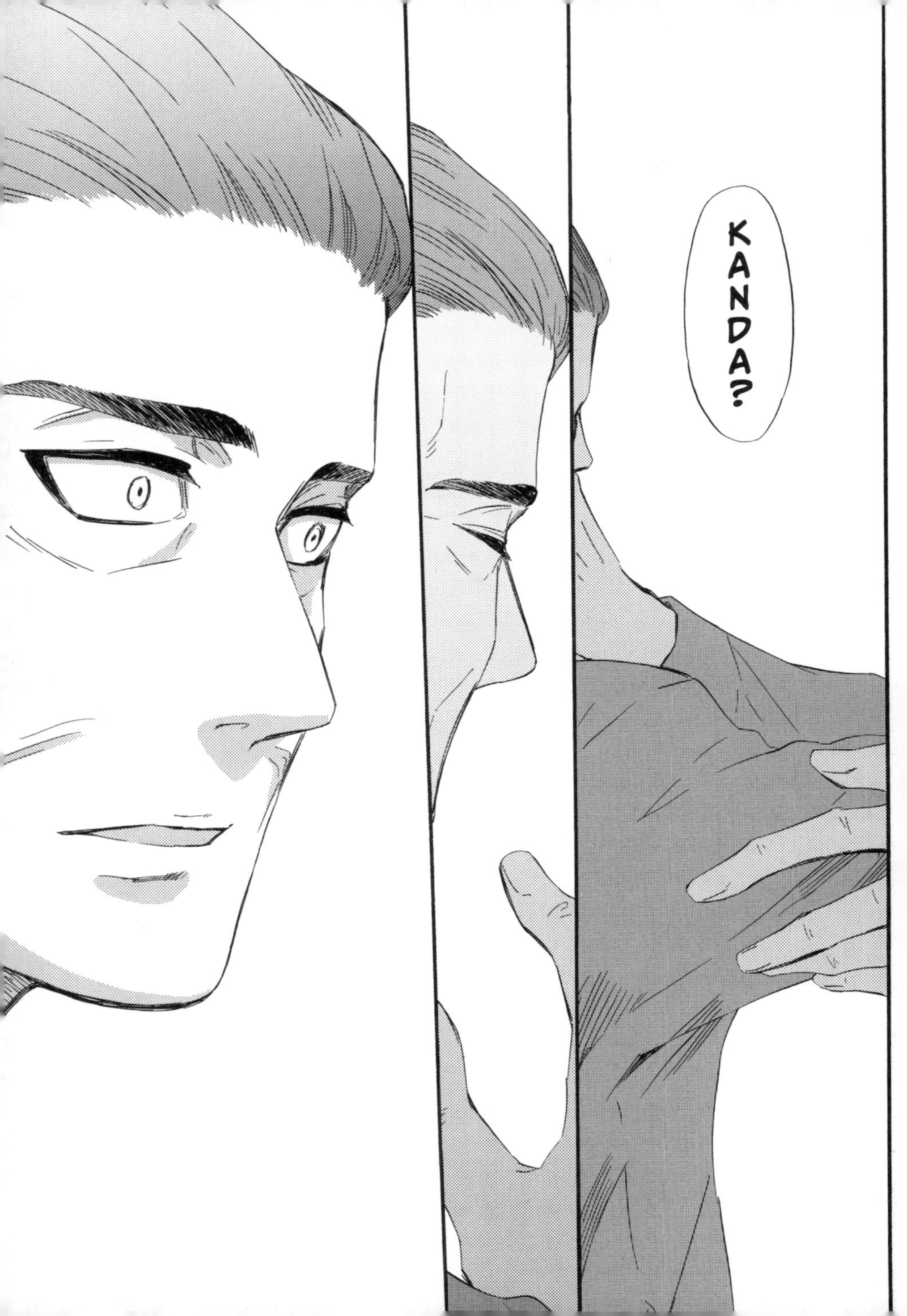
KANDA?

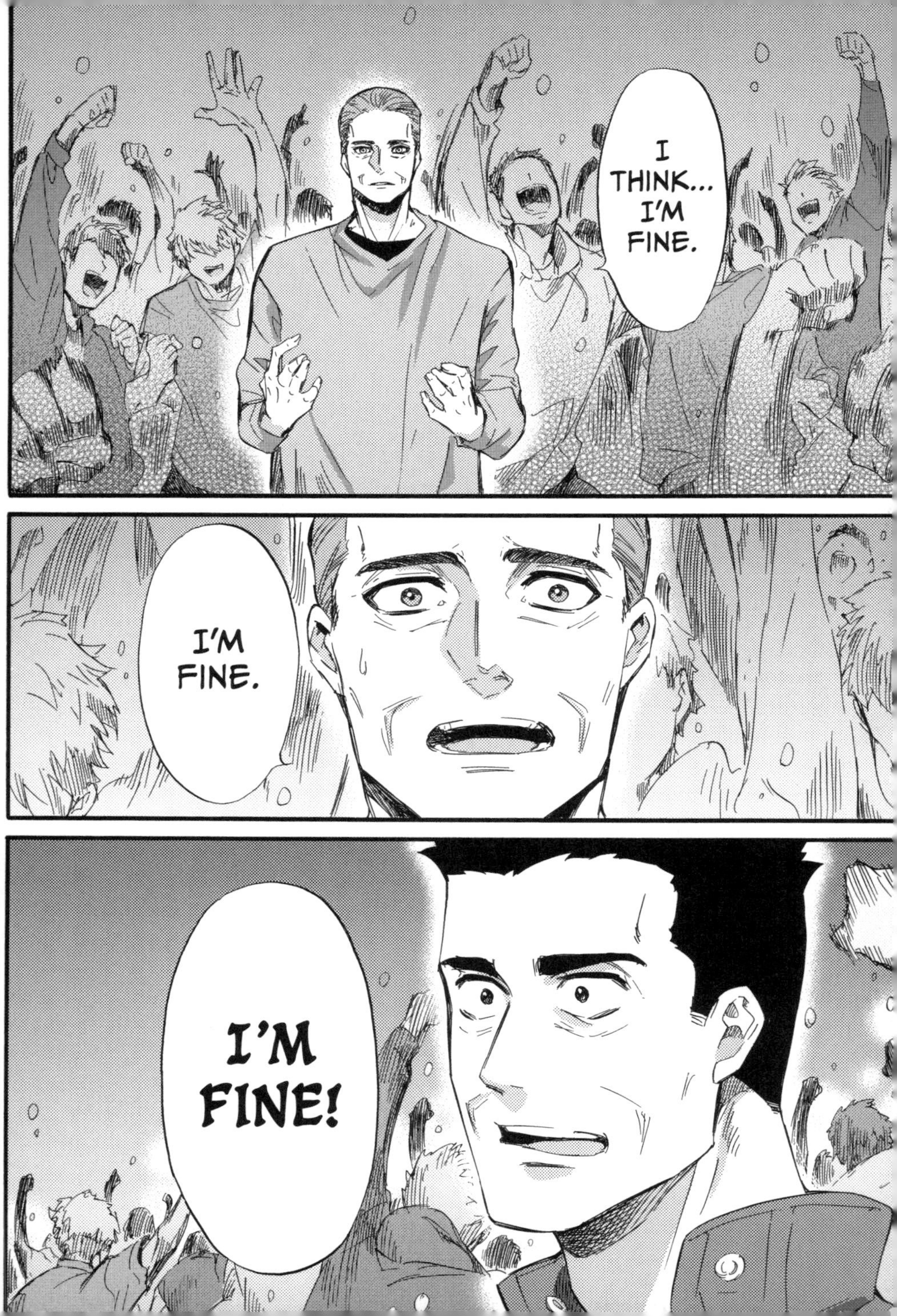
I THINK... I'M FINE.
I'M FINE.
I'M FINE!

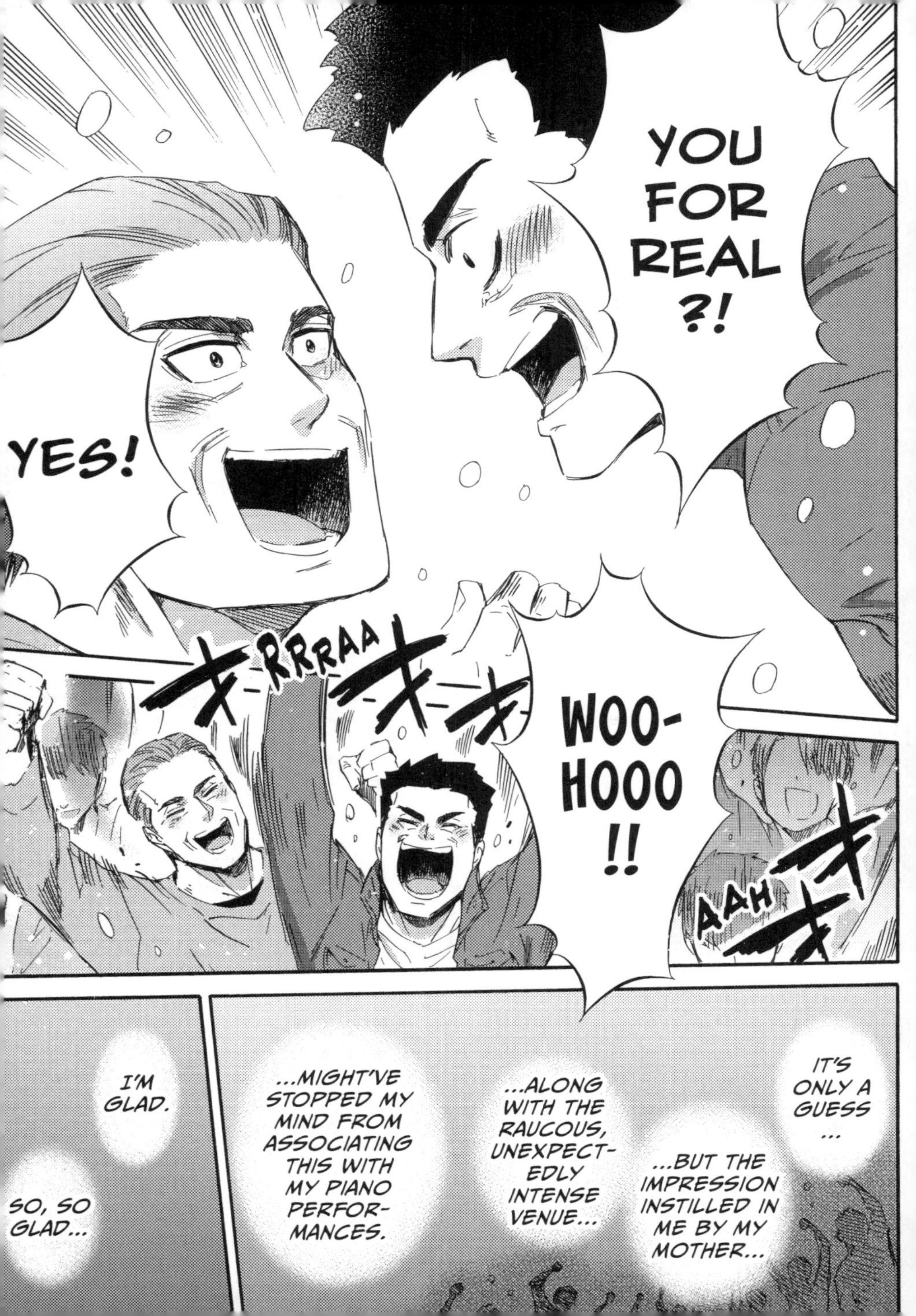
YOU FOR REAL?!
YES!
AAH
RRRAA
WOO-HOOO!!
IT'S ONLY A GUESS...
...BUT THE IMPRESSION INSTILLED IN ME BY MY MOTHER...
...ALONG WITH THE RAUCOUS, UNEXPECTEDLY INTENSE VENUE...
...MIGHT'VE STOPPED MY MIND FROM ASSOCIATING THIS WITH MY PIANO PERFORMANCES.
I'M GLAD.
SO, SO GLAD...

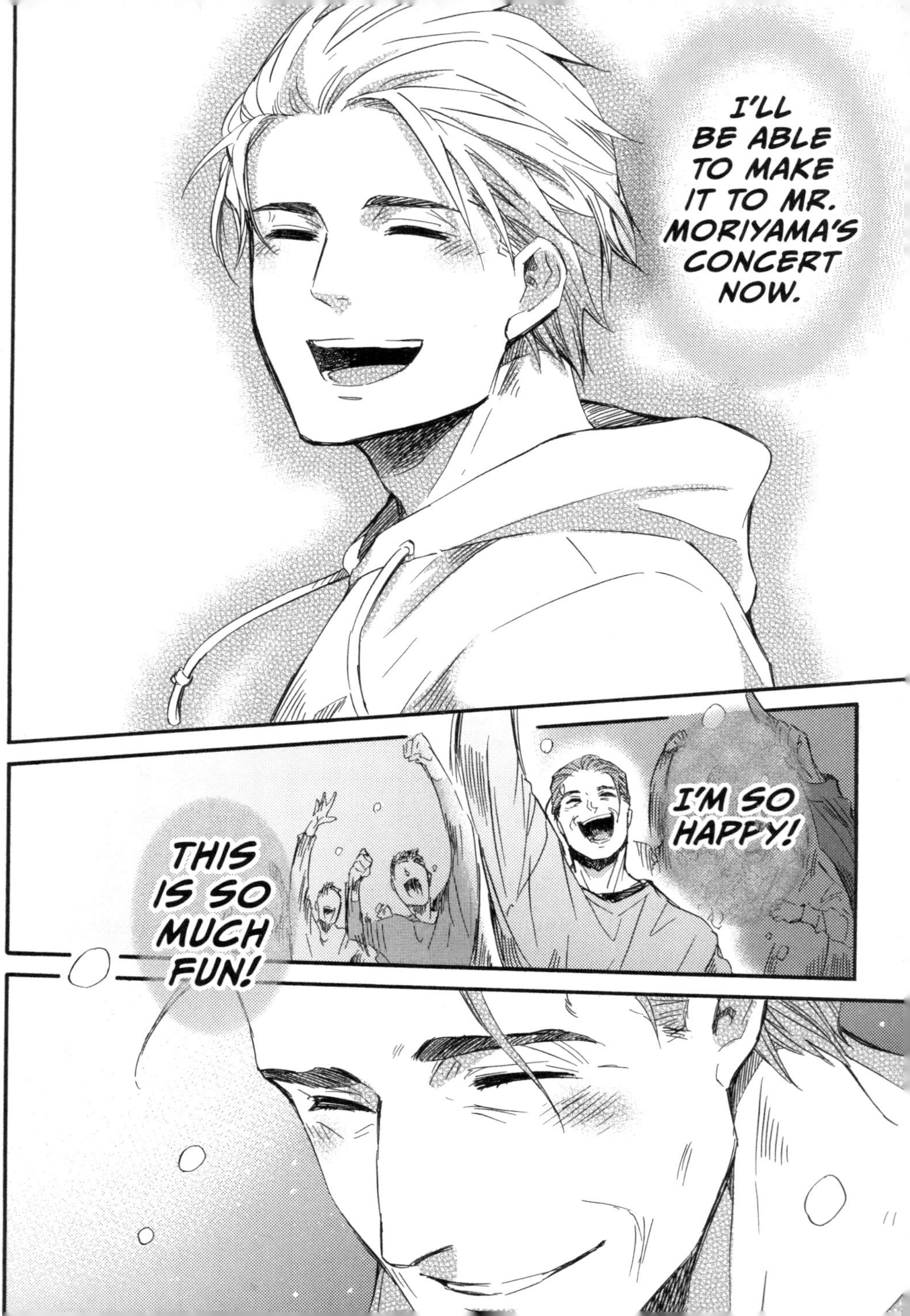
I'LL BE ABLE TO MAKE IT TO MR. MORIYAMA'S CONCERT NOW.
I'M SO HAPPY!
THIS IS SO MUCH FUN!

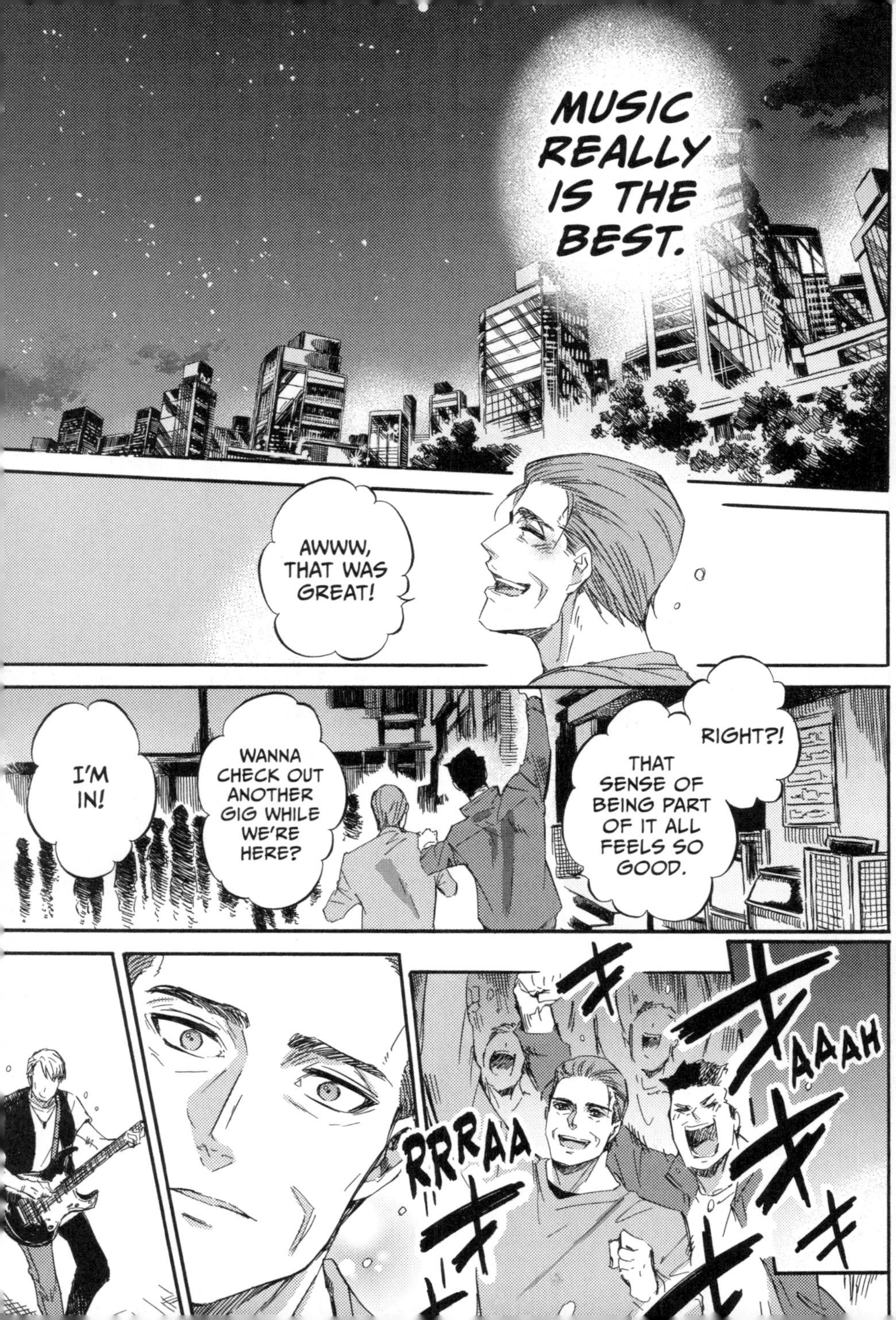
MUSIC REALLY IS THE BEST.
AWWW, THAT WAS GREAT!
RIGHT?!
THAT SENSE OF BEING PART OF IT ALL FEELS SO GOOD.
WANNA CHECK OUT ANOTHER GIG WHILE WE'RE HERE?
I'M IN!
AAAH
RRRAA

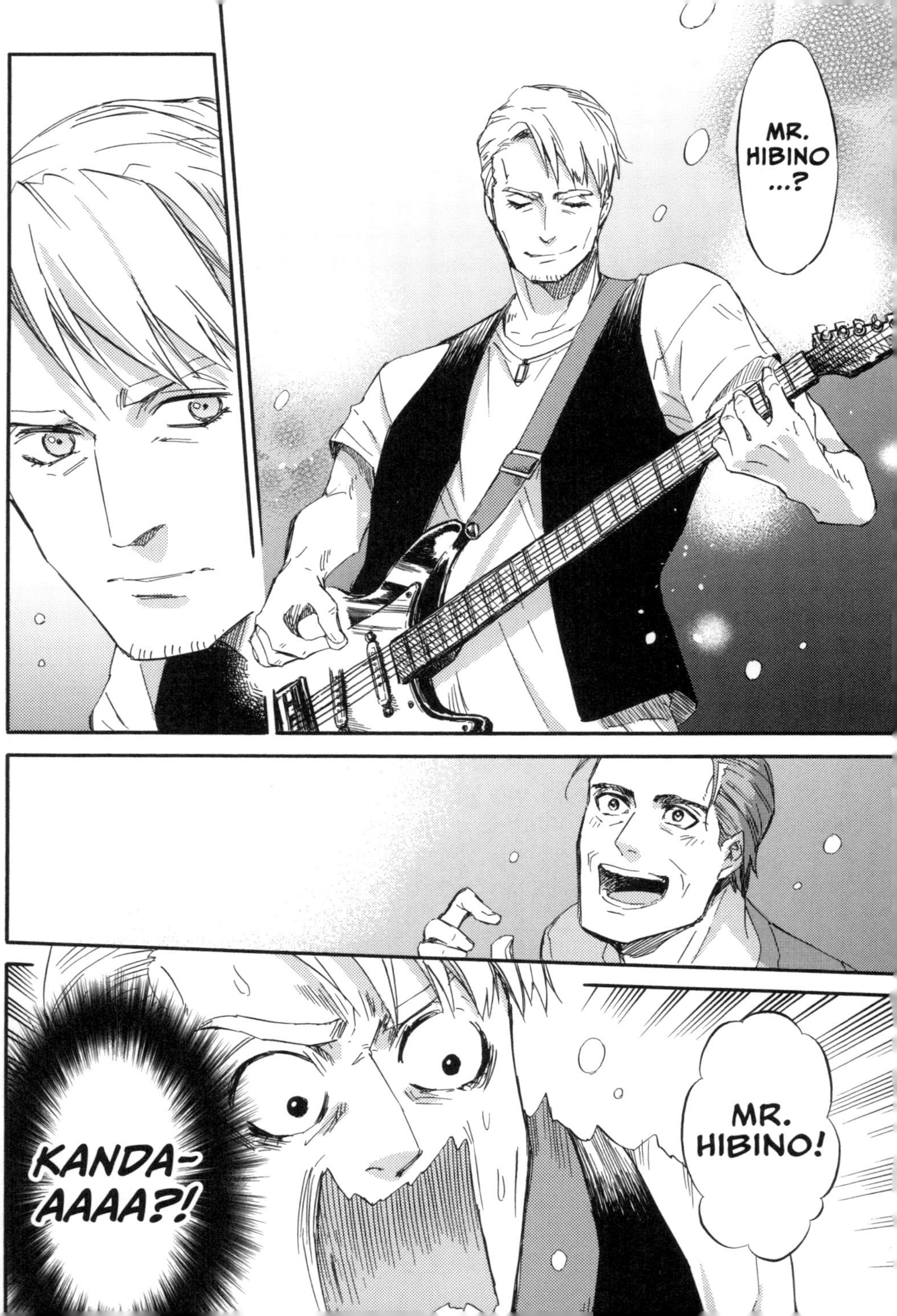
MR. HIBINO ...?
MR. HIBINO!
KANDA-AAAA?!

Chapter 46 The Ultimate Rival

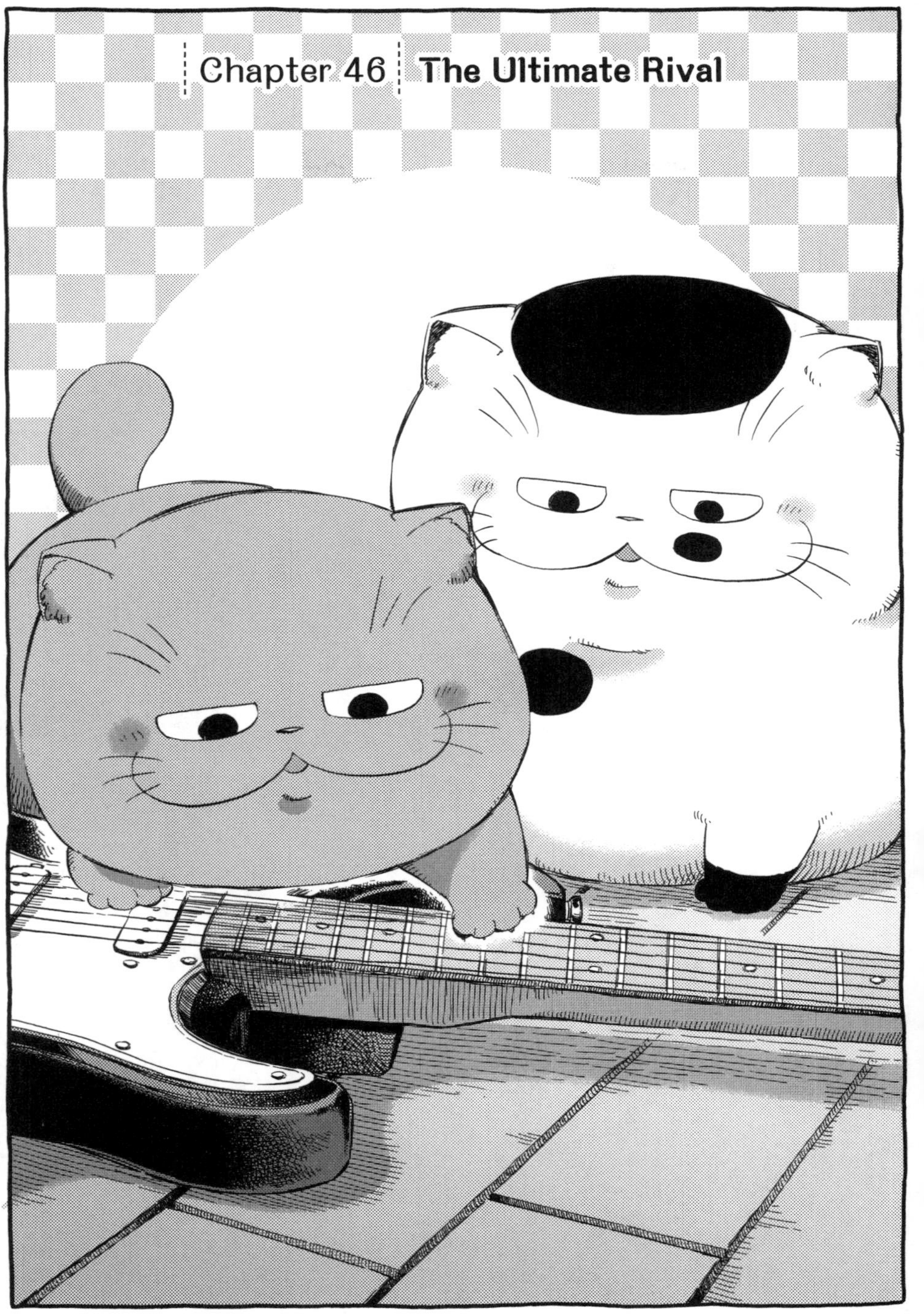

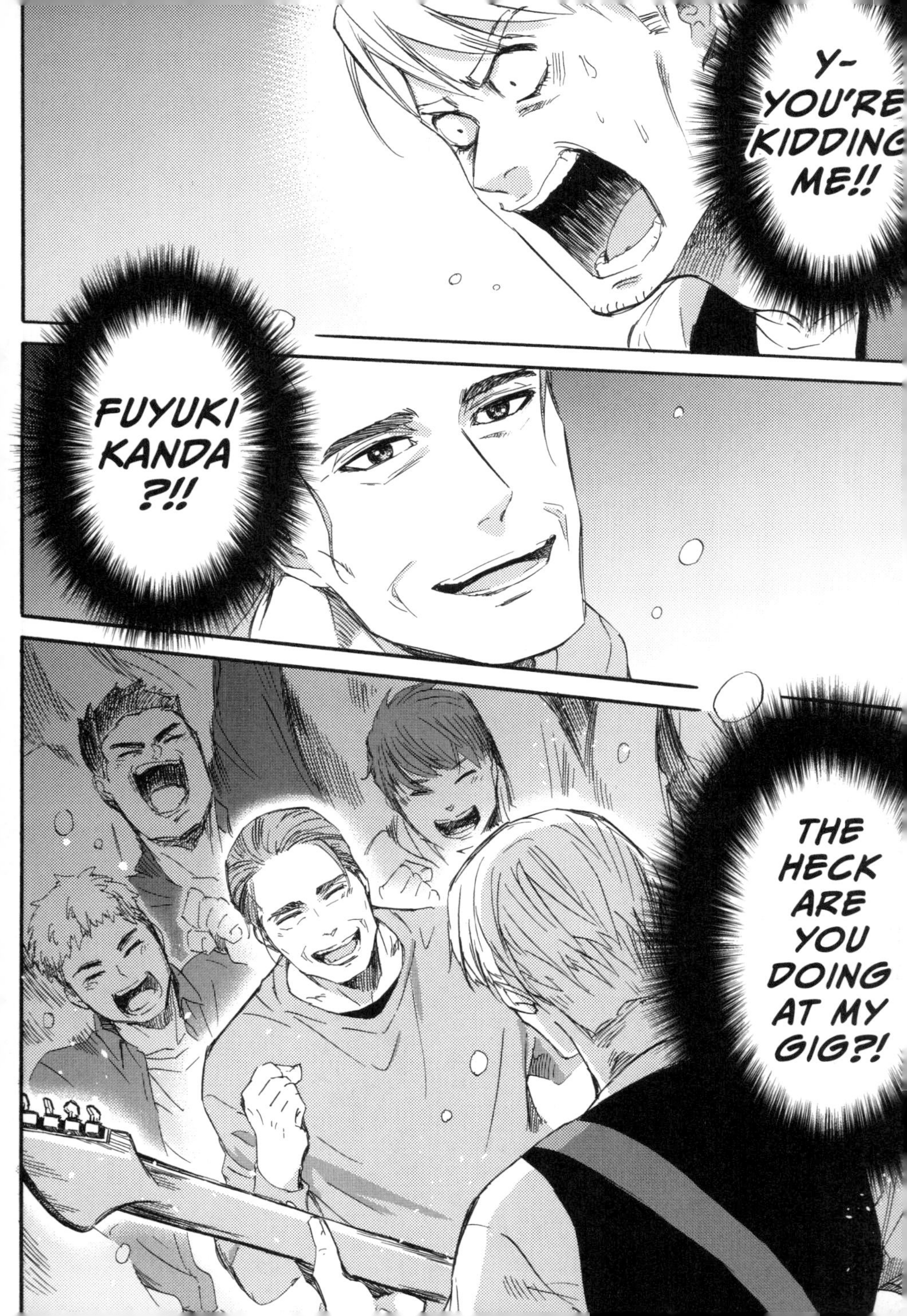
Y- YOU'RE KIDDING ME!!
FUYUKI KANDA ?!!
THE HECK ARE YOU DOING AT MY GIG?!

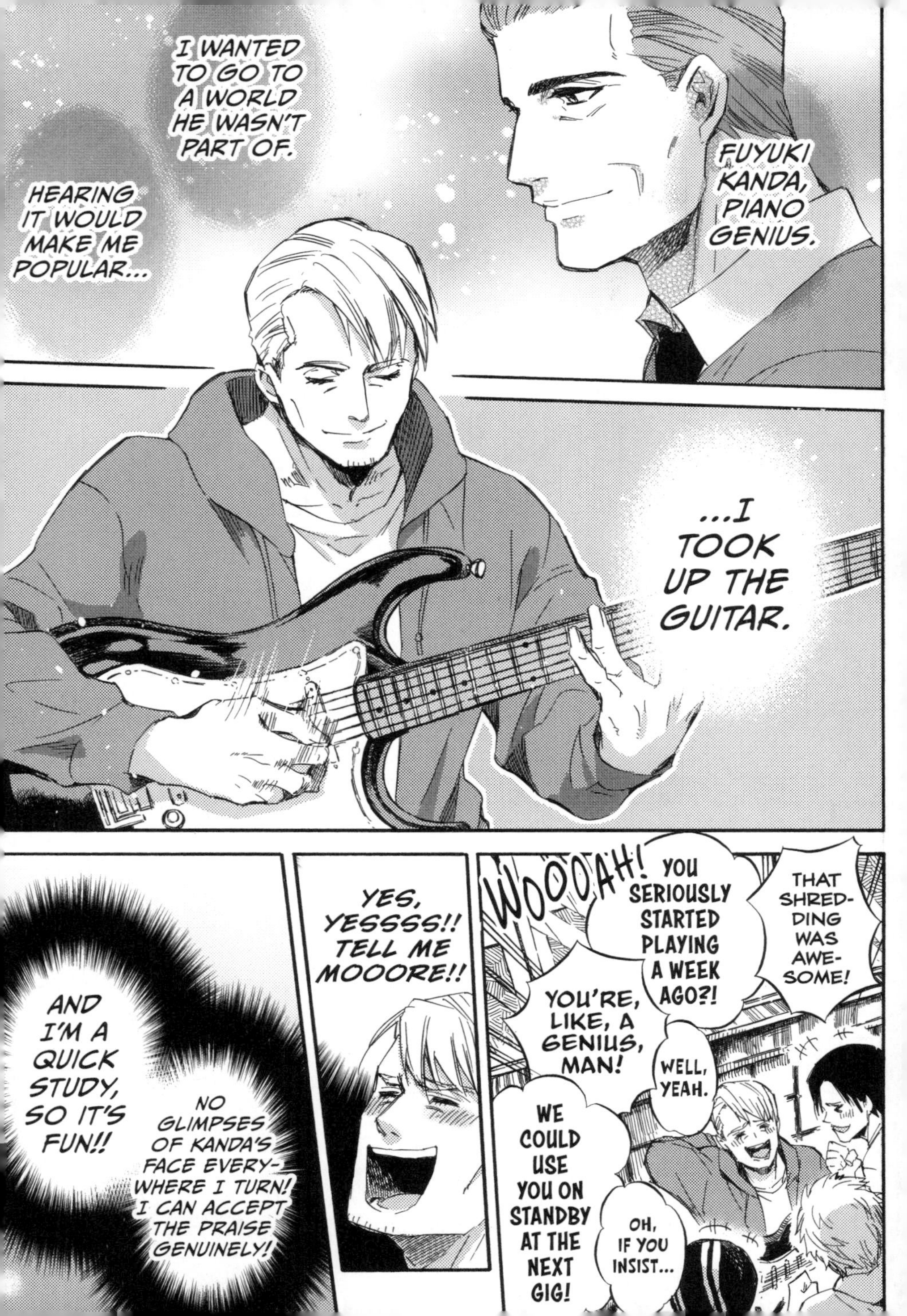
FUYUKI KANDA, PIANO GENIUS.
I WANTED TO GO TO A WORLD HE WASN'T PART OF.
HEARING IT WOULD MAKE ME POPULAR...
...I TOOK UP THE GUITAR.
THAT SHRED-DING WAS AWE-SOME!
WOOOAH!
YOU SERIOUSLY STARTED PLAYING A WEEK AGO?!
YOU'RE, LIKE, A GENIUS, MAN!
WELL, YEAH.
WE COULD USE YOU ON STANDBY AT THE NEXT GIG!
OH, IF YOU INSIST...
YES, YESSSS!! TELL ME MOOORE!!
AND I'M A QUICK STUDY, SO IT'S FUN!!
NO GLIMPSES OF KANDA'S FACE EVERY-WHERE I TURN! I CAN ACCEPT THE PRAISE GENUINELY!

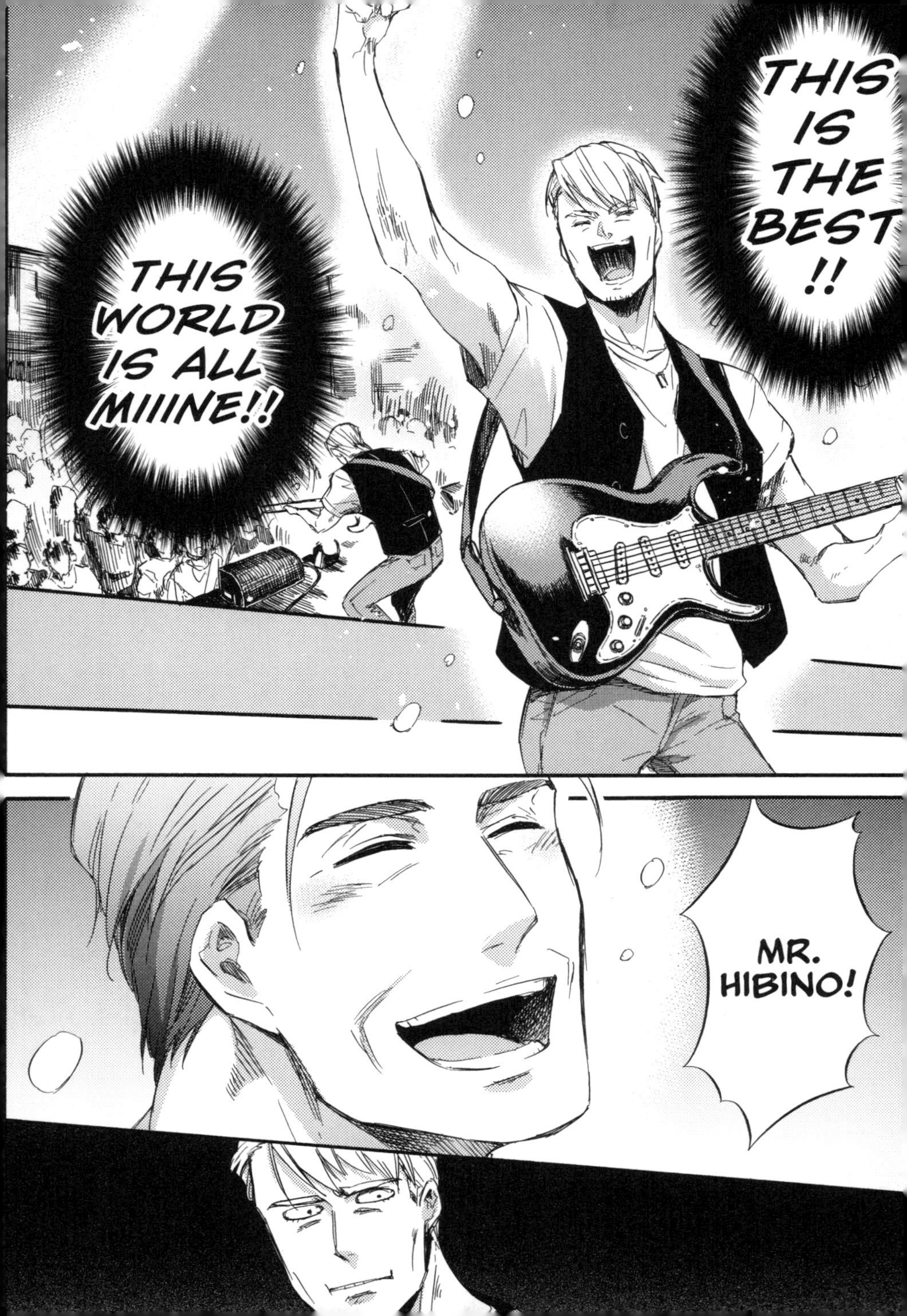
THIS IS THE BEST!!
THIS WORLD IS ALL MIIINE!!
MR. HIBINO!

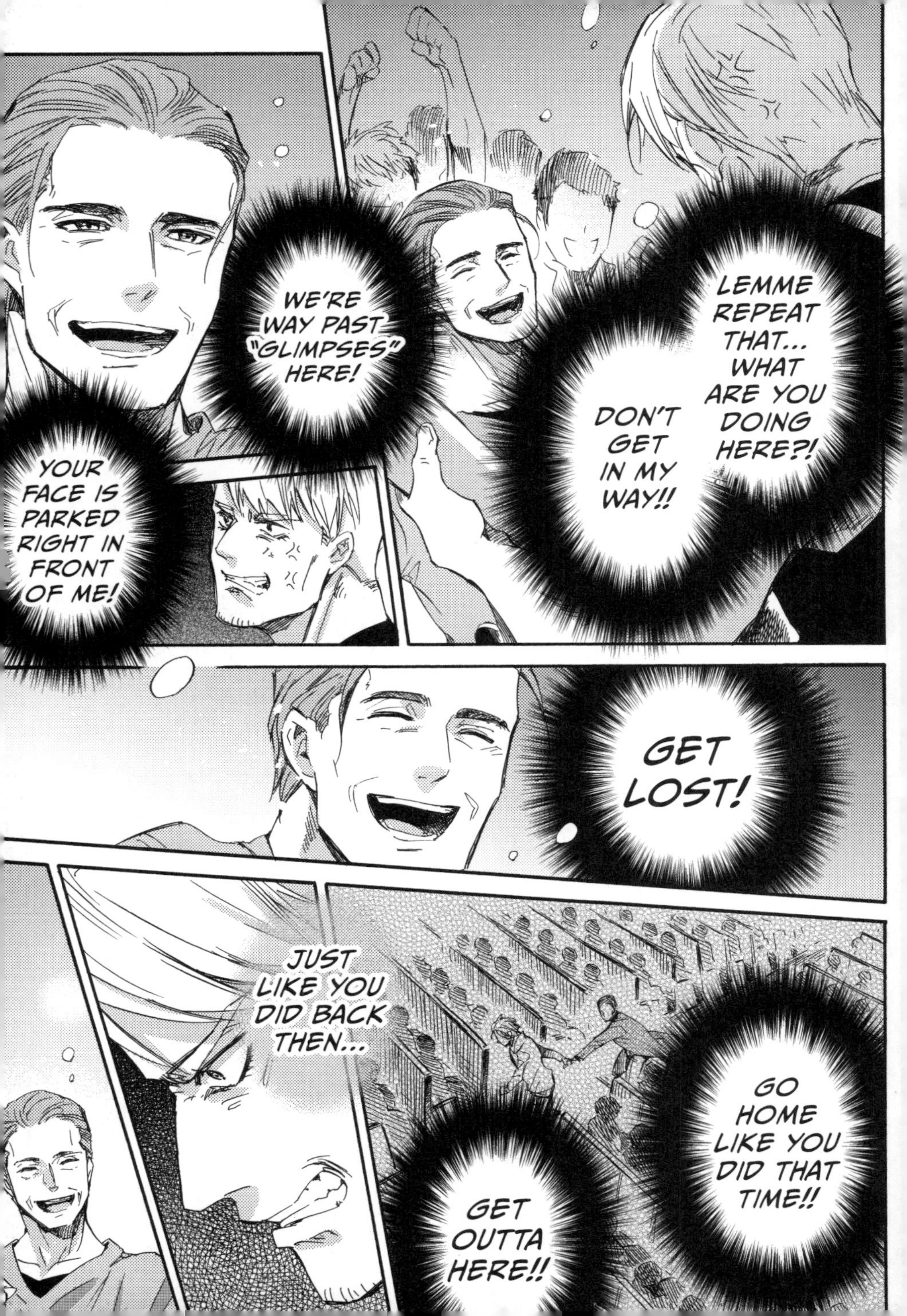
LEMME REPEAT THAT... WHAT ARE YOU DOING HERE?!
DON'T GET IN MY WAY!!
WE'RE WAY PAST "GLIMPSES" HERE!
YOUR FACE IS PARKED RIGHT IN FRONT OF ME!
GET LOST!
GO HOME LIKE YOU DID THAT TIME!!
GET OUTTA HERE!!
JUST LIKE YOU DID BACK THEN...

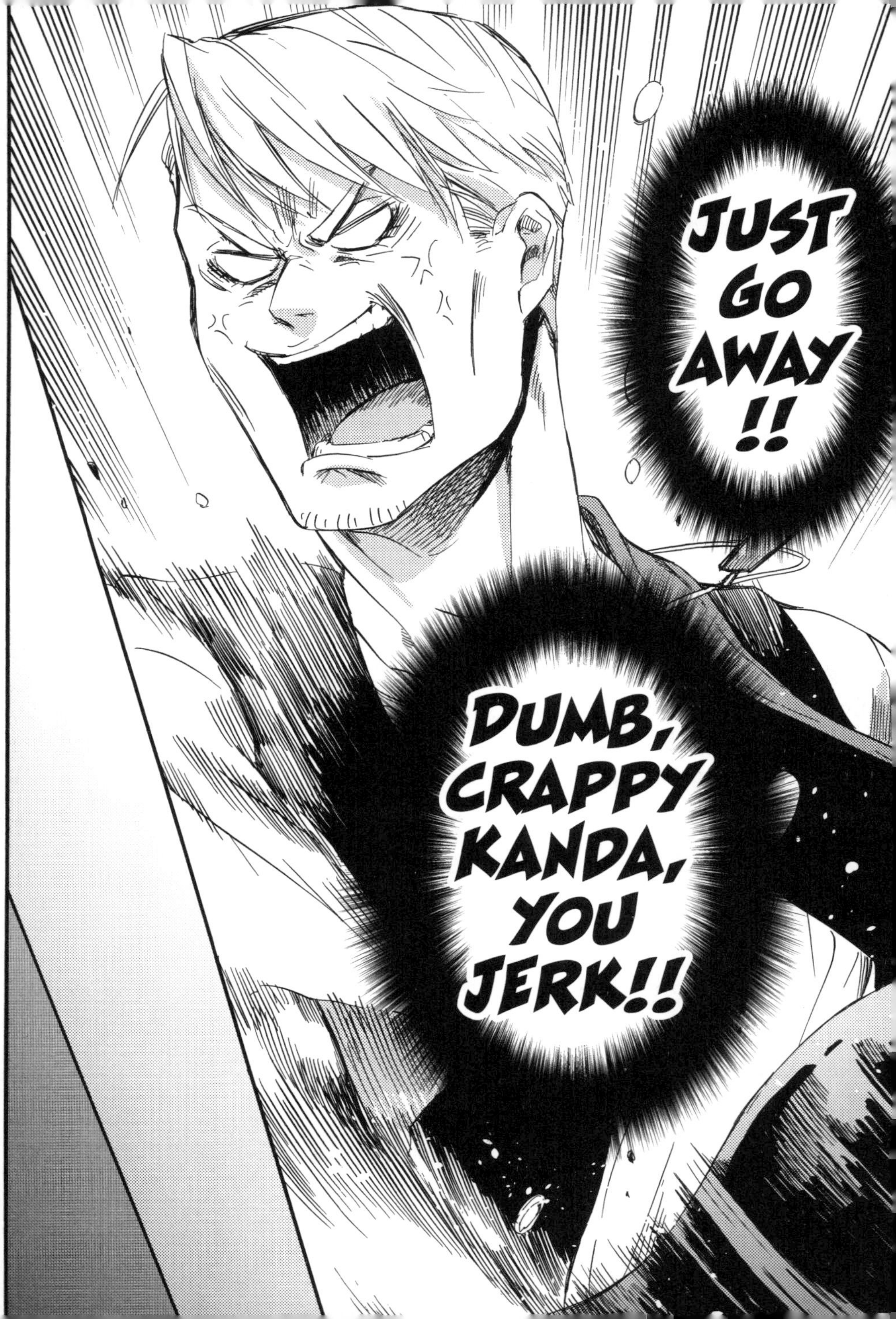
JUST GO AWAY!!
DUMB, CRAPPY KANDA, YOU JERK!!

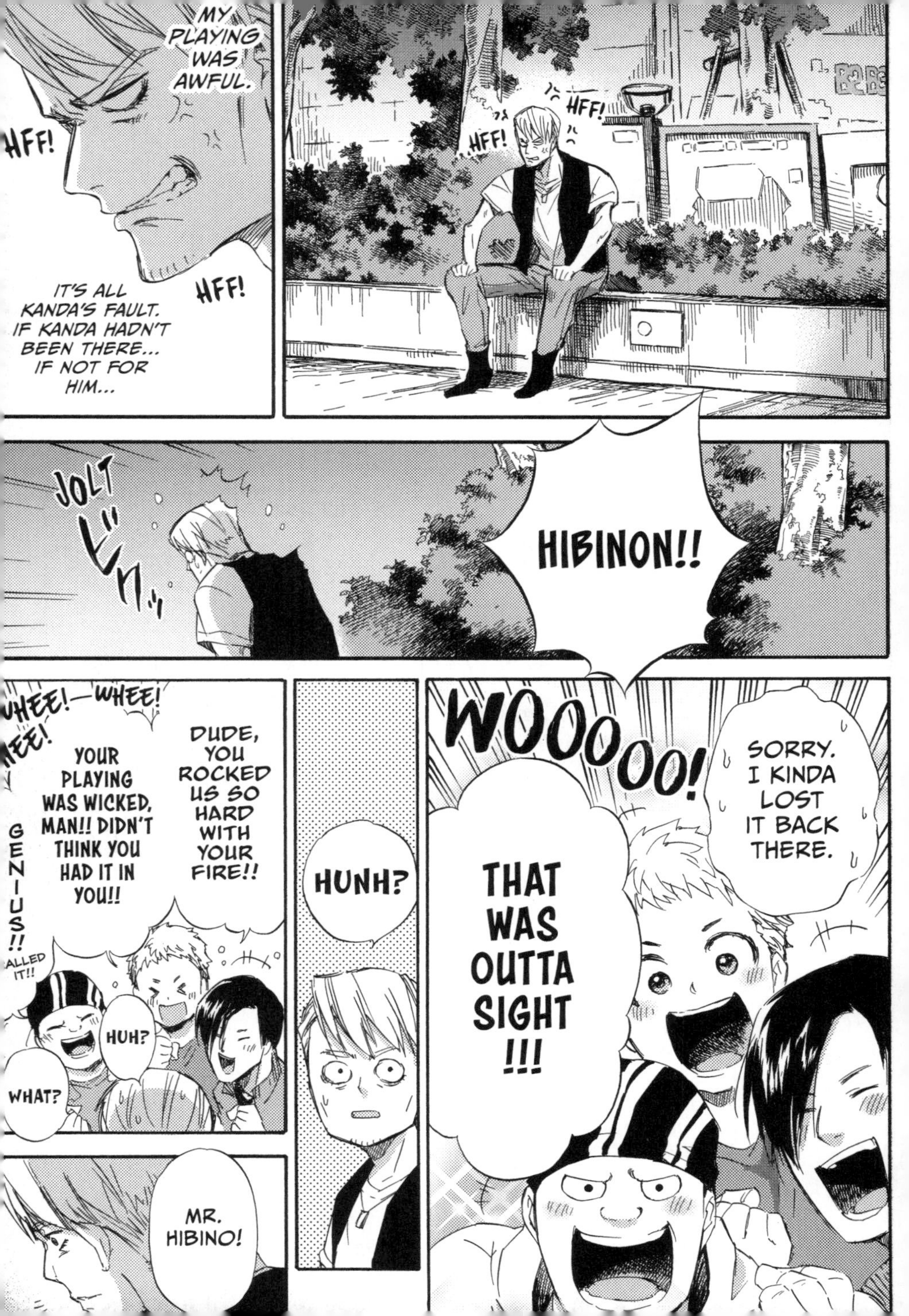
HFF!
HFF!
HFF!
MY PLAYING WAS AWFUL.
HFF!
HFF!
IT'S ALL KANDA'S FAULT. IF KANDA HADN'T BEEN THERE... IF NOT FOR HIM...
HIBINON!!
JOLT
SORRY. I KINDA LOST IT BACK THERE.
WOOOOOO!
THAT WAS OUTTA SIGHT!!!
HUNH?
WHEE!—WHEE!
HEE!
DUDE, YOU ROCKED US SO HARD WITH YOUR FIRE!!
YOUR PLAYING WAS WICKED, MAN!! DIDN'T THINK YOU HAD IT IN YOU!!
GENIUS!!
ALLED IT!!
HUH?
WHAT?
MR. HIBINO!

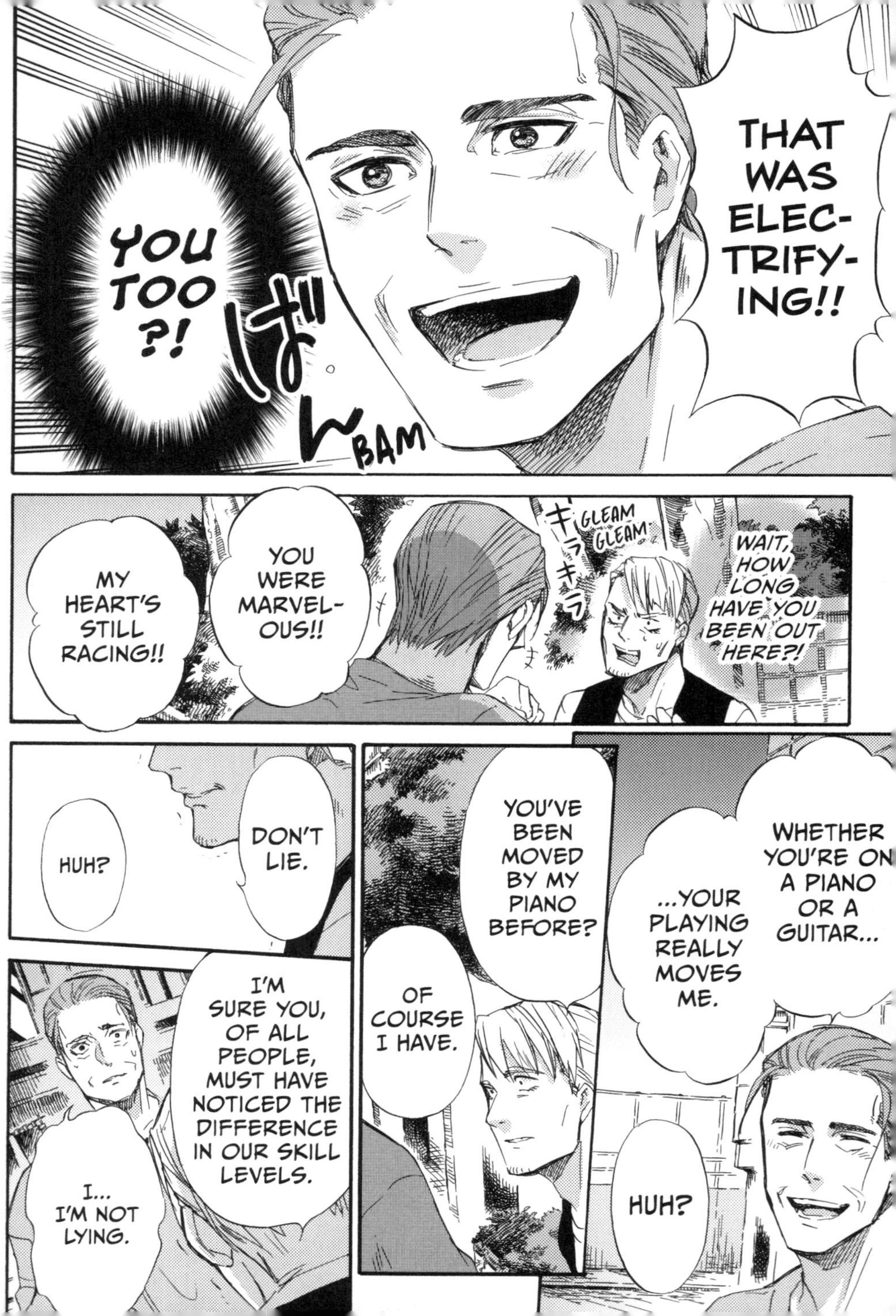
THAT WAS ELEC-TRIFY-ING!!
YOU TOO?!
ばん
BAM
WAIT, HOW LONG HAVE YOU BEEN OUT HERE?!
キラキラ
GLEAM GLEAM
YOU WERE MARVEL-OUS!!
MY HEART'S STILL RACING!!
WHETHER YOU'RE ON A PIANO OR A GUITAR...
...YOUR PLAYING REALLY MOVES ME.
HUH?
YOU'VE BEEN MOVED BY MY PIANO BEFORE?
OF COURSE I HAVE.
DON'T LIE.
HUH?
I'M SURE YOU, OF ALL PEOPLE, MUST HAVE NOTICED THE DIFFERENCE IN OUR SKILL LEVELS.
I... I'M NOT LYING.

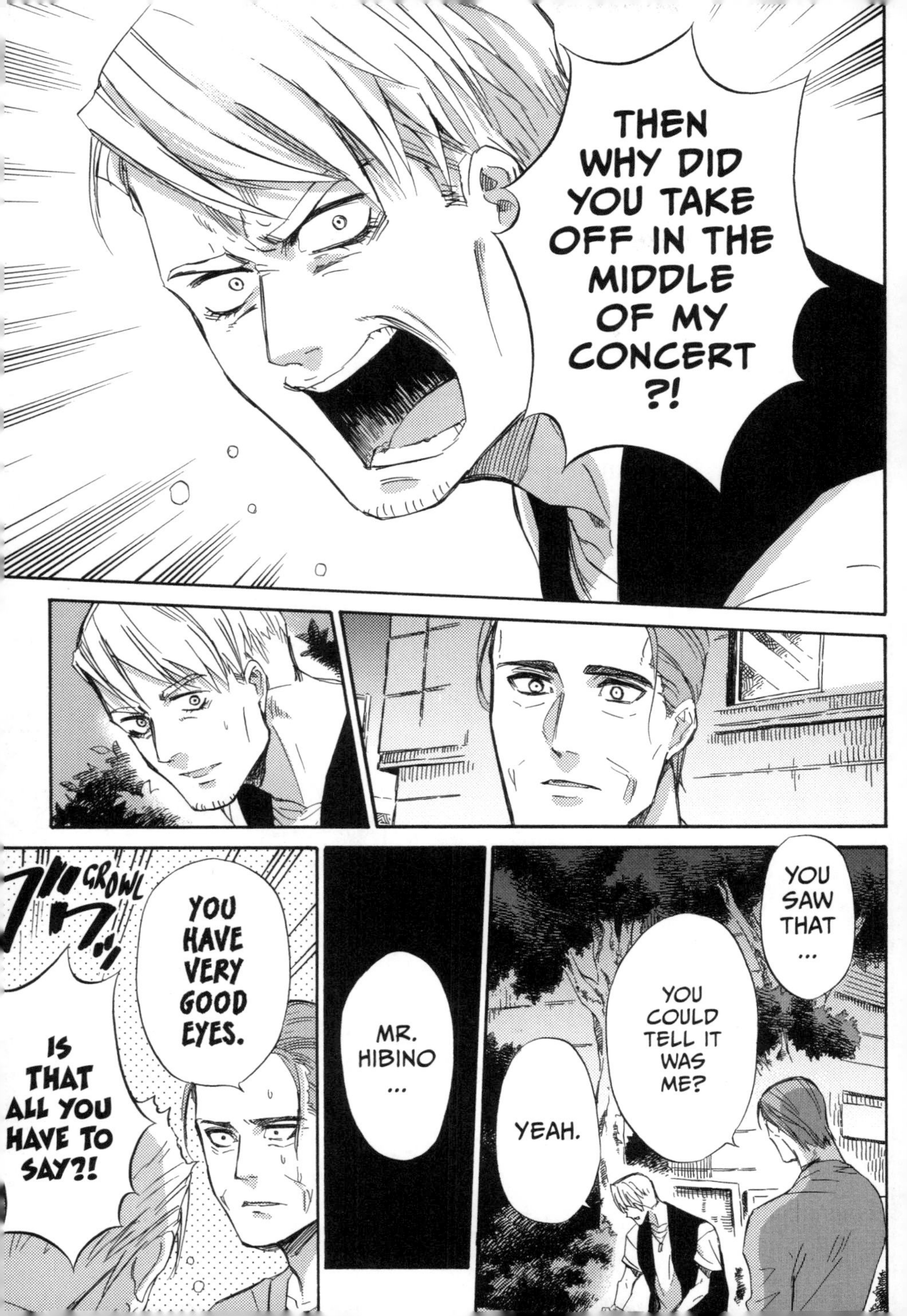
THEN WHY DID YOU TAKE OFF IN THE MIDDLE OF MY CONCERT ?!
YOU SAW THAT ...
YOU COULD TELL IT WAS ME?
YEAH.
MR. HIBINO ...
GROWL
YOU HAVE VERY GOOD EYES.
IS THAT ALL YOU HAVE TO SAY?!

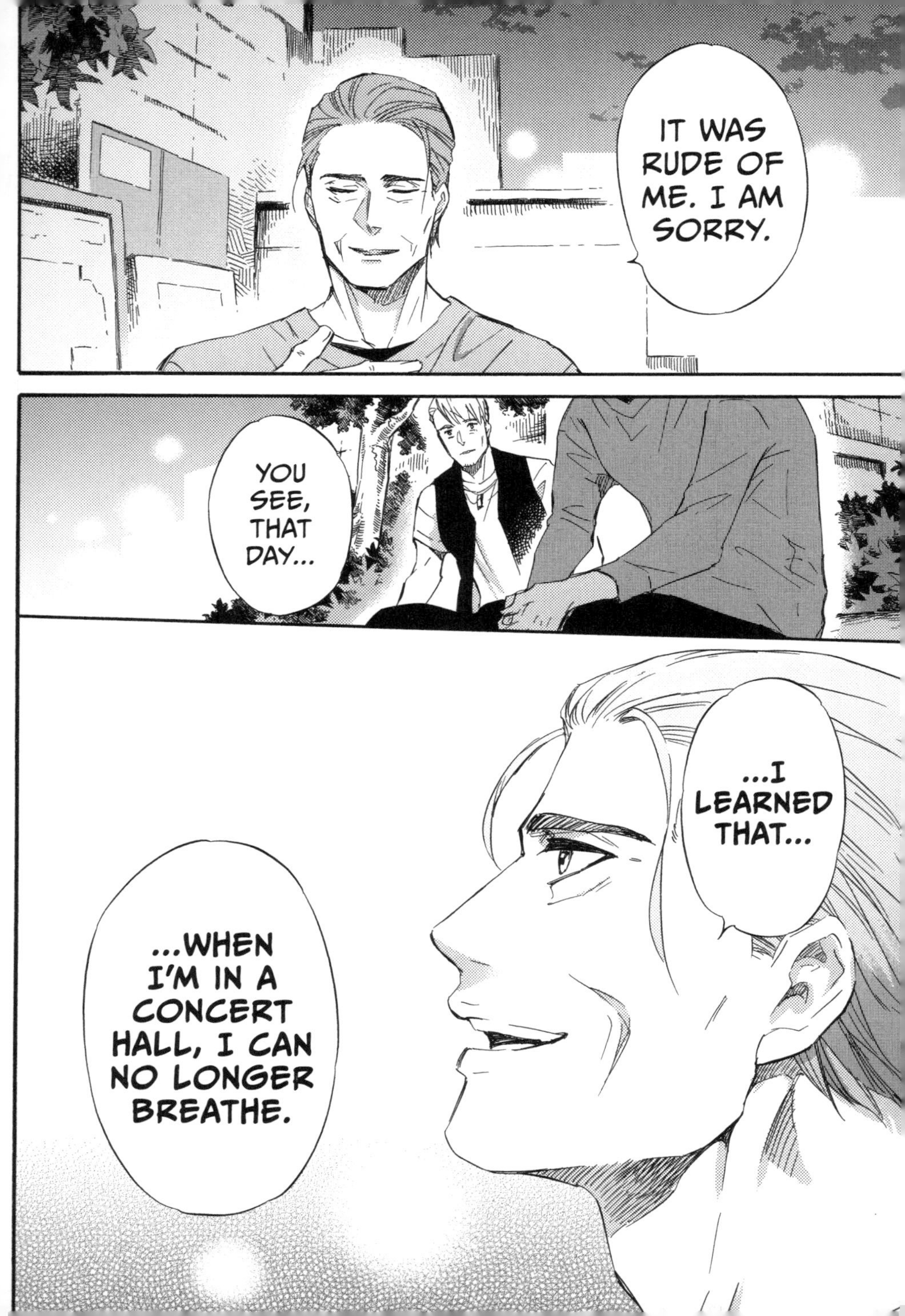
IT WAS RUDE OF ME. I AM SORRY.
YOU SEE, THAT DAY...
...I LEARNED THAT...
...WHEN I'M IN A CONCERT HALL, I CAN NO LONGER BREATHE.

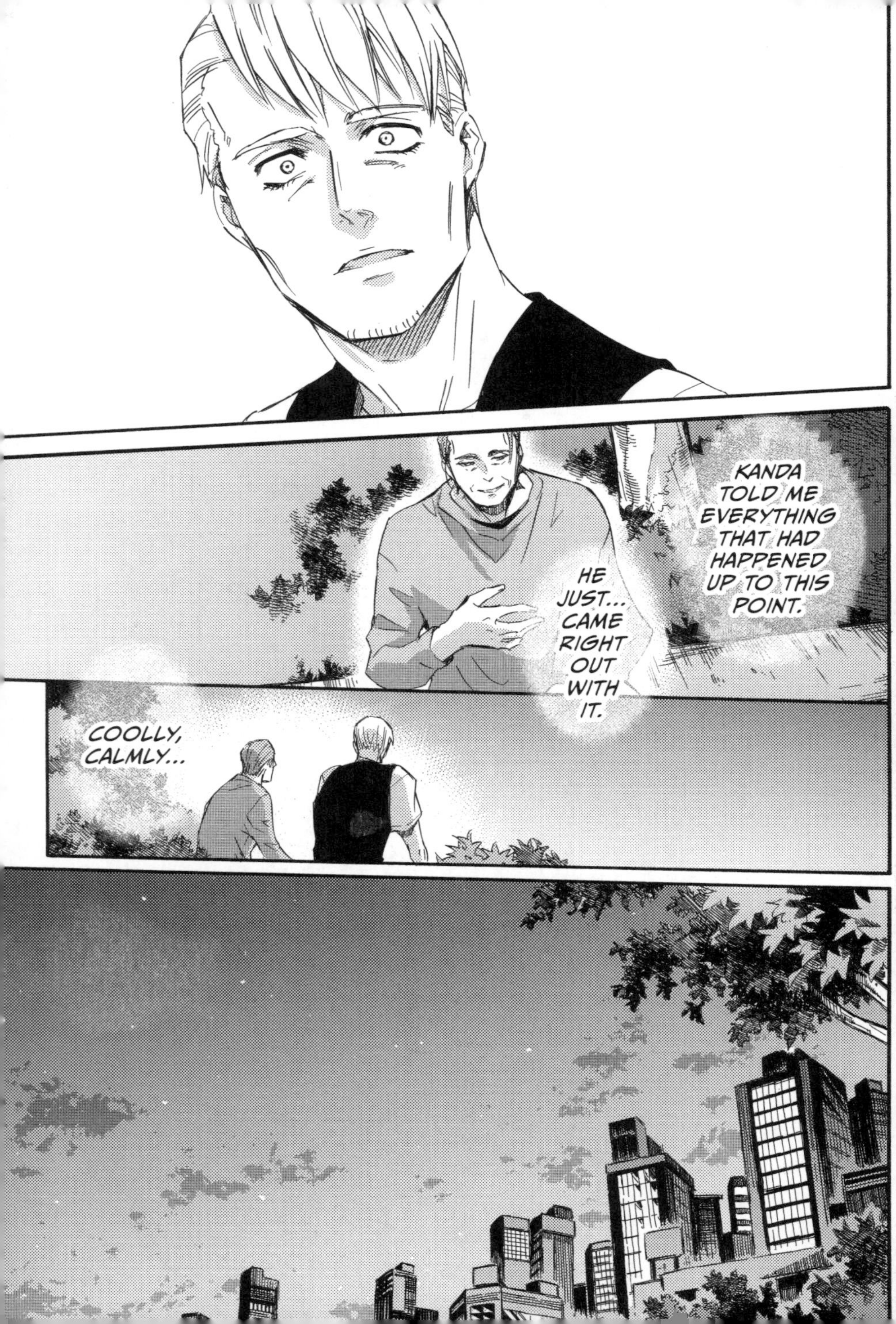
KANDA TOLD ME EVERYTHING THAT HAD HAPPENED UP TO THIS POINT.
HE JUST... CAME RIGHT OUT WITH IT.
COOLLY, CALMLY...

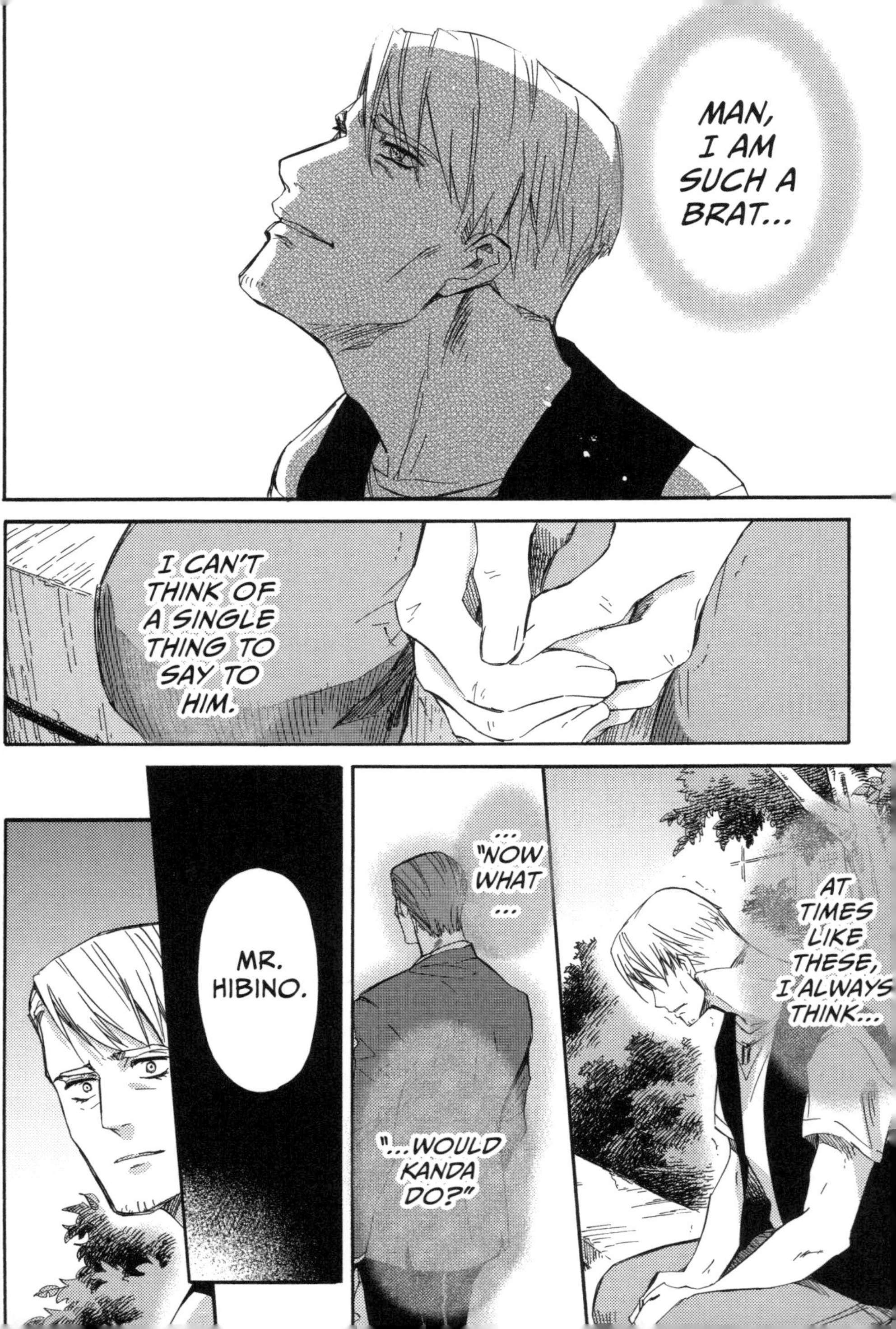
MAN, I AM SUCH A BRAT...
I CAN'T THINK OF A SINGLE THING TO SAY TO HIM.
AT TIMES LIKE THESE, I ALWAYS THINK...
... "NOW WHAT ...
"...WOULD KANDA DO?"
MR. HIBINO.

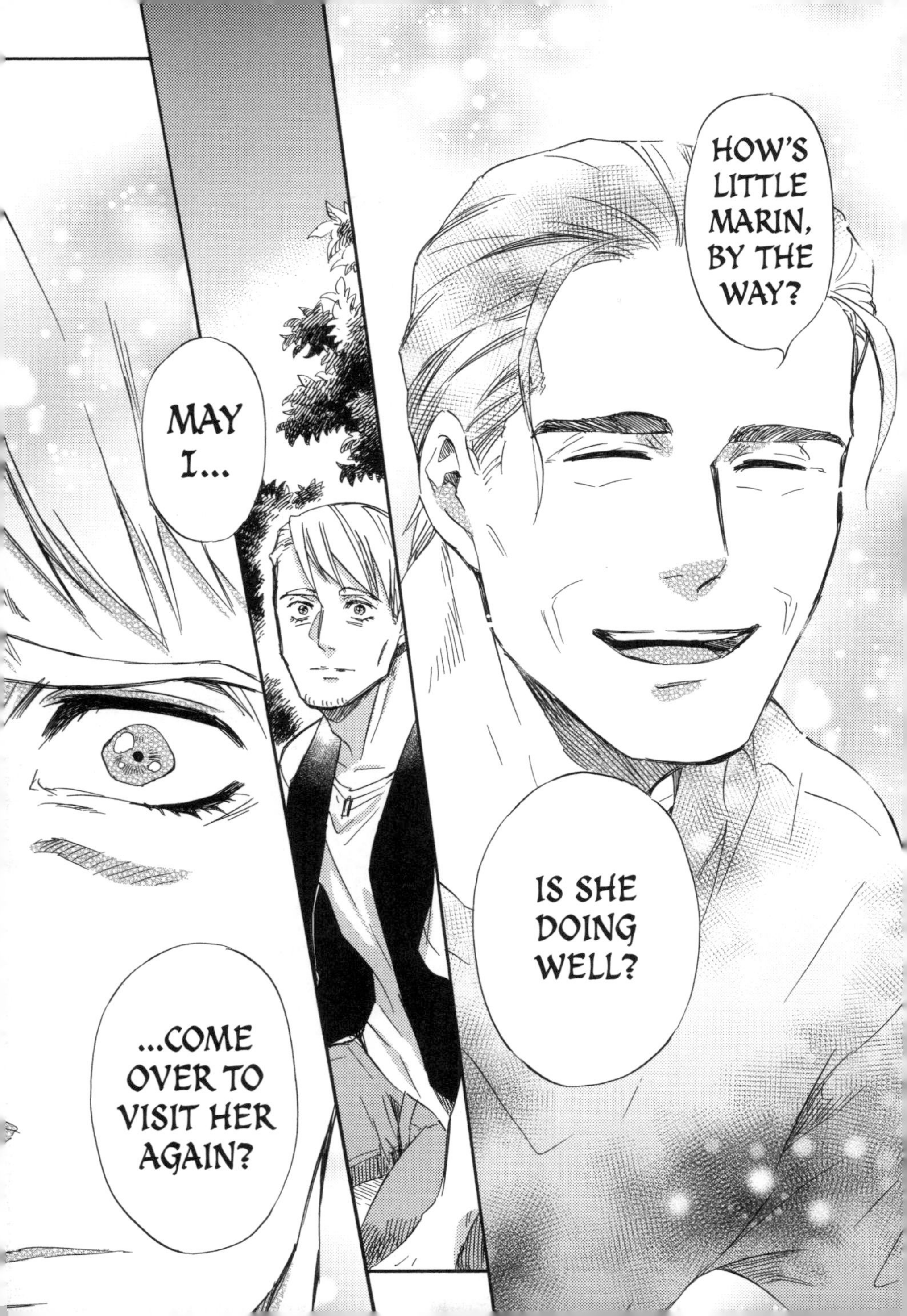
HOW'S LITTLE MARIN, BY THE WAY?
IS SHE DOING WELL?
MAY I...
...COME OVER TO VISIT HER AGAIN?

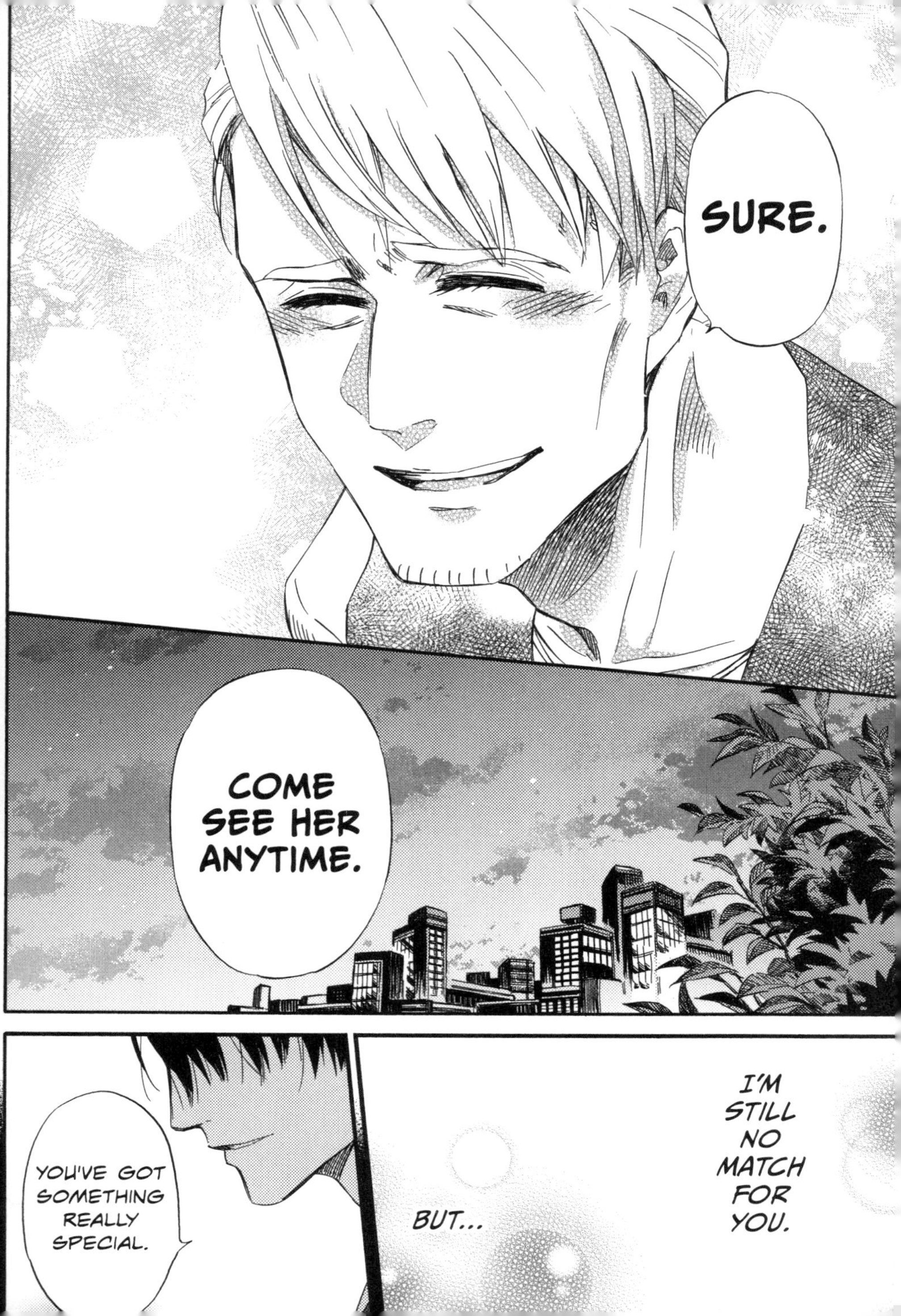
SURE.
COME SEE HER ANYTIME.
I'M STILL NO MATCH FOR YOU.
BUT...
YOU'VE GOT SOMETHING REALLY SPECIAL.

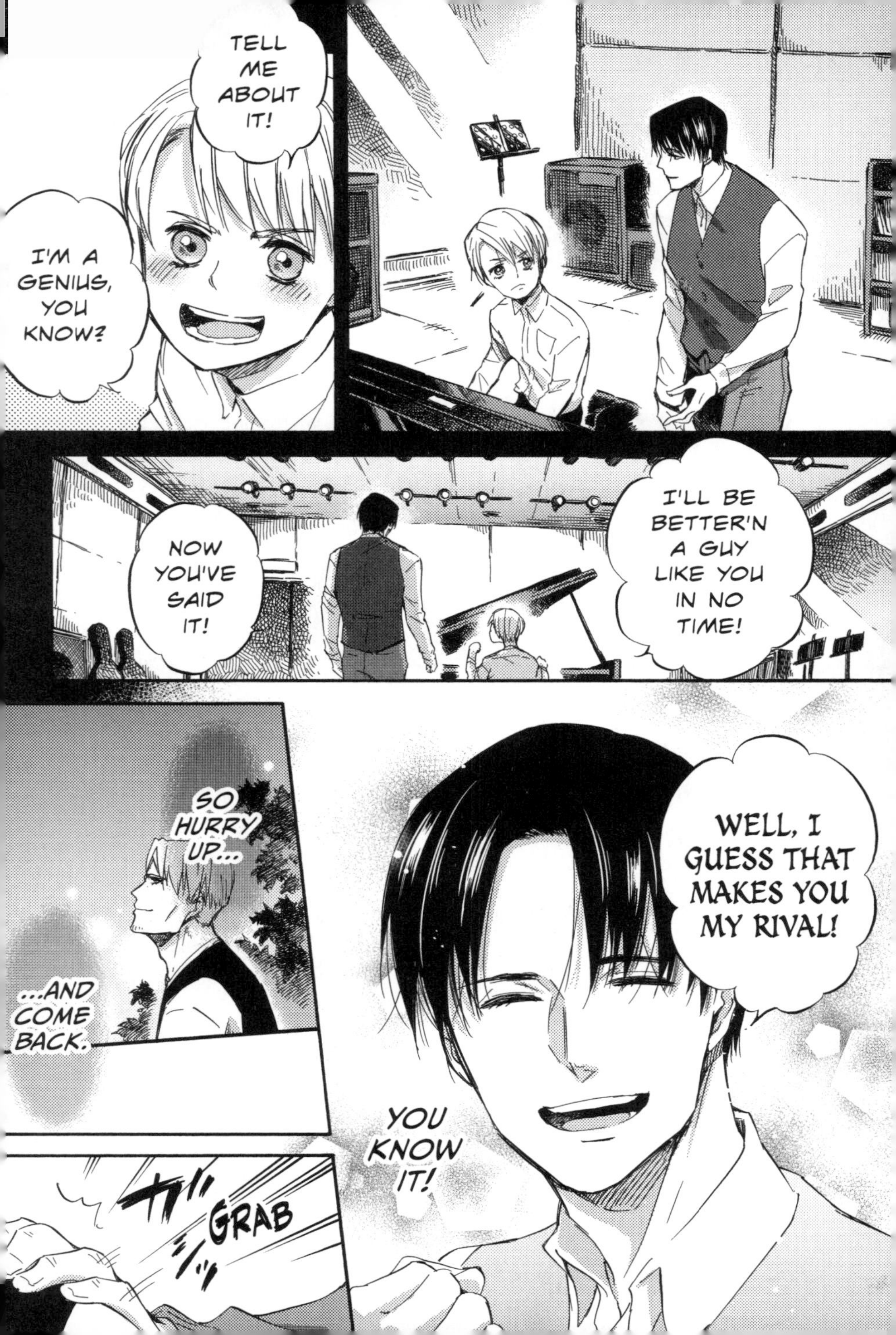
TELL ME ABOUT IT!
I'M A GENIUS, YOU KNOW?
I'LL BE BETTER'N A GUY LIKE YOU IN NO TIME!
NOW YOU'VE SAID IT!
WELL, I GUESS THAT MAKES YOU MY RIVAL!
YOU KNOW IT!
SO HURRY UP...
...AND COME BACK.
GRAB

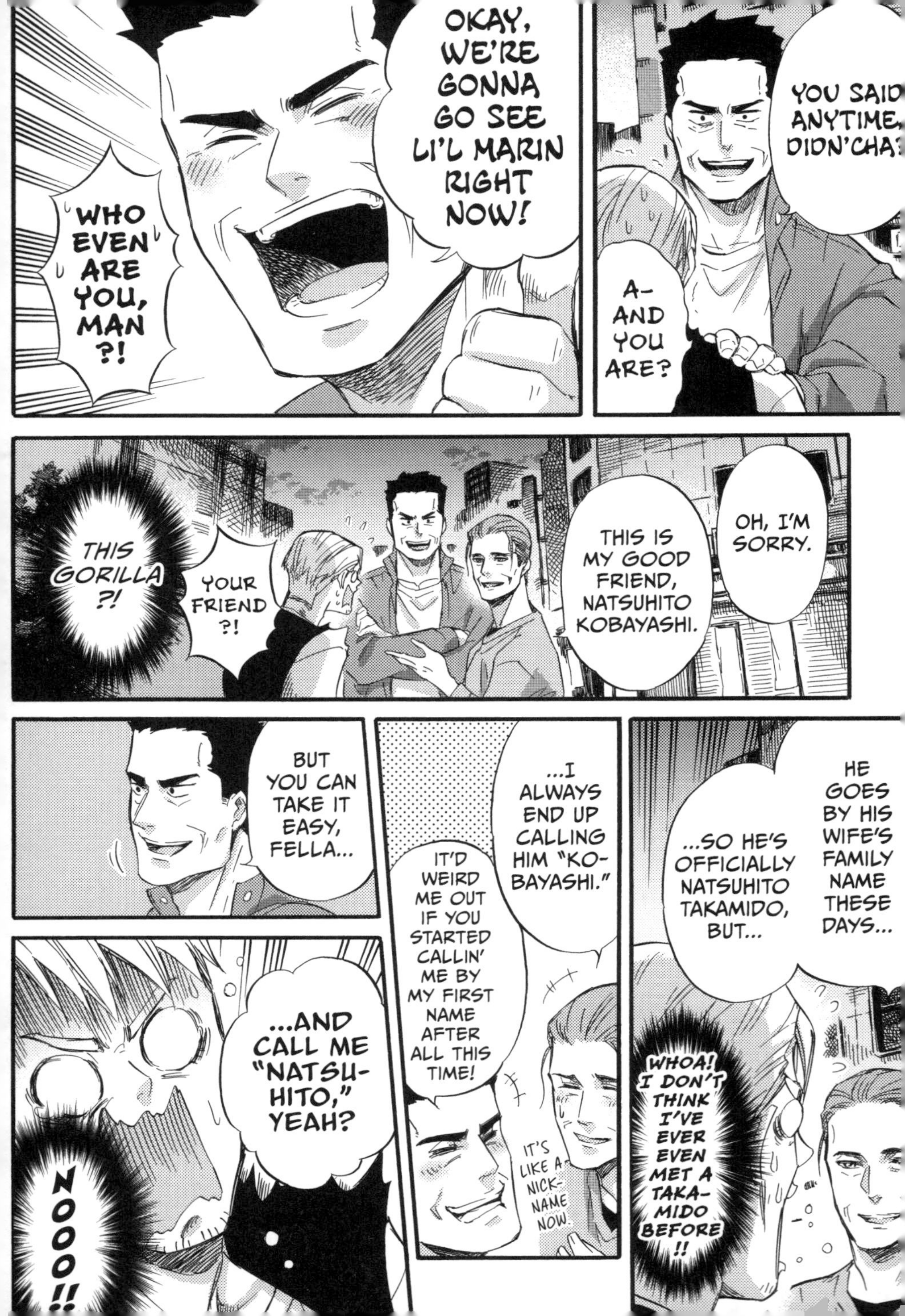
YOU SAID ANYTIME, DIDN'CHA?
A- AND YOU ARE?
OKAY, WE'RE GONNA GO SEE LI'L MARIN RIGHT NOW!
WHO EVEN ARE YOU, MAN?!
OH, I'M SORRY.
THIS IS MY GOOD FRIEND, NATSUHITO KOBAYASHI.
YOUR FRIEND?!
THIS GORILLA?!
HE GOES BY HIS WIFE'S FAMILY NAME THESE DAYS...
...SO HE'S OFFICIALLY NATSUHITO TAKAMIDO, BUT...
WHOA! I DON'T THINK I'VE EVER EVEN MET A TAKAMIDO BEFORE!!
...I ALWAYS END UP CALLING HIM "KO-BAYASHI."
IT'D WEIRD ME OUT IF YOU STARTED CALLIN' ME BY MY FIRST NAME AFTER ALL THIS TIME!
IT'S LIKE A NICK-NAME NOW.
BUT YOU CAN TAKE IT EASY, FELLA...
...AND CALL ME "NATSU-HITO," YEAH?
NOOOO!!

MARIN

BIRTHDAY: JUNE 12
HEIGHT: PLEASANTLY PLUMP
FAVORITE FOOD: GOURMET CRUNCHIES

FUKUMARU'S BIG SIS.
SHE HAS A CALM PERSONALITY.
A KITTY WHO LOVES HER OWNER, HIBINO.
SHE FOLLOWS HIM EVERYWHERE...
EVEN INTO THE BATHROOM, NATURALLY.

KANADE HIBINO

BIRTHDAY: SEPTEMBER 4
HEIGHT: 179CM (APPROX. 5'10½")
FAVORITE FOOD: COD ROE, NATTO

HE CAME TO LOVE HIS FAVORITES AS A
CHILD, WHEN HE WASN'T ALLOWED TO
USE KITCHEN KNIVES OR THE STOVE.

A PIANIST WHO SEES KANDA AS HIS RIVAL.
HE DOESN'T KNOW WHO HIS FATHER IS.

YOSHIHARU MORIYAMA

BIRTHDAY: MARCH 3
HEIGHT: 173CM (APPROX. 5'8")
FAVORITE FOOD: OMELET-ROLLED FRIED RICE,
SAKURA MOCHI

HE'S BEEN NUTS ABOUT FUYUKI KANDA FROM
THE MOMENT HE FIRST LAID EYES ON THE MAN.
HIS WEIRD T-SHIRTS ARE DESIGNED BY HIS DAD.
HE STARTED WEARING THEM BECAUSE THEY WERE
TOO CORNY, AND THEN BEING TOO CORNY
BECAME HIS THING.

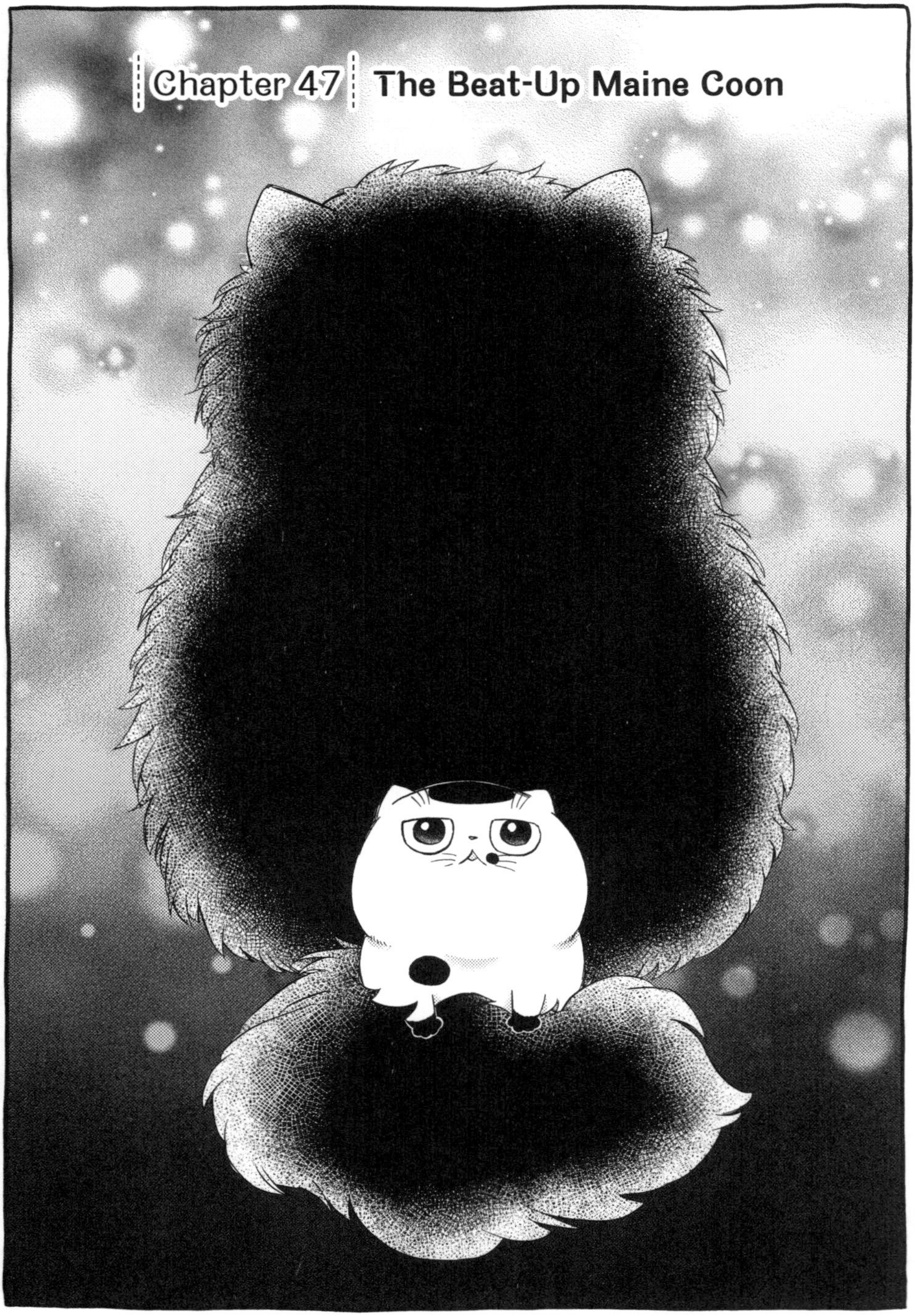
Chapter 47 The Beat-Up Maine Coon

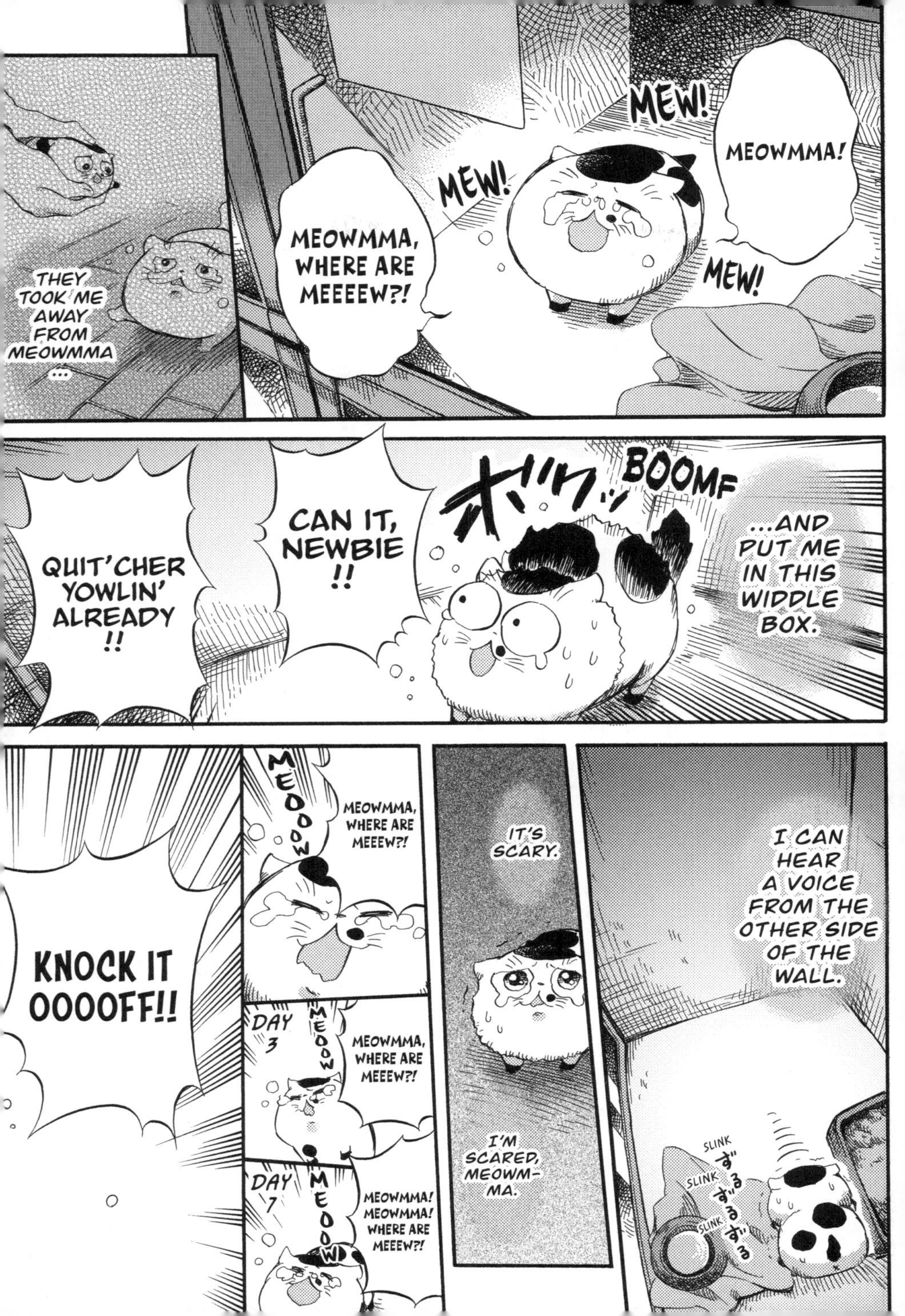
MEOWMMA!
MEW!
MEW!
MEW!
MEOWMMA, WHERE ARE MEEEEW?!
THEY TOOK ME AWAY FROM MEOWMMA ...
...AND PUT ME IN THIS WIDDLE BOX.
BOOMF
CAN IT, NEWBIE !!
QUIT'CHER YOWLIN' ALREADY !!
I CAN HEAR A VOICE FROM THE OTHER SIDE OF THE WALL.
SLINK ずる
SLINK ずる
SLINK ずる
ずる
IT'S SCARY.
I'M SCARED, MEOWMMA.
MEOOOW
MEOWMMA, WHERE ARE MEEEW?!
DAY 3
MEOOW
MEOWMMA, WHERE ARE MEEEW?!
DAY 7
MEOOOW
MEOWMMA! MEOWMMA! WHERE ARE MEEEW?!
KNOCK IT OOOOFF!!

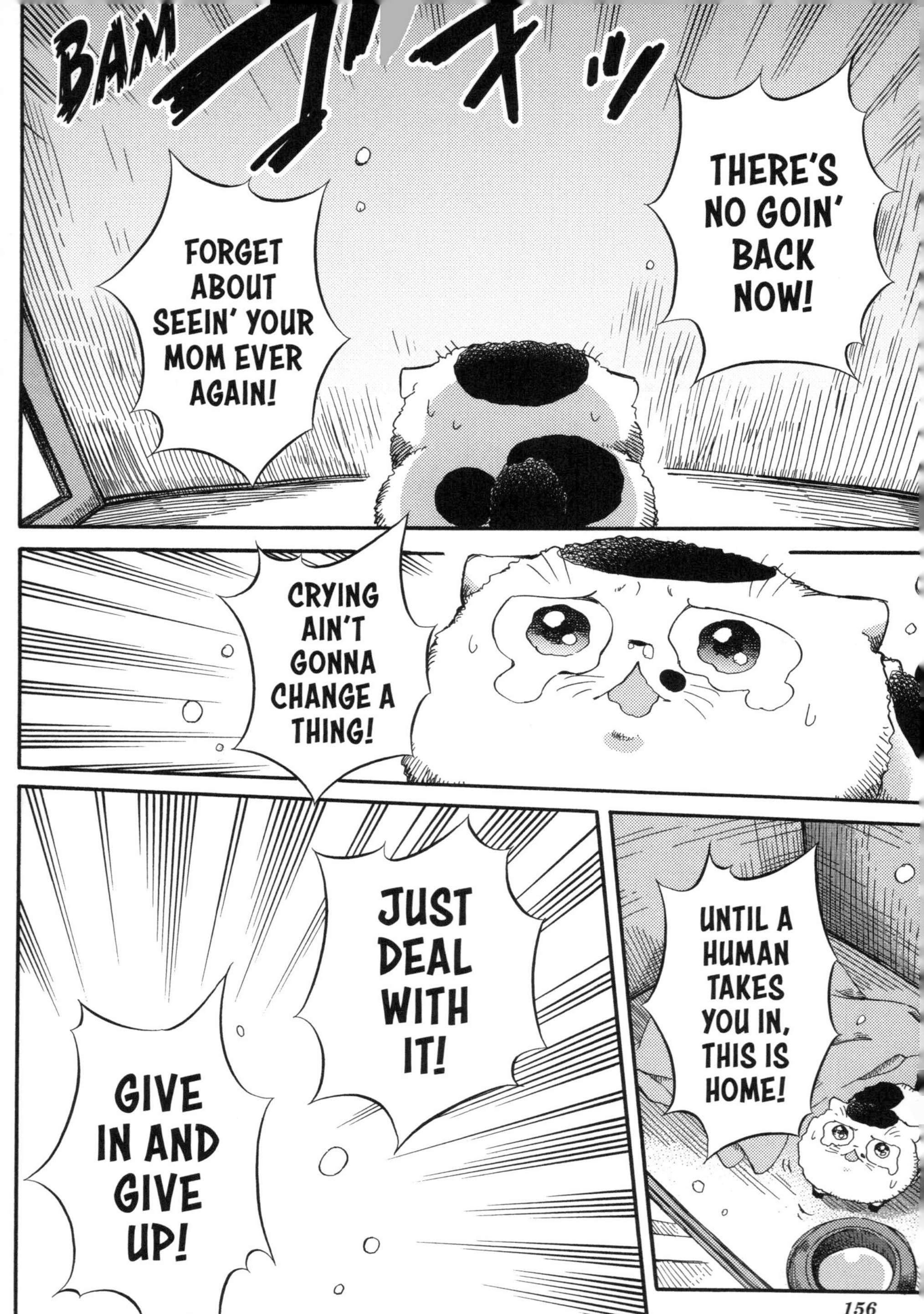
BAM
THERE'S NO GOIN' BACK NOW!
FORGET ABOUT SEEIN' YOUR MOM EVER AGAIN!
CRYING AIN'T GONNA CHANGE A THING!
UNTIL A HUMAN TAKES YOU IN, THIS IS HOME!
JUST DEAL WITH IT!
GIVE IN AND GIVE UP!

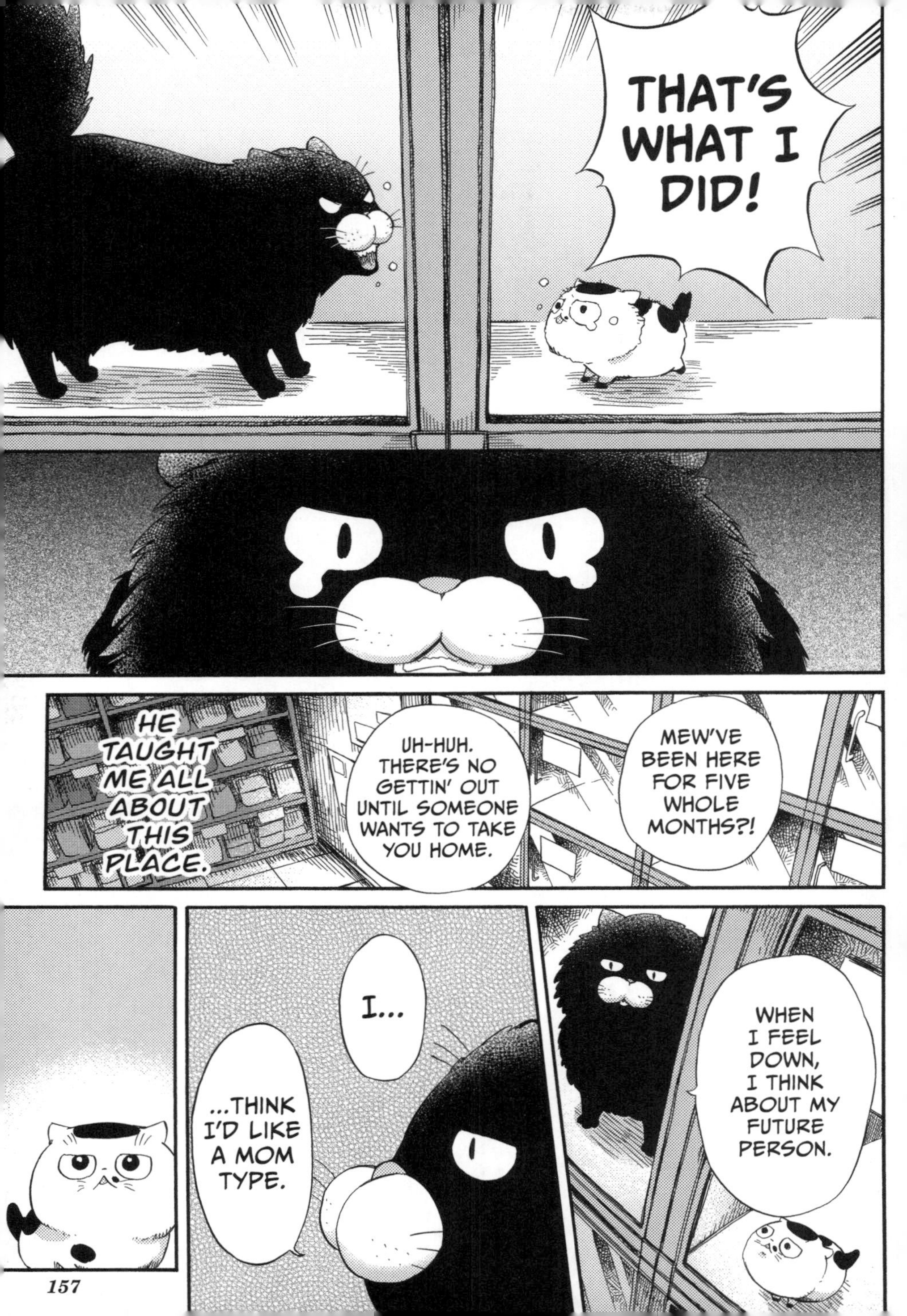
THAT'S WHAT I DID!
MEW'VE BEEN HERE FOR FIVE WHOLE MONTHS?!
UH-HUH. THERE'S NO GETTIN' OUT UNTIL SOMEONE WANTS TO TAKE YOU HOME.
HE TAUGHT ME ALL ABOUT THIS PLACE.
WHEN I FEEL DOWN, I THINK ABOUT MY FUTURE PERSON.
I...
...THINK I'D LIKE A MOM TYPE.

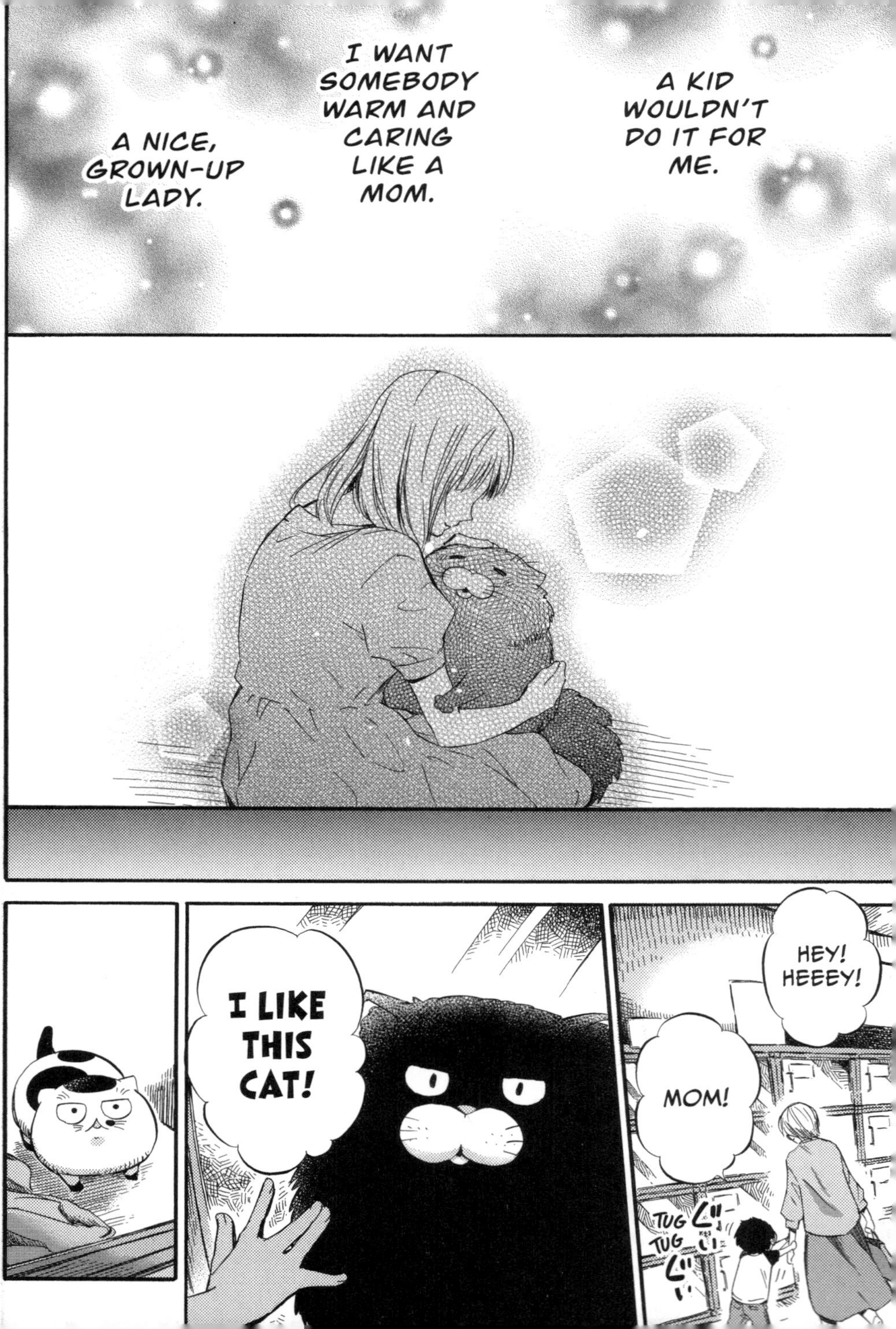
A KID WOULDN'T DO IT FOR ME.
I WANT SOMEBODY WARM AND CARING LIKE A MOM.
A NICE, GROWN-UP LADY.
HEY! HEEEY!
MOM!
TUG TUG
I LIKE THIS CAT!

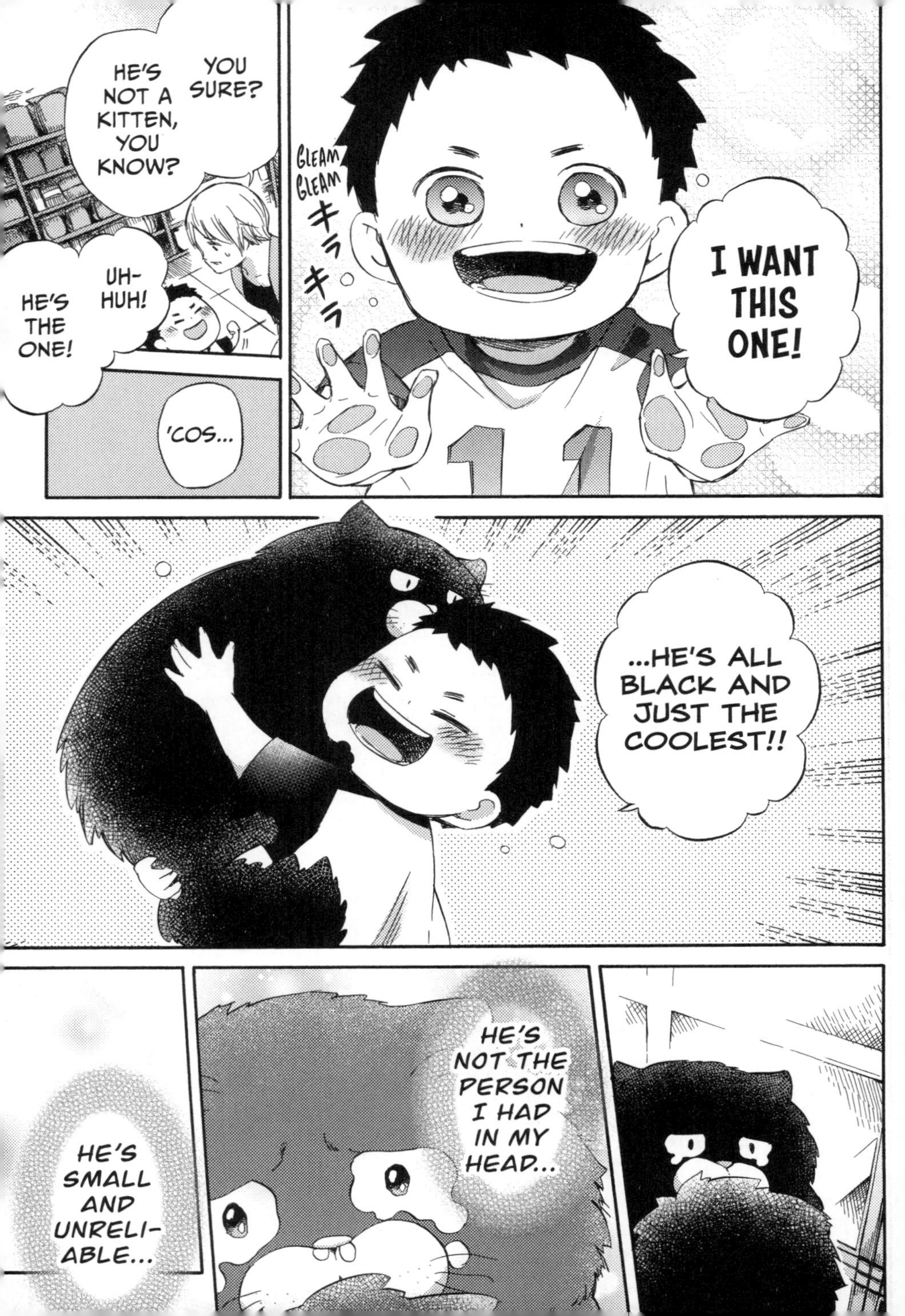
GLEAM GLEAM
キラキラ
I WANT THIS ONE!
YOU SURE?
HE'S NOT A KITTEN, YOU KNOW?
UH-HUH!
HE'S THE ONE!
'COS...
...HE'S ALL BLACK AND JUST THE COOLEST!!
HE'S NOT THE PERSON I HAD IN MY HEAD...
HE'S SMALL AND UNRELIABLE...

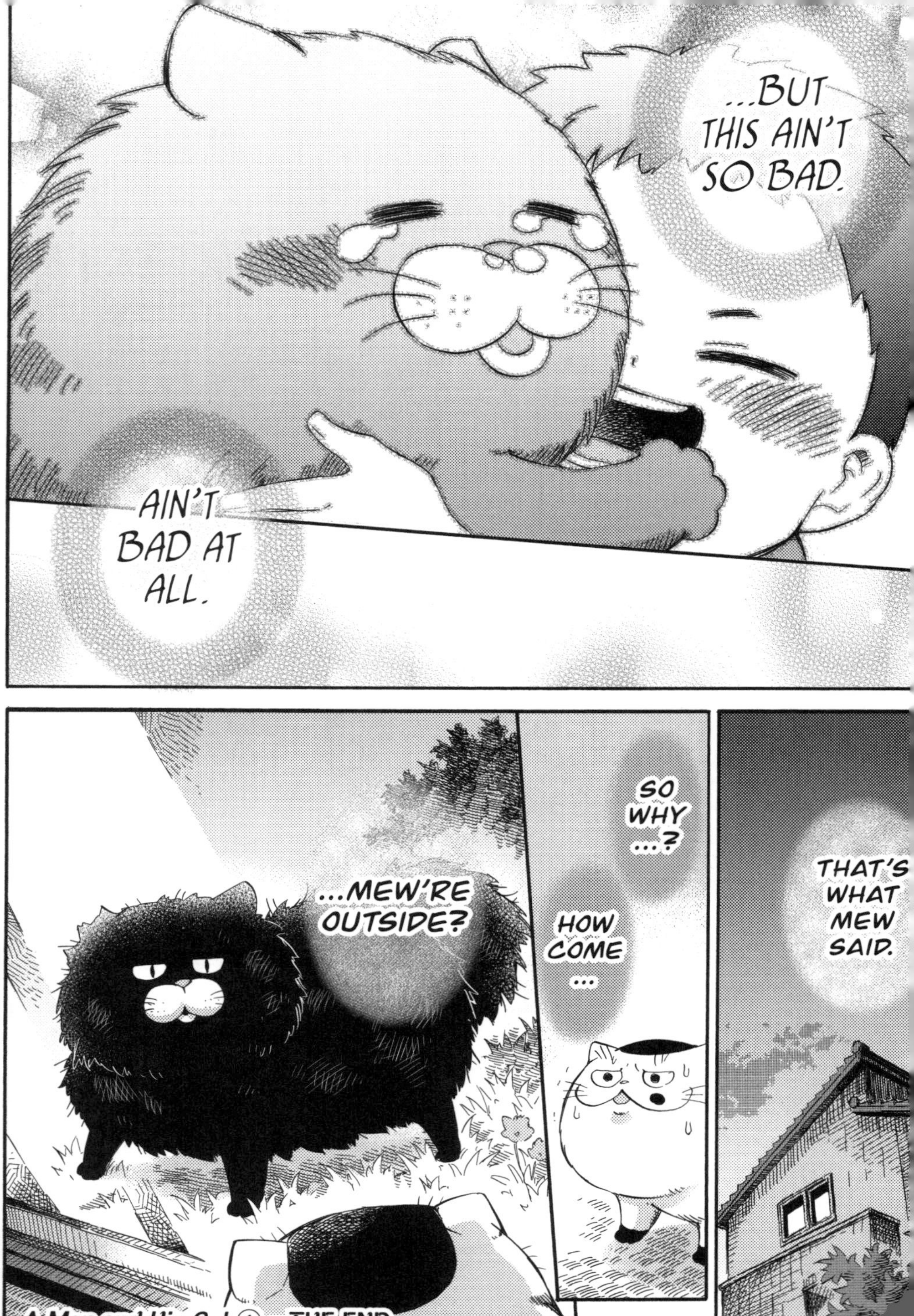
...BUT THIS AIN'T SO BAD.
AIN'T BAD AT ALL.
THAT'S WHAT MEW SAID.
SO WHY ...?
HOW COME ...
...MEW'RE OUTSIDE?

A Man and His Cat ④ – THE END

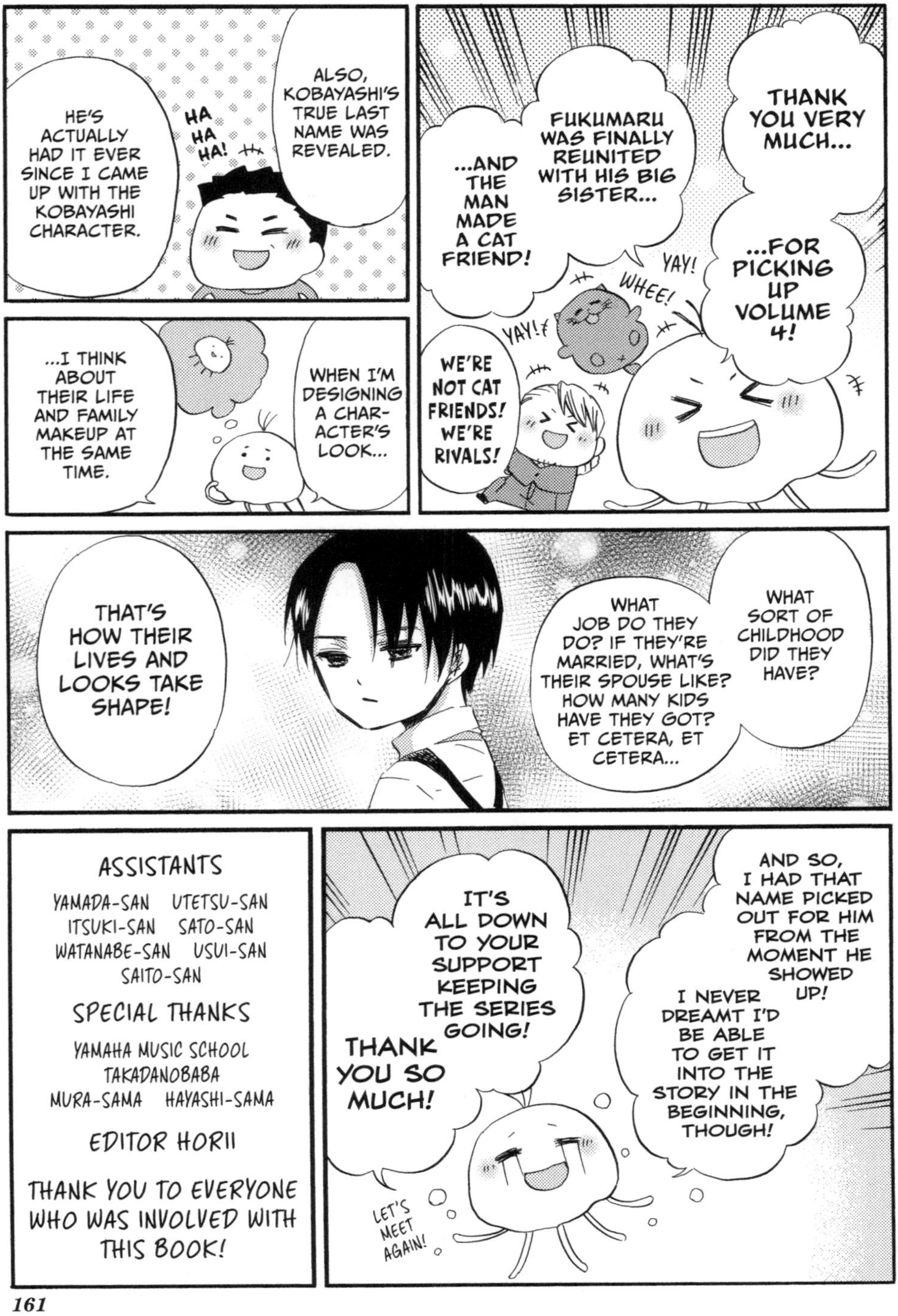
THANK YOU VERY MUCH...
...FOR PICKING UP VOLUME 4!
FUKUMARU WAS FINALLY REUNITED WITH HIS BIG SISTER...
...AND THE MAN MADE A CAT FRIEND!
YAY!
WHEE!
YAY!
WE'RE NOT CAT FRIENDS! WE'RE RIVALS!
ALSO, KOBAYASHI'S TRUE LAST NAME WAS REVEALED.
HA HA HA!
HE'S ACTUALLY HAD IT EVER SINCE I CAME UP WITH THE KOBAYASHI CHARACTER.
WHEN I'M DESIGNING A CHAR-ACTER'S LOOK...
...I THINK ABOUT THEIR LIFE AND FAMILY MAKEUP AT THE SAME TIME.
WHAT SORT OF CHILDHOOD DID THEY HAVE?
WHAT JOB DO THEY DO? IF THEY'RE MARRIED, WHAT'S THEIR SPOUSE LIKE? HOW MANY KIDS HAVE THEY GOT? ET CETERA, ET CETERA...
THAT'S HOW THEIR LIVES AND LOOKS TAKE SHAPE!
AND SO, I HAD THAT NAME PICKED OUT FOR HIM FROM THE MOMENT HE SHOWED UP!
I NEVER DREAMT I'D BE ABLE TO GET IT INTO THE STORY IN THE BEGINNING, THOUGH!
IT'S ALL DOWN TO YOUR SUPPORT KEEPING THE SERIES GOING!
THANK YOU SO MUCH!
LET'S MEET AGAIN!
ASSISTANTS
YAMADA-SAN UTETSU-SAN
ITSUKI-SAN SATO-SAN
WATANABE-SAN USUI-SAN
SAITO-SAN
SPECIAL THANKS
YAMAHA MUSIC SCHOOL
TAKADANOBABA
MURA-SAMA HAYASHI-SAMA
EDITOR HORII
THANK YOU TO EVERYONE WHO WAS INVOLVED WITH THIS BOOK!

 A Man & His Cat

4

Story and Art by
Umi Sakurai

Translation: **Taylor Engel**
Lettering: **Lys Blakeslee**
Cover Design: **Tania Biswas**
Editor: **Tania Biswas**

A MAN AND HIS CAT Volume 4
© 2020 Umi Sakurai/SQUARE ENIX CO., LTD.
First published in Japan in 2020 by SQUARE ENIX CO., LTD.
English translation rights arranged with SQUARE ENIX CO., LTD.
and SQUARE ENIX, INC.
English translation © 2021 by SQUARE ENIX CO., LTD.

ISBN: 978-1-64609-093-8

Library of Congress Cataloging-in-Publication data
is on file with the publisher.

Printed in the U.S.A.
First printing, September 2021
10 9 8 7 6 5 4 3 2 1

SQUARE ENIX
MANGA & BOOKS
www.square-enix-books.com

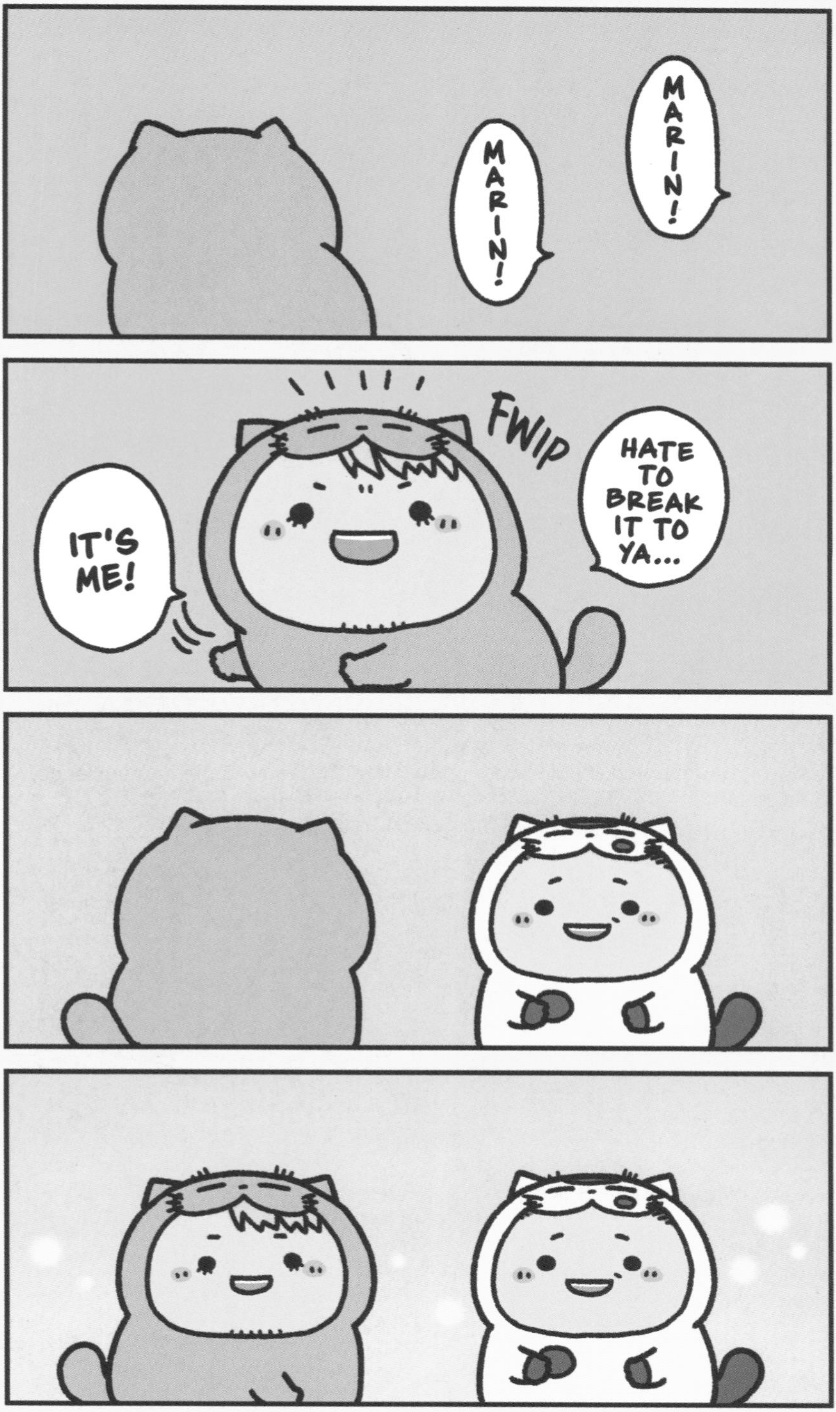
MARIN!
MARIN!
HATE TO BREAK IT TO YA...
FWIP
IT'S ME!

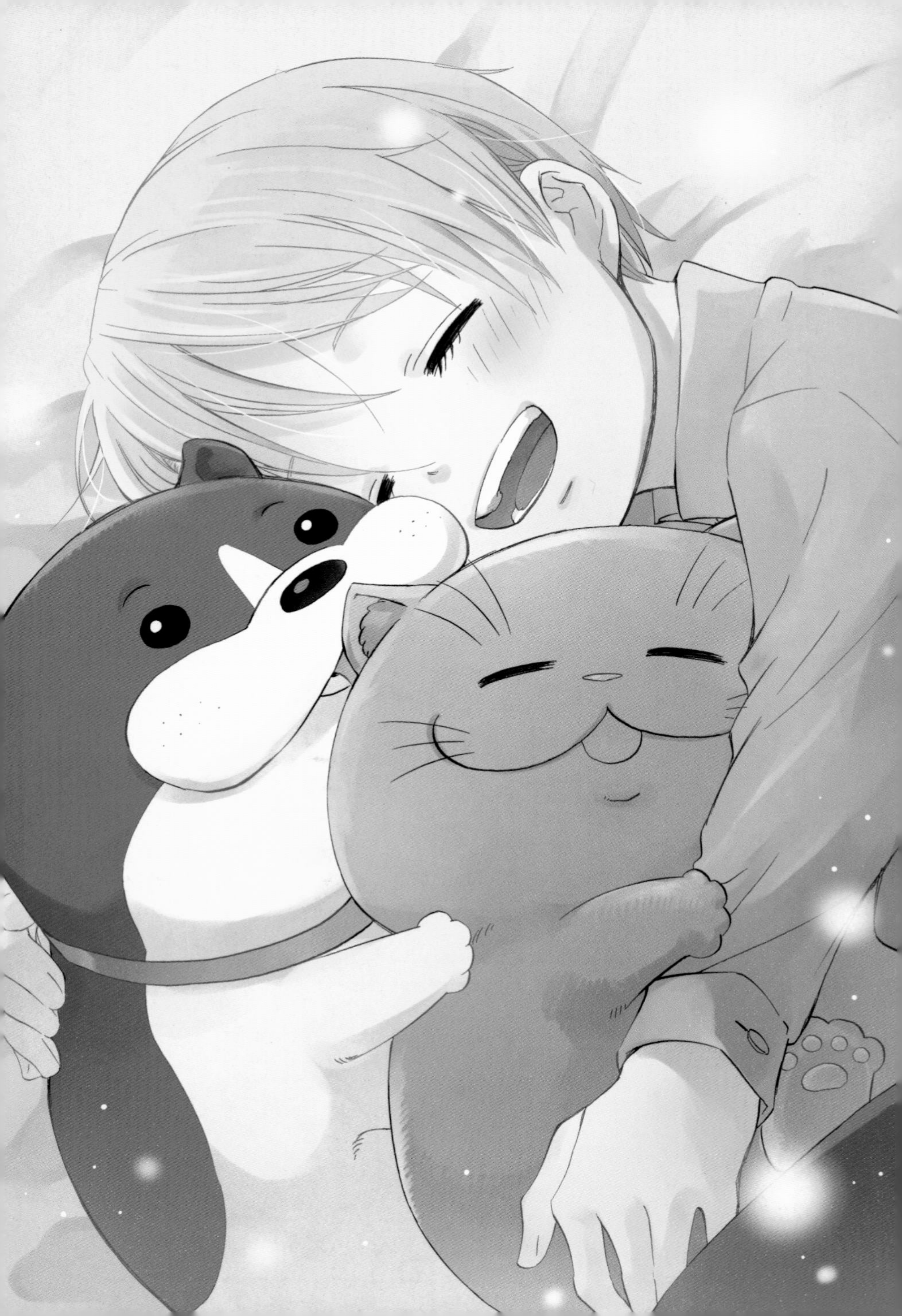